Managerial Skills in Organizations

CHAD T. LEWIS

Gemini Software, Training & Development

JOSEPH E. GARCIA

Western Washington University

SARAH M. JOBS

University of Washington

With *PHILIP C. LEWIS*
Gemini Software, Training & Development

ALLYN AND BACON
Boston   London   Toronto   Sydney   Tokyo   Singapore

Series Editor: John Peters
Senior Editorial Assistant: Carol Alper
Cover Administrator: Linda Dickinson
Composition Buyer: Superscript Associates
Manufacturing Buyer: Bill Alberti
Production Coordinator: Superscript Associates
Editorial-Production Service: TKM Productions

Photo Credits: Page 1: Spencer Grant, The Picture Cube; page 11: Ken Robert Buck, Stock, Boston; page 23: Patrick Reddy; page 47: Arthur Grace, Stock, Boston; page 56: Bruce Terami; page 83: Rob Crandall, Stock, Boston; page 105: R. J. MacLeod; page 121: Barbara Alper, Stock, Boston; page 132: Alan Kearney; page 147: Mark Antman, Stock, Boston; page 185: Peter Menzel, Stock, Boston; page 223: Robert V. Eckert, Jr., The Picture Cube; page 230: Eric D. Grunebaum; page 251: Peter Menzel, Stock, Boston; page 285: Anna Kaufman Moon, Stock, Boston; page 326: Chesley Bonestall/Space Art International.

Library of Congress Cataloging-in-Publication Data

Lewis, Chad T.
    Managerial skills in organizations / Chad T. Lewis, Joseph E.
  Garcia, Sarah M. Jobs.
      p. cm.
    ISBN 0-205-12336-8
    1. Management. 2. Organizational behavior. 3. Executive ability.
I. Garcia, Joseph E. II. Jobs, Sarah. III. Title.
HD31.L385 1990
658.4'09—dc20
89-28723
CIP

Contents

Chapter Three   *Motivation*   *47*

Chapter Six   *Performance Appraisal*   *147*

Chapter Seven   *Decision Making*   **185**

Chapter Eight   *Power*   **223**

Chapter Nine   Leadership   251

Preface

Managerial Skills in Organizations, along with its supporting activities and instructional aids, is particularly well suited for organizational behavior courses designed for students of management; for principles of management courses that emphasize the directing function of management; and for courses that make use of the emerging "managerial skills" approach.

The purpose of *Managerial Skills in Organizations* is to facilitate the teaching and learning of essential "people skills." Accordingly, this book:

- Is well researched. Recent developments in organizational behavior are provided (e.g., Graen's leader-member exchange theory, Fiedler's cognitive resource model, Kahneman and Tversky's prospect theory, Fisher and Ury's work on principled negotiation, Locke and Latham's work on goal setting, and so on).
- Provides more than theory. Theoretical coverage is followed by extrapolation to *practice.* Practical applications are outlined in chapter sections titled "Tips for the Manager" and in summary sections titled "Focus on Skills." Chapters also include commentaries from practicing managers.
- Recognizes that people skills are practiced in the context of individual, group, and organizational interactions. Each chapter is organized by these considerations.
- Provides margin terms, boxes, chapter endnotes, and a glossary to facilitate student understanding. Topics are also cross-referenced throughout the book.
- Includes supporting activities that provide for analysis of theory and practice of people skills (e.g., cases, roleplays, exercises, self-assessments, video tapes, and *Io Enterprises: A Microcomputer Simulation*).
- Includes a wide variety of instructional aids that complement different instructor styles. These aids include overhead masters, lecture

notes, and detailed instructions and teaching hints for using all supporting activities.

- Provides instructors with the opportunity to use a microcomputer simulation. *Io Enterprises* includes user-friendly instructions and a built-in word processor so that instructors can tailor program scenarios to their particular needs. (Students enjoy the simulation as it has them practicing people skills as managers of titanium mining operations on Io, the fifth moon of Jupiter, in the year 2086.)

In summary, the focus on *application* of theory makes this book distinctive and particularly relevant for training (as well as educating) present or prospective managers. Consequently, we hope and expect that *Managerial Skills in Organizations* will stay with students as they progress from a college/university degree program into the world of work.

We have worked hard to write a book that is stimulating for students to read. We also strived to develop supporting activities that will capture student attention, are pedagogically sound and well integrated with text material, and are easy for instructors to use and to adapt.

We welcome comments or suggestions. Please feel free to contact us c/o Allyn and Bacon, Simon & Schuster Higher Education Group, 160 Gould Street, Needham Heights, MA 02194-2310.

ACKNOWLEDGMENTS

Managerial Skills in Organizations could not have been successfully developed without considerable assistance.

We wish to thank Ken Keleman, management professor at Western Washington University; and Ken White, Jennifer Jones, and Diane Young, instructors at Everett Community College, for their helpful reviews of chapter content. James Van Dyck, a graduate of the Western Washington University business school, assisted in the development of managerial roleplays. Jacie Dalton, secretary at Western Washington University Management Department, and Stephanie Mangold, a student assistant, helped to keep the project on track.

Io Enterprises: A Microcomputer Simulation is a unique, optional part of the *Managerial Skills in Organizations* program. It provides instructors of the "people side" of management with the same pedagogy their colleagues in marketing and business policy have enjoyed for years. *Io Enterprises* would not have been possible without the programming skill, dedication, and creativity of Phil Lewis. We also wish to thank Allyn and Bacon Developmental Editor Allen Workman for seeing the possibilities inherent in *Io Enterprises*. We appreciated Allen's patience during the time the first version of the program was developed.

Each chapter of *Managerial Skills in Organizations* includes a commentary from a person working outside of academia. We asked these people to respond to an assigned chapter. Each volunteer was swamped with her or his own work, yet each person met the deadline. To each we give a resounding "thank you!":

- John Lewis, National Sales Manager—Bar Soap and Household Products, Procter & Gamble, Cincinnati, Ohio
- Chris Gobrecht, Women's Basketball Coach, University of Washington, Seattle, Washington
- Bob and Margaret Bavasi, President and Vice-President, Everett Giants (minor league baseball team), Everett, Washington
- Carlos Buhler, world renowned mountain climber, Bellingham, Washington
- Thomas Seeberg, Executive Director, Corporate Accounting, Siemens AG, Munich, West Germany
- Wallace Wong, Infant and Children's Wear Buyer, National Dollar Stores, Oakland, California
- Thomas Costagliola, President, Infinity Construction, Cambridge, Massachusetts
- Booth Gardner, Governor of the state of Washington, Olympia, Washington
- Tom Green, Consultant, Senn-Delaney and Associates, Long Beach, California

We also wish to thank outside reviewers of *Managerial Skills in Organizations*. These people returned necessary objectivity and accuracy to the manuscript. Our appreciation is extended to: Randy Boxx, University of Mississippi; Sonia Goltz, University of Notre Dame; Hazel Rosen, York University; and Grant T. Savage, Texas Technical University. We also thank Charles Walker, Harding University, for his thorough beta test of *Io Enterprises* software.

A special thank you goes to Lynda Griffiths of TKM Productions for her untiring attention to detail and creative vision. Finally, we thank Allyn and Bacon editor Jack Peters for his support and guidance. This ambitious project could not have succeeded without Jack's expert assistance and unflappable demeanor.

C. T. L.
J. E. G.
S. M. J.

CHAPTER ONE

Introduction

- **The Need to Improve the Teaching of "People Skills"**

- **Topic Selection/Book Organization**

- **Chapter Organization**

- **Conclusion**

Managerial Skills in Organizations is intended for use in undergraduate organizational behavior and management courses, as well as in "managerial skills" courses that emphasize the management of people. The focus on managerial skills is one of the distinctive features of this book. Consequently, the book also serves as a "real world" primer for practicing managers, as chapter content extrapolates from research in the lab or field, to actual practice in the workplace. In keeping with a focus on application, commentary from practicing managers is included throughout the various chapters. Guest contributors range from Booth Gardner, Governor of Washington State, to Wallace Wong, a buyer for a California-based retail department store chain.

This book is timely. Increasingly, students, professors, and employers are confirming that student success after graduation is as dependent on interpersonal skills as it is on any other set of skills associated with effective management (e.g., managing data, managing capital, etc.).

■ THE NEED TO IMPROVE THE TEACHING OF "PEOPLE SKILLS"

The teaching of people skills related to subjects such as leadership, motivation, communication, and conflict management has tended to receive short shrift in the typical business school curriculum. It is not surprising that a recent American Assembly of Collegiate Schools of Business study found that business schools need to do a better job of teaching people skills.[1]

This need to improve the status quo is underscored by comments of a recent business school graduate and Professor Willard Zangwill of the University of Chicago. The business school graduate complained that he could "crunch numbers to death, but didn't learn anything about managing, motivating, and leading people."[2] Professor Zangwill eloquently commented in a letter to the editor of *Business Week* that "the numbers are essential but can be quite misleading, and the classes I teach show that overreliance on them can lead to fatefully wrong decisions. People play the essential role, not numbers, and to be a world class company requires that (managerial) decision making strike a balance between the people and the numbers."[3]

Managerial Skills in Organizations will help professors to teach, and students to learn, people skills necessary for success in modern-day organizations. The book and accompanying materials facilitate teaching and learning because they extrapolate from the theory to the practice of effectively managing people.

"I'm a social scientist, Michael. That means I can't explain electricity or anything like that, but if you ever want to know about people I'm your man."

Research conducted by social scientists has contributed much to the productivity of people—the most important resource in all organizations.

Drawing by Handelsman; © 1986 The New Yorker Magazine, Inc.

THE NEED TO BALANCE THEORY AND PRACTICE

It is not easy to blend theory and practice when writing or teaching about people skills. Academicians are rightly accustomed to a guarded posture when it comes to applying theory. (Several roads usually lead to Rome when managers face challenges that involve human behavior.) Nevertheless, there are several good reasons why we were prescriptive as well as descriptive in writing this book.

An important part of the mission of a business school is to prepare students for success in modern-day organizations. This success is dependent on effective *practice* of skills as well as requisite *understanding* of underlying theory. This principle holds true whether one is discussing accounting, marketing, finance, or organizational behavior and management. As succinctly noted by Harold Geneen, the legendary CEO of International Telephone and Telegraph (ITT) for 17 years, "you cannot run a business, or anything else, on a theory."[4]

Emphasizing theory in organizational behavior and management courses may be a good way to educate future professors; it is a less effective way to *train* future managers. It can be difficult for students to extrapolate from the content of one or two required theoretical management and/or organizational behavior courses to actual practice on the job.

This criticism of a theoretical emphasis does not imply that the teaching of theory is wrong. It is *essential* that students understand concepts underlying practice. Indeed, management and organizational behavior coursework with an experiential emphasis is also limited. Students enjoy case studies, simulation, and exercises. However, without a tie to theory, students may be left with the sense of having been stimulated at the completion of an exercise or even a course, but with little else. Again, we return to the problem of extrapolation—the graduate, when faced with the problem of dealing with an angry customer, may wonder "Just *what* did that entertaining little exercise (or that stimulating two-hour lecture) I experienced in Management 302 really *mean?*"

In short, this book is prescriptive. It makes use of the emerging "managerial skills approach" because there is a need to better balance theory and practice in organizational behavior and management courses and seminars.

THE MANAGERIAL SKILLS APPROACH

The managerial skills approach used in *Managerial Skills in Organizations* integrates conceptual learning with specific skills. Applications are presented using skill assessment, learning, analysis, practice, and feedback.[5]

A *self-assessment* instrument is presented at the beginning of each chapter. Conceptual *learning* is promoted by chapters that thoroughly cover theoretical foundations. Vocabulary is highlighted in the text, defined in the margins at the point of presentation, and defined once again in the glossary. Videos tied to text content are also available.

Managerial skills are summarized throughout each chapter in sections titled "Tips for the Manager" and a "Focus on Skills" section concludes each chapter. Roleplays, exercises, case questions, and scenarios (part of *Io Enterprises: A Microcomputer Simulation*) reinforce managerial skills and provide the opportunity for *analysis* and *practice*. The provision of *feedback* is an integral part of all of these activities.

An Integrated Approach to Learning

The managerial skills approach is well-grounded in learning theory. People learn best when they can see interconnections among concepts they are trying to learn (*learning*); practical experience of trying to apply those concepts (*practice and feedback*); and the vicarious experience of watching others apply those concepts (*observation*).[6]

This book provides effective tools for learning, practice and feedback, and observation:

Learning . . . . Book chapters, prepared lectures, videos, overhead masters, self-assessment

Practice and feedback . . . . Self-assessment, cases, exercises, roleplay, simulation

Observation . . . . Exercises, roleplay, simulation

---

A Caveat

A couple of points need to be made regarding our application of the managerial skills approach. We attempted to avoid pitfalls associated with defining Truth only in terms of that which is observable by way of specific managerial behaviors. It is impossible to boil down all the relevant considerations related to the management of people to specific managerial behavior. Some broad and particularly integrative topics like leadership and organization development do not lend themselves well to application of specific managerial skills. Nevertheless, these topics are part of most organizational behavior and management courses. Should a managerial skills book avoid a topic simply because it defies inclusion within behavioral parameters? We think not. Throughout these chapters, where we cannot present managerial skills in terms of specific behavior, we offer instead "considerations" that lead to effective managerial practice.

Second, extrapolating from theory to practice requires interpretation. We expect readers to occasionally take exception to our interpretations. The *Managerial Skills in Organizations* program can accommodate differences of expert opinion. For example, professors will find it easy to rewrite and change answers of scenarios embedded in *Io Enterprises: A Microcomputer Program*. Lecture notes include designated space for commentary and modifications. Professors are also provided with the option of using a variety of roleplays, cases, and exercises. Instructors may also add their own material or interpretations without compromising the integrity of the program.

Keep in mind that *Managerial Skills in Organizations* is not a cookbook. Consider our prescriptions to be guidelines rather than inviolate recipes.

Io Enterprises: A Microcomputer Simulation

For years, marketing, finance, and business policy courses have had the benefit of computer-assisted simulations. These simulations provide students with the opportunity to practice skills within the relative safety of the classroom.

There is now a computer-assisted simulation for the practicing of people skills! *Io Enterprises: A Microcomputer Simulation* is an optional part of the *Managerial Skills in Organizations* package. In this user-friendly simulation, students serve as members of a management team overseeing titanium mining operations on Io, the fifth moon of Jupiter, in the year 2086. Increasing the productivity and profits of a mine requires making correct human resources decisions.

Io Enterprises allows professors to tailor scenarios involving application of people skills to the content of a specific course or seminar. Feedback is provided to students. Students practice people skills as they make decisions for their mine and as they participate as part of a twenty-first century management team.

Following is an excerpt from the student instructions:

Still, as the 21st century began, there were problems to overcome. Besides a burgeoning population to feed and house, the mineral resources of the planet were rapidly being depleted. Technology could solve many problems, but it could not replace planetary reserves of important minerals such as lead, nickel, and iron. Market forces, driven by the insatiable hunger of Earth industry, dictated a movement outward toward the stars. . . .

■ TOPIC SELECTION/
BOOK ORGANIZATION

The chapter titles of this book are:

1. Introduction
2. Communication
3. Motivation
4. Conflict Management
5. Stress
6. Performance Appraisal
7. Decision Making
8. Power
9. Leadership
10. Organization Development

(The last section of the book includes instructions for *Io Enterprises: A Microcomputer Simulation.*)

Selection of these topics was based on a 1986 analysis of organizational behavior texts used at 200 colleges and universities (conducted by Joe Garcia, Ken Keleman, and John Davis from Western Washington University, Bellingham, Washington). These topics are commonly covered in organizational behavior and management courses and seminars. As noted previously, topic selection was not constrained by limitations inherent in a focus on skills.

Chapter order was based on the extent to which skills learned in one chapter assist learning in a subsequent chapter. As an example, coverage of communication helps to facilitate coverage of conflict management. (Communication skills are an essential part of the effective management of conflict.) Communication and conflict management are placed before performance appraisal and decision making. Conflict management skills help during a performance review; communication skills are particularly important in group decision making. Professors are not bound by this chapter order, however; the first chapter of the instructor's manual provides other options for covering chapters.

Io Enterprises instructions are, of course, only relevant if professors decide to use the simulation. The simulation is only one (albeit exciting) component of the complete *Managerial Skills in Organizations* program.

CHAPTER ORGANIZATION

Each chapter in *Managerial Skills in Organizations* moves from individual, to group, and then to organizational considerations pertaining to the chapter topic. At times, these boundaries may seem artificial. For example, every individual and group interaction affects the organization. Nevertheless, we adopted this chapter organization because we felt it was not enough simply to have one or two chapters on "groups" and a chapter on "organizations." Managerial skills are practiced within the context of the individual manager, a group or groups, and the total organization. The chapter organization of the book makes this point very clear.

This chapter organization means some redundancy is unavoidable. Some subjects, such as MBO, goal setting, job redesign, job enrichment, two-factor theory, social loafing, and leader decision theory are covered in several chapters. However, definitions are kept consistent, subjects are cross-referenced, and the same subject is discussed from a *different* perspective in different chapters. For example, goal setting is discussed as a motivator in the motivation chapter, and as a necessary prerequisite to the conduct of job analysis in the performance appraisal chapter.

CONCLUSION

Professors will find *Managerial Skills in Organizations* very flexible to use. Chapter One in the Instructor's Manual provides a detailed account of the many ways to integrate supporting activities of the *Managerial Skills in Organizations* program in different courses. This chapter also includes ideas for using this book to conduct training in the field.

We have also written "to the student." Some purists may take exception to our use of humor and colloquial style. So be it. This is a book for students.

ENDNOTES

1. Porter, L. W., & McKibbin, L. E. *Management Education and Development.* New York: McGraw-Hill, 1988.

2. "Where the schools aren't doing their homework." *Business Week* (November 28, 1988): 84–92.

3. Zangwill, W. I. "Putting the B-school report to the test." (Letters to the Editor) *Business Week* (December 19, 1988): 9.

4. Geneen, H. *Managing.* Garden City, NY: Doubleday, 1984.

5. Whetten, D. A., & Cameron, K. S. *Developing Management Skills.* Glenview, IL: Scott, Foresman and Company, 1984.

6. Gioia, D. A., & Sims, H. P. "Videotapes and vicarious learning: A technology for effective training." In Goldstein and Pfeiffer (Eds.), *The 1985 Annual: Developing Human Resources.* San Diego, CA: University Associates, 1985.

CHAPTER TWO
Communication

- ■ *Self-Assessment: "Self-Esteem Scale"*
- ■ *Learning about Communication*
- ■ *Case: "Woes in the Warehouse"*
- ■ *Exercise: "Rumors"*

■ SELF-ASSESSMENT: "SELF-ESTEEM SCALE"

There is more to communication than meets the eye. Robert Keller and Winford Holland studied professional employees in three organizations and found that personality characteristics play an important role in how well people communicate.* One of the key characteristics they identified was self-esteem. Before reading on, please fill out the following assessment questionnaire as a first step in exploring your self-esteem and communication effectiveness.

Self-Esteem Scale

Please indicate the degree to which you agree with each of the following items by circling the appropriate value. There are no correct answers to these questions.

1. On the whole, I am satisfied with myself.

1	2	3	4	5
Strongly Agree	Agree	Neutral	Disagree	Strongly Disagree

2. At times I think I am no good at all.

1	2	3	4	5
Strongly Agree	Agree	Neutral	Disagree	Strongly Disagree

3. I feel that I have a number of good qualities.

1	2	3	4	5
Strongly Agree	Agree	Neutral	Disagree	Strongly Disagree

4. I am able to do things as well as most other people.

1	2	3	4	5
Strongly Agree	Agree	Neutral	Disagree	Strongly Disagree

5. I feel I do not have much to be proud of.

1	2	3	4	5
Strongly Agree	Agree	Neutral	Disagree	Strongly Disagree

6. I certainly feel useless at times.

1	2	3	4	5
Strongly Agree	Agree	Neutral	Disagree	Strongly Disagree

7. I feel that I am a person of worth, at least on an equal plane with others.

1	2	3	4	5
Strongly Agree	Agree	Neutral	Disagree	Strongly Disagree

8. I wish I could have more respect for myself.

1	2	3	4	5
Strongly Agree	Agree	Neutral	Disagree	Strongly Disagree

9. All in all, I am inclined to feel that I am a failure.

1	2	3	4	5
Strongly Agree	Agree	Neutral	Disagree	Strongly Disagree

10. I take a positive attitude toward myself.

1	2	3	4	5
Strongly Agree	Agree	Neutral	Disagree	Strongly Disagree

Scoring the Self-Esteem Scale

1. For items 1, 3, 4, 7, and 10 simply sum the circled values.

2. For items 2, 5, 6, 8, and 9 reverse the item values (i.e., 1 becomes 5, 2 becomes 4, 4 becomes 2, and 5 becomes 1). Using the reversed item values sum the circled values.

3. Sum the results of steps 1 and 2.

---

*Keller, R. T., & Holland, W. E. "Communication and innovators in research and development organizations." *Academy of Management Journal, 26* (1983): 742–749.

■ LEARNING ABOUT COMMUNICATION

Communication breakdowns contributed significantly to the Japanese attack on Pearl Harbor and the American nuclear attacks on Hiroshima and Nagasaki during World War II.

Prior to the attack on Pearl Harbor, U.S. Secretary of State Cordell Hull received translations of a series of intercepted Japanese messages from Japanese Foreign Minister Togo to U.S. Ambassador Nomura. These translations created the appearance that the Japanese had given up on negotiations and were committed to war with the United States. This was not the case, however. The actual content and tone of the messages were much more conciliatory than were their translations.

The highly stylized Japanese language used by diplomats was misunderstood by translators. (It's also possible that hastily trained translators wanted to make their copy "more readable and interesting.") These misunderstandings led directly to a hardening in the U.S. position and a breakdown in negotiations.[1] One month later, Japan and the United States were at war.

Four years later, the Potsdam Declaration called on a badly battered Japan to surrender. The Japanese government wanted to accept the terms of the declaration. However, for political reasons, the Japanese cabinet needed to delay the acceptance of terms. Consequently, Prime Minister Suzuki told the press that the cabinet was holding to a policy of *mokusatsu*. This term, which has no English counterpart, can mean to "withhold comment" or "to ignore."

Unfortunately, translators at the Domei News Agency chose the wrong meaning when translating the prime minister's comments into English. The world was led to believe that the Japanese government had decided to "ignore" the Potsdam Declaration. Shortly thereafter, Hiroshima and Nagasaki were destroyed by atomic bombs.[2]

Whether considering events surrounding global warfare forty-five years ago, or day-to-day correspondence with the person in the next office, it is easy to misunderstand seemingly straightforward communication.

Facilitating effective communication is an essential part of success in the workplace. Managers spend up to 80 percent of their day communicating.[3] In a recent survey 85 percent of 700 middle managers noted that it was a subordinate's communication skills that determined success or failure in critical situations.[4] Weitzel and Gaske cited 20 different studies that demonstrated that both employers and employees place high value on communication skills.[5] Effective communication is a necessary requirement for effective performance appraisal, conflict management, motivation of subordinates, decision making, and leadership. Effective communication is the cornerstone of individual, group, and organizational effectiveness.

Unfortunately, complaints regarding communication are common in all types of organizations across all organizational levels. Managers and subordinates often do not agree on whether they even met during the week![6] Up to 95 percent of high-ranking managers report believing they have a good grasp of employee problems. In contrast, only about 30 percent of subordinates agree that this is so.[7]

WHAT IS COMMUNICATION?

Communication problems are understandable in light of the complexity associated with even simple transmissions of information. Soon we will describe a model of the interpersonal communication process in detail. Before proceeding, though, we need to define communication.

Communication:
A process whereby symbols generated by people are received and responded to by other people.

Communication is a "process whereby symbols generated by people are received and responded to by other people."[8] In the context of this chapter, communication includes verbal, nonverbal, and written transmissions of information to the individuals and groups within an organization. The purpose of communication is to achieve meaning. Generally, communication is effective to the extent that the achievement of meaning is facilitated between and among people.

The purpose of communication in the workplace can be further understood by raising the question of *why* managers wish to achieve meaning. This question has an unlimited set of potential responses.[9] The basic position taken in this chapter is that the primary reason managers wish to achieve meaning in communication is to enhance individual, group, and organizational productivity.

The Spiritual Child

The "spiritual child" metaphor demonstrates that communication is a reciprocal process—with all parties responsible for creating and maintaining a unique, shared meaning. John Stewart describes the metaphor this way:

> Whenever you encounter someone, the two of you together create a spiritual child—*your relationship.* Unlike the creation of physical children, there are no contraceptives available for spiritual children; when two people meet, they always create a relationship of some sort. Also, unlike physical children, the spiritual child lives as long as at least one person lives. . . . The spiritual child can change drastically, but it can't be killed. . . .

> . . . If the (spiritual) child is born in a meeting characterized by manipulation, deceit, and exploitation, it will be deformed and ugly. If it's raised in that same atmosphere it can never be healthy. Often it can be nurtured back to health, but it takes a heavy commitment from both parents. On the other hand, if it's born and raised in an open caring atmosphere, it will grow healthy and strong. . . .
>
> I hope the spiritual child metaphor is useful for you. What it does for me is to give me another way to look at the relationship . . . between the persons. As a child, you are neither of your parents, but the result of their meeting, their contact. Similarly, the spiritual child who is born whenever two people communicate is an entity that emerges *between* them.[10]

There are specific behaviors and approaches that improve individual, group, and organizational communication and subsequent productivity. This chapter presents some of these behaviors and approaches, beginning in the next section with **interpersonal communication—** communication between two people.

Interpersonal communication: Communication between two people.

INDIVIDUAL CONSIDERATIONS IN COMMUNICATION

Wendell Johnson's classic article, "The Fateful Process of Mr. A Talking to Mr. B," concludes with the comment that people are a "noisy lot; and of what gets said among us, far more goes unheard and unheeded than seems possible. We have yet to learn on a grand scale how to use the wonders of speaking and listening in our own best interests and for the good of all our fellows. It is the finest art still to be mastered by men."[11]

As suggested by Professor Johnson, interpersonal communication is surprisingly complex. This complexity often contributes to a failure to achieve meaning.

Figure 2–1 outlines the **sender-receiver model,** a popular model depicting the interpersonal communication process. Bear in mind that this model only covers communication transactions between two people. The complexity of communication (and potential for failure to "achieve meaning") usually increases as more people participate in the process.

Sender-receiver model: Depicts parts of the interpersonal communication process: thought or feeling, encoding, transmission of a message, decoding, and thought or feeling.

The Sender-Receiver Model

The interpersonal communication process begins when one person wishes to transmit information to another person. This wish to transmit information need not be conscious, rational, or even eventually expressed using verbal or written language. A scowl, a smile, or a puzzled

Figure 2–1 The Sender-Receiver Model

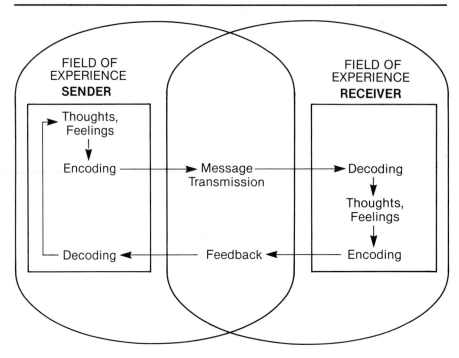

Communication is surprisingly complex. The inherent complexity of the communication process is compounded by differences in the "field of experience" of communicators.

Developed from discussion of communication models in: Bormann, Ernest G. (1980). *Communication Theory*. New York: Holt, Rinehart and Winston.

look are as much communication as a five-page single-spaced memo with headers or the Gettysburg Address.

Regardless of the communication vehicle used, the interpersonal communication process begins with a thought or a feeling that must be *encoded* before it can be transmitted. (Encoding literally means to put a message into code.) As noted previously, a sender can put a message into code using verbal, nonverbal, or written means.

After transmission, the receiver must *decode* the message. (Hmmm. . . I wonder what that scowl means? What is this five-page memo really saying? Was the Gettysburg Address really about soldiers dying for "freedom" or soldiers dying for "economic prosperity"?) After decoding, the message is then transformed into a thought or a feeling on the part of the receiver. The entire process is repeated when the receiver provides **feedback.** Feedback occurs during two-way communication when a receiver responds to the original sender of a message. (Feedback is also covered in Chapter Six, Performance Appraisal, and Chapter Three, Motivation.)

Feedback: Occurs during two-way communication when a receiver responds to the original sender of a communication.

In reviewing this model, it should be quite apparent that even very simple communication can be hampered because many parts of the communication process are private and not shared (e.g., thoughts and feelings, encoding, decoding). Only the actual verbal, nonverbal, or written transmission of a message is received.

Besides the inherent complexity of the communication process, the *field of experience* of communicators influences the achievement of meaning. "Field of experience" is broadly defined here to include perceptions, values, culture, attitudes, and opinions derived from previous experience.

For example, if you *think* that another person is angry with you, you may perceive an angry message, even if the person is not really angry. Misunderstandings may also occur because of difficulty understanding another person's culture or language (e.g., the Japanese language expression for "yes" can, depending on the context, actually mean "no"). You may find yourself communicating differently in one setting relative to another. Communication in a court of law differs from communication on a basketball court because people know from experience that these courts are very different. You may communicate differently in a quiet restaurant than in a noisy bus station.

To summarize, the sender-receiver model is useful in that it presents interpersonal communication as a multidimensional process involving many steps. This model can help us better understand communication breakdowns. The model also helps us to appreciate the complexity associated with sending and receiving even the simplest of messages. Conversely, the sender-receiver model does not capture the full richness of interpersonal communication, nor does it account for all threats to the achievement of meaning. The examples cited in the previous paragraphs just scratch the surface. Moreover, simply understanding the complexity of the communication process does not, by itself, improve interpersonal communication. Techniques for improving the quality of interpersonal communication are covered next.

Feedback and Active Listening

Active listening involves the timely and appropriate provision of feedback (defined previously) which improves the achievement of meaning between communicators. Some observations are in order before discussing active listening skills.

Active listening: Involves the timely and appropriate provision of feedback which facilitates achievement of meaning between communicators.

Imagine a situation involving one-way communication where you can only receive information without being allowed to provide feedback. You would be unable to ask questions to clarify a communicator's intent. You would not be able to add to the other person's understanding of the topic being discussed. The situation described would be much like being prohibited from asking questions of a speaker. You might not understand the material being covered, and the speaker might be completely unaware of your lack of understanding.

Two-way communication provides for feedback which often improves the accuracy of communication. This is because with feedback there is an opportunity to correct or otherwise refine communication leading to mutual understanding and agreement. An added advantage to two-way communication is that it is inherently more satisfying to communicators, who otherwise may feel stifled by one-way communication.

Clearly, feedback should be encouraged whenever interpersonal communication takes place. There are few situations one can conceive of where feedback would compromise the achievement of meaning in a communication between two people.

A lack of feedback can significantly affect the quality of communication. Problems with the communication *process* can interfere with interpretation of communication *content*. Managers improve communication accuracy by encouraging two-way communication. They should actively solicit and provide feedback from subordinates, customers, or anyone else affected by or who influences their position.

Paraphrasing and Perception Checking. Two communication techniques that improve two-way communication are paraphrasing and perception checking, both of which are *active listening skills*.[12] This is an appropriate term, because active listening skills supplement and enhance basic listening for the purpose of clarifying meaning. Paraphrasing and perception checking involve communication that helps the sender to clarify literal communication or intent.

Paraphrasing: Repeating back in your own words what you thought you heard the sender of a communication say.

Paraphrasing is repeating back in your own words what you thought you heard the sender say. "Noise" and the symbols used in a communication sometimes make it hard to understand a message, particularly a long and/or complex communication. The objective of paraphrasing is to ensure that the receiver got the message the sender actually sent.

Perception checking: Involves checking out what you thought another person meant by a communication.

Perception checking is similar to paraphrasing; the focus is on checking out what you perceive to be the intent of another person's communication. Here, the concern is not with *what* the person communicated as much as it is with what the other person *means*. For example, an employee might be consistently late to work. You might assume from this "communication" that the employee does not care much about his or her job. If you checked out this perception, however, you might find that the employee is extremely punctual and cares a great deal about his or her job. The problem was a temporary one associated with a breakdown in the local transit system.

Paraphrasing and perception checking work well together. You might have paraphrased Lincoln's Gettysburg Address this way:

"President Lincoln, did I hear you say that the founders of our country expressed the belief 78 years ago that all people are created equal, and the Battle of Gettysburg was fought and thousands of lives were lost to keep that ideal alive?"

President Lincoln might have stroked his beard, thought for a moment and then replied, "Yes, this is essentially what I said. However, 'four score and seven years ago' was 87, not 78, years ago."

Satisfied that you had accurately received the message, you could then proceed to check out the message's meaning:

"Because of the way your address tied a definition of 'freedom' to the lives lost at Gettysburg, it seems you did not intend to eulogize the 20,000 Confederate soldiers who died in this battle. Is this so? Also, was it your intent to include 'women' in your statement that 'all men are created equal'? As you know, women are not allowed to vote or to own property."

President Lincoln would then have had the opportunity to respond.

Put It in Writing and KISS.   Other approaches that can improve the clarity of communication and subsequent feedback are to put responses in writing and to follow the KISS Principle.

Written communication has the important advantage of being amenable to close review and analysis. You may still not understand what the sender meant, but there can be no doubt about the words (symbols) that were actually sent.

All forms of communication benefit when the **KISS Principle** is applied. There are many versions of the underlying meaning of this acronym. The one we particularly like is Keep It Short and Simple.[13] Baron sums up the advantages of adhering to the KISS Principle this way:

KISS Principle: Keep It Short and Simple.

> If we are exposed to more facts, ideas, or concepts than we can comfortably handle at a given time, much of this information is lost. In addition, the experience of having one's "cognitive circuits" overloaded is quite unpleasant. For these reasons, communicators who present too much (either by words or written comments) run the dual risk of failing to get their message across *and* annoying their audience. Thus, the moral for all would-be communicators is straightforward: avoid cramming too much information into written or verbal messages; doing so can be disastrous![14]

Commentary: "Communication"

W. John Lewis

One could argue that one's ability to succeed is in direct proportion with one's ability to communicate. In a company or organization, we must learn to effectively communicate internally (to our employees) and externally (to our customers). For this reason, communication could be viewed as the glue that binds a company or organization together or the solvent that drives it apart. Surely, in my role as a sales manager for Procter & Gamble, communication is a most valued and sought-after skill.

The 23 suggestions concerning managerial skills discussed at the close of this chapter can influence the final outcome of an effort. Based on my experience in business, at home, and in the community, I would group these suggestions into four interrelated but different categories. These include:

1. Having a clear picture of what you want to communicate
2. Developing a good understanding of the group to whom you will be communicating
3. Making an honest and straightforward attempt to gain feedback from the individual or group
4. Ensuring the communication leads to action or results

Know What to Communicate.   The ability for communication to enable an individual or an organization to generate results depends as much on what is communicated as the way in which it is communicated. For example, if we've done a perfectly good job of communicating the benefits of a new eye-care program to a group of employees when they're really interested in better dental care, the best communicator in the world won't gain the interest and support of that audience. But, expert communication skills could help you learn you've missed the target by paying careful attention to the group's body language.

Know Your Audience.   This chapter does a good job of underscoring the importance of knowing an audience's capacity to understand and comprehend as well as learning their interests. This is particularly appropriate for individuals managing and working within a vertical organization.

In a company, for example, middle managers could find themselves communicating to executive-level managers and to entry-level managers during the course of any day. This middle manager soon learns that the same approach to both groups will quickly lose the interest of one and fail to capture the interest of the other. Knowing what the individual or group is capable of understanding and the areas in which they have interest will ensure that you'll always capture the interest and communicate the desired message.

Get Candid Feedback.   The best way for any person to improve their communication skills is to get feedback either individually or from the group. One of the best ways I know is to get out from behind your desk and walk around among the group to which you have recently communicated. Interviewing people one-on-one or in small groups in their natural workplace will allow you to understand how people have responded to your message by listening to what they say and by interpreting their body language.

I've also learned that while it's certainly a good practice to follow verbal communication with a written confirmation, it is equally valid to follow written communication with a verbal confirmation. Early in my career, I learned it was pretty difficult to have a two-way conversation using memos, especially when dealing with sensitive issues.

Take Action. The final and perhaps most important rule I've learned in my career is to make certain the communication has led to the desired result. Whether it be a better understanding, an improved work process, or the introduction of a new program, it's important that the communication has led to something. As long as your words turn into action, people will always listen to you. It's when your words no longer lead to action, people no longer choose to listen.

While not necessarily a part of any one of the four rules but contained in all of them is the appropriateness of "walking the talk." This means living by your word or practicing what you preach. Call it what you will, it simply says that a good communicator not only speaks well and writes well, but also lives well.

W. John Lewis

John Lewis started his career with Procter & Gamble in Eugene, Oregon, in 1970, after graduating from the University of Washington with a bachelor's degree in business administration.

John has worked for Procter & Gamble for 18 years in various capacities, including sales representative, unit manager, district manager, and division manager. John is currently National Sales Manager of P & G's Bar Soap and Household Cleaning Products Division. In this capacity, he has overall sales responsibility in the United States for 14 of P & G's brands.

He regards himself as one of the very fortunate college graduates who made the right career and company decision straight out of school. John's career progress has clearly benefitted from the fit between his principles and values and those of Procter & Gamble. The P & G environment, coupled with John's intense interest in sales, has enabled him continually to work to be the best that he can be.

Reducing Defensiveness: Gibb's Suggestions and Other Advice

Sometimes neutral or even positive messages are communicated in such a way that the content sounds negative. This leads to unnecessary defensiveness on the part of the message receiver. Defensiveness on the part of one, both, or all parties to a particular communication puts up barriers to the achievement of meaning. It is as though people literally put up walls or don suits of armor, thereby making it very difficult for messages to get through.

After observing communication within groups for several years, Gibb was able to identify six types of defense-arousing communications and six types of contrasting **supportive communications** that seem to reduce defensiveness.[15] Figure 2–2 contrasts defensive and supportive communications.

Supportive communication: Is descriptive, problem oriented, honest, empathetic, equal, and tentative. Supportive communication is also timely and is "soft on people and hard on the problem."

Evaluation versus Description.   What is the difference between saying to someone, "You're always late to work!" versus "I've noticed that you've been late the last two days"? Both statements pertain to the same behavior. The real difference lies in *how* the message is communicated.

It is more constructive to describe behavior tentatively to another than it is to evaluate that behavior in an absolute fashion. It is also more constructive to send "I messages" than "you messages." I messages are less likely to lead to defensive behavior because they describe a person's behavior (lateness) rather than the person himself. If you must send a you message, soften it with a qualifier such as, "It seems to me that you. . . ."

Control versus Problem Orientation.   People become defensive when another person attempts to dictate a solution or a future activity.

Figure 2–2 Defense-Arousing versus Supportive Communication

Defense-arousing communication	Supportive communication
Evaluates behavior	Describes behavior
Is controlling	Shares problem solving
Manipulates	Is sincere and spontaneous
Is neutral and sterile	Is empathetic
"Talks down to . . ."	"Talks across to . . ."
Is certain	Is tentative

Supportive communication is also timely, invited, and is "soft on people, and hard on the problem."

Adapted from: Gibb, J. "Defensive communication." *Journal of Communication 11* (1961): 141–148.

"You'll do it because I told you so!" is probably the clearest example of this type of negative communication. Bases of control are many: a person may be the boss, a parent, a teacher, or simply someone who is louder and bigger than another party in a communication.

A contrasting, constructive approach is to let the other person participate in defining and solving the problem. The idea here is for communicators to find common ground, to find a "win-win" solution to a problem.

Manipulation versus Spontaneity (Honesty). Avoid communicating in a manipulative way. If others believe you are being manipulative, "the wall" will go up. The term *spontaneous* captures Gibb's intent. Spontaneous communication is not contrived; it is sincere and heartfelt. Keep in mind that creating the *appearance* of sincerity can be manipulative!

Neutrality versus Empathy. Remember the last time you interacted with a sterile, seemingly uncaring individual in an institutional setting? It may have been a clerk at a local state office, a physician, an Internal Revenue Service agent, or a professor. The studied neutrality of people in these settings can raise our defenses. We may find ourselves relating to these people as though they are machines, rather than thinking, feeling human beings.

In the workplace, managers are often guilty of indifference to the needs of subordinates. Sometimes managers believe such indifference is professional. However, it is quite possible to be constructively empathetic to employee concerns and still maintain professionalism. Managers can be empathetic, which involves looking at a situation from another's perspective, without compromising professionalism. Gibb found that empathy helps to remove the quality of indifference from communication and reduces defensiveness. Put yourself in the other person's shoes!

Superiority versus Equality. Think back to a boss with whom you enjoyed working. This boss probably made you feel as though the two of you were equals. Arrogant people, on the other hand, may cause you to become defensive and go on the attack.

We all have limitations and weaknesses. No one has cornered the market on brains, talent, or general ability regardless of their position on an organizational chart. Truly successful managers seem to realize this fact.

Certainty versus Provisionalism (Tentativeness). Do not be too sure you know the answer to a problem. Even if you are sure, listen to what others have to say. It is usually much more constructive to frame a problem or to raise an issue in a tentative way. For example, say, "It appears as though . . . , Don't you think . . . , I believe . . ." rather than, "I know that . . . , You're wrong . . . , I'm right . . . ."

Other Recommendations.   Constructive communication is usually invited. This means that a person offering a criticism or an idea to another is doing so by invitation, or by virtue of his or her position within the organization. We tend to be defensive when suggestions are offered by those who appear to lack expertise or are not appropriately positioned in the organization to offer advice. Consequently, when in doubt, determine whether or not communication is invited.

Constructive communication is also timely. You should try to avoid holding back adverse information or feelings, and then "dumping" this information during a conversation at a later date. On the other hand, sometimes it is constructive to let some time pass before providing feedback or advice. Waiting might allow an angry individual the time needed to cool off. An angry response from another person may have nothing to do with the content of your communication, but rather may be a function of bad timing.

Finally, one bit of advice that comes out of the conflict management literature is to reduce defensiveness by being "soft on people, and hard on the problem."[16] Try to attack the problem, not the person. If the person *is* the problem, Gibb's suggestions, as well as every other piece of advice offered to this point for improving the quality of communication, should be used. You may not always succeed in having constructive dialogue with another person, but the information supplied to this point will improve your chances.

Nonverbal Communication: Kinesics and Proxemics

Kinesics: Nonverbal communication.

Kinesics includes the whole gamut of nonverbal cues: eye contact, body posture, facial expression, gestures, and body movement. The study of kinesics was first popularized in a 1970 book entitled *Body Language* by Julius Fast.[17] This popular tradebook intrigued many people and probably also led to much frustration as people learned that interpreting "body language" was not an easy feat.

Kinesics is a highly speculative field. Even Julius Fast noted, "Unfortunately, something like kinesics, related facts on the way to becoming a science, also runs the risk of being exploited. For example, just how much can we really tell from crossed legs?"[18]

Although the topic of body language may be difficult to define and understand, there is no question about its importance. The way a message is *sent* is often more relevant than what is *said*.

Only a small portion of interpersonal communication is expressed in words. Most of our messages are expressed by facial expressions and posture (about 55 percent) and vocal intonation and inflection (38 percent); only about 7 percent of communication is verbal.[19] Judgments from visual cues are often more valid than judgments from vocal communication. When verbal and nonverbal messages differ, we tend to believe the nonverbal.[20] Also, judgments from visual cues in the environment are more accurate than judgments based on vocal cues.[21] It seems that it is more difficult to fool people nonverbally.

The importance of nonverbal communication cannot be overemphasized. Positive nonverbal behavior has a significant, positive effect on perceptions of observers relative to negative nonverbal behavior.

Imada and Hakel conducted a series of experimental trials where the same interviewee was asked the same questions by different interviewers. In half of the trials, the interviewee exhibited positive nonverbal cues. In the other half, negative nonverbal cues were displayed. In interviews where positive nonverbal cues were displayed (e.g., smiling, good eye contact, attentive body posture) the interviewee was liked more and was seen as being better qualified and more competent.[22]

It is relatively easy to build a convincing case for the importance of nonverbal communication. Describing positive nonverbal behavior in general terms is also not difficult. The difficulty lies in being specific about which nonverbal behavior is effective under particular circumstances.

Consider eye contact as an example. Under most circumstances making eye contact with another is perceived as a positive nonverbal behavior. However, too much eye contact can make another person uneasy. Indeed, to fix someone with a cold stare is usually a sign of hostility. In certain cultures, eye contact that is acceptable by Western standards might be perceived as being rude (e.g., in Japanese culture). The same thing can be said with regard to certain gestures.

Rather than provide you with a list of constructive nonverbal behaviors to be used in all circumstances, we offer an observation and a recommendation. First, the observation: It is impossible to avoid communication. Think about it. Everything you say, or do, or *are* sends a message. Now the recommendation: Never forget that body language, including voice intonation and inflection, usually plays a more important role in interpersonal communication than the words that are actually spoken. Managers should understand that appropriate nonverbal communication is embedded in context. Above all, the key to effective nonverbal communication is sensitivity to one's environment.

Positive Body Language

- Be physically alert.
- Maintain eye contact.
- Use an open, relaxed body posture.
- Minimize gestures and random movement.
- Reinforce the speaker (e.g., give head nods and other cues which communicate that you are listening).[23]

Sensitivity audit: Periodic assessment of what your nonverbal communication might be communicating to others.

Conduct a periodic, personal **sensitivity audit** to ascertain what your nonverbal communication might be saying to others. For example, when giving a presentation, notice if your audience is fidgeting or looking bored. Is the audience nodding their heads with approval? What's going on? In the process of conducting this sensitivity audit, consider whether your verbal and nonverbal communication is congruent. Work toward congruence between verbal and nonverbal communication for the purpose of clarifying communication.

Also observe the nonverbal communication of others. Be sure to use active listening skills (discussed previously) to check out nonverbal cues emanating from those around you. For example, if a person with whom you are communicating loudly and obviously yawns, don't get angry. Instead, check out the yawn: "Geez, Ralph, it looks like you're bored with what I'm saying." Ralph might respond by telling you that he stayed up all night in anticipation of your meeting. Ralph isn't bored, he's tired!

Proxemics: Study of the way people and animals use space.

Proxemics.   **Proxemics** is the study of the way people and animals use space. It is an interesting and important part of the study of nonverbal communication.

Anthropologist Edward T. Hall defined four distinct distances of which people are aware: intimate, personal, social, and public distances.[24] These distances range from skin contact up to 18 inches for intimate encounters, to 12 feet and beyond for public distance.

The implication of Hall's theory is to be mindful of the effect that personal distance has on those around you. Most communication in business meetings uses "social distance," which ranges from 4 to 12 feet. "Personal distance," 18 inches to 4 feet, is often employed in interpersonal communication.

As with other nonverbal communication, it is difficult to set rules for maintaining personal space. The effect of personal distance would be factored into the sensitivity audit described previously (e.g., Am I too close? Should I back-off? Is "personal distance" appropriate in *this setting* with *this person*?).

A related concern pertains to "touch." Touching, outside of incidental contact and handshakes (as part of a mutually understood greeting ritual) is always intimate. Sometimes it is appropriate to slap another on the back or touch an arm to emphasize a point. For the most part, however, at least in Western culture, managers should avoid extensive touching as part of their interpersonal communication repertoire.

Another application of proxemics concerns open versus closed **office design.** An office with an open design typically has the desk and chairs aligned so that there are no physical barriers between those sitting in the office. Conversely, offices with closed designs typically place a desk or other office furniture between people.

Office design: Layout of office furniture into a relatively open or closed format.

Studies indicate that people feel more welcome and comfortable in offices with an open design compared to offices with a closed design. Also, people tend to view the occupants of offices with an open design as being friendlier and more helpful.[25]

An open office design should be used by people in the helping professions (e.g., counselors, professors). The question of whether this statement extends to managers is debatable. We tend to favor open office design for most managers because such a design facilitates interpersonal communication. And, as noted at the beginning of this chapter, interpersonal communication is an important part of an effective manager's job.

Tips for the Manager. The primary purpose of communication in organizations is to achieve meaning for the purpose of facilitating individual, group, and organizational effectiveness. The communications process is complex. Much of the process is hidden (e.g., thoughts and feelings, encoding, decoding). Communicators also represent differing "fields of experience" that affect even the simplest of exchanges.

Consequently, managers should actively solicit feedback from others. Feedback helps managers to improve and otherwise assess the quality of their communications. Learning and practicing active listening skills such as paraphrasing and perception checking, putting things in writing, and practicing the KISS Principle also improve the quality of communication. Communication should be constructive and supportive. Such communication does not arouse defensive behavior in others.

Given the important and complex nature of nonverbal communication, managers should conduct a periodic sensitivity audit of their environment. They should check out nonverbal cues of others whenever there are doubts or questions with regard to meaning. Effective communicators are also mindful of the importance of personal space. Do not inappropriately violate the personal space of others, and do make use of office designs conducive to interpersonal communication.

COMMUNICATION IN GROUPS

Everything discussed to this point can be applied to communication within a group. Previously discussed skills that help improve the efficacy of interpersonal communication do the same within the context of a group process.

Group communication: Three or more persons who are interacting with one another in such a manner that each person influences and is influenced by each other person.

Keep in mind that participation within a group does not mean that **group communication** is taking place. Indeed, when two people pass notes or whisper with each other during a group meeting, group communication skills are not being practiced. Instead, interpersonal communication within a group is occurring. (You could also make the point that group communication skills are being poorly practiced.)

Much of the literature concerning group communication is actually concerned more with decision making.[26] In the workplace, groups usually convene to solve problems or to make decisions. (Group decision making is covered in detail in Chapter Seven, Decision Making.) A problem-solving and/or decision-making group is defined as three or more persons "who are interacting with one another in such a manner that each person influences and is influenced by each other person."[27]

It is important to note that groups need not be formed for formal purposes (to solve problems, make decisions, or disseminate information). Communication among members of a work group takes place for a wide variety of reasons which can be tied to the informal, as well as formal, organization. The emphasis of this section, however, is placed on communication among members of a **formal group.** A formal group is comprised of members brought together for the sole purpose of making decisions or solving problems.

Formal group: A group comprised of members brought together for the sole purpose of making decisions and solving problems.

Group Size and Communication

The question of optimum group size is related to *why* a group has convened in the first place. For example, information can be effectively communicated to very large groups convened to passively receive one-way communication (from several hundred students sitting in a lecture hall, to millions of people sitting in front of TV sets across the country). Effective two-way interaction among group members requires a smaller group size. Smaller groups (three to seven people) provide for more active information exchange relative to large groups.

Five to seven people is usually the best size for a problem-solving/decision-making group. Groups of four tend to set two pairs of people against each other, and a group of three tends to allow one person to "slide" from one position to another.[28] Scheidel and Crowell contend that a group of five people is "probably the smallest number in which the psychological forces tend to foster cooperation instead of setting the stage for contention."[29]

Bales's classic studies of small group interaction also support five to seven people as the optimum size for a problem-solving group.[30] In short, a group of five to seven persons is large enough to bring in a variety of ideas and small enough to function efficiently. Keep in mind, though, that five to seven group members is not a magic number! Sometimes the most important consideration in putting a group together is not group size, but the expertise and/or personal characteristics of group members.

Beware of Squeaky Wheels!

The more one verbally contributes to a group, the greater the likelihood that person will be perceived as being the leader (discussed further in Chapter Nine, Leadership). This is true *regardless* of the quality of what "the leader" communicates.[31] **"Squeaky wheels"** (talkative group members) do get the grease.

"Squeaky wheel": A talkative group member.

This phenomenon has a limit. Domination of verbal communication in a group can eventually lead to a reduction in the perceived leadership of the dominant person.[32] Essentially, as in the story of the "boy who cried wolf," group members can grow weary of listening to a dominant member.

The implications of the "squeaky wheel" phenomenon are straightforward. The *extent* of contribution by a group member should not be confused with the *quality* of contribution. In a problem-solving group, all members should actively solicit input from less talkative group members. This task is a particularly important part of the chairperson's job.

Listening

Probably the most important communications skill, whether in terms of interpersonal or group communication, is **listening.** Listening is a skill that involves the accurate receipt and interpretation of communication. Though active listening skills were discussed earlier, we will now go into more detail pertaining to group communication. Poor listening skills are sometimes less apparent, and more of a problem, in a group process than when two people are communicating verbally because there tends to be less accountability in a group.

Listening: A skill involving accurate receipt and interpretation of a communication.

Listening: A Lost Art?

Good, old-fashioned listening is an important part of effective communication. Yet, how often do we actually listen to what is being said by a speaker? And, if we're not listening, what are we thinking about? An answer to this question was presented at an American Psychological Association meeting in 1968 by Paul Cameron, then an Assistant Professor of Psychology at Wayne State University.

Professor Cameron collected the thoughts of his students at 21 random intervals during the course of a nine-week quarter. He discovered the following:

- About 20 percent of the students were pursuing erotic thoughts.
- Another 20 percent were reminiscing about something.
- About 40 percent were daydreaming, thinking about food or religion.
- Only 20 percent were paying attention to the lecture, and of this percentage only about half were actively listening (only 12 percent of the entire class!).

Keep in mind that there is a difference between *hearing* and *listening*. A person with a finely developed sense of hearing can be a poor listener, whereas a person with a hearing impairment can be an excellent listener.

A key impediment to effective listening lies in the difference between the speed at which we can talk and comprehend the spoken word. We think much faster than we talk. Unfortunately, people have a tendency to fill up this cognitive spare time by daydreaming or thinking about subjects other than those being communicated by a speaker at a given moment. A key to more effective listening is to use this "spare time" to better understand what the speaker is communicating.[33]

In a discussion of listening in small groups, Brilhart offers the following suggestions (which also apply to interpersonal communication):

1. Fully understand a question or statement of a fellow discussant before framing a reply. Try to avoid jumping to conclusions. Remember that you cannot listen both to your own "internal dialogue" as you think of what to say, and truly listen to what another person is saying.

2. Avoid becoming focused upon irrelevancies and distractions that do not relate to what the speaker is actually saying. Do not let the setting of a meeting or mannerisms of a group member distract from the content of the individual's presentation.

3. Do not become overly emotional or ego-involved.

4. Stay on the topic! Groups can easily become sidetracked. If sidetracking occurs, bring the group back to the topic at hand.

5. Keep using active listening skills—even if you disagree with a group member. You cannot effectively and constructively refute a position if you do not understand its basic tenets.[34]

Communication Networks and Rules

How communication flows through a group can be as important as what is said by group members.

Communication networks depict the flow of communication between and among members of a group. In centralized networks, information is communicated through a focal person; in decentralized networks, group members have direct access to each other. Figure 2–3 provides some examples of centralized and decentralized communication networks.

What communication network best facilitates group communication? The answer to this question is based on the situation and the nature of any decisions that must be made. Groups employing a centralized communication network, such as the "wheel" or the "Y," have been found to be effective at solving simple problems. Under these circumstances, groups make relatively few mistakes and solve problems quickly. When problems are relatively complex, decentralized networks such as the "comcon" or the "circle" are usually more effective.[35]

Highly centralized groups facing a complex problem do poorly because the channeling of all information through the facilitator creates an inefficient bottleneck. Also, resolution of complex problems benefits from direct sharing of information and other group resources, as occurs in a decentralized communication network typified by an open group communication process.

Research on satisfaction of group members has found that group members are more satisfied when communicating through a decentralized network. Baron notes that the reason for this is obvious: When individuals are left out of the group communication process they feel powerless and, consequently, dissatisfied.[36]

Implications of discussion of communication networks to this point seem straightforward. Use a centralized communication network when group tasks are relatively simple and use a decentralized network

Communication networks: Depict the flow of communication between and among members of a group. In centralized networks, communications flow through a focal person; in decentralized networks, group members have direct access to each other.

Figure 2–3 Communication Networks

CENTRALIZED
NETWORKS
(Information flows through a
central member)

DECENTRALIZED
NETWORKS
(There is no central member)

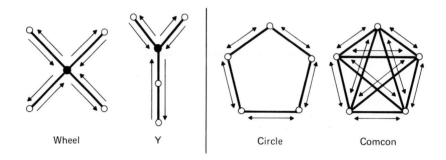

| Wheel | Y | Circle | Comcon |

→ = direction of information flow
● = central member
○ = peripheral member

Decentralized communication networks facilitate member satisfaction and are effective when dealing with relatively complex problems. Centralized networks are most effective when dealing with relatively simple, routine tasks.

Garcia, Joseph E.; Lewis, Chad T.; & Fiedler, Fred E. (1986). *People, Management, and Productivity.* Boston: Allyn and Bacon.

when tasks are relatively complex. If satisfaction of group members is important, a decentralized group communication process may be necessary even if group tasks are simple. Before moving on, however, these observations need to be qualified.

Laboratory studies of communication networks may have little to do with how groups communicate in reality. Brilhart has observed:

> Most of the so-called network studies of communication in task groups seem to be largely irrelevant to discussion groups in natural (as opposed to laboratory) settings. Persons passing notes through holes in plywood partitions (typical in network studies) to solve contrived problems im-

Bottlenecks frequently occur in highly centralized, overextended communication networks.

Drawing by Ziegler; © 1988 The New Yorker Magazine, Inc.

posed on them do not interact any more like persons in discussion groups than do baboons in a zoo interact like baboons in natural clans in a forest or veldt.[37]

Rather than think in terms of abstract communication networks, managers are better served if they approach group communication from the standpoint of **communication rules.** Communication rules define the communication process to be used by group members. If a relatively complex decision must be made, then a decentralized, consensus group communication process should be used. If the problem or the group's purpose is well defined, then a more centralized process using *Robert's Rules of Order* may be more effective. (See Chapter Seven, Decision Making, for further discussion of group decision making.)

Group communication using *Robert's Rules* is more centralized because it is channeled through a chairperson. In consensus decision making, group members communicate directly without going through a chairperson. This distinction between *Robert's Rules* and consensus processes is one of degree. In a natural situation (as opposed to the laboratory), group members still communicate with one another regardless of the communication rule employed. The difference lies in the amount of control exercised in the group communication process by the chairperson. *Robert's Rules*, or a comparable set of rules that control group

Communication rules:
Define the communication process to be used by group members.

communication, is *relatively* more centralized compared to consensus decision making.

In any event, it is important that communication rules (also referred to as *decision rules* in Chapter Seven, Decision Making), be they *Robert's Rules,* consensus, or some other approach, be clear to all group members at the outset of a meeting. It is also important that the group has an agenda (also discussed in Chapter Seven, Decision Making). Clear understanding of communication rules, together with an agenda, improve the group communication process. Communication rules facilitate the flow of information and the agenda provides direction.

Tips for the Manager. Although there is no "magic number" for the best group size, managers should try to keep the size of problem-solving/decision-making groups within five to seven members; should beware of "squeaky wheels"; and should encourage good listening skills. Group members should fully understand a communication from another member before framing a reply; avoid focusing on irrelevancies and distractions; not become overemotional or let ego get in the way; stay on the topic; and keep using active listening skills regardless of disagreement with a speaker.

Managers should use centralized communication when the group task is relatively simple. Decentralized communication, where group members are encouraged to communicate directly to other members in a relatively unstructured manner, is most effective when the group task is complex. Also, decentralized communication is usually more satisfying to group members. Consequently, managers should permit a relatively unstructured group process when a task is complex and/or when member satisfaction is particularly important.

Putting communication networks into action in real-world groups requires the use of communication rules (e.g., *Robert's Rules,* consensus). Accordingly, managers should be sure to clarify communication rules for group members. They should also set an agenda. Communication rules facilitate the flow of information, and an agenda helps to direct communication within the group.

ORGANIZATIONAL COMMUNICATION

As children, we used to play a game where we would whisper a message into the ear of a friend. This friend would then repeat the message to another friend. The process would be repeated down a long line of kids. You might recall that a message like, "The rain in Spain falls mainly on the plain" might end up like "A crane fell in the lane when hit by a plane." Problems with **organizational communication** are similar in principle to this example. Organizational communication is concerned with formal and informal vertical and horizontal communication within an organization.

Organizational communication: Is concerned with formal and informal, horizontal and vertical communication within an organization.

Good organizational communication begins at the interpersonal level. Application of the KISS Principle and use of active listening skills would have led to a more accurate result in the example cited above. The game we used to play as children did not provide for two-way communication. Keep in mind that organizational communication is the sum of its many communication parts. If interpersonal and group communication are not effective, then organizational communication— vertical or horizontal communication within an entire organization— also falters.

Poor Communications Didn't End with the Light Brigade

Ron Cuneo, Vice-President and General Manager of Honeywell Federal Systems Inc., tells the following story:

> The Charge of the Light Brigade during Great Britain's war with Russia in 1854 has long been memorialized in history and literature as one of the most gallant and courageous military acts ever. Into the valley of death rode the brave 600, school children learn from the Tennyson poem. But what is not taught in most schools is that this was a fool-hardy venture doomed from the start and made possible only because of a total lack of communication between the principals involved.
>
> The commanding general at Balaklava did indeed order a cavalry charge, but not into that "valley of death." His orders, carried to the Light Brigade by a captain, were totally misinterpreted. And to compound the blunder, when Lord Cardigan received those ill-fated and misconstrued orders he accepted them blindly, even though he knew they could spell only disaster.

Mr. Cuneo uses this lesson from history to emphasize a point: "To succeed in this market, we simply can't afford Light Brigade-style charges into the guns. And a major step in this direction is to talk with one another more often and more effectively."[38]

Vertical and Horizontal Communication

Vertical communication: Communication that flows through the organization in an upward or downward direction. Usually consists of management directives, information regarding changes in the environment (downward), or feedback (upward).

Horizontal communication: Communication across individuals and work groups at the same level within an organization. Facilitates coordination of efforts among organizational members.

Vertical communication in organizations refers to either upward or downward organizational communication. Downward communication consists of management directives or information regarding changes in the work environment. Upward communication consists of feedback from subordinates designed to keep managers in touch with what is happening (e.g., were directives carried out or orders followed?).

Horizontal communication in organizations flows *across* individuals and work groups. Its primary purpose is to facilitate coordination of efforts among organizational members. This coordination occurs within a work group or between groups and individuals.

Vertical communication is common in larger organizations. Large organizations tend to have "tall" organizational charts with several managerial layers. Vertical communication is more efficient under these circumstances. However, as noted previously, dissatisfaction results if people are excluded from communication flows. It is not surprising that such dissatisfaction often occurs in large organizations. (See Figure 2–4.)

Horizontal communication in a "tall" organization may be reduced because each department or division is jealously guarding its territory. Another problem associated with status differences in "tall" organizations is the tendency of subordinates to be hesitant to pass on

Figure 2–4 Organizational Communication

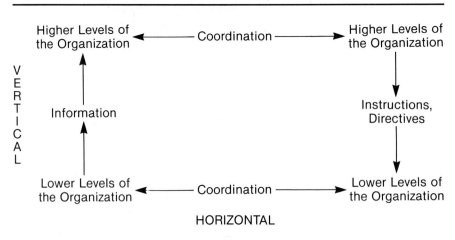

Notice that communication flows tend to be one-way in "tall" organizational structures.

bad news to superiors. As a result of this tendency, known as the **MUM Effect,** an organization could be on the verge of disaster and top management wouldn't know until it was too late![39]

There are no clear-cut solutions to organizational communication problems in large organizations. Managers should be mindful of the problems of vertical communication and should practice good communication techniques (as covered in this chapter), including solicitation of two-way communication whenever possible.

MUM Effect: Tendency of subordinates to be hesitant to pass on bad news to superiors.

Informal Communication Channels

To this point, discussion of organizational communication has focused on the formal organization depicted in an organizational chart. There is also an **informal organization.** No company document portrays the informal organization, as this "organization" is determined by the status, power, politics, friendship ties, and proximity of organization members.

Informal organization: Is determined by the status, power, and politics of organization members.

The communication channel that connects the informal organization is called the **grapevine.** The grapevine is an informal communication channel that exists in all organizations. The grapevine stems from the need of people to understand what is happening around them. It acts as an "escape valve" for employee tensions and is usually quite active in organizations undergoing considerable change. It is surprisingly accurate. One often-cited study found that about 80 percent of the information transmitted through the grapevine was correct.[40] Problems occur, however, because 20 percent of grapevine information is inaccurate, and because even if it is accurate, the information may not be understood in context.

Grapevine: The communications channel that connects the informal organization.

The grapevine is the communication channel that carries all *rumors.* Although it is difficult to combat rumors, managers can dispel rumors by providing accurate information, discrediting the source of a rumor, or helping subordinates to recall facts or experiences of their own that are contrary to the rumor.

Tips for the Manager.   Resolving communication problems associated with "tall" organizational structures is not a clear-cut proposition. By necessity, vertical communication flows (typical in "tall" organizations) tend to be one-way. Achieving mutual understanding, however, requires two-way communication. Consequently, managers in "tall" organizations should try to establish two-way communication when necessary, and always apply good interpersonal communication techniques, as covered in this chapter.

Managers should also not forget the grapevine! Combat rumors by providing accurate information, discrediting the source of a rumor, or encouraging subordinates to recall facts or experiences of their own that are contrary to the rumor.

SUMMARY: FOCUS ON SKILLS

Communication is defined as a process whereby symbols generated by people are received and responded to by other people.[41] The purpose of individual (interpersonal), group, and organizational communication is to achieve meaning for the purpose of improving individual, group, and organizational productivity.

Following are 23 suggestions for improving interpersonal, group, and organizational communication.

Managers should:

1. Keep in mind that communication is pervasive. It includes all nonverbal, written, and verbal attempts to achieve meaning.

2. Actively solicit feedback from others in the environment. On-going feedback can help managers to improve and otherwise assess the quality of their communications.

3. Learn and practice active listening skills such as paraphrasing and perception checking.

4. Understand that written communication can play an important role in clarifying communications.

5. Practice the KISS Principle in written and verbal communications.

6. Try to describe the behavior of others rather than critically evaluate. In this regard, it is more constructive to send "I messages" rather than "you messages."

7. Let others participate in problem definition and resolution. Do not overpower people; try to look for "win-win" solutions in a supportive, participative way.

8. Be honest in communications. Manipulative communication, or communication which is perceived to be manipulative, arouses defensive behavior in others.

9. Empathize! Stand in the other person's shoes. Cool indifference is seldom the best approach to communicating with an individual or a work group.

10. Try to avoid an air of superiority in communications with others. Remember the Japanese saying, "The pheasant that flies gets shot down."

11. Try to be tentative in comments to other people. For example, it is usually more constructive to say, "I believe . . ." than it is to say, "I know. . . ."

12. Remember that constructive communication is usually invited, timely, and is "soft on people and hard on the problem."

13. Conduct a periodic sensitivity audit of the environment. Ascertain the extent to which verbal and nonverbal communication is congruent, and the way in which communication is being perceived.

14. Check out discrepancies perceived in the verbal and nonverbal communication of others. Also check out nonverbal cues of others whenever there are doubts or questions with regard to meaning.

15. Be mindful of the importance of personal space. (Do not inappropriately violate the personal space of others.)

16. Use an open office design, intended to facilitate interpersonal communication with others.

17. Try to keep the size of problem-solving or decision-making groups within five to seven members.

18. Beware of "squeaky wheels." Do not confuse the extent of contribution by a group member with the quality of contribution.

19. Understand a communication from another group member before framing a reply; avoid focusing on irrelevancies and distractions; do not become overemotional or let ego get in the way; stay on the topic; and keep using active listening skills regardless of disagreement with a speaker.

20. Permit a relatively unstructured group communication process when a task is complex and/or when member satisfaction is particularly important.

21. Be sure to clarify communication rules for group members. Also set an agenda. Communication rules facilitate the flow of information, and an agenda provides direction for communication within the group.

22. Solicit two-way communication whenever possible and always apply good interpersonal communication techniques. Remember that good interpersonal communication improves organizational communication.

23. Never forget the grapevine! Combat rumors by providing accurate information, discrediting the source of a rumor, or encouraging subordinates to recall facts or experiences of their own that are contrary to the rumor.

■ CASE: "WOES IN THE WAREHOUSE"

Bill Wheels is the underground warehouse supervisor at the Overlake mine. He has four clerks who work for him. George Stevens is the regular day clerk. Kevin Davids is the clerk on the night shift. Bill Briggs works the graveyard shift. And Connie Neubauer is the fill-in clerk now working days with Stevens.

Last week Wheels met with each of the clerks to stress the importance of keeping the bins fully stocked to meet the needs of production and maintenance crews. Apparently, parts had not been moved from the receiving area to the bins near the warehouse service desk. Consequently, warehouse service was taking an excessive amount of time filling orders. Wheels felt if each clerk would keep the bins filled it would alleviate the problem.

He followed up his conversations with the following memo to the crew.

MEMO

TO: WAREHOUSE PERSONNEL
FROM: BILL WHEELS, WAREHOUSE SUPERVISOR
RE: INVENTORY REMINDER
DATE: FEB. 26, 1985

It is imperative that we maintain sufficient stores of materials in the bins to insure quality customer service. This is a high priority item.
  Let's keep with it.
  Thank you.

March 5, 1985: Stevens is upset over what has happened since his talk with Wheels. Now he comes in every morning and there is a load of parts on a pallet in the bins area. He tells Neubauer, "That good-for-nothing Briggs, I wish he would do his job."

"Well, what's the matter, George? Has Briggs messed you up?" asks Neubauer.

"Come on, Connie. Can't you see it? We get here just in time for the morning rush on equipment and parts every day. And ever since last week Briggs has been leaving us with a pallet in the aisles. That's just what we need. Something to fall over when the production and maintenance people are chewing us out for being slow."

"Should we tell Wheels about this?"

"Oh no! It will only upset him. He already has been getting grief from production and maintenance. He doesn't need to hear anything from us. Besides I don't want to be known as a squealer. Do you?"

"No way!"

March 7, 1985: On Thursday, after the management team meeting, Wheels runs into Dale Hartmann, night production foreman. Hartmann says, "Hey Wheels, you have trouble with your grave yard shift?"

"What are you talking about, Dale? My grave yard shift is fine!"

"Stop pulling my leg, Wheels. It's quite a stir."

"Well, what do you know, Mr. Super Snooper?"

"My sources tell me your dayshift doesn't get along with Mr. Briggs. He leaves the place a mess everyday and says he's just following your orders. Sounds like either he's playing you against the day crew or you have one very good soldier."

"Come off it, Hartmann. Where did you hear this trash?"

"One of your people—Davids. I think he works night shift."

"Just wonderful. I'll look into it."

Garcia, Joseph E.; Lewis, Chad T.; & Fiedler, Fred E. (1986). *People, Management, and Productivity.* Boston: Allyn and Bacon.

Case Questions

1. How could Wheels have been more effective in communicating his request to the crew?

2. What role did status play in keeping Wheels from finding out what was happening with his crew as a result of the memo?

3. How might Davids have found out about the situation with Briggs and the day shift?

4. What should Wheels do now that he is aware of his crew's problem?

■ EXERCISE: "RUMORS"

Verbal messages in organizations are distorted by a number of factors. These factors include the amount of information an individual can assimilate (leveling); interpretation of material based on an individual's personal frame of reference (assimilation); and attention to what is perceived to be the most important pieces of information (sharpening).

These three factors determine how well information is encoded and decoded across an organization. The purpose of this exercise is to observe how leveling, assimilation, and sharpening affect encoding and decoding of a message transmitted from one person to another over several iterations.

Consider the following questions as you participate in this exercise:

1. In what ways was the message leveled, sharpened, and assimilated? Which details were added or deleted? Why were these details added or deleted?
2. How could the messages have been more easily communicated and remembered?
3. What effect would two-way communication have had on the accuracy of the transmission of the message?

Forms

Your instructor may distribute rating forms on which you will note the occurrence of leveling, assimilation, and sharpening during transmission of information from one person to another.

Garcia, Joseph E.; Lewis, Chad T.; and Fiedler, Fred E. (1986). *People, Management, and Productivity.* Boston: Allyn and Bacon.

ENDNOTES

1. Toland, J. *The Rising Sun.* New York: Random House, 1970.

2. Coughlin, W. J. "The great mokusatsu mistake: Was this the deadliest error of our time?" In R. B. Adler and N. Towne (Eds.), *Looking Out/Looking In.* New York: Holt Rinehart and Winston, 1987.

3. Mintzberg, T. R. *The Nature of Managerial Work.* New York: Harper & Row, 1973.

4. Downs, C., & Conrad, C. A. "A critical incident study of effective subordinancy." *Journal of Business Communication 19* (1982): 27–28.

5. Weitzel, A. R., & Gaske, P. C. "An appraisal of communication career-related research." *Communication Education 33* (1984): 181–194.

6. Conrad, C. A. *Strategic Organizational Communication.* New York: Holt, Rinehart and Winston, 1985.

7. Likert, R. "Motivational approach to management development." *Harvard Business Review* (July-August 1959): 75–82.

8. King, S. W. "The nature of communication." In R. S. Cathcart and L. A. Samovar (Eds.), *Small Group Communication.* Dubuque, IA: Wm. C. Brown, 1988.

9. Scott, W. G., & Mitchell, T. R. *Organizational Theory: A Structural and Behavioral Analysis.* Homewood, IL: Irwin, 1976.

10. Stewart, J. *Bridges Not Walls* (2nd ed.). Reading, MA: Addison-Wesley, 1977, pp. 23–24. The spiritual child metaphor was developed by John Keltner and Loraine Halfen.

11. Johnson, W. "The fateful process of Mr. A talking to Mr. B." *Harvard Business Review* (January-February 1953): 56.

12. Rodgers, C. R. *On Becoming a Person.* Boston: Houghton Mifflin, 1961.

13. Bormann, E. *Interpersonal Communication in the Modern Organization* (2nd ed.), Englewood Cliffs, NJ: Prentice-Hall, 1982.

14. Baron, R. A. "Communication." In J. E. Garcia, C. T. Lewis, and F. E. Fiedler (Eds.), *People, Management, and Productivity.* Boston: Allyn and Bacon, 1986, p. 34.

15. Gibb, J. R. "Defensive communication." *Journal of Communication 11* (1961): 141–148.

16. Fisher, R., & Ury, W. *Getting to Yes: Negotiating Agreement Without Giving In.* Boston: Houghton-Mifflin, 1981.

17. Fast, J. *Body Language.* New York: Pocket Books, 1970.

18. Ibid., p. 146.

19. Mehrabian, A. *Tactics of Social Influence.* Englewood Cliffs, NJ: Prentice-Hall, 1972.

20. Ekman, P. *Telling Lies: Clues to Deceit in the Marketplace, Politics, and Marriage.* New York: Norton, 1985.

21. Burns, K. L., & Beier, E. G. "Significance of vocal and visual channels in the decoding of emotional meaning." *The Journal of Communication 23* (1973): 118–130.

22. Imada, A. S., & Hakel, M. D. "Influences of nonverbal communication and rater proximity on impressions and decisions in simulated employment interviews." *Journal of Applied Psychology 62* (1977): 295–300.

23. Adapted from: Brownell, J. *Building Active Listening Skills.* Englewood Cliffs, NJ: Prentice-Hall, 1986, p. 249.

24. Hall, E. T. *The Hidden Dimension.* New York: Doubleday, 1966.

25. Morrow, P. C., & McElroy, J. C. "Interior office design and visitor responses: A constructive replication." *The Journal of Applied Psychology 66* (1981): 646–650.

26. Hirokawa, R. Y., & Pace, R. "A descriptive investigation of the possible communication-based reasons for effective and ineffective group decision making." *Communication Monographs 50* (1983): 362–379.

27. Shaw, M. E. *Group Dynamics: The Psychology of Small Group Behavior* (3rd ed.). New York: McGraw-Hill, 1981.

28. Scheidel, T. M., & Crowell, L. *Discussing and Deciding.* New York: Macmillan, 1979.

29. Ibid., p. 12.

30. Bales, R. F. "In conference." *Harvard Business Review* (March-April 1954): 48. Also see: Bales, R. F., & Borgatta, E. F. "Size of group as a factor in the interaction profile." In A. P. Hare, E. F. Borgatta, and R. F. Bales (Eds.), *Small Groups.* New York: Knopf, 1956.

31. Haynes, E., & Meltzer, L. "Interpersonal judgements based on talkativeness: Fact or artifact? *Sociometry 35* (1972): 538–561.

32. Baird, J. E., & Weinberg, S. B. *Communication: The Essence of Group Synergy.* Dubuque, IA: Wm. C. Brown, 1977.

33. Adler, R. B., & Towne, N. *Looking Out/Looking In.* New York: Holt, Rinehart and Winston, 1987.

34. Brilhart, J. K. *Effective Group Discussion.* Dubuque, IA: Wm. C. Brown, 1982.

35. Shaw, M. E. "Communication networks fourteen years later." In L. Berkowitz (Ed.), *Group Processes.* New York: Academic Press, 1978.

36. Baron, "Communication."

37. Brilhart, *Effective Group Discussion,* p. 102.

38. Ron Cuneo, Vice-President and General Manager of Honeywell Federal Systems Inc. (Originally published in an employee publication titled *The Eagle.*)

39. Rosen, S., Grandison, R. J., & Stewart, J. E. "Discriminatory buckpassing: Delegating transmission of bad news." *Organizational Behavior and Human Performance 12* (1974): 249–263.

40. Walton, E. "How efficient is the grapevine?" *Personnel 28* (1961): 45–49.

41. King, "The nature of communication."

CHAPTER THREE

Motivation

■ *Self-Assessment: "Work Needs Inventory"*

■ *Learning about Motivation*

■ *Case: "The Mess"*

■ *Exercise: "Goals and Motivation"*

■ SELF-ASSESSMENT: "WORK NEEDS INVENTORY"

Instructions: Each of the following numbered items consists of three statements. For each separate item, rank each of the three statements according to how descriptive it is of *your own* feelings or opinions about work or of your behavior in a work environment. In the blanks provided to the right of the statements, write *1* for the statement that is *most* descriptive, *2* for the statement that is *next most descriptive,* and *3* for the statement that is *least descriptive.*

Some of the statements imply that you are presently a supervisor; if you are not a supervisor, evaluate these statements according to the way in which you believe you would feel, think, or behave if you were.

Rank

1. a. When solving a problem, I like to work by myself and be solely responsible for the solution. _____

   b. When solving a problem, I like to work as part of a team and find a team solution. _____

   c. When solving a problem, I like to work as part of a team, but only if I am in charge. _____

2. a. Managers should set challenging goals for their subordinates. _____

   b. Goals should be set through mutual agreement of team members. _____

   c. It is important to set goals that are within the average individual's capacity to achieve. _____

3. a. My co-workers would describe me as a good listener. _____

   b. People describe me as fluent. _____

   c. I tend to focus my conversations at work on job-related matters. _____

4. a. I enjoy discussions that are directed toward problem solving. _____

   b. I sometimes take an opposing point of view in a discussion just as a matter of interest. _____

   c. I enjoy discussions that enable me to know my fellow workers better. _____

5. a. I enjoy being perceived as a team member. _____

   b. Belonging to a specific team is not a priority with me. _____

   c. I enjoy my individuality; being seen as a team member does not interest me. _____

Rank

6. a. I like to have feedback about how well I have worked with others as a team member. _____

   b. I like to have specific feedback about how well I have done a job. _____

   c. I am the best judge of how well I have done a job; raises and/or promotions are the feedback that is important to me. _____

7. a. The most important aspect of performance analysis is the setting of future goals for an employee. _____

   b. The most important aspect of performance analysis is the planning of an employee's future development. _____

   c. The purpose of performance analysis is to isolate what an employee has done correctly and what mistakes he or she has made. _____

8. a. Conflict is a tool that can be used to arrive at the best possible solution to a problem. _____

   b. Conflict can be very healthy; it keeps people on their toes. _____

   c. Conflict should be controlled; teams whose members argue among themselves are seldom productive. _____

9. a. A factor of concern with any problem solution is its acceptability to the team that must implement it. _____

   b. If I am convinced that a problem solution will work, I expect it to be implemented and I accept responsibility for the consequences. _____

   c. If I find a problem solution that works, I want to implement it; prolonging discussion about it with team members is usually a waste of time. _____

10. a. If one of my subordinates does something incorrectly, I show him or her how to correct it. _____

    b. If one of my subordinates does something incorrectly, I discuss the situation with him or her, and we agree to correct it. _____

    c. If one of my subordinates does something incorrectly, I tell him or her to correct it. _____

11. a. People should use mistakes as learning tools and thus improve themselves. _____

    b. I make mistakes, but as long as I am right most of the time, I deserve my job. _____

Rank

   c. I do not like being wrong; I do not make the same mistake twice. _____

12. a. With hard work and the support of the right management, an individual can overcome most problems. _____

   b. Hard work can overcome most problems. _____

   c. A strong commitment can overcome most problems. _____

13. a. I focus more on my personal relationships with my peers and my supervisor than I do on my relationships with my subordinates. _____

   b. I spend time and effort developing and improving my personal relationships at work. _____

   c. I develop personal relationships at work only when they help me to complete my work tasks. _____

14. a. "Do not step on people on the way up; you may meet them on the way down." _____

   b. "Nothing succeeds like success." _____

   c. "Nobody remembers the name of the person who came in second in a race." _____

15. a. If I am right, I will win in the long run. _____

   b. If I am strong in my convictions, I will win in the long run. _____

   c. I try to be patient with people; doing so pays off in the long run. _____

16. a. Workers produce satisfactorily when their supervisors work alongside them. _____

   b. Workers' productivity increases when they have input regarding their job tasks. _____

   c. Workers must be challenged to reach new heights of excellence. _____

17. a. I enjoy convincing my fellow team members to do things my way. _____

   b. As long as a decision is right, whether it was an individual decision or a team decision is not important. _____

   c. For any decision to become final, all members of the team that will implement it should find it acceptable. _____

18. a. I work well when I have a personal relationship with my supervisor. _____

   b. I work well in situations in which I am my own boss. _____

   c. I work well when I have deadlines to meet. _____

Work-Needs Assessment Scoring Sheet

Instructions: Transfer your rankings from the inventory to this sheet. Then add the numbers in each vertical column and write the total in the blank provided. The column with the lowest total represents your first-priority need; the column with the next-lower total represents your second-priority need; and the column with the highest total represents your third-priority need.

Achievement Need	Affiliation Need	Power Need
1a _____	1b _____	1c _____
2c _____	2b _____	2a _____
3c _____	3a _____	3b _____
4a _____	4c _____	4b _____
5b _____	5a _____	5c _____
6b _____	6a _____	6c _____
7a _____	7b _____	7c _____
8a _____	8c _____	8b _____
9c _____	9a _____	9b _____
10a _____	10b _____	10c _____
11b _____	11a _____	11c _____
12b _____	12c _____	12a _____
13c _____	13b _____	13a _____
14b _____	14a _____	14c _____
15a _____	15c _____	15b _____
16a _____	16b _____	16c _____
17b _____	17c _____	17a _____
18c _____	18a _____	18b _____
Total _____	*Total* _____	*Total* _____

■ LEARNING ABOUT MOTIVATION

In the early days of the Polaroid company, research staffers were known to work vigorously through the night. Similarly, illustrators working for Walt Disney's *Snow White* and other classic cartoons put in enormous effort in creating animated scenes. In contrast, we hear managers complain about employees who arrive late and leave work early, and the popular media and trade press constantly remind us that work quality in the United States is not up to par.

Why is it that some people are willing to work long and hard while others seem disinterested and lackadaisical? The answer to this question lies in an understanding of motivation.

WHAT IS MOTIVATION?

Motivation is a psychological state that predisposes people to pursue or avoid certain activities and goals. Both energy and direction are essential components of motivation. (See Figure 3–1.) A person may have energy (be aroused), but not be motivated, because he or she lacks direction. Alternatively, a person who is directed may not put forth effort to reach a goal unless he or she is aroused.

Motivation plays a major role in improving work **performance** (actual output), which is an important (if not the most important) purpose of management.

Performance and Motivation

Think for a moment about your favorite activities. How much time do you devote to them? What makes those activities different from tasks you dislike? Is it because you have special talents that enable you to

Motivation: Psychological state that predisposes people to pursue or avoid certain activities and goals. Energy and direction are essential components of motivation.

Performance: Actual output. Effective performance requires both motivation and ability, as moderated by situational factors.

Figure 3–1 Elements of Motivation

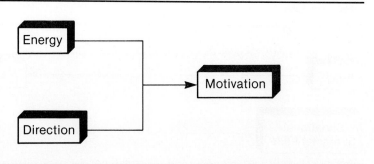

Energy and direction are essential components of motivation, an essential part of actual performance.

excel in performing the activity? Perhaps so, but one's *ability* to perform does not explain actual interest in an activity.

Think of all the people who like to sing even though they cannot carry a tune, or golfers who continue to play even though they are usually in the rough! The point is that motivation to perform a task is not the same as ability to accomplish the task successfully. We simply put more time and effort into tasks that we find motivating, regardless of innate talent or skill.

In short, motivation and actual performance are not the same thing. Effective performance requires ability *and* motivation, and is moderated by *situational characteristics*. (See Figure 3–2.) Consider someone who is highly motivated to become a dentist but has poor manual dexterity. It may be possible for Doctor Klutz to survive dental school. However, it is quite likely that Klutz's lack of skill will result in patients not receiving the best care. Another example can be seen in the manager who wants to be successful at leading others but does not know how to motivate subordinates.

Situational characteristics similarly affect performance. A mechanic, for example, may be highly motivated but cannot perform his or her job because of a scarcity of parts.

This chapter focuses only on the role that motivation plays in improving performance in organizations. However, one part of the performance equation, improving employee motivation, is an approach that can be accomplished on a regular basis by the typical manager. Improving work motivation does not usually require expensive modifications or disruptions to work flows. It often requires only the application of managerial skills.

Managers can improve employee motivation by recognizing and responding to employee needs; providing fair compensation and other rewards; setting clear, achievable, and acceptable goals; and offering

Figure 3–2 Contributors to Performance

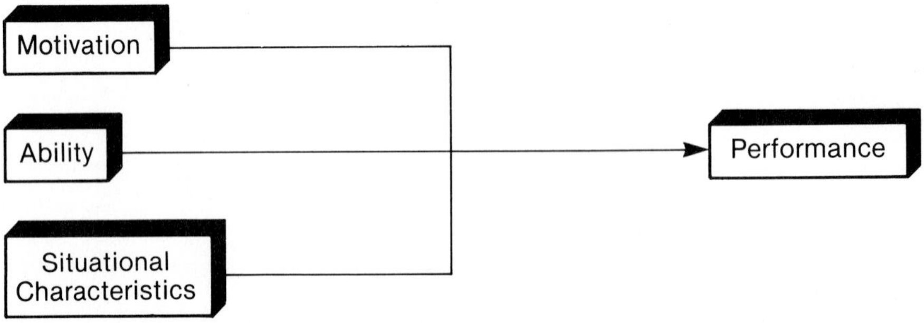

Motivation is only part of the performance equation. Ability to perform and situational characteristics also significantly influence performance.

Commentary: "Motivation"
Chris Gobrecht

The concepts of motivation, when analyzed, categorized, and theorized, can seem so complex and varied. When you consider that you are motivating *people*—very complex subjects, indeed—it's not hard to understand the complexities. Since motivation is such a critical aspect of athletic performance, coaches probably put more thought, preparation, and energy into motivating their people than the average leader.

Unfortunately, many leaders, including coaches, make the mistake of compartmentalizing the motivation aspect of their responsibilities. For this reason, the search seems always on for the latest gimmick, clever saying, threat, bribe, or reward. Although such things may play a role in the total motivation process, they are *far* from being the source for an individual's or group's motivation. True motivation is more a way of life than a tactic, more a daily occurrence than a year-end banquet, and much more related to the *expected* than the unexpected.

You have heard of the mountain climber who, when asked why he chose to undertake such an incredible task as scaling a mountain, replied, "because it is there." This gross understatement starkly reveals the true nature of human motivation. People do *not* act or fail to act for *no* reason, but often leaders fail to recognize or respond appropriately to the reasons.

Any leader's style of motivation will strongly reflect many of the attitudes and personality characteristics of that leader. Is it any wonder, then, that this stuff comes easily to some while others have to work at it? The important thing is to figure out the fundamentals of motivation and, while staying true to those fundamentals, perform them in a way that is compatible with your personality. One thing is for sure: *Nobody* responds to a phony.

I believe these fundamentals are at the heart of everything I do to aid the quest for the very best my basketball team has to offer:

1. Realize that the vast majority of people want to do the right thing. They want to be challenged, to excel, and to feel good about themselves at the end of the day. Superficial or too easily obtained positive reinforcement is not the answer; neither are unrealistic goals or skyscraper dreams. Give people something they can sink their teeth into—give them a way they can make a difference—then be sure that the fruits of their labor are obvious to them.

2. Respect people individually and collectively as a whole. There is *always* something to respect in a person. Make it obvious that you do, even as you may critically lambast or challenge the person to the height of his or her character. Downplay yourself and uplift them—if *you* are worthy of respect, you will get it without lobbying for it. People will not willingly work hard for self-promoting leaders.

3. *Know* what you want and *tell* them what you want. What often appears as a lack of motivation is in fact a lack of *information*. Most people want to please the person in charge, but can be frustrated and underutilized by a lack of direction. Clearly define your expectations. I am often asked, "How do you get your team to play

like that?" in reference to their all-out effort and willingness to do difficult things. The insinuation is that I must threaten them constantly or have some secret weapon to hold over their heads. My response is always the same: "We do it that way because we practice it that way and we practice it that way because nothing less is acceptable." Simple expectations are consistent and upheld!

4. Be *fair* and be *consistent*. Nothing shuts down a person's motivation faster than feeling he or she won't be treated fairly. This is a highly valued principle deeply instilled in most people. Consistency is so important for performance, but it is a learned ability. There has to be a standard for performance that is required day in and day out.

These are simple truths for what can be made a complex topic. All the gimmicks, rah-rah talk, incentive programs, or even pay raises in the world cannot take the place of these daily practices. Likewise, we have to be careful about not relying solely on doing things right and being a strong leader. Well-tuned motivational tactics and incentives can really put the icing on a rewarding experience for everyone.

Chris Gobrecht

Chris Gobrecht is the epitome of coaching success. In her first four seasons as the University of Washington women's basketball coach, Chris's teams compiled a 95–28 record. During this period, Gobrecht-led teams won one Pacific-10 championship as well as the last Northern Pacific Athletic Conference crown. Chris's peers have honored her twice for her achievements. She was voted Co-Coach of the Year in 1988 and Coach of the Year in 1987.

Chris is a 1977 graduate of the University of Southern California, graduating with a degree in public affairs. Following graduation, Chris worked as a Peace Corps volunteer for one year and taught English at St. Mary's College in Samoa. The Toledo, Ohio, native and her husband Bob are the parents of a son Eric and a daughter Madeline.

incentives valued by employees. This chapter addresses each of these topics, as well as other considerations pertaining to motivation.

MOTIVATION AND THE INDIVIDUAL

Managers frequently describe their most difficult problem as one of motivating an individual employee in their work group. "Why is it that I just can't get Miller to show a little enthusiasm?" is an often heard lament. An understanding of Miller's motivation can help to improve motivation leading to a gain in performance.

The following sections describe several theories of motivation as related to the individual. These theories explore how individual needs, expectations, and goals influence motivation and performance.

Needs as Motivators

People have a variety of *needs*. A need is the lack of something useful which, if present, would satisfy an individual. Needs for food, water, shelter, friendship, recognition, and self-expression are just a few examples of common needs. Motivational theories that address the role of needs agree that needs activate behavior.

A hungry person, for example, spends time and energy searching for food. Think of your behavior when you experience hunger. You probably find your way into the kitchen, check out the refrigerator or investigate the cookie jar. When you are lonely you might call a friend or a member of your family. You might go out to a common meeting place, perhaps the gym or coffee shop.

Having a need leads to arousal and requires finding an appropriate goal to satisfy the need. Put another way, a primary consideration in the need-based theories of David McClelland, Abraham Maslow, Clayton Alderfer, and Frederick Herzberg is that unmet needs motivate.

Need for Achievement

Professor David McClelland has studied a cluster of human needs that influence work motivation and leadership. Building on earlier work in personality theory, McClelland researched several important work-related needs, including the need for affiliation, the need for power, and the **need for achievement** (the need to exceed a performance standard).[1]

Need for achievement: The need to exceed a performance standard. High achievers tend to assume responsibility for tasks, seek task-relevant feedback, and prefer moderate risk situations.

Studies of need for achievement have demonstrated that those with a high need for achievement tend to concentrate more on personal accomplishments in comparison with low-need achievers. High-need achievers generally assume more responsibility for tasks, seek task-relevant feedback, and prefer moderate risk situations. Challenging tasks motivate high-need achievers.[2]

An intriguing aspect of McClelland's work are research findings that demonstrate the positive effects of need-achievement training on work motivation.[3] This training focuses on teaching people to think in achievement-oriented terms, to set high goals, and to develop self-awareness. Results of this program have demonstrated an increase in successful new business creation by a group of business people compared to an equivalent control group; an increase in the standard of living of a group of people living at the poverty level; and an improved level of effectiveness of a group of managers.

These efforts suggest that performance can be increased as a result of training that teaches people to focus on results. McClelland's training program was successful because it enabled individuals to focus their motivation. The components of this training can be applied to everyday life in organizations. Managers can remind or even train subordinates to think in terms of achievement, to set high goals, and to be sensitive to the effect of efforts on results. Managers should also match those with a high need for achievement with results-oriented jobs whenever possible (e.g., sales jobs).

Need Hierarchy Theories

Hierarchy of needs: Proposes that human needs are arrayed in a hierarchy ranging from primary needs (physiological and safety needs) to higher-order needs (social, esteem, and self-actualization needs).

According to Abraham Maslow's **hierarchy of needs,** human needs exist in a vertical structure, with basic needs such as hunger and thirst at the bottom of the hierarchy, and the need for esteem toward the top of the scale. (See Figure 3–3.)[4]

Only as lower-level needs are satisfied do higher-level needs take on motivational properties. For example, *physiological needs* such as hunger motivate to the extent an individual is hungry for food. Once fed, *safety needs* become motivators (e.g., the need for adequate shelter). Following safety needs on Maslow's hierarchy are *belongingness needs* (the need for meaningful social interaction with others) and *esteem needs* (the need for recognition). The need to *self-actualize* (the need to become all that you are capable of becoming) is at the highest level of

Figure 3–3 Maslow's Hierarchy of Needs

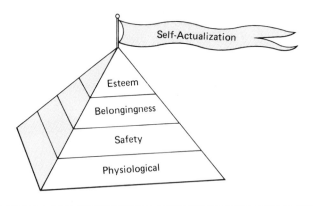

Maslow's hierarchy of needs is one of the most popular and intuitively appealing theories of motivation. According to this theory, unmet needs motivate, and progression up the needs hierarchy is blocked until all needs at a particular level have been met.

Garcia, Joseph E.; Lewis, Chad T.; & Fiedler, Fred E. (1986). *People, Management, and Productivity.* Boston: Allyn and Bacon.

Maslow's hierarchy. The unmet need to self-actualize motivates behavior only if all lower needs have been satisfied.

Maslow contended that most citizens in an affluent society will have satisfied lower-order needs, such as physiological needs and the need for safety. Consequently, unmet higher-order needs usually have greater motivational value in the North American workplace. An exception to this premise involves individuals who have experienced negative events such as job loss, rising financial obligations, or personal stress. Lower-order needs will serve as the primary source of motivation for people who have had such experiences. Essentially, under these circumstances, people have moved down the hierarchy of needs.

An attempt to improve on Maslow's theory is Clayton Alderfer's **ERG theory** of motivation.[5] This approach collapses Maslow's hierarchy into three needs: *existence, relatedness,* and *growth.* These needs correspond respectively to Maslow's physiological/safety, belongingness, and esteem/self-actualization needs.

ERG theory: Proposes three levels of human needs: existence, relatedness, and growth. Asserts that individuals move down the needs hierarchy if needs at a higher level have been frustrated.

In addition to simplifying Maslow's hierarchy of needs, Alderfer contends that individuals may remain at one level of a hierarchy if the satisfaction of higher-level needs is frustrated. In other words, higher-level unmet needs are not the only needs that motivate. An individual might remain at one level of the need hierarchy and remain motivated. Thus, Alderfer's model recognizes the flexible nature of needs in relation to motivation.

Although there has been little research support for the notion of a particular hierarchy of needs, Maslow and Alderfer's theories offer several useful concepts.[6] First, managers should help employees to satisfy unmet needs. In this regard, managers should consider nonfinancial rewards for employees who are well paid. Rewards such as recognition can be especially powerful sources of need satisfaction for these individuals. Second, managers should be aware that the importance of a particular need varies across circumstances. What motivates an employee on pay day, for example, may not motivate the same individual on some other day.

What Do Workers Want from Their Job?

A recent survey of members by the American Productivity and Quality Center found that having challenging work was rated as the most important motivating factor on their job. Following on the list, in ranked order, were: having your opinion matter, being recognized for a good job, and having pay reflect performance.[7]

What is your most important motivator?

Two-Factor Theory

According to Frederick Herzberg's **two-factor theory,** needs are satisfied by two types of job factors: *hygiene factors* and *motivators*.[8]

Hygiene factors are extrinsic to work and satisfy lower-level needs as identified by Maslow. These extrinsic factors include job security, company policies, quality of supervision, working conditions, and pay. In contrast, motivators are intrinsic to work. They serve to fulfill higher-level needs. Motivators exist in jobs that provide opportunities for achievement, recognition, responsibility, and advancement.

Herzberg differentiates between the effects of hygiene factors and motivators. The presence of hygiene factors, at best, only reduces job dissatisfaction. The presence of motivators, on the other hand, improves job satisfaction and work motivation. Herzberg has claimed that motivation and productivity problems are a result of managers relying too heavily on hygiene factors and underestimating the power of motivators.[9]

The results of research evaluating two-factor theory has not always supported the theory.[10] For example, two-factor theory regards pay as a hygiene factor, despite the fact that pay can serve as a source of recognition for achievement. Nevertheless, two-factor theory was the first theory to tie job conditions and outcomes with motivation and job satisfaction. This theory recognizes that human needs can be directly satisfied by work itself.

Expectancy Theory

An alternative view to need-based theories is the notion that motivation is largely determined by individual choice based on environmental factors. **Expectancy theory** embraces this view by describing the force of motivation as a function of an individual's perception that effort will lead to a required level of performance (*expectancy*); the likelihood that performance will lead to an outcome (*instrumentality*); and the overall attractiveness of the outcome (*valence*).[11]

Motivation is maximized to the extent that all three components of expectancy theory are high. For example, people will work hard if they feel a task can be accomplished; if they believe accomplishing the task will lead to a particular outcome; *and* if they value the outcome. Alternatively, the force of motivation is diminished if any *one* of these components is compromised.

You might work for a fair boss who provides rewards that you value highly. In this instance, instrumentality and valence are high—you know that preparing a report will lead to recognition you value highly. However, if expectancy is low—if you doubt you can actually prepare the technical report required by your boss—motivation will be low. No matter how fair your boss is, no matter how much you value recognition, your inability to conduct the mutlivariate statistical analysis required for the report will reduce your work motivation considerably.

Although expectancy theory has been found to predict individual motivation, it has been criticized on its assumption that behavior is largely a function of rational behavior.[12] Human motivation is not always rational. Critics of expectancy theory argue that the limited capacity of the human brain to store information, and the routine nature of day-to-day life, limits the usefulness of expectancy theory as an explanation of human motivation. After all, how much does the average person think about motivation on the way to work every morning? Moreover, most organizations provide a setting fully equipped with tasks that are familiar and routine. There are external control mechanisms (e.g., job orders, schedules, time cards) that provide direction and otherwise dictate the force of individual motivation throughout the day.

On the other hand, expectancy theory is especially useful for understanding motivation in situations that are nonroutine or where there are few social expectations for behavior.[13] Under these circumstances, cognitive processes affecting motivation are usually more deliberate and rational.

Goal-Setting Theory

Intention and choice are also central to the **goal-setting theory** of Edwin Locke and Gary Latham.[14] (See Chapter Six, Performance Appraisal, for further discussion of goal setting.) The process of setting a goal provides direction toward accomplishing a task. Specific and difficult-but-achievable goals have been demonstrated to lead to high levels of motivation and performance.[15] Telling an employee to "do your best" or to "give it the old college try" are not as effective as having in place a specific goal to increase sales by 15 percent by the next month. Moreover, a 15 percent sales increase, assuming it is achievable, will lead to greater motivation than a goal of 5 percent increase.

Goal-setting theory: According to this theory, setting specific, hard-but-achievable goals, accepted by subordinates, leads to higher performance than do vague goals or having no goals at all.

Hockey Team Uses Motivational Techniques to Win!

The application of goal setting, feedback, and praise recently improved the record of a college hockey team.

These techniques were applied in a recent study of motivation and performance. In the three years prior to the study, the team had performed poorly. This mediocre performance occurred despite the fact that the players were regarded as among the most highly talented in the school's history.

The researchers began by identifying a critical behavior for winning games. Legal body blocks (called *hits*) were determined to be the critical behavior based on discussion with team captains and other players. Next, the researchers used the first five games of the season to determine the team's base "hit rate" for comparison purposes. After obtaining the base hit rate, the motivational techniques of goal setting, feedback, and praise were introduced. A hard, but achievable hit-rate goal was established; feedback was provided on hits for each player for several games; and the coach was trained in giving praise to players for their hits.

As a result of these interventions, hits increased significantly, as did improvement in the team's win-loss record![16]

Effective goal setting requires goal commitment. Setting a goal has little bearing on motivation if an individual does not accept the goal. Individual participation in setting goals may lead to the adoption of more difficult goals and greater goal commitment; however, participation is not necessary for goal acceptance. Many studies have found that assigned goals can also lead to improved motivation and performance.[17]

In practice, deciding whether to use participation in goal setting depends on the relationship between the supervisor and employees, and the supervisor's need for employee input. When employees trust a supervisor's judgment, and the supervisor has adequate information upon which to make decisions, employee participation in goal setting is often not necessary.

Goal setting's success as a motivator requires the provision of *feedback*. Feedback provides information about progress toward the goal which improves performance by permitting individuals to adjust performance on the basis of goal-relevant information.[18] (See Chapters Two and Six, Communication and Performance Appraisal respectively, for further discussion of feedback.)

Goal-setting theory is consistent with *management by objectives* (MBO) in which an individual or department sets goals with time lines to direct the efforts of individuals or organizational units. In this sense, MBO is applicable as both a productivity enhancement tool and as a performance appraisal method. (See Chapter Six, Performance Appraisal, for further discussion of MBO.)

Tips for the Manager.   Improving work motivation is an excellent way to improve performance. Managers often have more control over the motivation of employees than over situational factors or the skill of subordinates.

David McClelland's work suggests that managers should remind employees to think in terms of achievement and become aware of the results of efforts on productivity. The work of Maslow and Alderfer asserts that individual differences exist in terms of where people are in a needs hierarchy. Managers should be sensitive to these differences. What motivates one employeee on a given day may not motivate another or the same employee on a different day! Based on need hierarchy theories and Herzberg's two-factor theory, it is plausible that higher-order social and esteem needs have more potency as motivators in the North American workplace because most people have already met primary needs.

In contrast to need-based theories that emphasize satisfaction of internal needs, expectancy theory and goal-setting theory see motivation arising out of deliberate, rational processes. According to expectancy theory, employees are motivated to the extent they believe they can do a job (expectancy) and believe that the job will lead to a valued outcome (instrumentality and valence). Goal-setting theory holds that employees are motivated to the extent they have specific, acceptable, and hard-but-achievable goals.

MOTIVATION AND GROUPS

The amount of effort put into tasks is not dependent entirely on individual needs or rational choice. The social context of organizations also plays an important role in affecting individual motivation. Consider the effect of the cheering crowd on the performance of an athlete or a co-worker's expectations on performance levels.

In the classic Hawthorne studies, conducted between 1927 and 1932, group expectations were found to have powerful effects on worker output.[19] In these studies, members of work groups put pressure on individuals to restrict output to a particular level. Employees who violated the expected output level were subject to name calling and "binging" from co-workers (binging involved hitting another employee as hard as possible on the upper arm). Employees who turned out too much work were called *rate busters;* those who turned out too little were labeled *chiselers.*

Although physical abuse and name calling may be less common today, group pressure continues to play an important part in motivation. The following sections describe several theories that explain how work groups influence individual motivation.

Equity Theory

Equity theory: States that people are motivated by fairness. Perceptions of fairness are based on comparisons made by employees with "comparison others" in terms of the ratio between job inputs and outputs.

Equity theory builds on the notion that fairness is a strongly felt social value and that people prefer to be treated fairly.[20] (See Chapter Six, Performance Appraisal, for further discussion of equity theory.)

Specifically, equity theory states that individuals compare the ratio of their inputs (e.g., education, experience) and outputs (e.g., pay, recognition) to the same ratio of inputs and outcomes for "comparison others." (See Figure 3–4.) Equity exists when these ratios are equal. People tend to be more satisfied when relationships with others are perceived to be equitable.[21]

Employees are motivated to restore equity when these ratios are unequal. When undercompensated, salaried individuals tend to reduce the quantity and quality of work. Individuals working on a piece-rate system are more likely to reduce the quantity of output. (See page 73 for a discussion of piece-rate pay.) Undercompensated individuals also tend to be absent from work more frequently.[22]

Laboratory studies of overpaid, salaried individuals have found that an increase in quantity and quality in output occurs, whereas overpaid piece-rate workers show only an increase in output quality. Studies conducted in the field, however, indicate that overcompensation

Figure 3–4 A Sample of Work Inputs and Outcomes

Work Inputs	Work Outcomes
Effort	Money
Time	Authority
Responsibility	Freedom
Work Experience	Status
Skill	Travel
Business Connections	Company Fringe Benefits (Car, Health Club)
Aptitude	
Attitude	Stock Options
Previous Training/Formal Degree	Retirement Package
Certification or License	Recognition

Equity theory contends that individuals compare the ratio of work inputs and outcomes with "comparison others." As can be seen from these lists, there are many inputs and outcomes to consider in maintaining equity in the workplace.

does not always result in employee attempts to restore equity.[23] Instead, individuals have a tendency to rationalize overcompensation by inflating their self-worth.[24] Overcompensated employees tend to believe they are worth an inflated salary.

Equity theory makes the point that comparisons are relative, not absolute. An employee could still be dissatisfied with a significant pay raise if a less productive "comparison other" receives an equal raise. It is important that managers maintain fairness in the workplace. This is a challenging task because equity is determined by internal *and* external comparisons to the organization. That is, employees compare their ratio of outputs to inputs with "comparison others" in comparable jobs outside, as well as within, the organization. Only consistent fair treatment of employees minimizes inequity and reduces dissatisfaction and motivation.

The Comparable Worth Controversy

A 1974 study conducted by Norman Willis and Associates found that employees in the state of Washington who worked in female-dominated job classes were paid 20 percent less than employees working in male-dominated job classes of comparable worth. Nevertheless, Washington state was *not* guilty of violating the Equal Pay Act of 1963. Why? Because this act prohibits gender-based pay discrimination only when employees are working in the *same* job. No provision existed for correcting pay inequity occurring when people worked in dissimilar jobs of comparable worth to an employer.

The Willis study was the beginning of the comparable worth movement in the United States. Proponents call for "equal pay for work of comparable worth" to an employer, as opposed to "equal pay for equal work." The comparable worth controversy is not as much about *more* pay, as it is about *fair* pay for people working in female-dominated job classes.[25]

Presence of Others

The mere presence of other people, termed the **social facilitation effect,** affects arousal and performance.[26] The presence of others increases arousal and aids performance on simple or well-learned tasks, but interferes with performance on complex or unfamiliar tasks. You may have experienced the negative impact of this effect when you stum-

Social facilitation effect: Is demonstrated when the presence of others increases arousal and facilitates performance on simple or well-learned tasks, but interferes on complex or unfamiliar tasks.

bled through a presentation before a group on a subject you had just mastered.

Social loafing: Occurs when the presence of others in a group leads to reduced individual effort and performance.

The presence of others also leads to reduced individual effort and performance through **social loafing.**[27] (See Chapter Seven, Decision Making, for further discussion of social loafing.) Social loafing is the reduction of individual effort that occurs in a group setting when individual contributions can be masked.

Social loafing has been demonstrated in a number of tasks including brainstorming, rope pulling, and evaluating essays.[28] It has been found that people put more effort into accomplishing a personnel evaluation task when told they may later have to explain their ratings.[29] Individuals also put forth more effort when told that their ratings would be the only ratings used by researchers. From a manager's perspective, these results highlight the importance of making individual group members accountable for results.

Social loafing, however, appears to occur primarily when tasks are routine and relatively uninteresting.[30] Intrinsically interesting tasks with no set method of solution are not likely to lead to social loafing. Requiring a high degree of accountability from group members for these type of tasks may actually interfere with performance!

In summary, social loafing and social facilitation effects suggest that managers give employees greater freedom on complex and nonroutine tasks where the presence of others and close supervision inhibit performance. Conversely, on routine tasks managers should introduce individual accountability into the group process.

Tips for the Manager. Equity theory acknowledges that people make comparisons with others to evaluate how fairly they are treated. Perceptions of inequity lead to attempts to restore equity, especially if individuals are undercompensated. Attempts to restore equity can reduce work motivation or otherwise adversely affect performance. Consequently, it is important that managers understand and remedy potential threats to equity.

Social facilitation and social loafing effects both show how the presence of others affects motivation and performance. The presence of others enhances performance only on straightforward tasks. Being around others tends to lower performance on complex or unusual tasks. The social loafing hypothesis states that when individuals perform in a group, individual effort is less than if the same person completed the task alone. Increasing individual accountability helps to offset social loafing.

MOTIVATION AND THE ORGANIZATION

Think about the traditional auto assembly plant in which the automobile moves down the line and hourly paid workers are assigned a single task to perform. Contrast this with a plant where teams of workers build entire automobiles. The assembly worker has a simple, boring task, and pay is a function of time spent at work. The autoworker who participates in building complete cars has a much more interesting and challenging job.[31]

Consider an employee who owns a company and whose personal fortune rises and falls with the profitability of the company. Unlike the typical salaried worker, the worker-owner knows that his or her income is a function of his or her own productivity.

The organizational arrangements described in the preceding paragraphs affect motivation differently. Alternatives to assembly line work represent organizational strategies to job design. Employee ownership is an example of an organizational reward system. The sections that follow describe how these organizational systems foster effective motivation.

Job Redesign

Too frequently, organizations do not consider the impact of job design on worker motivation (or worker stress; see Chapter Five, Stress). Jobs are often designed from a technical and efficiency perspective, and little attention is given to creating interesting and challenging work. Consequently, employee motivation suffers.

Job enrichment is one approach to designing work that is motivating. (See Chapter Ten, Organization Development, for further discussion of job enrichment.) Job enrichment was first made popular through Frederick Herzberg's two-factor theory of motivation (discussed previously in this chapter). Herzberg recommended that employers enrich work by building motivators into employee jobs. (Recall that motivators are intrinsic factors, such as opportunity for advancement and praise, that lead to satisfaction.)

Herzberg's theory of job enrichment was extended by Richard Hackman and Greg Oldham's **job characteristic model**.[32] According to this theory, jobs with a high degree of *skill variety, task identity, task significance, autonomy,* and *feedback* are considered to be high in motivating potential for employees who have high *growth needs*.[33] (Definitions of these terms can be found in the boxed insert on page 69; the model is outlined in Figure 3–5.) Managers should take these characteristics and the growth needs of employees into account when redesigning work to increase motivation.

Job characteristics model: An approach to redesigning jobs. Jobs with a high degree of skill variety, task identity, task significance, and autonomy are considered to have high motivating potential for employees with high growth needs.

Figure 3–5 The Job Characteristics Model

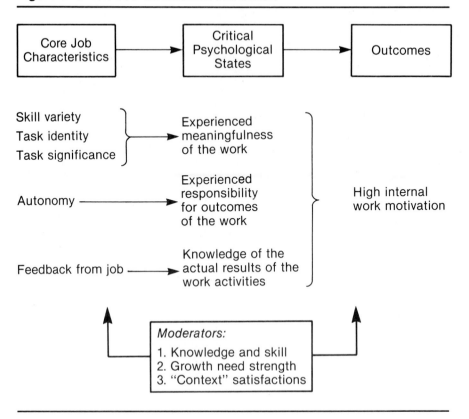

Note that knowledge and skill, growth need strength, and "context" satisfactions moderate the relationship between job characteristics and motivation.

Source: Hackman, R., & Oldham, G. R. *Work Redesign,* © 1980, Addison-Wesley Publishing Co., Inc., Reading, MA. Reprinted with permission.

The Job Characteristics Model

The motivating potential of a job is increased for employees with high growth needs when the following characteristics are present:

Skill Variety: The degree to which a job requires a variety of different activities involving the use of a number of different employee skills and talents.

> ***Task Identity:*** The degree to which a job requires completion of a "whole" and identifiable piece of work. That is, doing a job from beginning to end with a visible outcome.
>
> ***Task Significance:*** The degree to which a job has a substantial impact on the lives of other people, whether in the immediate organization or in the world at large.
>
> ***Autonomy:*** The degree to which a job provides substantial freedom, independence, and discretion to an individual to schedule work and to determine procedures to be used in carrying it out.
>
> ***Job Feedback:*** The degree to which carrying out work activities provides an individual with direct and clear information about the effectiveness of performance.[35]

Increasing the motivating potential of work will increase motivation of high growth-need employees if periodic feedback is provided to these employees; if employees have adequate knowledge and skill to do their jobs; and if context variables (e.g., pay, job security, and relations with co-workers) do not interfere with satisfaction.[34]

Redesigning work to increase motivation might involve having typists complete documents in their entirety for specific departments or individuals, in contrast with a typical arrangement where sections of unrelated documents are assigned among typists.

These typists would experience the entire piece of work (facilitating "task identity") and would understand the effect of their work on others (facilitating "task significance"). Typists should also be given considerable latitude (facilitating "autonomy") and be given the option of using different software to complete their work (facilitating "skill variety"). In this hypothetical situation, management should also provide adequate feedback to trained typists. There should also be no contextual problems to compromise satisfaction (such as inadequate pay).

Contextual variables, inadequate training, and/or the lack of high growth needs on the part of employees compromises the efficacy of job redesign. In the preceding example, typists with low growth needs might have been threatened by job redesign, perhaps regarding it as a management ploy to exploit workers. Also, the movitating potential of a redesigned job could be offset by inadequate pay or poor training. Managers need to be sensitive to these potential threats to job redesign. Do not assume, for example, that all employees are "ambitious."

Furthermore, redesigning jobs is not as simple as it might appear. Any change in the design of work affects other jobs in the organization.[36] For example, adding more autonomy to a line worker's job reduces the supervisor's responsibility for overseeing this employee's work. It may

Calvin and Hobbes   by Bill Watterson

Managers should be sensitive to individual differences in needs when assessing the motivating potential of jobs.

Source: CALVIN AND HOBBES COPYRIGHT 1988 UNIVERSAL PRESS SYNDICATE. Reprinted with permission. All rights reserved.

also reduce the supervisor's decision-making authority. Redesigning work may also turn out to be impractical and expensive, particularly if the organization has invested large sums of money in equipment or in developing a specific work process.

Job redesign is most likely to be successful for jobs that can be successfully modified within the context of the organization; for jobs that do not match employee growth needs; and in situations where managers and employees accept job redesign as a method for making work more satisfying and motivating.[37]

Organizational Behavior Modification

OB Mod: An approach to worker motivation based on principles of operant conditioning. OB Mod holds that organizational productivity can be improved by reinforcing desired employee behavior across the organization.

Organizational behavior modification (OB Mod) is an approach to worker motivation that is based on principles of *operant conditioning.*[38] The theory of operant conditioning contends that consequences of past behavior lead to, inhibit, or otherwise shape future behavior. For example, reinforcing (rewarding) a desired behavior in the present encourages the recurrence of this behavior in the future.

A reinforcer can be *positive* or *negative.* Positive reinforcement occurs when an attractive consequence is presented to an individual as a result of a behavior. Common positive reinforcers in the workplace include pay, praise, improved working conditions, and greater responsibility. Negative reinforcement is given when a noxious condition is removed or avoided as a result of an individual's behavior. An example of negative reinforcement in the workplace is seen when a domineering supervisor stops nagging when a report is completed on time. To reiterate, reinforcement of all types is intended to increase the future occurrence of a behavior.

Negative reinforcement is not *punishment*. Punishment occurs when a noxious consequence is delivered to an individual after a behavior occurs. Punishment, as opposed to reinforcement, is intended to *reduce* the occurrence of a behavior in the future.

Interestingly, supervisors can find themselves in an escalating cycle of punishment and negative reinforcement. For example, a supervisor receives negative reinforcement when he or she punishes an employee whose work station is untidy. The punishment (scolding the employee) leads to the reward (negative reinforcement occurring when the noxious condition of an untidy desk is removed). Under these circumstances, the supervisor is being reinforced for punishing employees and, consequently, will probably resort to punishment as a control mechanism in the future.

OB Mod emphasizes the use of positive reinforcement. Negative reinforcement tends to be less effective because it is usually associated with an accompanying negative response to the noxious condition in the environment (e.g., the nagging supervisor). The effect of punishment tends to be short lived and often leads to a counterproductive emotional response to the administrator of the punishment. Simply put, while punishment may satisfactorily moderate short-term behavior, employee resentment may lead to future problems between supervisor and employee.

Emery Air Freight and OB Mod

An outstanding testament to the success of organizational behavior modification was the success experienced by Emery Air Freight.

A significant improvement in customer service resulted when Emery managers began to reinforce desired behavior and provided feedback of results. Performance improved from 30 to 90 percent of a standard for responding to customer queries regarding service and schedules. This improvement resulted in an estimated savings of $650,000 per year for the company![39]

Reinforcement Schedules

An important aspect of operant conditioning is the **schedule of reinforcement.** Reinforcement is delivered on a *continuous reinforcement schedule* if a supervisor praises an assembly line employee every time the employee correctly assembles a part, or praises the employee at the same time every day. An *intermittent reinforcement schedule* occurs when reinforcement is applied sporadically, not after every previously designated behavior or time period.

Schedule of reinforcement: A plan used to distribute reinforcement. Includes continuous, intermittent, ratio, and interval schedules.

Intermittent schedules result in a slower rate of learning than do continuous schedules. However, intermittent reinforcement is more resistant to extinction of behavior caused by the removal of reinforcement. Also, continuous reinforcement is not very practical in most organizations because employee behavior cannot always be monitored. It is usually more practical to schedule reinforcement intermittently.

Reinforcement schedules are also distinguished on the basis of the functional relationship between the behavior and the reinforcement. Reinforcement that is administered based on the frequency with which a behavior occurs is called a *ratio schedule*. For example, sales personnel experience a ratio schedule of reinforcement when invited to join the "Gold Club" because sales exceeded a particular standard.

Reinforcement can also be administered using an *interval schedule*. This is reinforcement that is administered at periodic time intervals, contingent upon occurrence of desired behavior. A company that sponsors a company picnic every July 7th contingent on having had a "good year" is using an interval schedule of reinforcement.

Ratio schedules are preferable to interval schedules in the workplace. The problem with interval schedules is that the tie between actual performance and reinforcement is not as direct as it is with ratio reinforcement. Despite this inadequacy of interval schedules, it is interesting to note that most employees are paid on the basis of time intervals (e.g., hourly, weekly, or monthly wages) rather than on the basis of actual performance. For many employees, simply showing up for work is sufficient behavior to warrant payment of a weekly or monthly salary. It is not surprising to find that many employers are trying to find better ways to tie pay and actual performance together.

Social learning theory: Contends that behavior is influenced by observing the behavior of others.

In addition to operant conditioning, OB Mod incorporates **social learning theory,** which states that behavior is also influenced through observing others or modeling.[40] Modeling works when the observer views a person (model) with whom the observer can identify; the model performs a task which is followed by reinforcement; and the observer imitates and is then reinforced for performing the behavior. To be beneficial, social learning theory requires the modeling of appropriate behavior from top management on down. It is important to remember that employees tend to do as managers *do,* not as managers *say.*

In most organizations, behavioral consequences such as reinforcement and modeling occur unsystematically, promoting behavior that is not focused on the organization's goals. OB Mod attempts systematically to reinforce behavior consistent with organizational goals. First, behavior that is critical to organizational success is identified through systematic observation. Next, the incidence of these behaviors is compiled to form a baseline. Third, an organizational program of reinforcement of the critical behavior is implemented.

Finally, the effects of the program are recorded and compared with the baseline. OB Mod can be applied to a department or an entire organization. It is a powerful organizational tool for improving motivation and performance.

Reward Systems

An important reward for most workers is **pay.** Unfortunately, many organizations underutilize pay's effectiveness as a motivator.

Pay: Monetary compensation.

Cash Incentives: On the Way Out?

Cash incentives have been widely used in organizations to reward valued employees. These incentives are now coming under attack and some organizations are thinking of alternatives. Michael Weisman, President of Working Ideas Inc., a consulting firm, says that a $1,000 bonus represents little to an employee compared to a paid weekend vacation of the same value. The problem with the $1,000 bonus is that most employees use it to pay existing bills. The vacation, on the other hand, is memorable and the employee has something he or she values and associates with the company. Several companies have already shifted from cash incentives to vacations and even paid shopping sprees.[41]

Recent research indicates that to motivate employees effectively, the following conditions should exist in pay-based reward systems:

1. A high level of trust should exist between management and employees.
2. Performance should be measurable.
3. Pay distribution should reflect differences in performance.
4. Good performance should not be punished.[42]

Commission and Piece-Rate Pay Plans. Commission and piece-rate pay plans can be quite successful, particularly if the conditions described in the preceding paragraph are in place. **Commission pay** is based on a percentage of sales and is often used with sales personnel. **Piece-rate pay** is based on actual production; the more the employee produces the more she or he is paid. Being paid based on the number of flats of strawberries picked is an example of piece-rate pay.

There are drawbacks to these pay methods. Commissions can lead to unhealthy competition between sales personnel. Piece-rate systems

Commission pay: A compensation system where pay is based on a percentage of output (e.g., sales).

Piece-rate pay: A compensation system where pay is based on the number of units produced.

can cause workers to emphasize quantity over quality. With appropriate controls, both systems can work, but neither promotes cooperative efforts which may be more beneficial to the organization in the long run.

Gain-Sharing Plans.

Gain-sharing plans: Group or organizational pay plan that allows employees to share in the gains (profits) of a business enterprise (e.g., Scanlon Plan, ESOPs).

In contrast to individual plans such as piece-rate and commission systems, group plans do much to promote commitment to and cooperation between people in the organization. **Gain-sharing plans** allow employees to share in the profits of a business enterprise.

The Scanlon Plan, where employees set performance goals and share in bonuses when these targets are met, is an example of such a plan. Employee stock option plans (ESOPs) also engender commitment to the organization. Employees purchase stock in an ESOP at a discount based on eligibility criteria such as past performance or seniority. ESOPs are likely to be most effective when the company contributes significantly to the plan and management communicates the purpose and benefits of the plan to employees.[43] ESOPs do spur productivity. At Brunswick Corporation, for example, sales per employee increased by 50 percent after an ESOP was started in 1983.[44]

Alternative Pay Practices.

Alternative pay practices: Complement or otherwise modify traditional pay plans (such as cafeteria-style benefit programs, lump-sum salary increases, and skills-based evaluation).

Several **alternative pay practices** complement or otherwise modify traditional pay plans. These pay practices include *cafeteria-style benefits* in which employees select a package of benefits from several options (e.g., vacation and sick leave, insurance benefits). *Lump-sum payments,* where merit pay or salary increases are distributed in a one-time lump sum, and *skills-based evaluation,* where pay is tied to the number of jobs the individual is qualified to perform, are other alternative pay practices that are increasingly being used.[45]

These alternative pay practices all lead to increased satisfaction. However, there are some limitations to their use. Cafeteria plans and lump-sum increases are costly to administer. Skills-based evaluation requires an investment in training in order to enable individuals to qualify for a variety of jobs.

There is no simple answer to developing an effective reward system. Each approach has specific benefits and limitations for the organization. However, there is a general guideline to which managers should attend: For pay to be effective, it must be tied to effective performance. Professor Steven Kerr notes that "numerous examples exist of reward systems that are fouled up in that behaviors which are rewarded are those which the rewarder is trying to *discourage,* while the behavior he desires is not being rewarded at all."[46]

Tips for the Manager.   Managers need to consider the fit between employee needs and the job. Enriching a job for an employee with low growth needs would be ineffective. Also, managers should keep in mind that high growth-need employees require periodic feedback, must have adequate knowledge and skill to do their jobs, and context variables (e.g., pay, job security, relations with co-workers) cannot interfere with satisfaction.

The systematic use of positive reinforcement such as praise and recognition is also an effective method for increasing motivation. To implement OB Mod, managers should diagnose critical behaviors and record their occurrence before, during, and after the application of positive reinforcement.

Finally, formal reward systems in organizations promote motivation and commitment to the organization. Individual pay plans such as piece-rate or commission methods may lead people to maximize personal gain at the expense of the organization. Gain-sharing plans such as employee stock option plans (ESOPs) tend to orient employee effort toward the organization.

Alternative pay plans such as cafeteria systems are also effective motivators. The suitability of a particular plan, however, is dependent on the needs of the organization and the receptivity of employees. Most important, reward systems must be tied to effective performance and be viewed as fair.

SUMMARY: FOCUS ON SKILLS

Motivation is a psychological state that predisposes people to pursue or avoid certain activities or goals. Energy and direction are essential components of motivation.

Following are 18 suggestions for improving motivation at the individual, group, and organizational level.

Managers should:

1. Understand that individual performance is facilitated by three factors: motivation, ability, and situational characteristics.

2. Keep in mind that improving work motivation is an excellent way to improve performance. Managers often have more control over factors that influence motivation than they do over situational characteristics or the skill of subordinates.

3. Remind subordinates to think in terms of achievement, to set high goals, and to be aware of the effect of their efforts on

results. Match those with a high need for achievement with results-oriented jobs whenever possible.

4. Help employees meet unmet needs. Realize that most unmet needs in the workplace are higher-order needs related to needs for belongingness and esteem.

5. Be sensitive to individual differences in needs. What motivates one employee may not motivate another or even the same employee at another time!

6. Use coaching and training to increase employee belief that effort will lead to successful performance (to increase "expectancy"); ensure clear and consistent relationships between employee performance and work outcomes (to increase "instrumentality"); and provide outcomes that are valued by employees (to increase "valence").

7. Be sure that acceptable (to the employee), specific, hard-but-achievable goals are in place, and provide feedback to employees regarding progress and goal attainment.

8. Be fair. Keep in mind that employees perceptions of fair treatment are based on relative rather than absolute comparisons of "fair treatment" with other employees.

9. Combat social loafing by making individual group members accountable for their contribution to the group effort.

10. Increase accountability of group members if a group is involved in routine tasks. Avoid this practice if a group task requires a high degree of creativity.

11. Consider employee growth needs when enriching jobs. Employees with high growth needs are more receptive to job enrichment than are low growth-need employees.

12. Consider organizational effects when conducting job redesign. Redesigning a job or job class to increase its motivating potential can have a "ripple effect" throughout the organization.

13. Reinforce appropriate employee behavior with rewards such as praise, recognition, pay, and better working conditions.

14. Ratio reinforcement schedules tied to behavior are preferable to interval schedules tied to time periods. (Ratio schedules tie rewards to actual performance rather than to time periods.)

15. Remember that employees learn from and tend to imitate managerial behavior. Serve as a good role model for subordinates.

16. In implementing an OB Mod program be sure to identify critical behavior(s), establish a baseline, reinforce desired behavior, and evaluate the effect of the program.

17. To maximize the benefits of a pay-based reward system make sure that a high level of trust exists between management and employees, valid performance measures exist, pay distribution is related to performance, and desired performance is rewarded.

18. Always try to tie rewards to performance in a fair and consistent manner.

■ CASE: "THE MESS"

Curtis Taylor was great at digging out facts, following through on leads, and getting the company newsletter out on time each month. His initiative and the quality of his work were good examples to others in the public relations department of Bartt Engineering.

Curtis's manners and messiness, however, were deplorable. His desk, which was in the front office and visible to all visitors, looked like a hamburger stand's trash heap. There always seemed to be soggy paper cups, straws, and candy wrappers protruding from the landslide of papers. Worse than the chaos itself, though, was Curtis's penchant for borrowing books or documents then losing them in the rubble. And you could almost count on him to be rude or short on patience if anyone interrupted him.

Ron Landus, Curtis's supervisor, tried to explain to Curtis privately that while his work was acceptable, he needed to be more polite and better organized. Curtis said that he didn't care what other people thought about him or his desk and that he wanted to be judged on the basis of his work alone. He did concede, however, that he often had trouble finding things that he knew were on his desk. Ron stressed that Curtis needed to show some improvement in courtesy and cleanliness if he were to keep his job.

For several weeks, things seemed better. Curtis scowled a little in Ron's presence, but there were no more rude outbursts to guests, co-workers, or Ron. The top layer of debris on his desk got cleared away, although the improvement was barely noticeable to anyone who had not seen Curtis's desk before.

But a crisis came one afternoon when Carl Logan, the business office supervisor, stopped by to retrieve a file he had lent Curtis six weeks earlier. "Curtis, do you have that file I lent you for the statistics report you were working on?"

"It's probably here someplace," he answered, barely looking up from his desk.

"Well, I need it."

"If it shows up, I'll give it to you."

"I need it now, Curtis. I have a meeting in an hour, and I have to make copies of it to hand out."

Ron overhead the dialogue and intervened, apologizing to Carl and promising that he would have the file in 20 minutes. Then he and Curtis started to rummage through the debris, searching for the lost file.

"I think I have it," Curtis said pulling out a file with gum stuck to the cover and dripping with coffee.

"That does it," Ron said. He told Curtis to get his desk "spic and span" and to bring all borrowed books, files, and reports into his office before leaving for the day. Borrowed items would be returned, and he would try to salvage anything that was damaged.

When Curtis began slamming drawers and jamming things into the wastebasket, Ron wondered what he should say or do when Curtis came in.

By Grace Lander. Reprinted, by permission of publisher, from *Supervisory Management* (January) © 1985. American Management Association, New York. All rights reserved.

Case Questions

1. Which of Curtis Taylor's needs were being met by his job in public relations?

2. How did Ron Landus's behavior affect Curtis Taylor's performance?

3. What should Landus do to encourage and to facilitate a change in Taylor's behavior?

■ EXERCISE: "GOALS AND MOTIVATION"

Have you ever tried to achieve a formidable goal? Were you motivated to stick with the task or did you give up? These questions underscore the point that goal setting is important to motivating yourself and others. This exercise demonstrates relationships between goals and motivation.

Your instructor will be asking you to participate in one of three groups. You will engage in a task and then will analyze your group's performance. You will want to think about the following questions as you perform your task:

1. How did you feel about the goals your group was assigned?

2. How much effort did you expend to achieve your goals? Why?

3. What effect do you think feedback would have had on goal achievement?

Forms

Your instructor will hand out forms on which to record responses to the goal-setting task.

Used with permission from Farh, J. et al. (1987–1988). "Understanding goal setting: An in-class experiment." *The Organizational Behavior Teaching Review 12* (3), 75–79.

ENDNOTES

1. Murray, H. A. *Explorations in Personality.* New York: Oxford University Press, 1938. Also see: McClelland, D. C. *Assessing Human Motivation.* New York: General Learning Press, 1971; and McClelland, D. C., Atkinson, J. W., Clark, R. A., & Lowell, E. L. *The Achievement Motive.* New York: Appleton-Century-Crofts, 1953.

2. McClelland, D. C. *The Achieving Society.* Princeton, NJ: Van Nostrand, 1961.

3. McClelland, D. C. "Managing motivation to expand human freedom." *American Psychologist 33* (1978): 201–210.

4. Maslow, A. H. *Motivation and Personality.* New York: Harper & Row, 1954.

5. Alderfer, C. P. *Existence, Relatedness, and Growth: Human Needs in Organizational Settings.* New York: Free Press, 1972.

6. Wahba, M. A., & Bridwell, L. B. "Maslow reconsidered: A review of research on the needs hierarchy theory." *Organizational Behavior and Human Performance 15* (1976): 212–240.

7. *Wall Street Journal,* August 16, 1988.

8. Herzberg, F. *Work and the Nature of Man.* Cleveland, OH: World Publishing, 1966.

9. Herzberg, F. "One more time: How do you motivate employees?" *Harvard Business Review 46* (1968): 53–62.

10. Bockman, V. M. "The Herzberg controversy." *Personnel Psychology 24* (1971): 155–189.

11. Vroom, V. H. *Work and Motivation.* New York: John Wiley, 1964.

12. Ibid. Also see: Ilgen, D. R., Nebeker, D. M., & Pritchard, R. D. "Expectancy theory measures: An empirical comparison in an experimental simulation." *Organizational Behavior and Human Performance 28* (1981): 189–223; and Mitchell, T. R. "Expectancy models of job satisfaction, occupational preference, and effort: A theoretical methodological, and empirical appraisal." *Psychological Bulletin 81* (1974): 1053–1077.

13. Ajzen, I., & Fishbein, M. "Attitudinal and normative variables as predictive of specific behaviors." *Journal of Personality and Social Psychology 27* (1973): 41–57.

14. Locke, E. A. "Toward a theory of task motivation and incentives." *Organizational Behavior and Human Performance 3* (1968): 157–189. Also see: Locke, E. A., & Latham, G. P. *Goal-setting: A Motivational Technique That Works!* Englewood Cliffs, NJ: Prentice-Hall, 1984.

15. Locke, E. A., Shaw, K. N., Saari, L. M., & Latham, G. P. "Goal setting and task performance 1969–1980." *Psychological Bulletin 90* (1981): 125–152.

16. Anderson, D. C., Crowell, C. R., Doman, M., & Howard, G. S. "Performance posting, goal setting, and activity-contingent praise as applied to a university hockey team." *Journal of Applied Psychology 73* (1988): 87–95.

17. Locke et al., "Goal setting and task performance."

18. Tubbs, M. E. "Goal setting: A meta-analytic examination of the empirical evidence." *Journal of Applied Psychology 71* (1986): 474–483.

19. Roethlisberger, F. J., & Dickson, W. J. *Management and the Worker.* Cambridge, MA: Harvard University Press, 1949.

20. Adams, J. S. "Inequity in social exchange." In L. Berkowitz (Ed.), *Advances in Experimental Social Psychology* (Vol. 2). New York: Academic Press, 1965.

21. Walster, E. H., Walster, G. W., & Berscheid, E. *Equity: Theory and Research.* Boston: Allyn and Bacon, 1978.

22. Goodman, P. S., & Atkins, R. S. *Absenteeism.* San Francisco: Jossey-Bass, 1984.

23. Walster, Walster, & Berscheid. *Equity: Theory and Research.*

24. Mowday, R. T. "Equity theory predictions of behavior in organizations." In R. M. Steers & L. W. Porter (Eds.), *Motivation and Work Behavior* (4th ed.). New York: McGraw-Hill, 1987.

25. Lewis, C. T. "Assessing the validity of job evaluation." *Public Personnel Management 18* (1989): 45–63.

26. Zajonc, R. B. "Social facilitation." *Science 149* (1965): 269–274. Also see: Bond, C. F., & Titus, L. J. "Social facilitation: A meta-analysis of 241 studies." *Psychological Bulletin 94* (1983): 265–292.

27. Latane, B., Williams, K., & Hawkins, S. "Many hands make light the work: The causes and consequences of social loafing." *Journal of Personality and Social Psychology 37* (1979): 822–832.

28. Bartis, S., Szymanski, K., & Harkins, S. G. "Evaluation and performance: A two-edged knife." *Personality and Social Psychology Bulletin 14* (1988): 242–251.

29. Weldon, E., & Gargano, G. G. "Cognitive loafing: The effects of accountability and shared responsibility on cognitive effort." *Personality and Social Psychology Bulletin 14* (1988): 159–171.

30. Bartis, Szymanski, & Harkins. "Evaluation and performance."

31. Gyllenhammar, P. "How Volvo adapts work to people." *Harvard Business Review 55* (1977): 102–113.

32. Hackman, J. R., & Oldham, G. R. *Work Redesign.* Reading, MA: Addison-Wesley, 1980.

33. Glick, W. H., Jenkins, G. D., Jr., & Gupta, N. "Method versus substance: How strong are underlying relationships between job characteristics and attitudinal outcomes?" *Academy of Management Journal 29* (1986): 441–464.

34. Hackman & Oldham, *Work Redesign.*

35. Ibid.

36. Ibid.

37. Ibid.

38. Skinner, B. F. *Contingencies of Reinforcement: A Theoretical Analysis.* Englewood Cliffs, NJ: Prentice-Hall, 1969.

39. "At Emery Air Freight positive reinforcement boosts performance." *Organizational Dynamics 1* (1973): 41–50.

40. Bandura, A. *Social Learning Theory.* Englewood Cliffs, NJ: Prentice-Hall, 1977.

41. *Wall Street Journal,* August 17, 1988.

42. Lawler, E. E. III *Pay and Organizational Effectiveness.* New York: McGraw-Hill, 1971.

43. Klein, K. J., & Hall, R. J. "Correlates of employee satisfaction with stock ownership: Who likes ESOP most?" *Journal of Applied Psychology 73* (1988): 630–638.

44. Farrell, C., & Hoerr, J. "ESOPs: Are they good for you?" *Business Week,* May 15, 1989, 116–123.

45. Lawler, E. E. "New approaches to pay: Innovations that work." *Personnel 53* (1976): 11–23.

46. Kerr, S. "On the folly of rewarding A while hoping for B." *Academy of Management Journal 18* (1975): 769–783.

CHAPTER FOUR
Conflict and Its Management

- **Self-Assessment: "Conflict Management Style Survey"**
- **Learning about Conflict and Its Management**
- **Case: "A Woman in the House"**
- **Exercise: "The Ugli Orange"**

■ SELF-ASSESSMENT: "CONFLICT MANAGEMENT STYLE SURVEY"

Instructions: Choose a single frame of reference for answering all fifteen items (e.g., work-related conflicts, family conflicts, or social conflicts) and keep that frame of reference in mind when answering the items.

Allocate 10 points among the four alternative answers given for each of the fifteen items below.

Example: When the people I supervise become involved in a personal conflict, I usually:

Intervene to settle the dispute.	Call a meeting to talk over the problem.	Offer to help if I can.	Ignore the problem.
3	6	1	0

Be certain that your answers add up to 10.

1. When someone *I care about* is actively hostile toward me, i.e., yelling, threatening, abusive, etc., I tend to:

Respond in a hostile manner.	Try to persuade the person to give up his/her actively hostile behavior.	Stay and listen as long as possible.	Walk away.
_____	_____	_____	_____

2. When someone *who is relatively unimportant to me* is actively hostile toward me, i.e., yelling, threatening, abusive, etc., I tend to:

Respond in a hostile manner.	Try to persuade the person to give up his/her actively hostile behavior.	Stay and listen as long as possible.	Walk away.
_____	_____	_____	_____

3. When I observe people in conflicts in which anger, threats, hostility, and strong opinions are present, I tend to:

Become involved and take a position.	Attempt to mediate.	Observe to see what happens.	Leave as quickly as possible.
_____	_____	_____	_____

4. When I perceive another person as meeting his/her needs at my expense, I am apt to:

Work to do anything I can to change that person.	Rely on persuasion and "facts" when attempting to have that person change.	Work hard at changing how I relate to that person.	Accept the situation as it is.
_____	_____	_____	_____

5. When involved in an interpersonal dispute, my general pattern is to:

Draw the other person into seeing the problem as I do.	Examine the issues between us as logically as possible.	Look hard for a workable compromise.	Let time take its course and let the problem work itself out.
_____	_____	_____	_____

6. The quality that I value the most in dealing with conflict would be:

Emotional strength and security.	Intelligence.	Love and openness.	Patience.
_____	_____	_____	_____

7. Following a serious altercation with someone I care for deeply, I:

Strongly desire to go back and settle things my way.	Want to go back and work it out— whatever give-and-take is necessary.	Worry about it a lot but not plan to initiate further contact.	Let it lie and not plan to initiate further contact.
_____	_____	_____	_____

8. When I see a serious conflict developing between two people *I care about,* I tend to:

Express my disappoint- ment that this had to happen.	Attempt to persuade them to re- solve their differences.	Watch to see what devel- ops.	Leave the scene.
_____	_____	_____	_____

9. When I see a serious conflict developing between two people who are *relatively unimportant to me,* I tend to:

Express my disappoint- ment that this had to happen.	Attempt to persuade them to re- solve their differences.	Watch to see what devel- ops.	Leave the scene.
_____	_____	_____	_____

10. The feedback that I receive from most people about how I be- have when faced with conflict and opposition indicates that I:

Try hard to get my way.	Try to work out differ- ences coopera- tively.	Am easygo- ing and take a soft or con- ciliatory posi- tion.	Usually avoid the conflict.
_____	_____	_____	_____

11. When communicating with someone with whom I am having a serious conflict, I:

Try to over- power the other person with my speech.	Talk a little bit more than I listen.	Am an active listener (feeding back words and feelings).	Am a pas- sive listener (agreeing and apolo- gizing).
_____	_____	_____	_____

12. When involved in an unpleasant conflict, I:

Use humor with the other party.	Make an occa- sional quip or joke about the situation or the relationship.	Relate humor only to my- self.	Suppress all attempts at humor.
_____	_____	_____	_____

13. When someone does something that irritates me (e.g., smokes in a nonsmoking area or crowds in line in front of me), my tendency in communicating with the offending person is to:

Insist that the person look me in the eye.	Look the person directly in the eye and maintain eye contact.	Maintain intermittent eye contact.	Avoid looking directly at the person.
————	————	————	————

14.

Stand close and make physical contact.	Use my hands and body to illustrate my points.	Stand close to the person without touching him or her.	Stand back and keep my hands to myself.
————	————	————	————

15.

Use strong, direct language and tell the person to stop.	Try to persuade the person to stop.	Talk gently and tell the person what my feelings are.	Say and do nothing.
————	————	————	————

Conflict-Management Style Survey Scoring
and Interpretation Sheet

Instructions: When you have completed all fifteen items, add your scores vertically, resulting in four column totals. Put these on the blanks below.

Totals: _____   _____   _____   _____
            Column 1   Column 2   Column 3   Column 4

Using your total scores in each column, fill in the bar graph below.

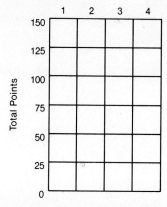

Now total your scores for Columns 1 and 2 and Columns 3 and 4.

                                         Score   Score
Column 1 + Column 2 = _____ A   Column 3 + Column 4 = _____ B

■ LEARNING ABOUT CONFLICT AND ITS MANAGEMENT

You have arranged a week-long trip to the mountains, complete with horses, camping gear, and a guide. Your "significant other" however, promised his mother that the two of you would pay her a visit in Detroit that week.

On the way to work you merge in front of another driver who takes exception to the maneuver and signals extreme displeasure. You let the gesture pass (though you entertained other thoughts).

At work, your assistant storms into your office with a problem. Apparently, a research and development team with whom your team had been working just completed a successful presentation to executive staff and were awarded bonuses for "exceptional problem solving." Your assistant is furious since your R&D team should have received recognition and shared in the bonus. (The two teams had worked closely together, each relying on the other for information and support.) Your entire work crew is now meeting at the water cooler, discussing how to get back at the other group.

Later, you explain to your boss that this bonus is likely to cause a serious rift between the two groups. Your boss accepts this explanation and agrees that recognition has been misdirected. She vows to talk to the executive staff and see that recognition and bonus dollars go to both teams.

Later that day, your counterpart from the other team comes by for a visit. He apologizes for slighting your group's efforts and suggests that the teams get together for a reconciliation party. You manage to avoid feeling suspicious and listen to what he has to say. Your competitor recognizes the talent available among your people. He wants to create a more collaborative working relationship between the two teams. You promise to present the invitation to your group and figure out ways to develop a mutually beneficial, future working relationship.

As can be seen from the preceding examples, conflict is pervasive and frequent because it occurs whenever and wherever people are gathered—from families, to work groups, to sports and volunteer groups. In the workplace, the ability to manage conflict effectively is an essential managerial skill. Up to 20 percent of a manager's time is spent actively managing conflict.[1]

WHAT IS CONFLICT?

Conflict is an incongruity of fit between the aspirations of interdependent parties. Definitions of conflict from different sources show the similarity of conflict as defined for individuals and groups:

Conflict: Occurs when there is an incongruity of fit between the aspirations of interdependent parties.

Conflict is:

"the interaction of interdependent people who perceive incompatible goals and interference from each other in achieving goals."[2]

"the process which begins when one party perceives that the other has frustrated or is about to frustrate some concern of his (or hers)."[3]

"the deliberate interaction of two or more complex social units which are attempting to define or redefine the terms of their interdependence."[4]

Note that each definition indicates that conflict begins as an interaction of at least two individuals or groups. These individuals or groups are interdependent. Conflict occurs during an interaction when one party is actually or potentially frustrating another party's aspirations (e.g., goals or needs). Most definitions of conflict have these elements in common.

Conflict can occur even though there is no actual interdependence or incongruity of fit between (or among) parties. The late Gilda Radner, former star of the television program "Saturday Night Live," made famous her portrayal of an elderly woman who misunderstood issues and proceeded to air her views about nonexistent problems on live television. When the announcer would break in to explain that the issue had been "rhinos visit the city" not "winos visit the city," Radner's character would look into the camera, smile sweetly, and say "Never mind."

This example may be humorous, but the problem is real. Conflict often occurs because of mistaken impressions or misinterpretations of what are otherwise benign actions or communications on the part of another.

Interdependence versus Independence

Interdependent relationships: Relationships where both (or all) parties must rely on one another to attain respective goals.

By definition, conflict occurs between (and among) interdependent parties. **Interdependent relationships** are relationships where parties must rely on one another to attain respective goals. Conflict is likely to be infrequent and constructive when interdependent parties have a close and accommodating relationship. Highly interdependent individuals and groups sharing incongruent goals may experience frequent and bitter conflict because they frustrate each other's aspirations. Under these conditions, establishing *independence,* as opposed to maintaining *interdependence,* effectively resolves conflict. When individuals and groups are unable to maintain a satisfactory "joint gain," one of the parties can resolve conflict by ending the relationship.

Unfortunately, the option of ending a relationship does not always exist. It may be necessary to maintain interdependence for a variety of reasons (e.g., financial ties in a business partnership, the need to maintain relations with a key supplier or customer, obligations inherent in international policies and business). The need to remain in interdependent relationships, coupled with the fact that it is impossible to resolve *all* conflict, means that conflict must be well *managed*.

Conflict Resolution versus Conflict Management

Attempts to resolve *all* conflict in an interdependent relationship can actually be counterproductive. (For example, a conflict-resolution strategy that calls for warring parties to "shake hands and stop fighting" might be a "quick fix," which does not provide for an understanding of issues necessary to long-term management of an interdependent relationship.) Although some conflict can be effectively resolved, managers should strive to maintain a *balance* between too much conflict, which is inherently destructive, and too little, which is counterproductive. The traditional view that all conflict should be eliminated is contrasted in Figure 4–1 with the current notion that some conflict is beneficial.[5]

Positive Effects of Conflict. There are several reasons why well-managed conflict is beneficial. An important benefit of conflict is that it signals a need for managerial attention and possible intervention. Conflict also brings concerns out into the open. Divergent views offered during decision making sharpen participant understanding of problem complexities and can lead to better outcomes as suggested by the old adage, "Two heads are better than one."

Business Partnerships and Conflict

A successful business partnership, like a successful marriage, requires the effective management of conflict. Poorly managed conflict results in the demise of otherwise successful business partnerships every day.

Estrangement among business partners has even fueled the growth of a new service industry—business dispute resolution and management. A few years back, Chicago attorney, Steven Levy, placed an ad in a trade publication that showed one man reaching into the company till while another had his hands around the thief's neck. The caption read, "Partner Problem? When it Comes to Money Sometimes Even Brothers Fight." A delighted Levy was inundated with responses for assistance.[6]

Figure 4–1 Traditional and Current Views of Conflict

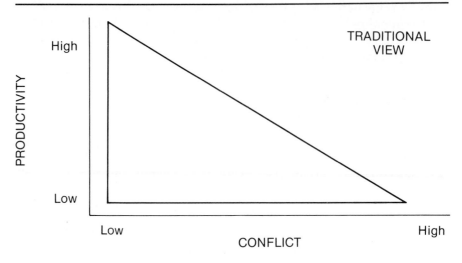

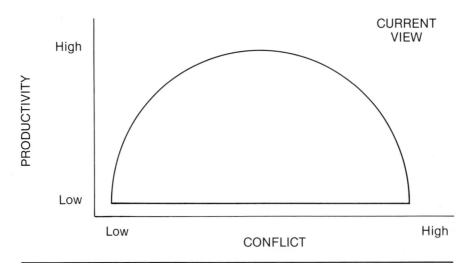

The traditional view of conflict does not take into account the benefits of a moderate amount of conflict to individual and group productivity. Some well-managed conflict is beneficial.

Adapted from Brown, L. D. (1983). *Managing Conflict at Organizational Interfaces.* Reading, MA: Addison-Wesley; and Gray, J. L., & Starke, F. A. (1988). *Organizational Behavior* (4th ed.). Columbus, OH: Merrill Publishing Company.

Conflict generally challenges individuals, heightens attention, increases the likelihood of innovation, provides for more careful consideration of new ideas, and encourages parties to monitor behavior more closely than they would under normal circumstances.[7] Well-*managed* conflict sharpens focus and can be stimulating and motivating.

The motivating aspects of conflict are pervasive and familiar. You have probably argued with a family member or friend over a historical or factual point and felt a strong desire to go to an encyclopedia or other reference to look up the correct answer to prove your point. You may have spent half a night solving a math problem just to prove you could do it after being challenged by a classmate or instructor. In the work setting, well-managed conflict provides the same kind of motivation and desire to prove oneself and to achieve.

INDIVIDUAL CONSIDERATIONS IN MANAGING CONFLICT

There are several ways to manage conflict, some more effective than others. Ruble and Thomas have classified **conflict management strategies** on the basis of *assertiveness* (behaviors intended to satisfy one's own concerns) and *cooperativeness* (behaviors intended to satisfy the concerns of others).[8] Figure 4–2 arrays conflict management approaches of avoidance, competitiveness, compromise, collaboration, and accommodation along the dimensions of assertiveness and cooperativeness.

Which approach best manages conflict? *Collaboration* would seem to be the best approach because it is high on both assertiveness and cooperativeness—all parties have their interests represented by a collaborative solution. The problem with this simplistic view, however, is that collaboration is effective primarily when interdependent parties are willing to ignore "power issues," have open-minded attitudes, and are mutually aware of the potential for conflict between or among parties.[9] Although collaboration is an ideal to work toward, other approaches can actually be more beneficial in the short term (e.g., collaboration is usually ineffective when conflict is rooted in value differences.[10] Under these circumstances, attempts to collaborate have the effect of emphasizing differences that are inherently irreconcilable).

Accommodation and *avoidance* are effective in handling temporary situations. You may choose to accommodate the rudeness of a temporary employee or a rude waiter at a restaurant because spending time and energy on a fleeting problem is not worth the trouble. Accommodation is also an effective approach when an issue is simply not important to the accommodating party. Avoidance can be a good way to temporarily handle the anger of another person or group. Heated

Conflict management strategies: Include avoidance, competitiveness, compromise, collaboration, and accommodation. These strategies involve different degrees of assertiveness and cooperativeness.

Figure 4–2 Conflict Management Strategies

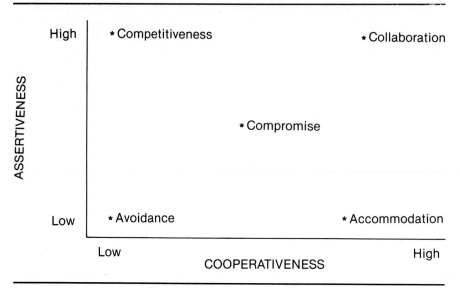

Collaboration, a conflict-management strategy high on both assertiveness and cooperativeness, is an ideal approach. However, circumstances sometimes dictate that other strategies be used.

From K. Thomas, Introduction, © 1978 by the Regents of the University of
California. Reprinted from the *California Management Review*, Vol. 21, No. 2.
By permission of the Regents.

exchanges tend to obscure substantive issues. Allowing people to "cool
off" by *temporarily* avoiding confrontation usually improves the quality
of a future exchange.

Peace for Our Time: The Failure of Accommodation

The Munich Agreement signed on September 30, 1938, by Adolf
Hitler of Germany, Neville Chamberlain of Great Britain,
Edourard Daladier of France, and Benito Mussolini of Italy was a
classic case of the failure of "accommodation" as a long-term conflict management strategy.

Britain and France believed that accommodating Adolf Hitler's drive to expand the boundaries of Germany would maintain
peace. Czechoslovakia was forced by this agreement to give a portion of its territory to Germany. Neville Chamberlain claimed

upon his return to Great Britain that the Munich Agreement meant "peace for our time."

Germany took over all of Czechoslovakia five months after the pact was signed, then invaded Poland to start World War II. This invasion took place on September 1, 1939, less than one year after the signing of the Munich Agreement!

A *competitive* (e.g., "power play") rather than collaborative strategy is indicated when self-interest has primacy, when ideological disputes need resolving, when an organizational "escape valve" is needed for independent parties, and when the vulnerability of any party is at issue.[11]

Compromise, rather than collaboration, has merit as a conflict-management strategy in the sense that it can be the "lesser of two (or several) conflict management evils." In a given situation, compromise may be more constructive than ignoring, accommodating, or trying to defeat an opponent.

In summary, no conflict-management approach is 100 percent effective under all circumstances. Ideally, a manager will be in a position where interdependent parties have relatively congruent goals, and where differences are not grounded in ideology, values, or in the belief that survival of any party is at stake. Under these circumstances, collaboration is the best long-term conflict-management strategy. A rationale for this assertion follows.

Collaboration: Constructive Confrontation

Before discussing the benefits of collaboration, we need to emphasize that collaboration does involve confrontation. This perspective may seem surprising as confrontation is often viewed as being negative. However, confrontation simply involves facing issues of mutual importance with another person or group.

Confrontation can be negative if one party attempts to win at the other party's expense. (This is the competitive strategy high on assertiveness and low on cooperativeness found in Figure 4–2.) A forced solution may not resolve the underlying substantive causes of conflict or the anger, frustration, and hostility that continues to build. The losing party in a confrontation may wait years to seek revenge, thinking he or she will "win" at last. Using force in a confrontation situation usually leads to a "win-lose" outcome. As noted previously, under certain circumstances a competitive approach to confrontation is necessary. However, unless actively engaged in trying to win a war or a contest, collaborating with others is much more constructive over time than is a competitive strategy.

"Well, Craigmeyer, I see we wasted our money sending you to that workshop on turning confrontations into constructive stepping stones for resolving conflict."

Constructive collaboration requires cooperation as well as competitiveness.

Reprinted by permission: Tribune Media Services.

Constructive collaboration leads to "win-win" outcomes which satisfy the needs of all those in conflict. Collaboration also helps to maintain a mutually satisfying relationship which, in turn, facilitates the future management of conflict.

Integrative versus Distributive Bargaining.   Walton and McKersie refer to constructive collaboration as **integrative bargaining**.[12] This approach to negotiation is a cooperative *and* assertive strategy used to maximize the joint gains of negotiating parties. Essentially, the idea is to find common or complementary interests and to adopt solutions that allow all parties to win.

Recall the classic story of two people fighting unnecessarily over an orange. If these people had explored mutual needs they would have determined that one wanted the orange peel (for baking) and the other wanted the fruit to eat. A power struggle could have been avoided and

Integrative bargaining: A cooperative *and* assertive negotiation strategy used to maximize joint gains of negotiating parties. Synonymous with *constructive collaboration.*

an integrative solution found if these parties collaborated. Do not assume that different needs or goals mean that mutual gain is impossible.

When conflicting parties do resort to a competitive strategy, bargaining becomes distributive. **Distributive bargaining** is used as an attempt to increase one's share of limited resources. In this traditional approach to bargaining, a competitive conflict-management strategy is employed; negotiating parties attempt to "get" as much of limited resources as possible. Invariably there is a winner and a loser.

Distributive bargaining: A traditional approach to bargaining that results in the distribution of limited resources and "win-lose" outcomes.

Getting to Yes: More on Constructive Collaboration

The previous section outlined conflict-management strategies and provided a rationale for *why* collaborative, integrative bargaining is an ideal approach to managing long-term relations between interdependent parties. This section will focus on *how* to collaborate successfully with another party.

Attitudinal Restructuring.   You might be thinking to yourself that parties attempting to collaborate through integrative bargaining are still likely to experience anger, frustration, and hostility toward one another. How does one mend fences during bargaining and yet still maintain momentum toward an integrative solution?

According to Walton and McKersie, one answer lies in **attitudinal restructuring.**[13] Attitudinal restructuring is intended to build bonds between individuals or groups by favorably influencing the attitudes of participants toward each other. For example, one party might unilaterally concede a point to give the other party evidence of good will in negotiations. Other attitude restructuring methods include open discussions of personal concerns or arranging for conflicting individuals to "pull together" to defeat a common enemy.

Attitudinal restructuring: Intended to build bonds between negotiating parties by building trust and favorably influencing the attitudes of participants toward each other.

Attitudinal Restructuring in the Middle East

Attitudes can be restructured in many ways. During 1977, Prime Minister Anwar Sadat of Egypt played a major role in establishing peace between the Israelis and Egyptians. Sadat, who four years previously had overseen a surprise attack on the Israeli homeland, traveled alone to Israel to speak face-to-face with Israeli Prime Minister Begin. His courage and vision did much to restructure attitudes held by Begin and his countrymen about the Egyptian enemy, and contributed significantly to the ultimate signing of an Egyptian-Israeli peace treaty.

Principled negotiation: When negotiating, involves separating the people from the problem; focusing on interests, not positions; inventing options for mutual gain; and using objective criteria.

Principled Negotiation.   Other bargaining skills should be used with attitudinal restructuring. Fisher and Ury have identified skills that help adversaries promote their interests for the purpose of creating and selecting options for mutual gain.[14] Fisher and Ury refer to their conflict management method as **principled negotiation:**

> The method of principled negotiation developed at the Harvard Negotiation Project is to decide issues on their merits rather than through a haggling process focused on what each side says it will and won't do. It suggests that you look for mutual gains wherever possible, and that where your interests conflict, you should insist that the result be based on some fair standards independent of the will of either side. The method of principled negotiation . . . employs no tricks and no posturing. Principled negotiation shows you how to obtain what you are entitled to and still be decent. . . .''[15]

Following is a discussion of the basic tenets of principled negotiation.

Principled Negotiation

1. Separate the people from the problem.
2. Focus on interests, not positions.
3. Invent options for mutual gain.
4. Use objective criteria.

Separate the People from the Problem.   Personal relations in negotiation tend to become tangled with substantive issues under consideration. Rather than attack problems, negotiators sometimes attack each other. This tactic not only compromises finding integrative solutions, but interferes with the maintenance of a long-term, interdependent relationship. As mentioned previously, maintaining a good working relationship after negotiations have been completed facilitates the *future* management of conflict.

Try to reframe personal attacks against you during negotiations as an attack on the problem. For example, let's say your boss, Harry, accuses you of being greedy because you ask for a modest pay raise. Rather than "go on the attack," you might respond by saying, "Harry, despite your contention that I am greedy, the fact remains that my productivity is up 10 percent and I haven't received a raise in three years." The *problem* in this situation isn't your greed—it is the fact that there is a lack of fit between your productivity and compensation. In

Fisher and Ury's words, try to be "hard on the problem, but soft on people."

Focus on Interests, Not Positions. Negotiations stall when people focus on *positions* (figuratively, when negotiators "draw lines in the sand" by taking an unwavering stand on an issue) rather than on *interests*.

Consider the example at the beginning of this chapter regarding a couple planning a vacation. She wanted to go camping; he wanted to visit his mother in Detroit. Each side argued a position that appeared to be incompatible. It is clearly impossible to go camping in the mountains and to visit Detroit at the same time. However, if this couple had focused on interests and concerns rather than respective positions, an integrative solution could have been found. Here is a summary of their interests and concerns:

She	He
I need peace and quiet; no family.	I need to see my family.
I need to spend quiet time with my mate.	I need to have excitement of others around.
I need exercise.	I need to be pampered.
I love horses.	Horses are nasty creatures.
I feel inadequate around his mother.	Mother is elderly and needs company.
If I give in, he'll think he can control me.	I'll feel guilty if I fail my mother.

In summary, she needs to feel she has control over her life, her mate's attention, and seclusion with him in an idyllic setting. On the other hand, he needs to provide security for his mother. He wants attention also, but primarily from his mother, not from his mate. This dutiful son wants to attend to his elderly mother.

An integrative solution is not possible if this couple holds fast to respective positions. However, by focusing on interests, a common meeting ground is possible. Perhaps this couple could pay a short visit to Detroit and stay in a hotel rather than in the family home, thereby providing more intimacy. Some of the visits to the mother could be from the son, giving his partner a chance to rest and to be alone (and to avoid her mother-in-law!). The vacation could be concluded by shortening the stay in Detroit to allow for a short visit to the mountains (without horses and long tiring days on the trail).

To summarize, try to avoid taking an intractable position in a negotiation. If in conflict with someone who has taken a seemingly intractable position, look behind his or her position to try to determine underlying needs. Respond to those needs in framing your replies.

Invent Options for Mutual Gain.   After identifying interests, it is necessary to create options that provide for mutual gain. Inventing options for mutual gain isn't as easy as the story of the vacationing couple might suggest. Stress associated with negotiation tends to reduce creativity.[16] People also fear being taken advantage of, looking foolish, having their ideas criticized, and feeling exposed.

Brainstorming is one strategy a negotiator can use to create options for mutual gain. (See Chapter Seven, Decision Making, for a detailed discussion of this technique.) Brainstorming allows for participants freely to propose alternatives for solving a problem. The key to effective brainstorming is separating the act of inventing options from critical evaluation of those options. Negotiators must be able to suggest any option—regardless of how impossible or crazy it might seem.

Look for dovetailing interests once all possible options have been placed on the table. Different needs per se do not mean that mutual gain is impossible, particularly if you find that your adversary only wants the orange peel while all you really want is the fruit.

Use Objective Criteria.   How would you determine the right price for a house you were planning to buy? Would you accept the realtor's word that a particular house is a good deal? Probably not. You would look at several houses and compare price versus amenities. You would also look for hidden costs such as costs associated with repairing a leaky roof, exterminating termites, or paying off liens against the property. You would also hunt for a low-interest loan. In short, you would not be satisfied that you had a good deal until you assessed a prospective purchase against a set of *objective criteria*.

Negotiators should evaluate differences against a set of objective criteria that seem fair and reasonable to all parties. Use of objective criteria allow negotiators to bring external data to bear on solving problems; problems and solutions can be better understood by all parties. The use of objective criteria by a negotiator also gives a position relatively more legitimacy.

When Principled Negotiation Does Not Work.   Unfortunately, there are times when "win-win" negotiation is difficult or impossible. As noted previously, when differences are rooted in value differences or ideological disputes, when an "escape valve" is needed, or when the vulnerability of any party is at issue, "win-lose" distributive bargaining often occurs. Sometimes an opponent simply does not want to cooperate.

Fisher and Ury recommend that negotiators use **negotiation jujitsu** when dealing with a difficult opponent. That is, when your opponent pushes you, don't push back. Instead, ask questions. Seek clarification. Reframe an attack on you as an attack on the problem. If absolutely necessary, make use of a **BATNA** (*Best Alternative To a Negotiated Agreement*). The more potent your BATNA, the better your bargaining leverage when dealing with a recalcitrant opponent. Examples of BATNAs include divorce, going on strike, quitting your job, and, quite literally, going to war.

Use the basic tenets of principled negotiation. Teach these principles to your opponent. As difficult as principled negotiation may seem, remember the example of Anwar Sadat (page 99). Sadat overcame his ideological differences, his vulnerability, and his country's need for an escape valve when he flew to Tel Aviv to meet with Begin. Once in Tel Aviv, Sadat found that he and Begin shared a strong mutual interest in peace.

Negotiation jujitsu: When negotiating with a difficult opponent, involves asking questions, seeking clarification, and reframing personal attacks as an attack on the problem.

BATNA: "Best alternative to a negotiated agreement."

Tips for the Manager.   Managers should view conflict as a potentially healthy condition to be managed. We say *potentially healthy* because well-managed conflict has a positive impact on a work group or individuals. For example, conflict signals a need for managerial attention. Managerial attention keeps problems from becoming worse.

Circumstances sometimes dictate use of conflict-management strategies other than collaboration. Managers should avoid conflict as a short-term tactic preceding use of a collaborative strategy and be accommodative when politically or practically expedient. A competitive strategy should be used as a last resort. ("Win-lose" bargaining is not conducive to maintenance of long-term relationships.) Compromise is never ideal, but should be employed when collaboration is not possible.

Traditional competitive, distributive bargaining leads to winners and losers because resources are perceived to be limited and joint gains are not considered. Collaborative, integrative bargaining, on the other hand, seeks outcomes satisfactory to all parties in a conflict situation.

Integrative bargaining usually requires some attitudinal restructuring in order to facilitate good relations and high trust between parties. Follow the basic tenets of principled negotiation when actually negotiating: separate people from the problem; focus on interests, not positions; invent options for mutual gain; and use objective criteria.

If dealing with a difficult opponent, employ negotiation jujitsu. If negotiations fail, employ a BATNA ("best alternative to a negotiated agreement").

GROUP CONSIDERATIONS IN MANAGING CONFLICT

If you attended summer camp as a child, you probably participated in competition between your cabin group and others. Remember how your group pulled together and by doing so achieved amazing accomplishments? Now think about competitions you have had with siblings or classmates. Do you remember how angry or frustrated you became if they bettered you or let you down? Do you recall being unsure of how to behave if you were the new kid on the block? If so, you experienced at an early age the powerful effects of inter- and intragroup conflict (conflict between and within groups respectively).

We'll begin by first discussing degrees of interdependence between groups. A discussion of norms and roles will follow, and we'll conclude with a discussion of what brings groups together or drives them apart. Communication, coordination and, ultimately, conflict between and among groups is affected for a variety of reasons.

Degree of Interdependence

Degree of interdependence: The degree of interdependence between groups in an organization. Groups have pooled (low), sequential (moderate), or reciprocal (high) interdependence with other groups.

The **degree of interdependence** differs among groups. Not all groups in an organization work closely with other groups. A group with *pooled interdependence,* for example, makes its contribution to the organization without relying on other groups within the organization.[17] (See Figure 4–3.) The plants that manufacture Boeing 767s and 747s have pooled interdependence, as each plant has independent inputs and does not rely on the other for its contribution to overall corporate profits.

Groups with *sequential interdependence* create outputs that become inputs for another group (Figure 4–3). One group is dependent on another for its input and the flow is in one direction.[18] Employees working

---

Commentary: "Conflict Management"

Margaret and Bob Bavasi

We must manage conflict within our business partnership and within our marriage. Prior to owning a minor league baseball team, we managed conflict as practicing attorneys within an inherently adversarial legal system. Margaret, in particular, while working as an attorney between 1981 and 1984, was involved in conflict management as a labor relations consultant.

We agree with the authors' observation that conflict can be resolved by leaving a situation or relationship if parties can truly become independent. Margaret was happy to leave a stressful law practice to take on the challenge of starting the Everett (Washington) Giants. This was an effective way for her to resolve irreconcilable conflict. Often, however, parties must remain interdependent. Under these circumstances, people need to know how to manage differences.

We believe that reconciling goals is an important prerequisite to effective conflict management. We think that managers could reduce or eliminate a lot of conflict by getting people to pull together from the start. Of course, this is often easier said than done.

It helps if all parties respect one another. Our marriage and business partnerships are solid because of mutual respect. The Northwest League, of which the Everett Giants is a part, succeeds only if team owners respect one another. Owners do not always agree, but if respect and commitment

exist, a necessary foundation for managing differences exists. It is very difficult to reconcile goals or to manage conflict if the other party is disrespectful or does not care.

Besides attending to goals and maintaining and earning the respect of adversaries, we think that using objective criteria is helpful. Do your homework! Conflict is reduced or avoided if people let data, rather than the strength of personalities, guide decision making. We should add that an important part of doing your homework is knowing your adversary's position as well as your own.

Above all, we agree with the chapter's emphasis on the value of "win-win" confrontations. If your confrontations are constantly of a "win-lose" variety, you may win several battles and still lose the war. Nobody likes to lose. We try to keep this in mind as we strive to make the Everett Giants the best franchise it can be for all involved: the Everett community, the fans, the staff members, ourselves, and, above all, the players and coaches without whom there would be no team.

Margaret and Bob Bavasi

Margaret Bavasi earned a BA degree in biology from Stephens College (Columbia, MO) and a Juris Doctorate from the San Diego School of Law. Margaret practiced employment relations

and labor law in the San Diego area between 1981 and 1984. She left this practice in 1984 to found the Everett Giants with her husband Bob. Margaret is Vice-President, Secretary, and Treasurer for the club.

Bob Bavasi earned a BA in psychology and a Juris Doctorate from the University of San Diego. Bob practiced civil litigation for the San Diego law firm of Thorsnes, Bartolotta, and McGuire between 1981 and 1984. Bob is the President of the Everett Giants.

The Everett Giants are the most successful affiliated franchise in Northwest League history in terms of winning percentage and fill ratio of their ballpark. *USA Today* has said that the Bavasis are aiming to "turn the Giants into the best little minor league franchise in the USA." Bob and Margaret live in Everett, Washington, with their three-year-old daughter, Haley.

Figure 4–3 Degrees of Group Interdependence

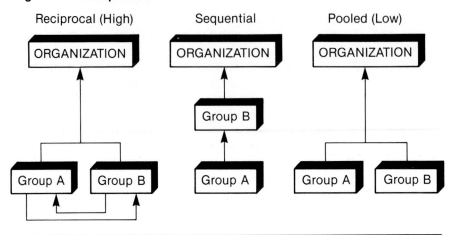

Degree of Interdependence:

The potential for intergroup conflict increases along with degree of interdependence.

Adapted from Thompson, J. D. (1967). *Organizations in Action.* New York: McGraw-Hill.

in a supply warehouse, for example, have sequential interdependence with those on the assembly line who actually assemble the product.

The highest interaction between groups results from *reciprocal interdependence* (Figure 4–3). In this case, groups trade inputs and outputs necessary to both; each is dependent on the other for their contribution to the organization.[19] The two R&D teams discussed in the example at the beginning of the chapter had reciprocal interdependence. Managers should keep in mind that conflict potential for groups with reciprocal interdependence is increased because these groups are highly interdependent yet often have different goals.

Norms and Roles

Conflict occurs when the behavior of an individual differs from the behavioral standards of the group. These behavioral standards are called **norms.** Put another way, norms are standards of behavior *expected for an individual within a group.*[20]

For example, a new employee might work late hours, volunteer for every committee possible, and skip scheduled breaks to do more work. This employee may be puzzled by the conflict his hard work has created

Norms: Standards of behavior expected for an individual within a group.

with less energetic fellow employees. After all, he's doing a good job! Nevertheless, there is a perceived incongruity between the aspirations of the individual and the aspirations of other group members.

As you might expect, work groups have different norms. The above example could be reversed; an unambitious employee could end up in a group with high production norms. Managers should try to understand the norms of the work group they are leading, and encourage establishment of norms that promote high productivity. We say *encourage* because ultimately norms are established by the group, not imposed by a manager. New employees should be helped to learn norms by including work group members in new employee orientation.

Standards of behavior expected for individuals *within a given position* are called **roles.** For example, by virtue of their position, mail sorters working in a mail room are expected to behave differently from members of top management.

Roles: Standards of behavior expected for individuals working in a given position.

Role conflict occurs when expectations from different roles are simultaneously incompatible. (See Chapter Five, Stress, for further discussion of role conflict.) For example, a single parent employed in a full-time job experiences role conflict to the extent there is conflict between the roles of "parent" and "employee." To whom does this person give her or his time and loyalty: family or work? Another example of role conflict occurs when you attempt to be both a friend *and* a boss (or a friend *and* a business associate).

Though some conflict should be expected in any role, managers can help reduce role conflict by clearly defining jobs and outlining expectations for subordinates. Such clarification helps people reconcile conflicting roles because roles and accompanying expectations can be better understood.

Group Cohesiveness

Group cohesiveness is the atmosphere of closeness that results in a group from common beliefs, attitudes, and goal directedness.[21] (See Chapters Five and Seven, Stress and Decision Making respectively, for further discussion of cohesiveness.)

Group cohesiveness: The atmosphere of closeness that results in a group from common beliefs, attitudes, and goal directedness.

High cohesiveness is generally regarded as a positive factor because member satisfaction is high. Factors that increase cohesiveness include agreement on group goals, frequency of interaction, personal attractiveness, intergroup competition (e.g., battling a common enemy makes a group more cohesive), and favorable evaluation of the group by an outside entity.[22] Factors that decrease cohesiveness include disagreement over goals, anything that decreases interaction of group members (e.g., excessive size, physical dispersion of members), fighting within the group, and domination of the group by one member or a clique.[23]

A poorly performing group can be turned around if group cohesiveness *and* constructive performance standards improve.[24] Note that high cohesiveness by itself does not mean that a group will be more productive or will make better decisions. (See Chapter Seven for a discussion of the detrimental effects of "groupthink.") For example, the output of a highly cohesive group engaged in sabotage will counter organizational objectives, as will the effectiveness of a cohesive group whose goal is to relax and to do as little work as possible.

Intraorganizational bargaining: Involves intragroup negotiation so that group members will accept outcomes negotiated with other groups by the group leader or negotiator.

Intraorganizational Bargaining. Managers can improve group cohesiveness by conducting **intraorganizational bargaining.** Intraorganizational bargaining involves intragroup negotiation (negotiation within the group) so that group members will accept outcomes negotiated by the group leader with other groups.

Intragroup conflict (as opposed to intergroup conflict) occurs when there is dissension and disagreement within the ranks. As articulated by Walton and McKersie, intraorganizational bargaining is intended to reduce the potential for intragroup conflict by building consensus within the group to a particular course of action.[25] Attaining this consensus, in turn, facilitates group cohesiveness and productivity, particularly if group members feel free to express views that may counter those of the negotiator.

Intraorganizational bargaining helps to align the needs of group members with each other and with the needs of the overall organization. A negotiator should bargain with the group he or she is representing as well as with an opponent. Never assume you have been successful as a negotiator simply because the other side agrees; your own membership must also be convinced! Conflict must be effectively managed within as well as outside the group.

Superordinate Goals

Superordinate goals: Higher-order goals that transcend differences between groups and lead groups to work together to solve a common problem.

Besides enhancing group cohesiveness, establishing **superordinate goals** also improves intergroup relations (relations between groups). Superordinate goals are higher-order goals that transcend individual group differences and compel groups to work together to solve a common problem.

Solidarity is increased within a group when attention is focused on overcoming an external problem (like a common enemy). In a classic study of superordinate goals, the Robber's Cave experiment, Sherif and Sherif found that when the seeds of intergroup conflict were sown—once a common enemy was recognized—the competing groups invariably pulled together.[26]

Sherif's experiment manipulated two gangs of 11- and 12-year-old

Superordinate goals facilitate group cohesiveness.

boys—the "Rattlers" and the "Eagles." Initially, the researchers promoted conflict between the groups by awarding prizes each time a group won a contest (treasure hunt, tug-of-war, etc.). Fighting and name calling between opposing group members became common. Later, the researchers introduced situations where cooperation to attain a goal important to both groups was necessary. For example, both groups were told the camp could not afford to rent a movie for both Eagles and Rattlers. Unless the two groups could agree on a film there would be no entertainment. By the end of the experiment, the introduction of superordinate goals had led to a cooperative climate between the groups.

An example of the successful application of superordinate goals in a real-world setting occurred recently in the Issaquah School District in Issaquah, Washington. Administrators, teachers, and parents worked together to save this financially strapped school district. Teachers and administrators agreed to pay cuts, students brought in their own supplies, and parents volunteered services. Soon, the district was "in the black." The positive experience of working together should also lead to more cooperative (and less competitive) future working relationships in the Issaquah School District, as competing parties learned the value of cooperating together for the common good.

Sherif's experiment and the example of the Issaquah School District suggest that managers can reduce intergroup conflict by establishing superordinate goals. This approach not only serves to promote harmony in the present, but can also result in better future working relationships.

Tips for the Manager. Managers should keep in mind that the more highly interdependent groups are, the greater the likelihood for intergroup conflict. Effective conflict management is particularly important under circumstances of reciprocal interdependence where inputs and outputs of two groups are tied together.

Managers should encourage group norms that promote high productivity. Also, managers can help to reduce role conflict by clearly defining jobs and outlining expectations for subordinates. Managers should also keep in mind that a poorly performing group can be turned around if group cohesiveness *and* constructive performance standards improve.

Conducting interorganizational bargaining and establishing superordinate goals are ways to facilitate group cohesiveness and constructive performance. Interorganizational bargaining involves bargaining with your own group as well as with an adversary. Establishing superordinate goals helps factions within a group or competing groups to pull together to attain a shared goal or goals.

ORGANIZATIONAL CONSIDERATIONS IN MANAGING CONFLICT

Promotive organizational climate: An organizational climate where interdependent parties perceive that gains or losses by one will result in gains or losses by another.

An objective of effectively managing conflict across all individuals and groups within an organization is the establishment of a **promotive organizational climate.** Organizational climate is defined as "the quality or property of the organizational environment that is perceived or experienced by organization members, and influences their behavior."[27] A promotive organizational climate is one where interdependent parties perceive that gains or losses by one will result in parallel gains or losses by another.[28] Integrative bargaining (as defined previously), and its resulting benefits, is encouraged by and leads to a promotive organizational climate.

Contrient organizational climate: An organizational climate where interdependent parties perceive that one party's gain will be another party's loss.

Conversely, a **contrient organizational climate** is one where interdependent parties perceive that one party's gain will be another party's loss. Contrient climates encourage and are caused by "win-lose" distributive bargaining among parties across an organization. Conflict tends to be nonproductive in a contrient environment because opposing groups and individuals work to defeat each other even if the overall organization suffers. Labor strikes and lockouts by management are good examples of the destructive effect of a contrient organizational climate.

Establishing and maintaining a promotive climate requires attention to how an organization is structured (e.g., the extent to which reporting relationships and responsibilities are clear across the organization) and to how people are treated (e.g., the extent to which employee needs are met).

Principles for Structuring an Organization

There are well-known, specific **organizing principles** developed to improve management, which help to manage conflict. Many years ago, Henri Fayol, a successful manager of a French mining company, introduced the principles of unity of command, the scalar principle, and the notion that authority should equal responsibility.[29] Another organizational principle that helps to manage conflict is having a manageable span of control in place for each manager.[30]

Organizing principles: Conflict-reducing principles that focus on organizational structure. Include unity of command, the scalar principle, maintaining balance between authority and responsibility, and maintaining a manageable span of control.

Unity of Command.   This principle states that all employees should report to only one boss. Perhaps you can recall the frustration felt when you were put in a job where you had more than one boss. Conflict in this situation could well have occurred not only between you and your supervisors, but also may have occurred between the bosses who were competing for your time.

The Scalar Principle.   Lines of authority and responsibility in an organization (the "chain of command") should be clear. When a chain of command is unclear, employees may approach the wrong supervisors for assistance and direction. Accountability for a given work area may be fuzzy, causing managers to blame one another if problems occur and to feel resentment if recognition goes to another party (as in the opening case involving the competing R&D teams).

Authority Should Equal Responsibility.   Responsibility (an obligation to act or to perform certain duties) should be balanced by authority (the power to act, usually based on one's formal position in an organization).

Have you ever been in a situation where you were responsible for doing a job but lacked the authority to carry out your responsibilities? An example of this situation occurs when a manager is responsible for the productivity of a work group but cannot hire (or fire) the people who work under him or her.

Span of Control.   Finally, each manager should have a manageable span of control. Having too many employees to supervise makes it difficult to maintain necessary control and leads to conflict when work group members fail to receive supervisory attention necessary to do their jobs. It was once felt that an ideal span of control existed (typically between five and eight employees). It is now apparent that the ideal span of control is entirely dependent on the nature of the work, the employees, and the capabilities of the manager.[31]

These organizing principles should be understood to be general guidelines rather than absolute rules.[32] There are exceptions to these rules. For example, a span of control excessive in one situation may be fine in another. Some organizational forms actually require that employees have two bosses (see the boxed insert on this page). Nevertheless, these principles serve well as general guidelines that help to manage conflict in most organizational situations.

Matrix Management

In recent years, matrix management has achieved considerable popularity (and notoriety!) as an organizational approach.

A matrix organization represents a hybrid of functional and product departmentation. All matrix organizations include a top manager who balances dual roles between functions and products, the matrix managers (functional and product bosses), and employees who report to two different bosses. Matrix management is usually used in high-tech companies where change is rapid and there is a strong need to communicate across functional and product areas. Matrix management helps the "left hand" (product teams) know what the "right hand" (functional areas) is doing and vice versa.

A matrix organization violates the principle of unity of command and the scalar principle as defined by Henri Fayol. It is not surprising to find that matrix management can lead to considerable conflict as matrix bosses compete for staff time and subordinates in the matrix are unsure of reporting lines in a given situation.[33] Nevertheless, the matrix works for some companies despite violating classic organizing principles.

Attention to People

Promotive organizational climates are also facilitated by managerial concern for the needs of people as well as concern for avoiding conflict inducting structure.

Classical management theorists like Fayol and Frederick Taylor (the father of scientific management; see Chapter Five, Stress, for further discussion of scientific management) have been rightly criticized for their emphasis on structure and managerial technique (e.g., time and motion studies) rather than to the needs of people. The advent of the human relations school management, the work of theorists such as Abraham Maslow and Frederick Herzberg, and the fact that the contemporary employee seeks and expects to find needs fulfillment in the workplace means that promotive organizational climates require managerial attention to the needs of individual employees.

Attending to structural needs and to the needs of people are very broad prescriptions for developing a promotive organizational climate. Generally, the effective manager effectively manages conflict. The practice of managerial skills covered in other chapters, together with the skills discussed in this chapter, improves conflict management at the individual and group level, thereby contributing to the establishment and maintenance of a promotive organizational climate.

Tips for the Manager. Effective conflict management across an organization leads to establishment of a promotive organizational climate. A promotive climate is one where interdependent parties perceive that gains or losses by one will result in gains or losses by another.

Establishing and maintaining a promotive organizational climate requires attention to how an organization is structured and to how people are treated. Conflict caused by structural problems will usually be reduced if managers adhere to principles pertaining to the unity of command, maintaining a clear chain of command, balancing responsibility and authority, and maintaining a manageable span of control. These organizing principles are not absolutes! Depending on circumstances, these principles can be violated (as in matrix management).

Promotive climates also require that managers attend to the needs of subordinates. Employees who feel their personal interests are considered are more willing to participate in processes that constructively manage conflict.

In summary, effective managers effectively manage conflict. The practice of managerial skills covered in other chapters also improves conflict management at the individual and group level, thereby contributing to the establishment and maintenance of a promotive organizational climate.

SUMMARY: FOCUS ON SKILLS

Conflict is defined as a perceived incongruity of fit between the aspirations of interdependent parties. Following are 22 suggestions for improving the quality of conflict management.

Managers should:

1. Know that it is not always possible to become truly independent from an adversary, nor can all "incongruities of fit" be resolved. Consequently, managers in interdependent relationships should focus on effectively managing conflict.

2. Keep in mind that effective conflict management can be beneficial to a work group or individual. Conflict signals the need for attention to a problem. Conflict also leads to sharpened attention and can contribute to higher levels of follower motivation.

3. Practice collaboration as a conflict management strategy whenever possible. Collaboration is high on assertiveness and cooperativeness. It leads to "win-win" integrative solutions in conflict situations.

4. Avoid conflict only as a short-term tactic preceding an attempt to use a collaborative strategy.

5. Accommodate conflict when politically or practically expedient.

6. Use a competitive strategy only when necessary. "Win-lose" propositions are not conducive to maintenance of long-term relationships.

7. Keep in mind that although compromise is never ideal it can be employed when collaboration is not possible and can be more effective than avoidance, accommodation, or competitive strategies.

8. Work on attitudinal restructuring with an opponent in order to facilitate good relations and to build high trust between parties.

9. Follow the basic tenets of principled negotiation when actually negotiating: separate people from the problem; focus upon interests, not positions; invent options for mutual gain; and use objective criteria.

10. When dealing with a difficult opponent, employ negotiation jujitsu and have a BATNA ready if negotiations break down. Put another way, if your opponent pushes you, don't push back. Ask questions. Seek clarification. Look behind your opponent's position. If negotiations fail, employ your BATNA ("best alternative to a negotiated agreement.")

11. Be mindful that effective conflict management is particularly important when leading a group that has reciprocal interdependence with another group.

12. Try to understand the norms of the group being led. Encourage establishment of norms that promote high productivity. Include group members in new employee orientation programs.

13. Help reduce role conflict by clearly defining jobs and outlining expectations for subordinates.

14. Know that a poorly performing group can be turned around if group cohesiveness *and* constructive performance standards are improved.

15. Conduct interorganizational bargaining as one way to improve group cohesiveness and constructive performance. Interorganizational bargaining requires that the manager (or other group representative) bargain with her or his group as well as with an adversary.

16. Never assume success as a negotiator simply because the other side agrees; your own membership must also be convinced.

17. Establish superordinate goals in order to build cohesiveness within your own group, to effectively manage conflict between groups, and to promote harmony with competing groups in the future.

18. Remember that establishing and maintaining a promotive organizational climate requires attention to how an organization is structured and to how people are treated across the organization.

19. Reduce conflict due to structural problems by adhering to principles pertaining to the unity of command, maintaining a clear chain of command, balancing responsibility and authority, and maintaining a manageable span of control.

20. Keep in mind that these organizing principles are not absolutes! Depending on circumstances, these principles can be violated (as in matrix management).

21. Attend to the needs of subordinates.

22. Realize that effective managers effectively manage conflict. The practice of managerial skills covered in other chapters of this text also contributes to effective conflict management across the individuals and groups within an organization.

■ CASE: "A WOMAN IN THE HOUSE"

"Herbie, Tom's transfer is official. You'll need to start the ball rolling on hiring a replacement," Stu advised. "The sooner you can find someone, the better."

"O.K., boss, I'll let personnel know right away," Herbie Victor replied.

As supervisor of the production planning group, Herbie was responsible for selecting Tom's successor. The three planning positions were traditionally held by men, but Herbie found himself interviewing several women for the position. As the latest female candidate left his office, Ron Bridges, one of the planners, stuck his head in the door. "You've interviewed a bunch of women, Herbie. You really wouldn't do that to us, would you?"

"Do what, Ron?"

"Hire a woman planner. A woman just couldn't do the job."

"Why, Ron, I never thought you were a male chauvinist," Herbie kidded. Both men laughed.

A few days later, Herbie did decide to hire a woman—Shirley Edwards, a recent college graduate with a degree in math. When Herbie took her around to meet the others in the department, Ron mumbled, "hello." He said he'd like to talk to Shirley but had a deadline to meet. "I'll drop by later," he added, "after I turn in this job." However, the afternoon found Ron working intently on his next project.

Shirley quickly caught on to the work, but Ron's attitude toward her continued to be icy. This bothered Herbie, but he felt that the problem would eventually disappear. Ron would just have to get used to working with a woman.

When Shirley had been in the position about six weeks, Herbie stopped by her desk to see how she felt about the job. "Oh, I'm very pleased," she replied. "This is the kind of work I've always wanted to do."

"Well, good. I've been pleased with your progress. If you keep on, you'll be a real asset to the planning group." As Herbie walked back to his office, he noticed Ron scowling. Ron obviously had overheard his conversation with Shirley.

Thereafter, the situation grew more and more unpleasant. Herbie frequently heard Ron and Shirley arguing. Once he heard the other planner tell Ron to give Shirley a break. "She's really a good worker, Ron," he said. "I don't see why you can't be nice to her." Finally, Stu summoned Herbie to his office to discuss the civil war that was raging in Herbie's department.

Stu told Herbie that the planners' feud had to stop. Because of it, the production planning group had missed two deadlines in the past two weeks. "Shirley seems capable enough, but I'm not sure that having her on staff is worth all this aggravation," Stu concluded.

Herbie didn't know what to do next. He wanted to keep Shirley, not only because she was a good worker, but also because she would have excellent grounds to level a discrimination charge if he fired her. But he just couldn't think of a way to make peace between her and Ron.

Case Questions

1. How did Herbie's behavior contribute to the conflict involving Ron and Shirley?
2. What strategies might Herbie use to manage the conflict he is experiencing with Ron?
3. Should Herbie use a competitive management strategy in this situation?

■ EXERCISE: "THE UGLI ORANGE"

Your goal in this exercise is to successfully take delivery of ugli oranges you require. There is a limited supply of oranges and you have a competitor with whom you must negotiate. You *must* find a solution to your problem. Much is at stake!

Your instructor will assign you either the role of Dr. Roland or the role of Dr. Jones. You will be given time to read your role. Then, 15 minutes will be provided for negotiation with your counterpart. Your instructor will probably want you to address the following questions as you negotiate:

1. What do you plan to do?
2. If you want to buy the oranges, what price will you offer?
3. To whom and how will the oranges be delivered?

Keep in mind that effective negotiation is facilitated by creative problem solving. Pay attention to the dynamics of your negotiations with your competitor. What factors contribute to successful negotiation? Conversely, what factors inhibit your progress?

Forms

Your instructor will distribute background information for your role as Dr. Roland or Dr. Jones.

Ugli orange exercise authored by Robert J. House, Joseph Frank Bernstein Professor of Organizational Studies, Wharton School of Management, University of Pennsylvania.

ENDNOTES

1. Thomas, K. W. "Conflict and conflict management." In M. D. Dunnette (Ed.), *Handbook of Industrial and Organizational Psychology.* Chicago: Rand McNally, 1976.

2. Walton, R. E., & McKersie, R. B. *Behavioral Theory of Labor Negotiations.* New York: McGraw-Hill, 1965.

3. Thomas, "Conflict and conflict management."

4. Frost, J., & Wilmot, W. *Interpersonal Conflict.* Dubuque, IA: Brown, 1978.

5. Robbins, A. C. "Conflict management and conflict resolution are not synonymous terms." *California Management Review 21* (1978): 67–75. Also see: Brown, L. D. *Managing Conflict at Organizational Interfaces.* Reading, MA: Addison-Wesley, 1983.

6. Mamis, R. A. "Sparring partners." *Inc.* (March 1984): 43–50.

7. Baron, R. A. *Behavior in Organizations.* Boston: Allyn and Bacon, 1986.

8. Ruble, T. L., & Thomas, K. W. "Support for a two dimensional model of conflict behavior." *Organizational Behavior and Human Performance 16* (1976): 143–155.

9. Derr, C. B. "Managing organizational conflict: Collaboration, bargaining, and power approaches." *California Management Review 21* (1978): 76–90.

10. Pondy, L. R. "Organizational conflict: Concepts and models." *Administrative Science Quarterly* (September 1967: 296–320). See also: Thomas, K. W. "Toward multi-dimensional values in teaching: The example of conflict behavior." *Academy of Management Review 15* (1977): 484–490.

11. Derr, "Managing organizational conflict."

12. Walton & McKersie, *Behavioral Theory.*

13. Ibid.

14. Fisher, R., & Ury, W. *Getting to Yes.* New York: Viking Penguin Inc., 1981.

15. Ibid.

16. Fiedler, F. E., & Garcia, J. E. *New Approaches to Leadership: Cognitive Resources and Organizational Performance.* New York: John Wiley & Sons, 1987.

17. Thompson, J. D. *Organizations in Action.* New York: McGraw-Hill, 1967. Also see: Miner, J. B. *Organizational Behavior.* New York: Random House, 1988.

18. Thompson, *Organizations in Action.*

19. Ibid.

20. Feldman, D. C. "The development and enforcement of group norms." *Academy of Management Review 9* (1984): 47–53.

21. O'Rielly, C. A., & Caldwell, O. F. "The impact of normative social influence and cohesiveness on task perceptions and attitudes: A social information processing approach." *Journal of Occupational Psychology 58* (1985): 193–206.

22. Lott, A. J., & Lott, B. E. "Group cohesiveness as interpersonal attraction: A review of relationships with antecedent and consequent variables." *Psychological Bulletin* (October 1965): 259–309.

23. Seashore, S. *Group Cohesiveness in the Industrial Work Group.* Ann Arbor: University of Michigan Institute for Social Research, 1954.

24. Schachter, S., Ellertson, N., McBride, D., & Gregory, D. "An experimental study of cohesiveness and productivity." *Human Relations 3* (1951): 229–238.

25. Walton & McKersie, *Behavioral Theory.*

26. Sherif, M., & Sherif, C. W. "The robber's cave study." In *An Outline of Social Psychology.* New York: Harper & Row, 1956.

27. Litwin, G. H. "Climate and motivation: An experimental study." In D. A. Kolb, I. M. Rubin, and J. M. McIntyre (Eds.), *Organizational Psychology.* Englewood Cliffs, NJ: Prentice-Hall, 1984.

28. Deutsch, M. *The Resolution of Conflict.* New Haven, CT: Yale University Press, 1973.

29. Translated into English: Fayol, H. *General and Industrial Administrative.* London: Sir Isaac Pitman & Sons, 1949.

30. Graicunas, V. A. "Relationships of Organizations." In L. Gulick and L. Urwick (Eds.), *Papers on the Science of Administration.* New York: Columbia University Press, 1947.

31. Woodward, J. *Industrial Organizations: Theory and Practice.* London: Oxford University Press, 1965.

32. Howell, W. C., & Dipboye, R. L. *Essentials of Industrial & Organizational Psychology.* Homewood, IL: The Dorsey Press, 1982.

33. Davis, S. M., & Lawrence, P. R. "Problems of matrix organization." *Harvard Business Review* (May/June 1978).

CHAPTER FIVE

Stress

- **Self-Assessment: "Coronary-Prone Behavior"**

- **Learning about Stress**

- **Case: "Time—Not on His Side"**

- **Exercise: "Coping with Stress"**

■ SELF-ASSESSMENT: "CORONARY-PRONE BEHAVIOR"

For each of the following items, please select the alternative that best fits your situation.

1. How do you feel about competition on the job?
   __ a. Enjoy it.
   __ b. Dislike it.

2. Do you consider yourself to be hard driving?
   __ a. Yes.
   __ b. No.

3. How is your temper?
   __ a. Hard to control.
   __ b. Easy to control.

4. How often are there deadlines on your job?
   __ a. Daily or more.
   __ b. Less than weekly.

5. Do you set deadlines or quotas for yourself at home or at work?
   __ a. At least once a week.
   __ b. Less than once a week.

6. How important is it to you personally to get ahead in life?
   __ a. Very important.
   __ b. Not very important.

7. How many hours do you spend on overtime work at home?
   __ a. More than eight per week.
   __ b. Less than eight per week.

8. How often did you take vacations in the past five years?
   __ a. Less than one per year.
   __ b. More than one per year.

9. How much time do you usually spend on an average vacation?
   __ a. Less than five days.
   __ b. More than five days.

10. Do you usually wake up rested?
    __ a. No.
    __ b. Yes.

Scoring the Measure
of Coronary-Prone Behavior

Simply sum up the number of times you selected choice A.

Reprinted from L. D. Young and J. J. Barboriak, "Reliability of a brief scale for assessment of coronary-prone behavior and standard measures of Type A behavior," *Perceptual and Motor Skills,* 55 (1982):1039–1042.

■ LEARNING ABOUT STRESS

* Stan works as a production supervisor in a midsize electronics firm that produces computer components. Employed fresh out of college five years ago, he has since been identified as a rising star by the company's management development program. Stan puts in 50-hour weeks just to keep up with the everyday demands of his job. In addition, he serves as the advisor to the company's quality-control program.

Just last week, Stan's boss appointed him head of a new committee charged with promoting and monitoring safe work practices throughout the plant. This assignment, although an honor, requires that Stan sacrifice even more time away from his wife and their new baby.

* Anita owns and manages a specialty gift shop recently relocated at a new suburban mall. Unfortunately, the move hurt her business—overhead costs doubled and sales did not keep pace. Anita can't switch to a less expensive location because she has an obligation to honor a three-year lease at the mall.

To cover longer mall hours, Anita had to hire two full-time employees. Before the move she was able to work with a minimum of part-time help and still give valued customers personal attention. But much to Anita's frustration, her new employees don't seem to care or to understand how good customer relations contribute to the survival of a business.

* Thom is a purchasing agent at the local hospital. Although his work is demanding, the benefits and retirement program are attractive, so Thom has stayed with the hospital for the past 15 years. Content with his situation, he has long enjoyed a sense of job security.

However, Thom's life was radically disrupted last month when a large hospital management corporation acquired the hospital. Thom soon learned exactly where he stood. He was informed soon after the takeover that the corporate office would absorb his duties. At age 55, Thom was unemployed.

Stress! Stan, Anita, and Thom know the feeling. Along with countless other people, difficult work situations translate into sometimes overwhelming, detrimental stress. Work-related stress leads to losses in productivity, job dissatisfaction, conflict, and poor morale in the organization.[1] Stress also causes health problems, particularly coronary heart disease, ulcers, depression, and generally poor physical and mental well-being. One conservative estimate places the annual cost of stress in the United States at $100 billion.[2]

The Rising Cost of Stress

The psychological effects of stress cost business more and more each year. Worker compensation claims for mental stress in California grew from 1,282 in 1980 to 7,838 in 1987. Similarly, a nationally based study of 32 states found a fivefold increase in stress-related claims over five years. In response to this expensive epidemic, companies are increasingly turning to stress-management programs as a cost-containment measure.[3]

WHAT IS STRESS?

Stress: A condition in which demands threaten an individual's ability to obtain valued outcomes.

Stressors: Events that place demands on the individual.

Stress is experienced whenever a person is confronted with a demand or challenge that threatens his or her ability to attain valued outcomes.[4] Stressful events—events that place demands on us—are called **stressors.** Examples of stressors include noise, extreme cold, and excessive time pressures. Although stressors often lead to the negative outcomes associated with stress, individual differences in personality and ability to cope with environmental demands influence stress outcomes.[5] As you will see, some people are less susceptible to the wear and tear of stress than others.

Not all stress is negative; stressors can also lead to positive effects. For example, the opportunity for personally satisfying gain can be seen as a positive stressor.[6] Earning a college degree—finding money for tuition, sitting through classes, taking exams, writing papers, and so on—is stressful. But this stress can be quite positive to the extent that it encourages performance and otherwise challenges the individual in a positive way. We cannot eliminate all stress. Instead, we should try to understand stress—its causes and effects—for the purpose of better managing its inevitable onset. (See Figure 5–1.)

Stress pervades all levels of an organization. Life events bring stress to us as individuals. Coworker relations can cause or relieve stress experienced in groups. And organizational policy and structure influence stress levels within organizations. We will now look at stress from the perspectives of the individual, the group, and the organization.

STRESS AND THE INDIVIDUAL

Susceptibility to dysfunction caused by stress can be great or small, depending on the way individuals respond to stressors. Not everyone

Figure 5–1 A Basic Model of Stress

STRESSORS → **INDIVIDUAL CHARACTERISTICS** → **OUTCOMES**

Individual	Type A	Absenteeism
Hassles	Hardiness	Alienation
Life change	Coping style	Anxiety
		Boredom
Group		Depression
Role overload		Disease
Role underload		Dissatisfaction
Interrole conflict		Fatigue
Intrarole conflict		Heart disease
Role ambiguity		Hypertension
Poor relationships		Lack of sleep
		Low self-worth
Organizational		Physical strain
Impoverished work		Substance abuse
Hazardous work		Tardiness
Shift work		
Lack of participation		
Rigid organizational structure		
Change and reorganization		

Stress is a pervasive, potentially harmful phenomenon that needs to be well managed at individual, group, and organizational levels.

reacts with the same level of intensity when experiencing stress. Individual differences in this regard account for the variation in how effectively we cope with stress.

General Adaptation Syndrome

Think of the last time you experienced a significant stress. You can probably recall experiencing heightened mental alertness, a racing heartbeat, and rapid breathing when the stressor presented itself. These physical reactions characterize the *fight-or-flight* response. The introduction of a stressor prompts this response, which is a state of arousal that mobilizes the body's resources to cope with stress. The fight-or-flight response is only the first part of a generalized reaction to stress known as the **General Adaptation Syndrome** (G.A.S.).[7] Stressors normally trigger a three-phase set of reactions that form the G.A.S.:

1. Alarm—Resources are marshalled to combat the stress (fight or flight).

General Adaptation Syndrome (G.A.S.): A generalized physical response to a stressor. The three stages are alarm (fight or flight), resistance, and exhaustion.

2. Resistance—Adaptation to the stressor occurs, increasing susceptibility to disease.

3. Exhaustion—Resources are depleted, disease processes are engaged, and exhaustion sets in.

Through the G.A.S., we actively respond and adapt to stressors. Despite the importance of adaptation, repeated or prolonged activation of the G.A.S. depletes personal resources, leading to psychological exhaustion and physical disease. Repeated activation of G.A.S. has also been associated with the development of heart disease.[8]

Type-A Behavior

Type-A behavior pattern: A set of personality traits typified by competitiveness, achievement focus, fatigue suppression, persistence, and impatience.

Some people are distinguished by personality traits that fall into the **Type-A behavior pattern.** Type-A personalities have a strong need to control their environment, and they exhibit low tolerance for interruptions at work. More competitive than Type-Bs, Type-As also persist longer at tasks, suppress fatigue, focus on achievement, and lack patience. Type As generally exhibit high levels of hostility, anger, and distrust, and display an especially strong fight-or-flight response. These individuals are at greater risk for coronary heart disease.[9]

Properly managing the Type-A behavior pattern benefits both the individual and the organization. Research into the effective treatment of Type-A behavior suggests a multidimensional approach. Type As are advised to monitor and reduce their mistrust of others, use humor and relaxation to overcome the intensity of the stress response, and learn to treat others with kindness.[10]

Hardiness

Hardiness: A personality trait associated with feelings of control, commitment, and challenge.

One personality trait that mitigates the effects of stress is hardiness.[11] **Hardiness** is associated with feelings of commitment, control, and challenge. *Commitment* concerns the extent to which one is involved in life events—feelings of commitment reflect a sense of purpose in life. *Control* is the ability to influence events—belief in one's power to control is necessary to the development of an active approach to coping with stressors. And *challenge* is associated with opportunity—one who perceives stressors as opportunities will be stronger in the face of stress than one who sees stressors as demands or obstacles.

Several studies have shown that managers who rated high in feelings of commitment, control, and challenge were less prone to physical ailments under stress.[12] Thus, it can be said that developing these attitudes at work leads to hardiness, or a greater resilience and resistance to stress.

Where Do All the Type-A Managers Go?

The profile of the Type-A manager seems to correspond with the popular image of the successful executive. Hard-driving, competitive, impatient, and dedicated to work, Type As are generally expected to make a positive impact and rise to leadership positions. But recent research contradicts this assumption.

Type Bs, not Type As, are more heavily represented at top executive levels of organizations. Type As rise easily from the bottom ranks but tend to reach a plateau at middle management. A possible explanation is that Type As are unable to adjust to high-level jobs because such jobs require patience and an ability to deal with uncertainty and complexity over extended time periods.[13]

Individual Stressors

Stressors come in all sizes and shapes. Particularly troublesome are stressors that lead to increased risk of physical health problems. Life change events fall into this category.[14] Simply put, **life change events** are major incidents that require people to make sweeping adjustments in their lives. Events linked with subsequent risk of physical illness include the death of a spouse, divorce, being fired, and experiencing a change in financial status. Research shows that both negative and positive changes create stress, but negative life changes have a more devastating impact on health.[15]

Life change events: Incidents that cause individuals to make major adjustments in their lives.

Everyday irritations, or hassles, add further to the problems of stress. Ongoing worries such as keeping house, balancing the checkbook, and feeling socially isolated contribute significantly to future ill health and maladjustment.[16] Hassles are equally rampant in the workplace. (See the boxed insert concerning office stressors.) Managers should work to reduce the frequency of everyday work hassles to enhance their own health and adjustment as well as that of others.

Office Stressors

A recent poll of company managers found that the following workplace characteristics generate consistently high levels of stress:

- Demands on time
- Excessive workload
- Dealing with organizational politics
- Responsibility for subordinates.[17]

Managing Individual Stress

Coping: The dynamic efforts one makes in response to stressors.

Effective stress management is largely a matter of how well people cope. **Coping** is defined as the dynamic efforts individuals make to manage specific demands that exceed individual resources.[18] This definition differentiates coping from stable traits, such as hardiness and the Type-A behavior pattern discussed previously, and from overlearned responses or experiences. Through coping, we actively pursue strategies to deal with stressors.

Coping efforts begin after potential stressors have been appraised. A stressor is appraised first in terms of its likely impact, and second in terms of the resources that might be used to manage it. If the initial appraisal shows that the potential stressor merits no concern, then there is no relevant need for continued appraisal. On the other hand, if a stressful situation has a potential for impact, then examining how to deal with the stressor becomes relevant.

The way stressors are appraised affects individual coping strategies.[19] Stressors viewed as being intractable lead to a greater use of emotional coping efforts. *Emotion-focused coping* strategies regulate emotions stemming from a stressful situation. For example, we may cope with an apparently intractable problem by increasing distress through self-blame, or by reducing distress through distancing and even deceiving oneself about the magnitude of the stressor.

In contrast, *problem-focused coping* strategies direct attention to the active management of the stressor. Relied upon when stressors appear malleable, problem-focused strategies include manipulating the environment, learning new skills, or changing goals. Finally, one can cope with stress through *symptom management,* or controlling physical reactions to stress. Relaxation techniques are a form of symptom management. Individuals tend to favor symptom management when coping with personal life changes.[20]

In summary, coping with stress is a function of a two-stage appraisal process. Stressors to be reckoned with trigger three types of coping strategies: emotion-focused coping, problem-focused coping, and symptom management. Although all three have utility, recent research indicates that proactive problem-focused coping strategies tend to lead to more favorable results.[21]

Individual Stress Management Techniques. Four stress management techniques recommended for individuals are *relaxation, exercise, time management,* and *eliminating stressors.* Relaxation and exercise direct coping inward, focusing on emotions and symptom management. Time management and the elimination of stressors are more outward-directed, anticipating stressful events through a problem-focused approach. A discussion of these techniques follows.

Relaxation techniques serve to reduce the negative effects of physical reactions to stress.[22] Through the use of medical technology or biofeedback, individuals learn to control heart rate, blood pressure, and muscle tension. Relaxation training may also include the use of deep-breathing exercises and meditation. Once learned, these techniques should be used to counteract the arousal and upset resulting from a stressful situation.

Exercise as a stress management technique means, specifically, regular daily activity equivalent to one hour of walking at three to three-and-a-half miles per hour. The benefits of exercise as it relates to good physical health are widely accepted. Its usefulness in dealing with stress is also well accepted. Exercise increases resistance to stress symptoms through fitness, the development of a greater sense of control over the environment, and a more positive self-concept.[23]

Time management focuses on the effective use of time; as a stress management technique, it is more or less preventative. Successful time management entails organizing tasks according to their importance and urgency. By setting priorities with realistic goals, people can address important demands and reduce the amount of effort wasted on peripheral issues.

Effective time management is an important part of effective stress management.

Commentary: "Stress"

Carlos Buhler

In contrast with some other situations, the stress of mountaineering is controllable. That is, climbers regulate stress by choosing which mountain to climb and the style in which it will be climbed. An experienced climber might select Mount Baker, a 10,600-

foot volcano in Washington state as a worthy objective. A decision to make an ascent on a clear day in July, following a well-traveled route with a team of competent companions has quite different effects upon stress levels than a decision to make a solo ascent in the dead of winter by way of the precipitous North Ridge.

Hardships of a winter climb—in the cold, deep snow, and alone on a steep, ice-laden route exposed to the ever-present danger of avalanches—are much more stress inducing for most climbers than an easier summer ascent. In this regard, experience and relative capability to handle stress make a difference. For example, the positive consequences of stress would probably not be found on a winter ascent of Mt. Baker for the novice climber. An implication of this example is that successful stress management requires managing limitations within the context of environmental challenges—some self-imposed, others not.

Successful stress management, whether while climbing a mountain or managing an organization, also involves problem solving. As a general rule for both climbers and managers, the more complex the problem, the greater the stress. The problem for climbers is how to get safely up a mountain and back down again by the chosen route. The solution to this problem can be found in the series of actions taken to make the ascent possible within the confines of the group's self-limitations, including the capacity to handle a given level of stress. In this regard, I particularly agree with the chapter's comment that proactive problem-focused coping strategies represent an effective way to deal with stress.

To conclude, it is the process by which we limit and maintain control over tactics that regulates the stress and challenge at work. A key point here is that we really cannot eliminate stress. Instead, we should adopt problem-focused approaches to *managing* stress, within the context of environmental or individual limitations, so that its stimulating aspects compliment, rather than overwhelm, our lives.

Carlos Buhler

Carlos Buhler is one of the most accomplished mountain climbers in the world. His career spans 18 years with major ascents on four continents. He draws from experience gained on 22 expeditions to Alaska, Ecuador, Peru, Bolivia, Argentina, Uganda, Kenya, Pakistan, Nepal, China, and the Soviet Union. In 1983, Carlos climbed Mt. Everest with the American team that made the first ascent of the Kangshung (East) Face from Tibet. It was Everest's last unclimbed face and its ascent established the mountain's most technically demanding route. Most recently, on May 3, 1988, he became the first American to stand atop Kangchenjunga (28,168 feet, Nepal), the world's third highest mountain, while leading an ultra-light team up its difficult and dangerous North Wall.

Carlos earned a B.S. in Environmental Education at Western Washington University in 1978. Between climbs, he is actively involved in applying his leadership experience in mountaineering to help companies worldwide to solve problems in organizational development and managerial performance.

Time Management

Following are just a few of several time-management techniques covered in self-help books and seminars:

1. Find quiet time during each day to reflect on where you've been and where you would like to go.

2. Handle each piece of paper only once.

3. Set goals! Make a daily "to do" list.

4. Prioritize goals.

5. Put your time and effort into activities that bring the best return in terms of your goals.

6. Learn to say "no."

7. Try to arrive five minutes early to all appointments.

Finally, changing a stressful situation by eliminating stressors is an effective stress management technique. There are many ways to eliminate or to moderate stressors. For example, you can prepare in advance for an encounter you know will be stressful. Or you can alter patterns of behavior, such as taking a longer but less congested route to work to ease stress caused by traffic jams. Or you can diffuse the impact of a stressor by redistributing it over a period of time (e.g., using a monthly schedule to pay bills).

Tips for the Manager. Effective stress management requires that managers know how to recognize the physical reactions associated with stress. Identifying the General Adaptation Syndrome begins the process of understanding and managing stressful situations.

Managers should recognize that individual differences in susceptibility to stress exist and can be identified. Type-A individuals, particularly those with hostility, will benefit from relaxation training and the development of trust in others. In contrast, people who have high levels of commitment, control, and challenge are hardier and, consequently, more resistant to stress. Managers should strive to create an environment that nurtures attitudes of commitment, control, and challenge.

Stressors such as major life change and everyday work hassles also contribute to the demands of work. Managers should keep in mind that structuring one's life to reduce hassles and, to the extent possible, minimizing the effects of life change are beneficial to the individual in the organization. Managers should also encourage proactive stress management approaches involving problem-focused coping and effective symptom management.

STRESS AND THE GROUP

Many aspects of organizational life—particularly stress and well-being—are affected by participation in groups. Groups often require that individuals fill roles that are too large or contradictory. Groups may isolate members, creating feelings of disengagement. Effective management of groups adds to both quality of life and productivity of teams in an organization.

Roles

All members of groups perform within the context of a role. A *role* is a set of behaviors expected of an individual who occupies a position in a group. (See Chapter Four, Conflict Management, for further discussion of roles.) For example, a professor is expected by students to play the role of an expert in his or her subject matter. Students, in turn, are expected to act as though they have an interest in learning material presented in class.

People in groups experience stress when they cannot fulfill role expectations. For instance, stress develops when a professor is expected to be all things to his or her students—expert, evaluator, friend, confidant, advisor, and entertainer. A student also feels stress in the face of conflicting messages about his or her role from professors, sorority sisters or fraternity brothers, and parents. In these examples, the professor suffers from role overload and the student suffers from role conflict. Stress also results from role underload and role ambiguity. Incongruent role demands—role overload, underload, and role conflict—are associated with physical strain and job dissatisfaction.[24]

Role overload: A condition in which role demands exceed the individual's ability to respond.

Role underload: A condition in which the individual's abilities are underutilized due to a lack of expectations.

Role Overload and Underload.   As described above, **role overload** exists when an individual is required to fill too many roles—when group demands exceed a group member's time limits or personal energies. In contrast, **role underload** is characterized by a lack of expectations from the group. Whereas role overload causes the stressed individual to feel rushed and harassed, role underload leads to a low sense of self-worth, alienation, and boredom.

Role Conflict. Role conflict (see Chapter Four, Conflict Management, for further discussion of role conflict) comes in two forms: interrole conflict and intrarole conflict. **Interrole conflict** exists when a person tries or is expected to play two or more roles that are incompatible. For example, an individual suffers interrole conflict when he or she discovers that the demands of effective parenthood conflict with the demands of working as an upwardly mobile professional.

Interrole conflict: Exists when a person is expected to play two or more incompatible roles.

   Intrarole conflict is generated by incompatible demands made on the same role by different groups. Middle managers face intrarole conflict when the boss expects them to supervise and evaluate workers but the workers expect them to perform as listener and advocate. Boundary spanners, such as purchasing agents and brokers, are particularly vulnerable to intrarole conflict because their clients and work groups usually have adversarial expectations.

Intrarole conflict: Exists when different people expect incompatible behaviors from the same role.

Role Ambiguity. **Role ambiguity** is defined as confusion about the requirements of a role. Lack of a clear job description and vaguely drawn duties cause high levels of role ambiguity, to the frustration of both the roleplayer and the other group members. The roleplayer suffers because he or she doesn't know what is expected, and the other group members suffer because they don't know how to act or work with the ambiguously defined person.

Role ambiguity: A state of confusion about the nature of a role.

Women, Work, and Role Conflict

As more women have moved into the world of paid work, fears that holding a job would lead to divorce have not been supported. A 15-year study of 2,742 women found that age, education, wages, and attitudes toward work had no effect on divorce rates. However, divorce was predicted by the number of hours spent on the job by married women. Apparently, high work involvement for women remains incompatible with husbands' expectations of wives and marriage.[25]

Work-Group Relations

Groups vary in the degree to which members like each other and choose to associate. Members of highly *cohesive groups* spend time together and enjoy each other's company. Such groups typically share high levels of trust and communication.

One negative effect of group cohesiveness is pressure to conform with group preferences. Conformity pressure reduces the quality of group decisions and may serve to limit input by group members. (See Chapter Seven, Decision Making, for a discussion of "groupthink.") On the other hand, people derive pleasure and support from cohesive groups. The **social support** found in groups cushions individuals from the effects of stress. Social support can help people increase self-esteem, cope with specific demands, satisfy social needs, and obtain resources.[26]

Social support: The helpfulness derived from others in a group.

In contrast, fragmented and conflict-laden groups produce stress instead of support; interactions become costly ordeals as each disagreement takes on a win-lose quality. (See Chapter Four, Conflict Management, for a discussion of "win-lose" confrontations.) Managers should strive to build cohesive, supportive teams where some disagreement among group members is perceived as being constructive.

Tips for the Manager.   Poorly understood role expectations serve as a primary source of stress in groups. Individual stress caused by role conflict, role overload and underload, and role ambiguity all contribute to stress within a group. Managers should increase clarity in role descriptions, and assess and adjust role expectations in number and quality to combat the problems of inappropriate role expectations.

Work-group stress also comes from poor coworker relationships. Jealousies and rivalries lead to fragmented and stressful groups where little cohesiveness, trust, or mutual support is present to provide security and relief. Work-group stress can be moderated if managers are successful in building group *esprit de corps* and teamwork.

STRESS AND THE ORGANIZATION

The level of work stress is largely a function of organizational structure and practices. Some industries and occupations are more stressful than others. In fact, a study comparing the incidence of stress-related illness across occupations found construction laborers, secretaries, inspectors, *managers*, waiters, and waitresses to have high rates of stress-induced disease. The study found that although both white- and blue-collar occupations were susceptible to stress, jobs that were lower in socioeconomic level tended to be more stressful.[27] The organization and content of work in these occupations appears to create high levels of stress.

Some of the more prominent organizational factors that influence stress are the design of work, participation in decision making, organizational structure, and organizational life stage and change.

Design of Work

Experts in the design of work have historically made a priority of optimizing work processes. This concern dates back to Frederick Taylor and the development of **scientific management.**[28] Under Taylor's approach, work was divided into its smallest components and piece-rate pay was introduced as a performance reward. Scientific management led to the creation of assembly line jobs and work that treated the worker as a machine. Such jobs are quite stressful and dissatisfying. Managers should attempt to redesign and enrich jobs to make work more interesting and less stressful.[29] (See Chapters Three and Ten, Motivation and Organization Development respectively, for further discussion of job redesign and job enrichment.)

Even in the age of robotics, much work is done in unpleasant working conditions. Firefighters run into burning buildings, miners work in noise and darkness, foundry workers perform in extreme heat, and word processors spend long hours watching video display terminals. Although special equipment and clothing protect these workers from direct health hazards, their jobs still make for a demanding, dangerous, and generally hostile workplace. Organizations should find ways to compensate for unpleasant working conditions. For example, managers should attempt to create pleasant working conditions, including adequate breaks and pleasant environments (e.g., attractive cafeterias and clean locker rooms), so employees can better manage job-related stress.

Work Schedules. In the United States most employees work on a five-day, 40-hour week schedule. Perhaps the largest number of employees who vary from this schedule are shift workers. These workers usually put in five days at 40 hours but their hours vary to include afternoons and nights. **Shift work** entails rotating work hours over a standard period of time. A shift worker might work 7:00 A.M. to 3:00 P.M. for two weeks, 3:00 P.M. to 11:00 P.M. for two weeks, and 11:00 P.M. to 7:00 A.M. for two weeks. Obviously, whenever workers change shifts they must adjust to working and sleeping at different times of the day.

Not surprisingly, shift work has disruptive effects on physiological and social well-being. Major changes in sleep schedules result in physical complaints such as loss of sleep, fatigue, and reduced appetite.[30] In addition, shift workers usually try to further adjust their sleep schedules on off days to participate in daytime activities with friends and family, adding to the problems of altered sleep patterns. The emotional impact of rotating shifts exceeds that of stable shift work. Studies indicate that the change in routine is stressful and leads to increased absenteeism and tardiness.[31]

Scientific management: A methodology used for optimizing work processes and reducing inefficiency through techniques such as work simplification.

Shift work: A work schedule in which employees work different hours or shifts, rotating from one set of work hours to another at regular time intervals.

In some cases, though, eliminating or reducing shift work may conflict with the need to maintain an around-the-clock operation. Police departments and hospitals, for example, must employ people day and night, Sundays and holidays. But this conflict need not inhibit efforts to reduce the negative consequences of shift work. Managers should consider using stable shifts rather than rotating shifts; some workers prefer "off" shifts. If rotating shifts are required, then workers should be kept on each shift long enough to settle into and enjoy some stability before the next rotation.

Participation in Decision Making

Decision making in organizations ranges from autocratic and "top-down" to participative and "bottom-up." Although these extremes rarely if ever exist in reality, organizations and departments do vary greatly in the degree of participation encouraged. **Participation** in decision making means direct employee involvement in the processes of goal setting, problem identification, decision making and implementation. (See Chapter Seven, Decision Making, for further discussion of participatory decision making.)

Participation: Direct involvement in the processes of goal setting, problem identification, decision making, and implementation in work processes.

Research on participation in decision making consistently shows that a low level of participation results in employee dissatisfaction, poor physical health, and psychological maladjustment such as depression and excessive drinking.[32] On the other hand, participation in decision making tends to increase an employee's sense of self-worth and creates ownership of organizational events and motivation to perform.

Mergers and Stress

Corporate mergers and acquisitions have become commonplace in today's business world. Although the financial benefits can be attractive, the management of mergers is a difficult task at best. Mergers create a great deal of stress and result in massive defections of talented executives who fear for their careers. Corporate culture clashes are frequently reported as a major source of merger-related stress. One strategy used to reduce merger stress involves the creation of a joint management transition team to include divergent input into the planning process and address fears and uncertainty about the future of the newly created organization.[33]

Organizational Structure

Organizational structure, or the allocation of work, responsibility, and authority within an organization, has much to do with stress levels across an organization. In tall, hierarchical organizations, managerial control over events is governed by formal rules and prescribed channels of communication. A particularly bureaucratic organization requires mountains of paperwork to justify and record proposals and decisions, plus approval in writing from department heads who are often only peripherally affected by a proposed action.

Organizational structure: The formal allocation of work, responsibility, and authority in an organization.

In contrast, flat organizations with fewer layers of management offer employees greater opportunity to control their work and participate in decision making. Informal communication is accepted, and there are few rules that serve as barriers to obtaining approval for actions. Not surprisingly, employees from flat organizations report lower stress and greater satisfaction with work than do employees from tall organizations.[34] (See Chapter Two, Communication, for further discussion of this point.)

Organizational Life Stage and Change

An organization, comprised of people and functioning in a dynamic environment, has a life of its own; as such, it goes through stages of growth, stabilization, and decline. As an organization enters each stage, its members confront unfamiliar and unique problems. For example, the *growth stage* presents the challenge of finding and integrating managerial talent to collect and disseminate the technical knowledge that accounts for the existence of the young organization. The *decline stage* calls on management to reduce the size of the organization effectively and humanely. Thus, each organizational life stage leads to stress and requires special expertise and proactive efforts.

Contributing to the stressful effects of each organizational life stage is the rate at which the organization passes through its stages. Rapid changes, like the overnight turns induced by mergers and acquisitions, exacerbate stress. Success, then, depends on communicating the purpose of a change, listening to people's concerns about the change, and incorporating employee input into the management of change.[35]

Organizational Strategies for Stress Management

Organizations have an implicit responsibility to provide employees with the resources needed to perform their jobs. Given the stressful nature of work and the potential losses to productivity and quality of life, organizations should offer assistance to prevent and ameliorate the dysfunctional effects of stress.

Indeed, a number of organizational programs have been promoted and used to this effect. Among them are stress-prevention efforts such as *wellness programs* that include physical activities and diet workshops, *stress management education,* and *career development programs* to help employees adjust to the dynamic relationship between their interests and the needs of the organization. More direct actions include changing the physical work environment and reorganizing work processes to create more enriched work.

Other approaches are reactive, as when an organization finances medical support for stress-induced diseases such as hypertension, or offer *Employee Assistance Programs (EAP),* which provide psychological counseling and drug rehabilitation for distressed workers.

Tips for the Manager. Managers should keep in mind that work processes that enrich and challenge employees lead to greater health and individual satisfaction. Jobs that reduce workers to machines produce unwanted stress.

Although some occupations require exposure to noxious conditions, managers can also alleviate negative stress associated with unattractive work by providing adequate rest breaks in pleasant surroundings. Managers should also try to minimize the disruption of sleep patterns resulting from shift work by increasing the length of time between shift rotations.

Lack of participation in decision making leads to dissatisfaction with work and poor health. Consequently, managers should use participative decision-making methods when possible and appropriate. Finally, changes in organizations as they develop serve as potential stress points. Preparing for these changes by developing expertise and including people in the change process will promote a more healthy, stress-resistant organizational climate.

SUMMARY: FOCUS ON SKILLS

Stress is a condition in which demands threaten the attainment of valued outcomes. Exposure to stress leads to lessened quality of life, physical disease, and maladjustment. The cost of stress-related ailments to organizations is staggering. Understanding and effectively managing stress in organizations is a critical management skill.

Following are 18 suggestions for managing stress across an organization.

Managers should:

1. Recognize physical signs of stress such as the fight-or-flight response and the other phases of the General Adaptation Syndrome.
2. Understand that personality differences govern individuals' tolerance and responses to stress. Some people do better with stress than others.
3. Help reduce the negative attributes of the Type-A behavior pattern through relaxation and building trust.
4. Find ways to increase employee hardiness by nurturing feelings of commitment, control, and challenge.
5. Use techniques such as relaxation and exercise to manage feelings and symptoms associated with stress.
6. Reduce the number of workday hassles and, to the extent possible, minimize the effects of major life changes.
7. Deal directly with stress by using time management techniques and eliminating stressors.
8. Set clear expectations for team members' behavior and roles.
9. Adjust role expectations to manageable and acceptable levels for unit members.
10. Clarify and negotiate realistic and compatible role expectations among work group members.
11. Develop a supportive and cooperative group climate.
12. Design jobs that enrich and challenge employees. Work to redesign boring and repetitive jobs.
13. Reduce employee exposure to hazardous work. Where this is impossible, provide adequate rest periods in pleasant surroundings.
14. Minimize the disruptions of shift work by increasing the length of time workers remain on a shift before rotating the schedule.
15. Encourage employee participation in decision making.
16. Where possible, create organizations with a minimum number of management levels. Avoid bureaucracy and red tape.
17. Anticipate change in the organization. Prepare employees for change, and develop expertise to provide direction in the management of change.
18. Include employees, especially those affected by change, in the management of change.

■ CASE: "TIME—NOT ON HIS SIDE"

Carlo Gardonia, the machine shop supervisor at Perfect Parts Company, got to his office at 9:15 A.M. in a bad mood. He had overslept, forfeited breakfast, and received a speeding ticket on his way to work.

As soon as he got in, he received a phone call from Ralph Mason, the plant superintendent. Ralph was worried because the scrap and rework rates in Carlo's area were soaring.

Carlo agreed to check on the problem, but he knew that the low pay scale was the leading cause. Other plants in the area had higher pay scales and were attracting better qualified workers. Carlo's department attracted only people with undeveloped skills who, after on-the-job training, invariably went over to another plant at higher pay. The result was the high scrap rate, high rework costs, and high turnover.

On his way to the plant floor Carlo passed Bill, his assistant, and asked him whether he had done the variance report on the previous month's overtime figures. "No," Bill replied, "I just don't understand. . . ."

"Never mind," Carlo said. "It has to be completed today, so I'll do it myself. You do it next time."

Then Carlo remembered that he had to check a new machine that wasn't working properly. After he adjusted the machine, he worked along with the men and women—the most enjoyable part of his day—in a effort to show them how to cut down on scrap and avoid rework.

When he finally returned to his office, he began to work on the variance report but was interrupted by a call from the personnel department. The raise that Carlo had requested for his assistant had been turned down. Carlo shouted, "How do you expect me to keep good people?" and slammed the receiver down.

Carlo left for lunch at 1:30 P.M., his first opportunity to do so, and returned at 2:00 P.M. looking tired and worn out. As he passed his secretary he remarked that she looked a bit pale and drawn. "You men are all alike," she began, and then she launched into a tirade about men in general and her former boyfriend in particular. Carlo realized that he had said the wrong thing and tried to calm her down. Finally, Carlo managed to indicate tactfully that he had a lot to do and slipped into his office.

At 2:35, Carlo's secretary reminded him that he was supposed to be in a production meeting that had started at 2:30. During the meeting that dragged on until 4:30, Carlo became drowsy and struggled to remain awake and alert.

After the meeting, one of the men in his department approached Carlo to complain about the unfair distribution of overtime. Carlo promised to investigate the matter and talk to him the next day. Then he returned to his office to finish the variance report that he had started. As he sat down, he wondered if he was running the job or if the job was running him.

Case Questions

1. What is the impact of nonwork events on Carlo Gardonia's work performance?
2. How do organizational policies affect Gardonia's work-related stress?
3. What would you recommend that Carlo do to more effectively manage his stress?

■ EXERCISE: "COPING WITH STRESS"

List two significant stressful events you have experienced during the past six months.

1.

2.

Then, briefly describe how you dealt with these stressors:

Stressor #1

Emotion Focused Coping

Problem Focused Coping

Symptom Management

Stressor #2

Emotion Focused Coping

Problem Focused Coping

Symptom Management

How successful were your efforts?

Stressor #1

Stressor #2

How might you have dealt with these stressors differently?

1.

2.

ENDNOTES

1. McLean, A. A. *Work Stress.* Reading, MA: Addison-Wesley, 1979.

2. Ivancevich, J. M., & Matteson, M. T. *Organizational Behavior and Management.* Plano, TX: Business Publications Inc., 1987.

3. Labor Letter. "Mental stress exacts a rising toll in the workplace." *Wall Street Journal*, Dec. 28, 1988, p. 1.

4. McGrath, J. E. "Stress and behavior in organizations." In M. D. Dunnette (Ed.), *The Handbook of Industrial and Organizational Psychology.* Chicago: Rand McNally, 1976.

5. Ivancevich, J. M., & Matteson, M. M. *Stress at Work.* Glenview, IL: Scott, Foresman, 1980.

6. Schuler, R. R. "Definition and conceptualization of stress in organizations." *Organizational Behavior and Human Performance, 25* (1980): 184–215.

7. Selye, H. *Stress Without Distress.* New York: J. B. Lippincott, 1974.

8. Williams, R. "The trusting heart." *Psychology Today, 23* (1989): 36–42.

9. Friedman, M., & Rosenman, R. H. *Type A and your heart.* New York, NY: Knopf, 1974. See also: Matthews, K. A. "Psychological perspectives on Type A behavior patterns." *Psychological Bulletin, 91* (1982): 293–323. See also: Williams, "The Trusting Heart." See also: Kirnmeyer, S. L. "Coping with competing demands: Interruption and the Type A pattern." *Journal of Applied Psychology, 73* (1988): 621–629.

10. Williams, "The Trusting Heart."

11. Kobasa, S. C. "Stressful life events, personality and health: An inquiry into hardiness." *Journal of Personality and Social Psychology, 37* (1979): 1–11.

12. Kobasa, S. C.; Maddi, S. R.; & Kahn, S. "Hardiness and health: A prospective study." *Journal of Personality and Social Psychology, 42* (1982): 168–177. See also: Kobasa, "Stressful Life Events, Personality and Health."

13. "Type-A managers stuck in the middle." *Wall Street Journal*, June 17, 1988, p. 1.

14. Holmes, T. H., & Rahe, R. H. "The social readjustment rating scale." *Journal of Psychosomatic Medicine, 11* (1967): 213–218. See also: Stern, G. S.; McCants, T. R.; & Pettine, P. W. "Stress and illness: Controllable and uncontrollable life events' relative contributions." *Personality and Social Psychology Bulletin, 8* (1982): 140–145.

15. Stern, McCants, & Pettine, "Stress and Illness."

16. Lazarus, R. S.; De Longis, A.; Folkman, S.; & Gruen, R. "Stress and adaptational outcomes." *American Psychologist, 40* (1985): 770–779.

17. "Rough day at the office." *US News and World Report*, July 25, 1988, p. 66.

18. Lazarus, R. S., & Folkman, S. *Stress, appraisal, and coping.* New York: Springer Publishing Co., 1984.

19. Folkman, S., & Lazarus, R. S. "An analysis of coping in a middle aged community sample." *Journal of Health and Social Behavior, 21* (1980): 219–239.

20. Latack, J. C. "Coping with job stress: Measures and future directions for scale development." *Journal of Applied Psychology, 71* (1986): 377–385.

21. Folkman, S., & Lazarus, R. C. "Coping as a mediator of emotion." *Journal of Personality and Social Psychology* (1988): 466–475.

22. Murphy, L. R. "Occupational stress management: A review and reappraisal." *Journal of Occupational Psychology* (1984): 1–15.

23. Baun, W. B.; Bernacki, E. J.; & Herd, J. A. "Corporate health and fitness programs and the prevention of work stress." In J. C. Quick, R. S. Bhagat, J. E. Dalton, & J. D. Quick (Eds.), *Work Stress: Health Care Systems in the Workplace.* New York: Praeger, 1987.

24. Cooke, R. A., & Rousseau, D. M. "Stress and strain from family roles and work role expectations." *Journal of Applied Psychology, 69* (1984): 252–260.

25. Bozzi, V. "Love and labor lost." *Psychology Today* (April 1988): 16.

26. Cohen, S., & Wills, T. A. "Stress, social support, and the buffering hypothesis." *Psychological Bulletin, 98* (1985): 310–357.

27. Smith, M. M.; Colligan, R. W.; Horning, R. W.; & Hurrell, J. *Occupational comparison of stress related disease incidence.* Cincinnati, OH: National Institute for Occupational Safety and Health, March 1978.

28. Taylor, F. W. *Scientific Management.* New York: Harper & Row, 1911.

29. McLean, *Work Stress.* See also: Herzberg, F.; Mausner, B; & Snyderman, B. *The Motivation to Work.* New York: Wiley, 1959. See also: Hackman, J. R., & Oldham, G. R. *Work Redesign.* Reading, MA: Addison-Wesley, 1980.

30. Meers, A.; Maasen, A.; & Verhagen, P. "Subjective health after four months and after six years of shift work." *Ergonomics, 21* (1978): 857–859. See also: Hood, J. C., & Milazzo, N. "Shiftwork, stress and well-being." *Personnel Administrator* (December 1978): 95–105.

31. Jamal, M. "Shiftwork related to job attitudes, social participation, and

withdrawal behavior: A study of nurses and industrial workers." *Personnel Psychology, 34* (1981): 535–547.

32. Margolis, B. L.; Kroes, W. H.; & Quinn, R. P. "Job stress: An unlisted occupational hazard." *Journal of Occupational Medicine, 16* (1974): 654–661. See also: French, J. R. P., & Caplan, R. D. "Organizational stress and strain." In A. J. Marrow (Ed.), *The Failure of Success,* New York: AMACOM, 1972. See also: Shaw, J. B., & Riskin, J. H. "Predicting job stress using data from the P.A.Q." *Journal of Applied Psychology, 68* (1983): 253–261.

33. Marks, M. L., & Mirvis, P. H. "The merger syndrome." *Psychology Today* (October 1986): 36–42.

34. Ivancevich, J. M., & Donnelly, J. H., Jr. "Relation of organizational structure to job satisfaction, anxiety-stress and performance." *Administrative Science Quarterly, 20* (1975): 272–280.

35. Cummings, T. G., & Huse, E. F. *Organization Development and Change* (4th ed.). St. Paul, MN: West Publishing, 1989.

CHAPTER SIX
Performance Appraisal

- ■ *Self-Assessment: "Locus of Control"*
- ■ *Learning about Performance Appraisal*
- ■ *Case: "Games Planners Play"*
- ■ *Exercise: "Rating Performance"*

■ SELF-ASSESSMENT: "LOCUS OF CONTROL"

The information generated by performance appraisal serves as performance feedback to both the organization and the individual. Research has demonstrated that our beliefs about how our actions are related to the environment play a role in our response to performance feedback information.* Please fill out the following self-assessment inventory to gain an insight into how your personal beliefs influence how you manage performance feedback.

For each of the following pairs, select the item that you most agree with.

1. _____ a. Promotions are earned through hard work and persistence.

   _____ b. Making a lot of money is largely a matter of breaks.

2. _____ a. In my experience I have noticed that there is usually a direct connection between how hard I study and the grades I get.

   _____ b. Many times the reactions of teachers seems haphazard to me.

3. _____ a. The number of divorces indicates that more and more people are not trying to make their marriages work.

   _____ b. Marriage is largely a gamble.

4. _____ a. When I am right I can convince others.

   _____ b. It is silly to think that one can really change another person's basic attitudes.

5. _____ a. In our society an individual's future earning power is dependent upon his or her ability.

   _____ b. Getting promoted is really a matter of being a little luckier than the next guy.

6. _____ a. If one knows how to deal with people they are really quite easily led.

   _____ b. I have little influence over the way other people behave.

7. _____ a. In my case the grades I make are the results of my own efforts; luck has little or nothing to do with it.

   _____ b. Sometimes I feel that I have little to do with the grades I get.

8. _____ a. People like me can change the course of world affairs if we make ourselves heard.

_____ b. It is only wishful thinking to believe that one can really influence what happens in society at large.

9. _____ a. I am the master of my fate.

_____ b. A great deal that happens to me is probably a matter of chance.

10. _____ a. Getting along with people is a skill that must be practiced.

_____ b. It is almost impossible to figure out how to please some people.

Scoring Your Locus of Control Scale:

Simply sum the number of times you selected choice A.

Rotter, J. B. "External and internal control." _Psychology Today_ (June 1971): 37–59. Reprinted with permission from Psychology Today Magazine, © 1971 (PT Partners, L. P.).

*Basgall, J. A., & Snyder, C. R. "Excuses in waiting: External locus of control and reactions to success-failure feedback." _Journal of Personality and Social Psychology, 54_ (1988): 656–662.

■ LEARNING ABOUT PERFORMANCE APPRAISAL

Performance appraisal is an important part of organizational life regardless of organization type; parents evaluate children, teachers evaluate students, friends evaluate each other, and managers evaluate subordinates.

In the workplace, performance appraisal may be highly subjective and sporadic, and may appear to be unrelated to human resource decisions. Written appraisal policies and procedures may not exist. Nevertheless, it is impossible for managers *not* to judge subordinates. No one truly escapes evaluation. The real issue is not whether performance appraisal occurs; rather, it is with how well the appraisal is conducted.

WHAT IS PERFORMANCE APPRAISAL?

Performance appraisal is defined as the assessment of employee performance. Performance appraisal directly effects productivity by identifying standards upon which to base employee performance. Performance appraisal results also influence other human resource management areas affecting productivity. These areas include compensation, training and development, and staffing (e.g., transfer, promotion, and termination decisions).

Performance appraisal: The assessment of employee performance.

Performance appraisal is affected by legal issues and requirements. In today's litigious environment, managers also need to understand legal requirements and issues pertaining to performance appraisal. In this regard, besides influencing productivity, the proper application of performance appraisal helps protect the organization from legal reprisals.

Goal Setting and Job Analysis

An understanding of goal setting and job analysis is important to the understanding of the successful application of a performance appraisal review system. Performance appraisal should be based on requirements of the job identified through job analysis. In turn, job analysis results should be used to calibrate job content with the goals of the organization (or individual or department or work group, as the case may be).

The Importance of Goal Setting. *Goals* are statements of direction. Goals describe desired states or end results. In large organizations, it is common to speak of a "hierarchy of objectives" or a "cascading of goals," which arrays goals from the top to the bottom of the organization. Performance appraisal helps managers to assess the effectiveness of human resources strategies intended to attain goals. In this sense, goals provide a purpose and direction for conducting performance appraisal.

Goal setting: The process of setting goals. Goals are statements of direction that describe desired states or end results.

Goal setting is also a powerful motivational technique.[1] (See Chapter Three, Motivation, for further discussion of goal setting.) As such, goal setting contributes to an important objective of performance appraisal, which is to improve individual productivity. Productivity is facilitated to the extent that goals are clear, acceptable, specific, and "hard, but achievable." (A vague "do-your-best" approach to goal setting is not effective.) Also, it is very important to provide feedback to employees. Feedback and goal setting are so important that these topics will be discussed again in this chapter. (See Figure 6–1.)

Job analysis: Involves the measurement and recording of work activities associated with a job. This analysis includes determination of tools used and assessment of working conditions.

The Importance of Job Analysis.   **Job analysis** involves the measurement and recording of work activities associated with a job. This analysis includes determination of tools used and assessment of working conditions. Job analysis procedures, results, and updates should be reduced to writing and available in the event employees have questions or a third-party review becomes necessary (e.g., from an Equal Employment Opportunity Commission investigator).

Job description: A written description of all work activities associated with a job (e.g., responsibilities, duties, reporting lines).

Job analysis should lead to development of a written **job description** for each job in an administrative unit. A job description describes all work activities associated with a position. Job descriptions should

Figure 6–1 Steps Leading to Selection of an Appraisal Method

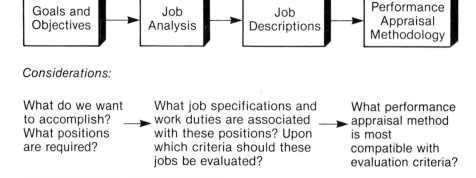

Job analysis leads to the development of job descriptions, which include specifications (e.g., education, skills) required for a given job. The job description also serves as the basis for justifying evaluation criteria—standards—upon which to assess performance.

include job specifications and should serve as the basis for **evaluation criteria**.

   Job specifications indicate minimum qualifications, such as work experience and education, necessary for an employee to perform a job adequately. Evaluation criteria are defined as standards against which to assess a ratee's atttributes, motives, abilities, skills, knowledge, or behaviors.[2] The appropriateness of different kinds of evaluation criteria will be covered in the next section when we discuss performance appraisal methodology.

INDIVIDUAL CONSIDERATIONS IN APPRAISING PERFORMANCE

After goals have been set, jobs analyzed, and evaluation criteria identified, the next step in designing a performance appraisal system is to develop an appraisal method. Performance appraisal methodology is concerned with *how* evaluation is conducted.

Appraisal Methods: Problems with Subjectivity

There has been considerable debate regarding the benefits of different appraisal methods. Some people, particularly those in academic and legal environments, prefer performance appraisal that employs definable, observable evaluation criteria based on employee behavior or output. These evaluation criteria are referred to as *performance criteria*. "Typing speed" and "production output" are examples of performance criteria.

   Many managers like the ease of use and simplicity of appraisal based on the use of *personal criteria*. Personal criteria are based on traits or innate characteristics of employees. Examples of personal criteria include personality traits such as dependability, loyalty, team play, and initiative.

   Figure 6–2 illustrates a **graphic rating scale** that makes use of personal criteria. Graphic rating scales display either a continuum or discrete categories of potential performance for each job dimension. These scales are often anchored by using adjectives (as in Figure 6–2), numbers (e.g., a scale of 1 to 5), or descriptions of behavior. An *anchor* is a description of a level of performance along a scale; a *dimension* is a discrete component of job performance such as "intelligence" or "skill."

Use of Personal Criteria.
Performance appraisal methods that rely on personal criteria lead to vague feedback. It is especially difficult to provide specific, meaningful feedback on personality traits (that the

Evaluation criteria: Evaluate standards against which to assess an employee's attributes, motives, abilities, skills, knowledge, or behavior.

Job specifications: Indicate minimum qualifications, such as work experience and education, necessary for an employee to perform a job adequately.

Graphic rating scale: Displays a continuum or discrete categories of potential performance for each job dimension. Scales can be anchored using adjectives, numbers, or descriptions of behavior.

Figure 6–2 Use of Personal Criteria

Name _____   Date _____

Rater _____   Department _____

	Excellent	Good	Fair	Poor
1. Team play	____	____	____	____
2. Dependability	____	____	____	____
3. Cooperation	____	____	____	____
4. Quality of work	____	____	____	____
OVERALL PERFORMANCE	____	____	____	____

Traits like "team play," "dependability," and "cooperation" may not contribute much to actual performance. Note that "quality of work" does relate to performance, but it is ill defined. What does "good" or "fair" quality of work really mean?

employee usually cannot change anyway). Moreover, performance feedback that does occur is compromised because actual behavior or performance can only be described in general terms (i.e., "Bob's work performance was fair"). Keep in mind that *specific* feedback is an important part of performance appraisal because it contributes to employee development and increased productivity.[3]

Another problem with using personal evaluation criteria concerns potential legal challenges based on the results of performance appraisal. Relatively subjective performance appraisal methods have not been well received by the courts. In *Albermarle Paper Company* v. *Moody,* the U.S. Supreme Court determined that performance appraisal ratings were legally "tests," and found that Albermarle Paper Company's rating procedures were too vague and overly influenced by individual interpretation to be valid.[4] In *Rowe* v. *General Motors,* the Fifth Circuit Court of Appeals found that subjective determinations of "ability, merit, and capacity" had an adverse impact on black employees.[5]

Performance appraisal that evaluates observable, measurable behavior or output associated with a job, based on the dictates of a job description developed through job analysis, stands on firmer legal ground than does appraisal that focuses on personal characteristics of the ratee.

Performance appraisal that emphasizes personal criteria also results in more employee dissatisfaction than do approaches that focus on behavior and performance.[6] In this situation, ratees may understandably feel that their personality is being criticized rather than their work performance. It is also more difficult to train raters when personal criteria are used. Raters can be trained to observe performance, but cannot be trained to observe and record accurately a personality trait such as "loyalty."

The primary advantage of incorporating personal criteria into an appraisal instrument is that appraisal instruments tend to be easy to design, understand, and use. These advantages may prove to be illusionary, however, if productivity is reduced and legal challenges occur.

Less Subjective Appraisal Methods

A less subjective way to anchor rating scales is to use specific, observable employee behavior. Our use of the term *less subjective* is particularly appropriate because it emphasizes the fact that all performance appraisal involves some subjective judgment. Evaluating performance is not cut and dried. Ultimately, individual raters make *judgments* about individual ratees. The rater is not just a passive recorder of information, but actually functions as an evaluator–judge.[7]

BARS and BOS. Two less subjective modifications of the basic graphic rating scale format are behaviorally anchored rating scales **(BARS)** and behavior observation scales **(BOS)**. BARS and BOS focus on evaluating specific *behaviors* rather than traits or characteristics.[8]

BARS: Requires that raters judge behavior associated with a dimension of a job.

BOS: Requires that raters respond to all behaviors associated with a job dimension. In doing so, raters indicate the frequency with which behaviors occur.

BARS require that raters judge behavioral anchors associated with a dimension of a job. In contrast to BARS, BOS require that raters indicate the *frequency* that different behaviors occur, and must respond to *all* behaviors associated with a position. Please note the differences between BARS and BOS in Figure 6–3.

Personal criteria are not explicitly included in these instruments. This does not mean that personal criteria are excluded as evaluation criteria altogether. However, rather than frame a scale item in terms of, say, an innate characteristic such as an employee's "attitude," BARS and BOS instrument developers identify observable behaviors and output levels that employees with "good" ("bad," "indifferent," etc.) attitudes normally exhibit.

BARS and BOS emphasize observable, measurable behavior. In other words, these instruments focus on what people *do* rather than on who people *are*. Constructive criticism can be provided that pertains to behavior on the job rather than to the person. Besides increasing ratee satisfaction, this advantage plays an important role in increasing productivity because, as noted previously, specific feedback tied to goal performance improves productivity.

The primary problem with BARS and BOS is that these methods are costly to develop and maintain (see Figure 6–4). A different instru-

Figure 6–3 Less Subjective Appraisal Methods: BARS and BOS

An example of a behaviorally anchored rating scale (BARS):

LEADERSHIP—THE DEMONSTRATED ABILITY
TO MOTIVATE OTHERS

Leadership — The Demonstrated Ability to Motivate Others

7 — This employee leads work groups that consistently exceed stated performance goals. Criticisms of leadership style by subordinates are exceedingly rare regardless of circumstances.

5 — Work groups usually exceed performance goals. Criticisms of leadership style would not be expected under normal circumstances.

3 — Performance of work groups is often less than established standards. Criticisms of leadership style are sometimes heard by management. Group performance is occasionally impeded by conflict with the leader. Formal grievances may have been filed.

1 — Group performance is deficient. Goals are seldom met. Criticisms of leadership style occur at frequent intervals. Formal grievances can be expected to have been filed.

An example of a behavior observation scale (BOS):

LEADERSHIP—THE DEMONSTRATED ABILITY
TO MOTIVATE OTHERS

Maintains composure under stress.

| Almost Never | 1 | 2 | 3 | 4 | 5 | Almost Always |

Deals effectively with employee problems (listens, takes action, follows through).

Almost Never   1   2   3   4   5   Almost Always

Treats workers fairly (assigns job evenly, plays no favorites).

Almost Never   1   2   3   4   5   Almost Always

Represents subordinates fairly to upper management levels (e.g., investigates problems, backs subordinates up where appropriate, protects subordinates from inappropriate pressure).

Almost Never   1   2   3   4   5   Almost Always

Maintains cooperation with other foremen (e.g., shares information, leaves area in good shape for next shift).

Almost Never   1   2   3   4   5   Almost Always

Total = _____

Note that both BARS and BOS focus upon observable behavior. Compare these instruments to the classification instrument in Figure 6–2.

Figure 6–4 Developing BARS

1. Conduct job analysis.
2. Prepare incidents of employee behavior on the job.
3. Cluster incidents into job dimensions (such as "leadership"). Have two knowledgeable groups cluster incidents. Retain incidents where there is agreement between groups regarding incident/dimension fit.
4. Write behavioral anchors for each job dimension based on these incidents. Have one of the groups reach consensus on assignment of behavioral anchors to a BARS scale for each dimension. Remove ambiguous anchors and dimensions.
5. Check scales to assure clarity and to add any necessary anchors.

The development of behavioral observation scales (BOS) differs in that developers place the *frequency* with which behaviors should occur on a Likert-type scale (usually 5–7 points). A good description of BOS instrument development, and the benefits of performance-based performance appraisal, can be found in Latham, G. P., Wexley, K. N. *Increasing Productivity Through Performance Appraisal.* Reading, MA: Addison-Wesley, 1981.

ment may be required for each position because behavioral requirements usually differ by position. Of course, if behaviors are the same across a class of jobs, one instrument can suffice.

Management by Objectives. Management by Objectives (MBO) focuses on results, using employee output as the evaluation criterion. The MBO process is outlined in Figure 6–5. At the individual level, supervisors and subordinates participate in goal setting, review progress periodically, and adjust activities and/or goals as necessary. This cycle is then repeated at a predetermined time, usually tied to the organization's budget cycle.

The distinction between MBO and behavioral performance appraisal methods (e.g., BARS or BOS) is not as great as you might think.

MBO: Performance appraisal that uses output as an evaluation criterion. Managers and subordinates participate in setting objectives, review progress periodically, and adjust activities and/or objectives as necessary.

Figure 6–5 The MBO Process

Top management support and commitment is an important part of a successful MBO program.

Both appraisal approaches ultimately focus on performance. The primary difference between MBO and behaviorally oriented performance appraisal is that MBO does not explicitly define the behaviors that drive performance. MBO defines performance in terms of goal attainment rather than in terms of productive behaviors *leading* to goal attainment.

Other Performance Appraisal Methods

There is a wide range of other performance appraisal methods available, aside from MBO and graphic rating scales. Following is a representative list.

Weighted Checklists: A list of adjectives is provided for each position and points are awarded for each favorable adjective the rater checks.

Critical Incidents: Successful performance is based on practice of behavior deemed "critical" to success on the job. The standard for determining critical behavior is derived from managers, and sometimes employees, writing incidents that describe effective and ineffective behavior.

Ranking Techniques: Employees are evaluated on a relative rather than absolute standard. Employees are compared and ranked by performance.

Assessment Centers: This method involves evaluation of job candidates through systematic interviewing, tests, exercises, and simulation. It was first used to select officers by the German High Command during World War II.

MBO can be used to evaluate performance at all levels of the organization, but it might be particularly effective for higher-level managerial positions where specific behaviors required to reach specific goals are difficult to identify.

One of the most important advantages of using MBO is its relative simplicity. It does not *require* the moderating steps of identifying behaviors that lead to outputs which, in turn, contribute directly or indirectly to goal attainment. Rating forms are used in MBO, but these forms lead with the goal, then follow with "action steps" (e.g., behaviors) necessary to reach the goal. The focus is on results rather than process. Evaluation criteria are always output-based.

From the goal-setting literature cited earlier, we know that a focus on results, by itself, improves productivity. The MBO process also enhances productivity because it often improves communication. One of the often cited advantages of MBO is that it facilitates constructive, results-oriented communication between managers and subordinates.[9]

There is little if any literature that addresses the use of MBO and potential legal problems. The emphasis on output rather than characteristics of the individual employee means that MBO is more resistant to employee claims of "unfair discrimination" than general classification methods. Managers should still make sure that clear linkages exist between job analysis, resulting job descriptions, performance criteria, and performance appraisal. For example, performance objectives assigned to an individual employee should be traceable to a job description developed through the process of job analysis. Employees working in the same position should not be assigned widely disparate goals. A rationale for unusual or widely disparate goals should always be documented.

There are disadvantages associated with MBO. Because the focus is on results, the process sometimes suffers. The means do not always justify the ends. For example, hard-sell approaches that focus on achieving sales targets may alienate customers and hurt future sales. Employees may resort to unethical behavior in the pursuit of goals.

MBO appraisal systems are also plagued by goal manipulations. In order to "look good," some managers set easy goals for their departments and for individual employees. Differences in goal difficulty creates problems when top management compares departments or individuals across an organization. Did Bob really outperform Ted or did Bob instead benefit from easier goals? Is Carol's department really more productive or did Alice's department face an overwhelming and inherently unfair goal burden?

Problems associated with goal manipulation and resulting inequities became exacerbated by compensation plans that tie merit pay to goal attainment.[10] Merit pay (pay for performance) can improve productivity across an organization. It is important, however, that performance standards be clear and equitable.

An often cited problem with MBO concerns the paperwork and meetings it produces. Managers and subordinates often become disgusted with meetings and forms, which, taken to excess, can compromise the productivity they are intended to promote. Carroll and Schneier cite the case of a manager who exclaimed, "I thought I was hired to make refrigerators—now I find that I am managing a paper factory!"[11]

MBO, like other performance appraisal methods, has its strengths and weaknesses. There are no easy answers to the problems associated with MBO. However, the probability of MBO succeeding is enhanced to the extent that "game playing" is recognized and discouraged; performance standards are clear, measurable, and relatively uniform in terms of difficulty across the organization; and top management understands and is committed to MBO.

Behavior and Output versus Personal Traits: Concluding Remarks

To this point, we have argued that performance appraisal based on appraising behavior and/or output (e.g., use of performance criteria) is superior to appraisal based on personality traits (e.g., use of personal criteria).

While advancing this argument, we need also to point out that personal criteria cannot always be translated into behaviors. Imagine the difficulty inherent in translating the personal criterion of "charisma" into measurable behavior! Managers should not avoid incorporating an important personal criterion into performance appraisal simply because it is difficult to measure. If a given position description is simply overwhelmed by the requirement for abstract personal traits, as is sometimes the case with managerial positions, top management might consider using an MBO format that focuses on results rather than process.

Major reviews of the performance appraisal literature have also shown no consistent advantage of one performance appraisal method over another in terms of rater accuracy.[12] However, these findings are not inconsistent with a focus on behavior and/or output in appraising performance. A focus on behavior and performance still leads to the provision of specific feedback, which does improve productivity and provides better protection from legal reprisals.

Goals should still be set and jobs analyzed; specific, periodic feedback should be provided; and raters should be trained. If these steps do not occur or are poorly done, performance appraisal will fail to increase employee productivity, *regardless* of the performance appraisal method used.

Commentary: "Performance Appraisal"

Thomas Seeberg

Leadership and cooperation within a company like Siemens are basically determined by the quality of communication between superiors and staff. The superior has to have daily discussions with his or her staff members in connection with their respective assignments. However, because of a lack of time, these discussions are usually restricted to topics of immediate concern.

Even though tasks and problems of cooperation are often discussed in bigger meetings in a broader organizational context and time frame, such meetings do not focus on scrutinizing in detail questions such as a particular member's attitude, the special difficulties of an assignment, or the achievements and long-range objectives of the employee or his or her career.

The communication of such topics in relation to the individual's work and professional situation, called *performance appraisal,* is extremely important as a means of giving a staff member a sense of direction in his or her work. Performance appraisal also strengthens commitment to and identification with the company and its corporate goals.

The performance appraisal principles Siemens has developed for management-level staff have proven to be most efficient for heading a staff of mostly managerial and highly qualified people. The method called *Staff Dialogue* takes place annually. It is particularly suited to assist both the superior and the subordinate in the following:

1. Clarify the employee's responsibilities and objectives within the larger corporate context.
2. Come to an understanding with regard to the criteria for evaluation that will be applied to achievements, so that the manager knows what is expected of him or her and where his or her efforts should be concentrated.
3. Review the manager's assignment and career with reference to special ability and personal interests, and possibly decide on concrete measures for advancement.

A prerequisite for a successful Staff Dialogue is that the discussion be candid but remain objective and constructive for both partners and not deteriorate into a battle of generalities, or turn into a debate about subjective impressions and opinions that cannot be verified. Consequently, the five phases of a "Staff Dialogue"—Contact, Orientation, Analysis, Consequences and Measures, and Summary—should be specifically structured and should focus on tangible *performance.* Thus, regular Staff Dialogues can be a source of cumulative experience that leads to lasting improvement in the effectiveness of an individual's work.

Thomas Seeberg

Thomas Seeberg graduated from the University of Cologne/West Germany with a Master's Degree in Business Administration. He completed his formal education by graduating from the University of Fribourg/Switzerland with a Ph.D. in economics. After passing the exam as "Wirtschaftsprufer" (German CPA), he became a junior partner of KAROLI-WirtschaftsprufungGmbH, a major German accounting firm. In 1978, Dr. Seeberg accepted an offer by Siemens AG, looking for new challenges in industry.

At Siemens, Dr. Seeberg has held various positions in the accounting area. He served as manager in the corporate accounting department and as a Controller of major subsidiaries in the U.S. and Germany. Since 1988, he has served as Executive Director of the corporate accounting function.

Dr. Seeberg feels he made the right career and company decision, combining his strong interest in accounting with the multinational activities of one of the largest companies in the world.

The Performance Review: Feedback!

A **performance review** occurs whenever a manager and a subordinate discuss performance appraisal results. Performance reviews are effective to the extent they are specific, timely, impersonal, noticeable, and frequent.[13]

Specific feedback involves relaying to employees precisely what they did well (or not so well). Speaking in general terms, such as "Well, Michael, you did a good job on the Anderson account but you could have done better with the Higgins account," fails to tell Michael how his performance could have been improved. What is meant by "good" or "bad"? Specific behavior or performance measures ("Michael, you completed executive summaries for all meetings with Mr. Anderson") or ("Michael, you were late to all four meetings with Mr. Higgins") are much more informative and more likely to help Michael improve his performance in the future.

Feedback should be *timely*. Often, deviations from preferred behavior and performance can be corrected so that individual or group objectives can be reached. Productivity is increased to the extent that deviations from standards are corrected in a timely manner.

Feedback should be relatively *impersonal*. As noted previously, feedback based on personality traits leads to ratee dissatisfaction. Performance appraisal based on behavior and/or output eliminates this problem to a large extent. Even if the performance appraisal emphasizes personal criteria, the rater can still try to emphasize that he or she is critiquing performance on the job rather than innate characteristics of the employee.

Performance review: Occurs whenever a manager and a subordinate discuss performance appraisal results.

"Keep up the good work, whatever it is, whoever you are."

Specificity improves the quality of the performance review. This employee is not likely to be more productive in the future.

Drawing by Stevenson; © 1988, The New Yorker Magazine, Inc.

Feedback needs to be *noticeable*. Obviously, if feedback is to improve productivity, it must be acknowledged by the ratee. Carroll and Schneier suggest that employees might be encouraged to "test their own performance and give themselves feedback." Another idea is to have ratees write an acknowledgment to supervisors based on the results of a performance review. This acknowledgment might take the form of a personal action plan—steps to correct deficiencies and ways to build on past successes.

Frequent performance review can contribute significantly to the success of a performance appraisal system. Frequent feedback is *not* the same thing as close supervision. Performance review sessions should be planned and should take place so that privacy between rater and ratee is maintained. Frequent reviews tell employees that management is committed to performance appraisal and is not simply paying "lip service" to a management fad. Frequent reviews also provide for timely corrective action. Carroll and Schneier cite several studies indicating that frequent feedback contributes to higher employee satisfaction with supervisors.

Frequent performance review is a relative term. What is frequent (and necessary) for one employee may not be for another. Cummings and Schwab feel that the method used and the timing of review should depend primarily on the results of past appraisal. Accordingly, they developed a set of performance review approaches called **DAP-MAP-RAP**.[14]

These authors suggest using a developmental action plan (DAP) if past performance has been good. Performance review should occur at the completion of projects. A maintenance action plan (MAP) should be used if performance has been satisfactory. Performance review in this situation should occur on a periodic basis two or three times a year. A remedial action plan (RAP) should be used if performance has been poor. RAP calls for frequent performance review.

DAP-MAP-RAP: A performance review method that bases timing, content, and action following a review on past employee performance. Reviews are developmental, maintenance, or remedial in nature, depending upon performance.

Beware of Negative Feedback! Negative feedback can actually *reduce* productivity. Meyer, Kay, and French found that subordinates who "received an above-average number of criticisms . . . generally showed *less* goal achievement 10 to 12 weeks later than those who had received fewer criticisms."[15] These findings are consistent with our earlier discussion of *increased* employee dissatisfaction resulting from negative feedback.[16]

How should a manager convey negative feedback? Clearly, avoiding feedback is not the solution to this problem. At the same time, the primary purpose of a performance appraisal system is to increase productivity; however, the Meyer, Kay, and French study indicates that negative feedback may hurt productivity. How can the problem of conveying negative feedback be reconciled?

It is difficult to criticize performance constructively. Nevertheless, employees are more receptive to negative feedback if they are allowed to participate in the performance review, if plans and objectives are discussed, and if employees are evaluated on factors relevant to their work.[17]

The Importance of Rater Training

An otherwise well-conceived appraisal system could still fail if raters are not adequately trained. Our discussion of training begins with a review of **rating error.** Rating error takes place whenever a systematic recording of invalid impressions by raters occurs. Common errors include contrast effects, leniency, central tendency, severity and halo errors, and attributional biases.

Rating error: A systematic recording of invalid impressions by raters. Examples of rating errors include contrast effects, leniency, central tendency, severity, halo effects, and attributional biases.

An employee could be doing a good job and still receive a poor evaluation because his or her performance was implicitly compared with the superior performance of another employee doing comparable work. *Contrast effect errors* occur when such comparisons are not explicitly intended but still affect appraisal outcomes. For example, instructors who promise to grade students on the basis of a standard scale rather than on a curve should not be influenced by overall class performance when grading an individual student.

Is a student "above average" if he or she earns a grade-point average of over 3.0? You might think so. A letter grade of B (or 3.0) usually means above-average performance has occurred. However, *average* grades at many colleges and universities run above 3.0! "Grade inflation" is one example of a *leniency error.* Leniency errors occur when raters consistently and inaccurately evaluate ratees near the top of a scale. Evaluations can also be consistently in the middle or at the bottom of a scale. Psychologists refer to these as *central tendency* and *severity* errors, respectively.

Keep in mind that all individuals in a work group sometimes do poor, average, or excellent work. Individual ratings that reflect this consistency are *not* invalid. Under such circumstances it is more valid, for example, to speak of a "leniency effect" rather than a leniency "er-

Halo effects occur when a rater overgeneralizes from one aspect of an employee's performance to all aspects of the employee's performance. A person who does a good job of "meeting the public" might also be rated as doing a good job of record keeping when, in fact, his or her record-keeping performance has been very poor.

The Lake Wobegon Effect

All kinds of tests are subject to rating errors. According to Chester E. Finn, Assistant Secretary for Educational Research and Improvement, parents and children are being fooled by standardized achievement tests in which most student's scores are declared above average. Finn has labeled this phenomenon the "Lake Wobegon Effect."

In the mythical town of Lake Wobegon (invented by author and radio personality Garrison Keillor), "all of the women are strong, all of the men are good-looking, and all of the children are above average."[19]

Finally, employees may receive differential treatment because of the *attributional bias* of a rater. For example, Maria might be deemed successful because she is a "hard worker" and might be promoted. Susan, employed in the same job and doing the same level of work, might be perceived by the same rater to be simply "lucky" and be denied a promotion. The search for attributions typically occurs when people are unable to categorize observed behavior clearly. Because we live in a complex world characterized by imperfect information, "attributions" are a daily fact of life.

Inaccurate attributions in performance appraisal can be traced to inadequate or otherwise incomplete information about the ratee. Under these circumstances, the rater's personality plays an important role in filling in missing information. In this regard, performance ratings are often as much a function of the personality of the rater as they are a function of the performance of the ratee![20]

Reducing Rater Error.   **Training programs** are systematic, structured attempts to improve the validity of rating by training raters so that rater error is reduced. One of the most important considerations in training raters is to focus training on *what* to observe rather than "how to" or "how not to" rate.[21]

   For example, a training program that teaches raters how to rate performance by avoiding leniency could result in highly invalid ratings. What if a particular group of ratees all exhibit superior performance? What if the performance of a particular group of ratees does not approximate a normal distribution of performance? Teaching raters how to do evaluation by requiring that ratings be given that fall within a bell-shaped curve would be invalid in this instance.

   Raters should be trained to focus on observable behavior and output and to ignore factors that do not relate to the job.[22] A focus on teaching managers to observe behavior correctly is critical to increasing rater accuracy.[23] Seen from this perspective, performance appraisal based on performance criteria is much more amenable to rater training than is appraisal based on personal criteria (e.g., personality traits).

   Traits such as enthusiasm and intelligence are difficult to observe explicitly. Consequently, the rater must overrely on subjective judgment of what constitutes "enthusiasm" and "intelligence." An overemphasis on subjective judgment contributes to rater error, particularly attributional bias. Enthusiastic and intelligent behaviors, on the other hand, can be defined and raters can be trained to observe their occurrence in the job setting. This observation underscores another reason to build performance appraisal systems around performance rather than employee personality.

   Incorporating discussion, practice, and feedback into training seems to help raters become more accurate.[24] (Interestingly, the lecture method is relatively ineffective.[25]) A program described by Latham, Wexley, and Pursell trained raters in "what to observe" and involved discussion, feedback, and practice.[26] Participants were trained in the use of a performance appraisal rating scale, then observed and rated "employees" on videotape. Differences in ratings among workshop participants were then argued in a discussion led by a trainer.

   Next, the trainer provided the correct ratings, including a rationale for assigning ratings to different behaviors. Workshop participants then considered actual examples of behaviors and rating errors in everyday life, and discussed ways of overcoming the rating errors being studied. A follow-up to this study indicated that rater errors were still sharply reduced six months after the initial training had been provided. Raters should be trained; however, despite the reported success of the

Training programs: Systematic, structured attempts to improve the validity of performance appraisal ratings by training raters.

Latham, Wexley, and Pursell program, no study has empirically confirmed which training program is *most* effective.[27]

Finally, raters should also be trained in how to conduct an effective performance review. Communication and conflict management skills, covered in Chapters Two and Four respectively, play an important role in "leveling with employees" without "leveling them."

Tips for the Manager.   Performance appraisal methodology should be based on evaluation criteria (performance and personal criteria) developed through goal setting and job analysis.

Appraisal methods based on performance rather than personal criteria tend to be more effective at facilitating individual productivity; are more resistant to legal challenges based on claims of unfair discrimination; and lessen employee dissatisfaction during the performance review. Managers should strive to keep performance appraisal from becoming an end in itself. When using MBO, keep in mind the importance of avoiding goal manipulation and busywork.

Feedback is an essential part of an effective performance appraisal review system. Managers should provide feedback to employees that is specific, timely, impersonal, noticeable, and frequent. To mitigate counterproductive effects of negative feedback, managers should provide employees with the opportunity to participate in the performance review, discuss plans and objectives, and evaluate employees on factors relevant to their work.

Raters should be trained. A variety of rater errors—halo, leniency, severity and central tendency errors, contrast, and attributional biases—can compromise validity and undermine productivity, which performance appraisal is intended to promote. This is not to suggest that rating error can be avoided entirely; it can't. However, the validity of performance appraisal can be *improved* through training. Managers should be provided with detailed instruction in the use of a specific performance appraisal methodology; be trained in specifically what to observe; receive practice in actually rating subordinates; and be provided with feedback pertaining to results. Managers should also be provided with training in communications and conflict management skills in order to conduct effective performance reviews.

GROUP CONSIDERATIONS IN APPRAISING PERFORMANCE

Although the focus of a performance appraisal system lies in the individual domain, there are also group considerations that should be taken into account.

Peer Evaluation

Performance appraisal is usually conducted by an immediate supervisor. Approximately 93 percent of performance appraisal programs require immediate supervisors to take responsibility for evaluating employee performance.[28] **Peer evaluation,** performance appraisal conducted by co-workers, is not a common practice despite favorable reviews regarding the validity and resistance from bias of this approach.[29]

Peer evaluation: Performance appraisal conducted by co-workers.

Peers often have a good understanding of work requirements and are often in a better position to observe work performance than are supervisors. Problems with peer assessment include friendship bias and the adverse effect of negative feedback on ratees. Also, co-workers often do not want to be responsible for evaluating peers.

Cascio has noted that friendship bias and the counterproductive effect of negative feedback by peers might be significantly reduced if performance criteria are clearly specified.[30] (Again, more justification for using performance-based appraisals such as MBO, BARS, and BOS!) Peer assessment should also be avoided within highly competitive work groups because of possible self-serving manipulation of results.

In any event, peer evaluation could be used in conjunction with other rating efforts by management and/or self-ratings by the employee. In this context, peer evaluation could be viewed as a way to validate performance appraisal results from other sources rather than as an evaluation end in itself.

Interdependent Work Groups: Some Considerations

A managerial emphasis on providing differential rewards in interdependent work groups (e.g., football teams, new product venture teams) is counterproductive.[31] Such a practice can lead to destructive competition within a group which must rely on cooperation in order to succeed. (*Interdependent work groups* are groups where individual members must depend on each other to accomplish work objectives. An example of a *differential reward* is pay based on individual effort. See Chapters Three and Four, Motivation and Conflict and Its Management respectively, for discussion related to these concepts.)

This observation suggests that managers should practice performance appraisal that accounts for interdependence of a work group. Using performance appraisal results to provide "pay for performance" might significantly improve the productivity of a sales staff. The same approach would prove disastrous if applied to an interdependent construction crew.

Performance-based evaluation of individual, independent salespeople working in well-defined territories is a much more straightforward proposition than is evaluating individual performance within a highly interdependent construction crew. Even if well-trained managers apply all performance appraisal suggestions provided to this point (e.g., set goals, conduct job analyses, write job descriptions, develop and apply performance-based appraisal methods, provide feedback), the productivity of a construction crew could still be compromised unless group objectives are implemented.

Group objectives: Objectives set for the entire group. Particularly relevant for interdependent work groups.

Group Objectives.   Generally, **group objectives** should be used in interdependent work groups where it is impossible to partial out individual effort. As with other MBO formats, the use of group objectives means that evaluation focuses on results rather than process.

Group performance objectives are particularly effective when used with temporary work groups (project teams) in work environments characterized by rapid change. Group measures are also more functional for operating-level employees who are motivated by affiliation with co-workers—a situation where productivity is highly dependent on group norms.[32]

Equity Theory

Equity theory (also discussed in Chapter Three, Motivation) states that people want to be treated fairly. Specifically, this theory holds that individuals compare the ratio of their inputs into a job (e.g., education, experience, effort) and outputs from a job (e.g., pay, praise) with the ratio of inputs and outputs of "comparison others."[33] The standard used by employees for judging fairness is relative rather than absolute. For example, an employee could be dissatisfied with a "good" performance appraisal rating if a less productive co-worker receives an "excellent" rating.

How does one conduct fair performance appraisal? The answer to this question lies in what has been discussed thus far. Setting goals, conducting job analyses, preparing job descriptions, emphasizing performance measures, and conducting constructive performance reviews all contribute to the conduct of equitable and valid performance appraisal. In this sense, equity should be regarded as a *by-product*, rather than as an express objective, of effective performance appraisal.

Tips for the Manager.   Managers should consider using peer evaluation as only one source (not as the only source) of information. Managers should also consider using an MBO format, with group objectives, in highly interdependent groups. Additionally, managers should keep in mind that productivity could be undermined if group members believe performance appraisal is unfair. Equity theory indicates that comparisons are made on the basis of relative rather than absolute standards. Giving an employee a "very good" rating may actually cause dissatisfaction if another employee receives an "outstanding" rating for doing the same quality of work.

ORGANIZATIONAL CONSIDERATIONS IN APPRAISING PERFORMANCE

Our discussion of organizational considerations includes a reiteration of the importance of goal setting, a review of the necessity of a systems perspective, and concludes with consideration of a contingency approach to performance appraisal based on the dictates of the job and nature of the organization.

Goal Setting (Again!)

Performance appraisal is not an end in itself, but rather a means to the end of attaining organizational, group, and individual objectives. Performance appraisal at all levels of an organization is rendered impotent if the organization, and the parts that comprise it, lack direction. It is not enough to use performance appraisal simply to "increase productivity" at the individual or group level. Productivity increases should be tied to organizational objectives (e.g., to increase sales, market share, profits, quality, customer service, etc.).

A Systems Perspective

Seen from a **systems perspective,** performance appraisal should be viewed as part of a human resources system rather than as an independent process. Performance appraisal affects other human resources areas pertaining to promotion, transfer, compensation, training and development, and employee termination.

Systems perspective: Views the different parts of an organization in terms of how they function together.

Performance appraisal also stands as a system by itself. The effectiveness of a performance appraisal system is not a function of any one part (such as instrumentation), but rather is dependent on how well all the parts (e.g., goals, job analyses, methods, training, etc.) work together.

Method/Job/Organization Fit

Finally, what about method/job/organization fit? Job analysis, preparation of job descriptions, performance review, and training are common components of any performance appraisal system. However, what about the methodology? Should an organization (or its sub-units) use BARS, BOS, MBO, or a combination or modification of these methods? Are some appraisal methods superior for certain types of jobs or certain types of organizations?

We believe if it is unduly difficult (or impossible) to identify behaviors that drive output, or if personal criteria cannot be "translated" into behavioral standards, then MBO methodology may be necessary. This may be the case for many managerial jobs. Conversely, a behavioral methodology (e.g., BAR) may work well with lower-ranking employees because job duties (behaviors) are relatively well defined.

Contingency approach: Indicates that the performance appraisal method used should be based on the capability to define work outcomes and behaviors associated with a given job or job family.

A Contingency Approach.   One writer has developed a **contingency approach** for identifying the most appropriate performance appraisal methodology. Cynthia Lee believes that the performance appraisal method chosen should be based on the relationship between "availability of reliable and valid performance measures" and "knowledge of transformation process."[34] These terms refer respectively to the capability to define work outcomes clearly, and the capability to define behaviors associated with a given job.

With some jobs it is relatively easy to identify outcomes, but not the behaviors that lead to the outcome (e.g., sales personnel); or it is relatively easy to identify behaviors, but not outcomes (e.g., astronauts); or it is relatively easy to identify both behaviors and outcomes (e.g., assembly-line workers). With some jobs it is not possible to identify either (e.g., foreign service agents). According to Lee, the performance appraisal method employed should take into account these factors (see Figure 6–6).

Note that Lee does not consider the use of appraisal methods that use personal criteria. For example, rather than rely on personal characteristics to evaluate researchers or foreign service agents, she recommends that the right people be hired and trained for the job in the first place, since in these jobs it is difficult to evaluate performance objectively.

Lee's theory has not been empirically tested. It is offered only to illustrate that the "right" performance evaluation method depends on the nature of the job. To this idea should be added the notion that the right performance appraisal method also depends very much on the nature of the organization.

Organic organization: Characterized by unstable, rapidly changing technology and markets.

Mechanistic organization: Characterized by relatively stable technology and markets.

Organic versus Mechanistic Organizations.   An **organic organization** characterized by unstable, rapidly changing technology and markets would benefit from a different performance appraisal method, relative to a **mechanistic organization** characterized by relatively stable technology and markets. (Distinction between these organizational types is made by Burns and Stalker.[35] See Chapter Ten, Organization Development, for further discussion.)

An MBO approach involving significant employee participation in goal setting may be more effective in an organic organization staffed by research personnel, than in a relatively mechanistic organization populated by assembly-line workers. This is because work behaviors are

Figure 6–6 A Contingency Approach

Availability of Reliable and Valid Performance Measures	Knowledge of the Transformation Process	
	High	*Low*
High	1. Behavior or output control: e.g., assembly line workers, clerks	2. Output control: e.g., recruiters, sales, insurance agents, teachers, computer programmers
Low	3. Behavior control: e.g., reporters, bank tellers, astronauts, managers	4. Extensive selection and training procedures: e.g., researcher, foreign service agents

The capability to clearly define work *outcomes* ("availability of reliable and valid performance measures") and capability to define *behaviors* associated with a given job ("knowledge of transformation process") should be considered in selecting a performance appraisal method. These capabilities are based on the nature and purpose of the organization and the work processes that serve organizational objectives.

Reprinted with permission from Lee, C. (1985). Increasing performance appraisal effectiveness: Matching task types, appraisal processes, and rater training. *Academy of Management Review, 10,* 322–331.

relatively more difficult to define in an organic organization. Also, employee satisfaction caused by participation in goal setting may be a more significant contributor to productivity in the organic situation. On the other hand, performance appraisal of assembly-line workers may be more effective if evaluation focuses on behaviors or output.

Tips for the Manager. This section returned briefly to the subject of goal setting. It is important that managers tie the direction of the organization to the purpose and practice of performance appraisal.

Taking a systems perspective is important to the understanding and practice of effective performance appraisal. Appraisal is part of a total human resources system, as organizational compensation, promotion, transfer, training, and termination decisions are all affected by appraisal of performance. The components of a performance appraisal process also constitute a system. Job analysis, preparation of job descriptions, provision of feedback through the performance review, and training all need to take place for performance appraisal to be effective.

Choosing the right performance appraisal method is also important to the healthy functioning of organizational systems. The selection of the right performance appraisal method depends on the clarity of performance measures associated with a given job (whether output can be clearly defined); knowledge of work processes that lead to goal attainment (whether work behaviors can be well defined); and the nature of the organization (whether organic or mechanistic).

SUMMARY: FOCUS ON SKILLS

Performance appraisal is defined as the assessment of employee performance. The primary purpose of performance appraisal is to improve productivity across an organization for the purpose of attaining individual, group, and organizational goals. A secondary purpose is to protect the organization from legal reprisals.

Following are 17 suggestions for conducting effective, valid performance appraisal.

Managers should:

1. Establish specific and "hard but achievable" goals.
2. Analyze jobs. Use job analysis results to modify job content based on goals.
3. Use job analysis as the basis for preparing written job descriptions, which include job specifications and evaluation criteria.
4. As much as possible, employ evaluation criteria that define a "good" or "poor" appraisal in terms of behavior and output (e.g., performance criteria) rather than in terms of individual personality (e.g., personal criteria).
5. Try to translate personal criteria into behaviorally defined scales when possible. If this is difficult or impossible to do, consider using an MBO format.
6. When using MBO, keep in mind the importance of avoiding goal manipulation and busywork across the organization.

7. Provide feedback to employees that is specific, timely, impersonal, noticeable, and frequent.

8. Base frequency of feedback on needs and past performance of the employee. Remedial action programs (RAP) involve frequent review using detailed standards; maintenance action programs (MAP) involve periodic review two or three times a year; and developmental action programs (DAP) involve appraisal at the conclusion of projects.

9. Give employees the opportunity to participate in the performance review. Discuss plans and objectives, and evaluate employees on factors relevant to their work.

10. Participate in training (or make possible training for others) that provides practice in actually rating subordinates, discussion of the method being learned, and feedback of results.

11. Learn communications and conflict management skills in order to "level" with employees during the performance review without "leveling them."

12. Consider incorporating peer evaluation from work-group members into performance appraisal as only one source (not as the only source) of information.

13. Consider using an MBO format, with group objectives, in highly interdependent groups.

14. Keep in mind that productivity could be undermined if group members believe performance appraisal is unfair.

15. Set goals! This is true at the organizational, group, and individual levels.

16. Maintain linkages between performance appraisal and organizational systems. This perspective holds true whether looking at performance appraisal within the context of a human resources system, or at the parts that comprise the performance appraisal system itself.

17. Consider adopting behavior or output-based methodology founded on the dictates of a job (or job class) and the nature of the organization (e.g., organic or mechanistic). No one method is ideal for all organizations and for all jobs within them.

■ CASE: "GAMES PLANNERS PLAY"

In 1974 Walcon Manufacturing Corporation adopted an approach to MBO that integrates objective-setting and budgeting. It includes the following steps which are designed to produce a complete set of objectives and budgets for the company by July 1st, the start of each fiscal year:

1. Each department submits its proposed objectives for the coming year to the executive committee, comprising the five top executives, by April 1st.
2. After review, discussion, negotiation, and perhaps modification, the executive committee approves a set of objectives.
3. After approval, each department submits the financial data for its objectives to the executive committee by May 1st.
   a. The Sales Department forecasts sales. Estimated new sales plus the backlog of inventory provide the basis for projecting total shipments for the coming year.
   b. The Manufacturing Department estimates production and provides an estimate of gross profit based on the estimated costs and revenues for each job.
   c. All so-called "overhead" departments, e.g., administrative departments such as Purchasing and Personnel, submit their own budgets. Special program expenses, such as research and development, are also prepared.
4. The planning staff then combines all these data and issues the new company plan by June 1st.

The trouble is that the Sales Department understates its objectives so that it will look good by surpassing them. Manufacturing does the same thing: It understates the anticipated gross profit for each job. This gives them a chance to exceed the objective. It also provides a reserve to meet unanticipated expenses.

The overhead departments always seem to ask for a larger budget and more employees than can possibly be supported by revenues projected by the sales forecast. The department heads are asked to make cuts. They never cut their budgets enough, so top management cuts them all across-the-board by, say, 10 percent.

What happens as a result of a low sales forecast is that we have too much work for the number of employees and the amount of money our budgets allowed. In an attempt to satisfy customers, however, top management authorizes overtime or subcontracting plus occasional special expenditures for air freight and other hurry-up efforts. These expenditures reduce gross profits.

As for the overhead departments, they are imposed upon by all this scrambling. Purchasing and Personnel, for example, are asked for special fast services. They usually try to help, but they often fail to meet their original objectives because of these added burdens. Sometimes they aren't very cooperative precisely because cooperation in coping with this annual emergency will interfere with their meeting their own objectives. In any event, they claim that the budget cuts caused any failures they do experience. They always inflate next year's estimates so that what is cut is more likely to be fat.

This happens every year.

From instructor's manual, to accompany *Organizational Behavior and the Practice of Management,* 4th ed., by David R. Hampton, Charles E. Summer, and Ross A. Webber. Copyright © 1982 by Scott, Foresman and Company. Reprinted by permission.

Case Question

1. How would you advise Walcon to cope with their problems?

■ EXERCISE: "RATING PERFORMANCE"

In this exercise, your job is to rate the performance of three first-line supervisors using behavioral observation scales (BOS). Your instructor will hand out case reports for Andrew, Betsy, and Cal. You will use these reports to rate the performance of each of these supervisors.

After scoring each BOS subscale for a job dimension (such as "supervision and planning"), you will have an opportunity to discuss the importance of accuracy in conducting an appraisal.

Forms

Instructions: The following checklists for Andrew, Betsy, and Cal contain performance-related job behaviors that have been identified as being critical to the success of first-line mine supervisors on Io, the fifth moon of Jupiter, in the year 2086. Read each scale item carefully. Then make your judgments on the basis of dependable knowledge obtained from the case report for the supervisor being rated.

Circle the number that best indicates the extent to which the supervisor demonstrated the critical job behavior. For each scale, a 5 represents "Almost always" (or 90–100 percent of the time); a 4 represents "Frequently" (or 80–89 percent of the time); a 3 represents "Sometimes" (or 70–79 percent of the time); a 2 represents "Seldom" (or 40–69 percent of the time); and a 1 represents "Almost never" (or 0–39 percent of the time).

An example of a scale item is shown below. If the supervisor being rated has followed safety procedures most of the time, you should circle 5. If the supervisor followed safety procedures about half the time, you should circle 2.

Behavioral Observation Scale for First-Line Supervisors at Io Enterprises

Supervisor: *Andrew*

I. Technical Competence

1. Knows technical aspects of the job (e.g., basics of ground characteristics, equipment operation and maintenance).
   Almost never   1   2   3   4   5   Almost always

2. Seeks guidance when necessary to fill out information gaps.
   Almost never   1   2   3   4   5   Almost always

3. Attends to equipment maintenance even when difficult.
   Almost never   1   2   3   4   5   Almost always

4. Communicates effectively in written and oral form.
   Almost never   1   2   3   4   5   Almost always

5. Provides complete, orderly paperwork in a timely fashion (e.g., reports, time cards, work orders, safety forms).
   Almost never   1   2   3   4   5   Almost always

TOTAL Part I _____

II. Supervision and Planning

1. Assigns priorities to jobs and allows sufficient time for accomplishment.
   Almost never   1   2   3   4   5   Almost always

2. Develops plans and procedures for jobs ahead of time (e.g., moving machinery, equipment repair, preventive maintenance).
   Almost never   1   2   3   4   5   Almost always

3. Stays appropriately close to the crew to monitor work flow and accomplishment.
   Almost never   1   2   3   4   5   Almost always

4. Works to upgrade personnel (e.g., builds skills, recognizes competencies).
   Almost never   1   2   3   4   5   Almost always

5. Allows crew to develop good working relationship (e.g., helps integrate new crew members).
   Almost never   1   2   3   4   5   Almost always

TOTAL Part II _____

III. Leadership

1. Provides accurate and timely feedback (e.g., praise, constructive criticism).
   Almost never   1   2   3   4   5   Almost always

2. Builds and maintains rapport with crew members (e.g., is friendly, does not use abusive language, reprimands in private).
   Almost never   1   2   3   4   5   Almost always

3. Helps out crew with work on occasion (e.g., helps carry tools, reports instrument readings).
   Almost never   1   2   3   4   5   Almost always

4. Maintains composure under stress.
   Almost never   1   2   3   4   5   Almost always

5. Cooperates with other supervisors (e.g., communicates, leaves work area ready for next shift).
   Almost never   1   2   3   4   5   Almost always

TOTAL Part III _____

IV. Safety

1. Follows approved safe work practices (e.g., knows safety regulations and company policies, requires use of protective equipment).
   Almost never   1   2   3   4   5   Almost always

2. Maintains a safe pace and work flow.
   Almost never   1   2   3   4   5   Almost always

3. Gives feedback for safety behavior (e.g., praises working safely, does not punish reporting of unsafe conditions or accidents).
   Almost never   1   2   3   4   5   Almost always

4. Maintains a clean and hazard free work area.
   Almost never   1   2   3   4   5   Almost always

5. Regularly holds safety meetings.
   Almost never   1   2   3   4   5   Almost always

TOTAL Part IV _____   **TOTAL** _____

Behavioral Observation Scale for First-Line Supervisors at Io Enterprises

Supervisor: *Betsy*

I. Technical Competence

1. Knows technical aspects of the job (e.g., basics of ground characteristics, equipment operation and maintenance).
   Almost never   1   2   3   4   5   Almost always

2. Seeks guidance when necessary to fill out information gaps.
   Almost never   1   2   3   4   5   Almost always

3. Attends to equipment maintenance even when difficult.
   Almost never   1   2   3   4   5   Almost always

4. Communicates effectively in written and oral form.
   Almost never　　1　　2　　3　　4　　5　　Almost always

5. Provides complete, orderly paperwork in a timely fashion (e.g., reports, time cards, work orders, safety forms).
   Almost never　　1　　2　　3　　4　　5　　Almost always

TOTAL Part I _____

II. Supervision and Planning

1. Assigns priorities to jobs and allows sufficient time for accomplishment.
   Almost never　　1　　2　　3　　4　　5　　Almost always

2. Develops plans and procedures for jobs ahead of time (e.g., moving machinery, equipment repair, preventive maintenance).
   Almost never　　1　　2　　3　　4　　5　　Almost always

3. Stays appropriately close to the crew to monitor work flow and accomplishment.
   Almost never　　1　　2　　3　　4　　5　　Almost always

4. Works to upgrade personnel (e.g., builds skills, recognizes competencies).
   Almost never　　1　　2　　3　　4　　5　　Almost always

5. Allows crew to develop good working relationship (e.g., helps integrate new crew members).
   Almost never　　1　　2　　3　　4　　5　　Almost always

TOTAL Part II _____

III. Leadership

1. Provides accurate and timely feedback (e.g., praise, constructive criticism).
   Almost never　　1　　2　　3　　4　　5　　Almost always

2. Builds and maintains rapport with crew members (e.g., is friendly, does not use abusive language, reprimands in private).
   Almost never　　1　　2　　3　　4　　5　　Almost always

3. Helps out crew with work on occasion (e.g., helps carry tools, reports instrument readings).
   Almost never　　1　　2　　3　　4　　5　　Almost always

4. Maintains composure under stress.
   Almost never　　1　　2　　3　　4　　5　　Almost always

5. Cooperates with other supervisors (e.g., communicates, leaves work area ready for next shift).
   Almost never　　1　　2　　3　　4　　5　　Almost always

TOTAL Part III _____

IV. Safety

1. Follows approved safe work practices (e.g., knows safety regulations and company policies, requires use of protective equipment).
   Almost never   1   2   3   4   5   Almost always
2. Maintains a safe pace and work flow.
   Almost never   1   2   3   4   5   Almost always
3. Gives feedback for safety behavior (e.g., praises working safely, does not punish reporting of unsafe conditions or accidents).
   Almost never   1   2   3   4   5   Almost always
4. Maintains a clean and hazard free work area.
   Almost never   1   2   3   4   5   Almost always
5. Regularly holds safety meetings.
   Almost never   1   2   3   4   5   Almost always

TOTAL Part IV _____   **TOTAL** _____

Behavioral Observation Scale for First-Line Supervisors at Io Enterprises

Supervisor: *Cal*

I. Technical Competence

1. Knows technical aspects of the job (e.g., basics of ground characteristics, equipment operation and maintenance).
   Almost never   1   2   3   4   5   Almost always
2. Seeks guidance when necessary to fill out information gaps.
   Almost never   1   2   3   4   5   Almost always
3. Attends to equipment maintenance even when difficult.
   Almost never   1   2   3   4   5   Almost always
4. Communicates effectively in written and oral form.
   Almost never   1   2   3   4   5   Almost always
5. Provides completely, orderly paperwork in a timely fashion (e.g., reports, time cards, work orders, safety forms).
   Almost never   1   2   3   4   5   Almost always

TOTAL Part I _____

II. Supervision and Planning

1. Assigns priorities to jobs and allows sufficient time for accomplishment.
   Almost never   1   2   3   4   5   Almost always

2. Develops plans and procedures for jobs ahead of time (e.g., moving machinery, equipment repair, preventive maintenance).
Almost never 1 2 3 4 5 Almost   always

3. Stays appropriately close to the crew to monitor work flow and accomplishment.
Almost never 1 2 3 4 5 Almost always

4. Works to upgrade personnel (e.g., build skills, recognizes competencies).
Almost never 1 2 3 4 5 Almost always

5. Allows crew to develop good working relationship (e.g., helps integrate new crew members).
Almost never 1 2 3 4 5 Almost always

TOTAL Part II _____

III. Leadership

1. Provides accurate and timely feedback (e.g., praise, constructive criticism).
Almost never 1 2 3 4 5 Almost always

2. Builds and maintains rapport with crew members (e.g., is friendly, does not use abusive language, reprimands in private).
Almost never 1 2 3 4 5 Almost always

3. Helps out crew with work on occasion (e.g., helps carry tools, reports instrument readings).
Almost never 1 2 3 4 5 Almost always

4. Maintains composure under stress.
Almost never 1 2 3 4 5 Almost always

5. Cooperates with other supervisors (e.g., communicates, leaves work area ready for next shift).
Almost never 1 2 3 4 5 Almost always

TOTAL Part III _____

IV. Safety

1. Follows approved safe work practices (e.g., knows safety regulations and company policies, requires use of protective equipment).
Almost never 1 2 3 4 5 Almost always

2. Maintains a safe pace and work flow.
Almost never 1 2 3 4 5 Almost always

3. Gives feedback for safety behavior (e.g., praises working safely, does not punish reporting of unsafe conditions or accidents).
Almost never 1 2 3 4 5 Almost always

4. Maintains a clean and hazard free work area.
   Almost never   1   2   3   4   5   Almost always
5. Regularly holds safety meetings.
   Almost never   1   2   3   4   5   Almost always

TOTAL Part IV _____   **TOTAL** _____

ENDNOTES

1. Locke, E. A., & Latham, G. P. *Goal-setting: A Motivational Technique That Works!* Englewood Cliffs, NJ: Prentice-Hall, 1984.

2. Smith, P. C. "Behaviors, results, and organizational effectiveness: The problem of criteria." In M. D. Dunnette (ed.), *Handbook of Industrial and Organizational Psychology.* Chicago: Rand-McNally, 1976.

3. Locke, E. A. "Toward a theory of task motivation and incentives." *Organizational Behavior and Human Performance, 3* (1968): 157–189. See also: Locke and Latham, *Goal-setting.*

4. *Albermarle Paper Company* v. *Moody.* U.S. Supreme Court Nos. 74–389 and 74–428, 10 FEP Cases 1181, 1975.

5. *Rowe* v. *General Motors.* 4 FEP 445, 1972.

6. Burke, R. J.; Weitzel, W.; & Weir, T. "Characteristics of effective employee performance review and development interviews: Replication and extension." *Personnel Psychology, 31* (1978): 903–919.

7. Nathan, B. R., & Alexander, R. A. "The role of inferential accuracy in performance rating." *Academy of Management Review, 10* (1985): 109–115.

8. Latham, G. P.; Fay C. H.; & Saari, L. M. "The development of behavioral observation scales for appraising the performance of foremen." *Personnel Psychology, 32* (1979): 299–311. See also: Latham, G. P., & Wexley, K. N. *Increasing Productivity Through Performance Appraisal.* Reading, MA: Addison-Wesley, 1981; and Smith, P. C., & Kendall, L. M. "Retranslation of expectations: An approach to the construction of unambiguous anchors for rating scales." *Journal of Applied Psychology, 47* (1963): 149–155.

9. Carroll, S. J., & Tosi, H. L. "Goal characteristics and personality factors in a management by objective program." *Administrative Science Quarterly, 15* (1970): 295–305.

10. Carroll, S. J., & Schneier, C. E. *Performance Appraisal and Review Systems.* Glenview, IL: Scott, Foresman and Company, 1982.

11. Ibid., p. 10.

12. Landy, F. J., & Farr, J. L. "Performance rating." *Psychological Bulletin, 87* (1980): 72–107.

13. Carroll & Schneier, *Performance Appraisal.*

14. Cummings, L. L., & Schwab, D. P. *Performance in Organizations: Determinants and Appraisal.* Glenview, IL: Scott, Foresman and Company, 1973.

15. Meyer, H., Kay, E., & French, J. R. P. "Split roles in performance appraisal." *Harvard Business Review, 43* (1965): 123–129.

16. Burke, Weitzel, & Weir, "Characteristics of effective employees."

17. Dipboye, R. L., & Pontbriand, R. "Correlates of employee reactions to performance appraisals and appraisal systems." *Journal of Applied Psychology (Short Notes), 66* (1981): 248–251.

18. Hakel, M. D. "An appraisal of performance appraisal: Sniping with a shotgun." Paper presented at Scientist-Practitioner Conference in IO Psychology, Virginia Beach, VA, 1980. See also: Cascio, W. F. *Applied Psychology in Personnel Management* (3rd ed.). Englewood Cliffs, NJ: Prentice-Hall, 1987.

19. "Norms above average in standardized tests," *The Herald* (Everett, WA), February 10, 1988, p. 1.

20. Hakel, M. D. "Normative personality factors recovered from ratings of personality descriptors: The beholder's eye." *Personnel Psychology, 27* (1974): 409–421.

21. Bernadin, H. J., & Pence, E. C. "Effects of rater training: Creating new response sets and decreasing accuracy." *Journal of Applied Psychology, 65* (1980): 60–66.

22. Fay, C. H., & Latham, G. P. "Effects of training and rating scales on rating errors." *Personnel Psychology, 35* (1982): 105–116.

23. Hedge, J. W., & Kavanagh, M. J. (1988). "Improving the accuracy of performance evaluations: Comparisons of three methods of performance appraiser training." *Journal of Applied Psychology, 73* (1988): 68–73.

24. Latham, G. P.; Cummings, L. L.; and Mitchell, T. R. "Behavioral strategies to improve productivity." *Organizational Dynamics, 9* (1981): 4–23.

25. Smith, D. E. "Training programs for performance appraisal: A review." *Academy of Management Review, 11* (1986): 22–40.

26. Latham, G. P.; Wexley, K. N.; & Pursell, E. D. "Training managers to minimize rating errors in the observation of behavior." *Journal of Applied Psychology, 60* (1975): 550–555.

27. Smith, "Training programs."

28. Bernadin, N. J., & Beatty, R. W. *Performance Appraisal: Assessing Human Behavior at Work.* Boston: Kent, 1984.

29. Cascio, *Applied Psychology.*

30. Ibid.

31. Miller, L., & Hamblin, R. "Interdependence, differential rewarding and productivity." *American Sociological Review, 28* (1963): 768–778.

32. Carroll & Schneier, *Performance Appraisal.*

33. Adams, J. S. "Inequity in social exchange." In L. Berkowitz (Ed.), *Advances in Experimental Social Psychology.* New York: Academic Press, 1965.

34. Lee, C. "Increasing performance appraisal effectiveness: Matching task types, appraisal process, and rater training." *Academy of Management Review, 10* (1985): 322–331.

35. Burns, T., & Stalker, G. *The Management of Innovation.* London: Tavistock, 1961.

CHAPTER SEVEN

Decision Making

- ■ *Self-Assessment: "Cognitive Styles"*
- ■ *Learning about Decision Making*
- ■ *Case: "By the Light of the Moon"*
- ■ *Exercise: "Consensus Building"*

■ SELF-ASSESSMENT: "COGNITIVE STYLES"

Please respond to the following questions. You may want to indicate your responses on a separate sheet of paper. The key for diagnosing your responses is presented below. There are no "right" or "wrong" responses to any of these items.

PART I. Circle the response that comes closest to how you usually feel or act.

1. Are you more careful about:
   a. people's feelings
   b. their rights

2. Do you usually get on better with:
   a. imaginative people
   b. realistic people

3. Which of these two is the higher compliment:
   a. a person has real feeling
   b. a person is consistently reasonable

4. In doing something with many other people, does it appeal more to you:
   a. to do it in the accepted way
   b. to invent a way of your own

5. Do you get more annoyed at:
   a. fancy theories
   b. people who don't like theories

6. It is higher praise to call someone:
   a. a person of vision
   b. a person of common sense

7. Do you more often let:
   a. your heart rule your head
   b. your head rule your heart

8. Do you think it a worse fault:
   a. to show too much warmth
   b. to be unsympathetic

9. If you were a teacher, would you rather teach:
   a. courses involving theory
   b. fact courses

PART II. Which word in the following pair appeals to you more? Circle A or B.

10. a. compassion
    b. foresight

11. a. justice
    b. mercy
12. a. production
    b. design
13. a. gentle
    b. firm
14. a. uncritical
    b. critical
15. a. literal
    b. figurative
16. a. imaginative
    b. matter-of-fact

Scoring Key

This key is to be used to diagnose your responses to the questionnaire. Count one point for each response on the following four scales. Then, total the number of points recorded in each column. Score classifications are indicated below.

Sensation	Intuition	Thinking	Feeling
2 b __	2 a __	1 b __	1 a __
4 a __	4 b __	3 b __	3 a __
5 a __	5 b __	7 b __	7 a __
6 b __	6 a __	8 a __	8 b __
9 b __	9 a __	10 b __	10 a __
12 a __	12 b __	11 a __	11 b __
15 a __	15 b __	13 b __	13 a __
16 b __	16 a __	14 b __	14 a __

■ LEARNING ABOUT DECISION MAKING

You played a part in the decision to read this chapter, even if this reading was assigned to you by another person. Had you not registered for this course you might now be watching TV or eating sushi. Determining *where* to read this chapter was a decision almost certainly left up to you. You might now be sitting in a library, on a couch at home, or in a classroom.

The above examples may seem trivial. Nevertheless, they make the point that decision making is a part of everything we do. Even not making a decision is making a decision! Making decisions is easy with abundant resources and certain outcomes. One simply picks the outcome with the highest actual return. Most of the time we are not so lucky. Instead, people must make decisions every day under conditions of uncertainty involving the allocation of scarce resources (e.g., time, money).

A second point to be made about decision making builds on the first point. We not only must make decisions on an ongoing basis, we must also strive to make the *right decisions* under conditions of uncertainty and scarce resources. Making the right decisions under these circumstances is an essential part of effective management. This chapter focuses on behaviors and techniques that help managers or prospective managers make the right decisions.

A Caveat

Before proceeding, a caution is in order. The study of decision making has led to relatively few clear conclusions regarding how to make the "right" decisions. The challenges have been threefold.

First, decision making should always be understood in context. A particular mix of manager, subordinates, environmental setting(s), and the nature of the decision(s) to be made can lead to the need for an "exception to the rule." For example, allowing subordinates to participate in decision making is often a good idea because it facilitates employee satisfaction. Under certain circumstances, however, managers should make decisions themselves. (This point will be discussed in more detail later in the chapter.) Keep in mind that the suggestions offered in the chapter are general guidelines for decision making rather than inviolate rules.

A second related concern is that decision makers are often not rational. Even if hard and fast decision-making rules existed, people often would not follow them. We are not machines. Rational input-output models of decision making look good on paper, but in practice managers often rely on intuition. In a classic study that contrasted the way managers should behave with the way they actually behave, it was found that most managers make decisions quickly and unsystematically, relying on "soft" information and intuition.[1] Intuition certainly has a place in managerial decision making. Another study found that only *1* out of a sample of 200 managers denied using intuition in making decisions![2] Nevertheless, training in systematic decision making helps managers to become even more effective.

A third problem with identifying effective approaches for managerial decision making concerns the sheer mass of information available on the subject of decision making. A case in point can be found in a recent *Academy of Management Review* article. The authors found some 400 articles that could be related to employee participation in decision making, which is only one facet of the decision-making literature![3]

Gleaning effective managerial behaviors and techniques from this weight of information is made more troublesome because much of the decision-making literature is normative—describing how decisions *should be* made on the basis of a theoretical ideal. Even when the literature is descriptive—describing how effective decisions are actually made—connections between description and application are sometimes difficult to make. In this chapter we build on normative and descriptive material to support suggestions for improving managerial decision making.

The next section begins by defining decision making and the decision-making process. You will then find a discussion of when to conduct systematic, analytic decision making and when to rely more on intuition.

WHAT IS DECISION MAKING?

Decision making: Involves solving a problem or otherwise attaining a goal by choosing among alternative courses of action.

Decision making is solving a problem or otherwise attaining a goal by choosing among alternative courses of action. Once an alternative has been selected for implementation, a decision has been made. The **decision-making process** adds to this definition of decision making by including "implementation of an alternative," and "evaluation" (see Figure 7–1).

Decision-making process: Steps are: definition of the problem, consideration and selection of an alternative, implementation, and evaluation.

Following the Steps in Order.　　Have you ever tried to define a problem before gathering information, or tried to solve a problem before it was even defined? You may have occasionally been guilty of selecting the first alternative that comes to mind, rather than searching for a better way to solve a problem. These are common mistakes made by individuals and groups. These errors occur because of a failure to work through the decision-making process in order. Learn the steps in the decision-making process outlined in Figure 7–1, and cover the steps in order

Figure 7–1 The Decision-Making Process

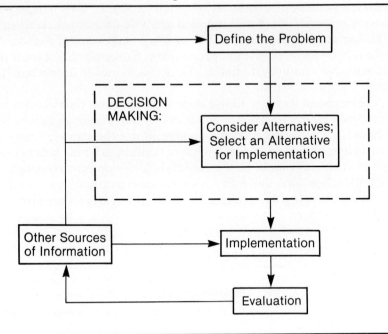

Variations of this model are found throughout the literature. The concept of a decision-making *process* was described as early as 1910 in John Dewey's work *How We Think*. (Perhaps this book would have been more appropriately titled, *How We Sometimes Think* or *How We Should Think*.)

when making and following through on some decisions. Notice we said *some decisions* because, otherwise, our advice would seem a bit unrealistic given the large number and nature of the decisions we make every day.

The Nature of Decisions: Decision Strategies.   Clearly, some decisions are more important than others and require more attention to a systematic, information-driven approach. It is not necessary to "haul out the heavy artillery of careful, hard analysis for decisions of minor importance."[4] A decision to eat pizza rather than tofu should not require a systematic decision-making approach as outlined in Figure 7–1.

A useful framework for assessing the nature of decisions, and an aid in determining when to be analytic and when to be intuitive, was developed by Lee Beach and Terence Mitchell. According to these researchers, decision makers use one of three different **decision strategies:** aided analytic, unaided analytic, or nonanalytic.[5]

Decision strategies: The decision strategy selected (aided analytic, unaided analytic, or nonanalytic) should be based on the decision environment and characteristics of the decision.

Aided and unaided analytic decisions require the use of a systematic decision-making process as outlined in Figure 7–1. The primary difference between aided and unaided analytic decision-making strategies is that aided analytic decision making makes use of aids such as computer models or statistical projections. Nonanalytic decision making is intuitive and unsystematic. The decision maker does what "feels right."

The decision strategy to use depends in part on the decision environment and characteristics of the decision (see Figure 7–2). The basic idea here is that the decision maker should use the strategy that takes the least time and effort to reach what is thought to be the best decision. Analytic strategies should be selected if the decision is irreversible, very important, when time and other resources are available, and when the decision maker is highly accountable. Analytic strategies are also called

Figure 7–2 The Nature of Decisions

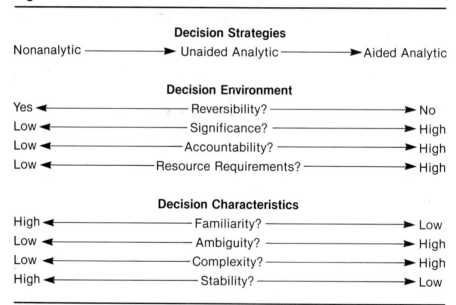

This model provides justification for *contingency planning*—plans developed in response to *potential* problems. Aided analytic decisions require a high degree of time and other resources. Contingency plans help decision makers to solve problems when aided analytic decisions must be made and time and other resources are low.

Adapted from Beach, L. R., & Mitchell, T. R. "A contingency model for the selection of decision strategies." *Academy of Management Review, 3* (1978): 439–449.

for as decision characteristics become less familiar, more ambiguous, complex, and unstable.

To summarize, be sure to follow the steps (in order) in the decision-making process for decisions that require an analytic approach (e.g., outlined in Figure 7–1). There is a need for balance. The literature suggests that managers depend on intuitive decision making, relative to what would be expected.[6] On the other hand, as noted by Beach and Mitchell, intuitive decision making is fine for many of the everyday decisions we must make.

Our discussion of individual, group, and organizational considerations in decision making will focus on analytic decision making. Intuitive decision making (e.g., deciding to eat pizza rather than tofu) is something you already know how to do.

INDIVIDUAL CONSIDERATIONS IN DECISION MAKING

Defining the problem to solve is the most important part of an analytic decision-making process. All else in the process flows from this essential first step. (Note: The first step in the decision-making process does not always involve the defining of problems in a negative sense. "Taking advantage of an opportunity" represents one type of "problem" that can be very positive.)

Step One: Defining the Problem

Two considerations that facilitate clear problem definition when making analytic decisions are (1) avoiding the **garbage in–garbage out syndrome** and (2) being mindful of cognitive traps associated with the way a problem is framed.

Garbage In–Garbage Out.   All steps in the decision-making process benefit from the use of relevant, valid information. If you put good information into the decision loop, your chances of making a good decision will improve. Conversely, if you put "garbage in" you will get "garbage out." To the extent that information is invalid, problem definition is usually invalid, and the remaining steps in the decision-making process suffer accordingly.

Another related concept concerns checking out assumptions. Sometimes decision making is flawed by not checking out information because it is *assumed* to be valid. It is not possible to gather all information relating to a particular problem, nor is it possible to eliminate assumptions. However, an effective decision maker tries to define a

Garbage in–garbage out syndrome: All steps in the decision-making process benefit from using relevant, valid information. If you put "garbage in" you'll usually get "garbage out."

problem before trying to solve it, and uses the best information he or she can gather in the process.

The Information Industry

Decision making should be guided by the best information a decision maker can find. This basic principle is well understood by U.S. business managers. Expenditures on market research now exceed $2 billion a year in the U.S. economy. Usually the research helps; sometimes it doesn't. The wrong information is sometimes collected, information is misinterpreted, or some factor beyond the control of the decision maker affects decision quality.

Coca-Cola conducted exhaustive taste tests in developing the New Coke, but failed to assess one crucial factor: brand loyalty. The unveiling of the New Coke is one of the best-known marketing flops of all time, standing next to the Ford Edsel. The Edsel fiasco involved another product that had been extensively researched. *Star Wars*, one of the most successful films of all time, would not have reached the theatres if film director George Lucas had listened to market researchers.

It is tough to find good, reliable data. Some businesses have hired University of Arizona anthropology professor William Rathje to rummage through consumers' garbage. According to Rathje, a major problem is that "dogs and cats sometimes eat our data."[7]

Framing the Problem.   Even if the best information is available and an analytic decision-making process is being used, judgmental errors can still be made because of problems with *framing the problem*. By *framed*, we mean the way in which a problem is expressed.

According to the work of Daniel Kahneman and Amos Tversky, people tend to avoid risks when seeking gains, but choose risks to avoid sure losses. For example, choose between:

A. A sure gain of $3000.

B. An 80 percent chance of winning $4000 and a 20 percent chance of winning nothing.

In this situation, most people are risk aversive and select option A. People go for the "sure thing" in this example even though option B has a higher expected payoff (.80 × $4000 = $3200).

Now, choose between:

A. A sure loss of $3000.
B. An 80 percent chance of losing $4000 and a 20 percent chance of losing nothing.

In this example, Kahneman and Tversky found the preferences were reversed relative to the first example. More than 90 percent of the participants in their study went for option B—the risky gamble![8]

This "framing effect" is commonplace. For example, in labor negotiations individuals are more likely to choose a negotiated settlement when a problem is framed positively in terms of potential gains than when it is framed negatively in terms of potential losses.[9] When negotiators evaluate the prospect of losses, they behave in a more risk-seeking manner and are more willing to choose the risky option of arbitration rather than take what apears to be a certain loss.

Consider also the manner in which a doctor presents the problem of a possible surgery, an attorney presents the problem of a potential law suit, or an accountant presents the prospect of losing money on a new business venture. The manner in which problems are framed by the doctor, attorney, and accountant can significantly affect decisions that are ultimately made.

Kahneman and Tversky's work suggests that, when possible, decision makers should use a frame that takes the broader view of a problem. Framing problems can also be reduced if decision makers are *aware* of the framing effect and if they reframe the same problem from different perspectives.

Commentary: "Decision Making"

Wallace Wong

One of the most important parts of business decision making is using good information. Information should be used to guide business decision making regardless of business type, whether you're talking about General Motors or a neighborhood lemonade stand.

For example, the manager of a retail clothing store needs information to plan a successful sale. Do customers of the store tend to be affluent, or do they wait until payday to shop (usually the first and 15th of each month)? An affluent customer might also pay

$20 or more for a silk tie—not so for low-income customers who are looking for a $5.99 special! Merchandise must also meet the needs of customers. For example, white colors in children's clothing are often not attractive to budget-minded shoppers because they soil easily. Large sizes will not move well if your store is located in Chinatown.

As a buyer for National Dollar Stores, I am constantly concerned with understanding National's customers. I must make customer-related decisions every day that rely on this understanding.

Poor decisions also occur because companies lose sight of fundamentals pertaining to their niche. In recent years, J. C. Penney, Sears Roebuck, and Montgomery Ward all tried to change their merchandising image to become like Bloomingdale's, Macy's, and Saks Fifth Avenue. This strategy has had mixed results. Sears, for example, is returning to its previous niche.

Another important part of successful decision making in business is *education.*

You could have the best information in the world, yet not know how to use it! Learn how to make good decisions.

In my field, one can get educated by reading trade journals, enrolling in courses, and learning on the job. Education is more important to business decision making now than ever before. This is true, in part, because the pace of business has increased. There is less time to deliberate before decisions must be made, and the competition is very keen.

As for myself, having no more than a high-school diploma and speaking English as a second language, I have learned to appreciate the benefits of a good education. Well-educated, experienced people usually make better business decisions than people who are only well educated or who only have experience.

This chapter includes some good advice, helpful for furthering one's education. I particularly agree with the suggestion to define a problem before you try to solve it.

Wallace Wong

Wallace Wong started his career in retailing with the National Dollar Stores in 1943. (National was founded in 1903 in Vallejo, California. A picture of the founder, Mr. Joe Shoong, is located in the Museum of Successful Immigrant Merchants at the base of the Statue of Liberty.) National is a chain of 40 stores located in California, Arizona, Texas, and Hawaii.

Of Mr. Wong's 46 years of experience in retailing, 37 have been with National. Over the years with National, he worked his way to the top, moving from the position of salesman to store manager, district supervisor, corporate operations manager, and, finally, to his current position as an infants and children's wear buyer.

Mr. Wong's secret to success is: "I have enjoyed my work. The days have been like hours and the years like weeks."

Step Two:
Considering and Selecting an Alternative

Once the problem has been defined, the decision maker (or group) should consider alternatives—prospective courses of action for solving the problem.

Consideration and selection of an alternative would seem to be a straightforward proposition—simply consider all alternatives and implement the alternative that best solves the problem. In reality, there is a significant difference between this normative view of decision making and the way people actually behave. Herbert Simon claims that consideration of alternatives is "bounded" by our limited capability to carry information.

Simon's **bounded rationality model** asserts that it is impossible for decision makers to consider *all* alternatives.[10] Instead, people tend to focus on only a few alternatives and ultimately select the alternative that is minimally sufficient to address the problem. In short, decision makers tend to "satisfice" rather than "maximize" in considering and selecting alternatives.

Bounded rationality model: People tend to focus on only a few alternatives, and eventually select the first alternative minimally sufficient to solve a problem.

Some satisficing behavior is unavoidable. We do not have access to all possible contingencies in making decisions. Additionally, overworking a problem can result in "analysis paralysis," leading to inaction by the decision maker. Nonanalytic decision making also does not require systematic consideration of alternatives. Despite these barriers, the use of a systematic approach to alternative consideration and selection benefits analytic decision making.

Systematic Consideration of Alternatives: The Expected Value (EV) Model.

The **expected value** model (and its variations) has two primary components: (1) the probability that a given action or actions will lead to a particular outcome and (2) the value the decision maker places on the outcome. The expected value model is governed by the *maximization rule*, which states that decision makers will select the alternative with the highest expected value.

Expected value: The expected value of an alternative is a function of the probability that a given action will lead to an outcome, and the value of the outcome to the decision maker(s).

The principle of expected value and the maximization rule can be illustrated by building on the Kahneman and Tversky example cited previously:

Potential Gain		Probability (%)		Expected Value
a. $3000	×	100	=	$3000
b. $4000	×	.80	=	$3200
c. $7500	×	.70	=	$5250

According to this example, a rational decision maker would select option C because of the maximization rule's dictate that the alternative with the highest expected value be chosen.

The concept of "expected value" can be broadened into the development of a *decision tree,* which graphically portrays the expected value of several possible alternatives. Graphing a decision tree allows the decision maker to consider *several* probabilities associated with a given alternative. Figure 7–3 outlines a decision tree justifying a decision to study for an upcoming exam.

As you can see in Figure 7–3, there is about a 90 percent chance that you will pass the exam if you study, and about a 10 percent chance of failure. In contrast, if you do not study, you have about a 30 percent chance of passing the exam, and about a 70 percent chance of failing.

You weigh the attractiveness of passing versus the unattractiveness of failing on a five-point scale. Let's say in this case you decide that passing the exam is slightly more attractive ($+3$ for passing versus $+2$ for failing). As a result of using this analytic decision process, you find that the expected value of studying is higher than it is for not studying (expected value of studying $= 2.90$; of not studying $= 2.30$). Consequently, you decide to study and earn an A on the exam!

In constructing decision trees, keep in mind that measures of attractiveness can be monetary amounts, as in the Kahneman and Tversky example, or can be expressed as a scale, as in the Figure 7–3

Figure 7–3 A Decision Tree

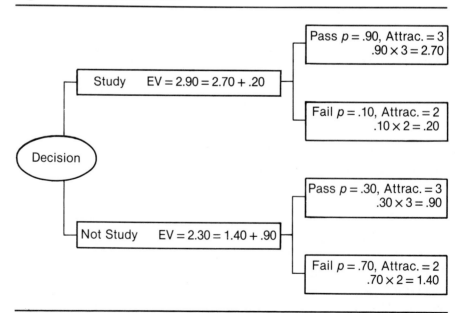

Adapted from Garcia, J. E.; Lewis, C. T.; & Fiedler, F. E. *Instructor's Manual for People, Management, and Productivity.* Boston: Allyn and Bacon, 1986, p. 46.

example. Also, do not confuse the expected value determination with your *actual* return based on the option chosen.

If the five-point attractiveness scale used in Figure 7–3 was stated in terms of dollars, your actual return might have been $2.70 (study and pass); $.20 (study and fail); $.90 (not study and pass), *or* $1.40 (not study and fail). The expected value computation pertains to the value of one alternative relative to another (e.g., 2.90 versus 2.30 in the example provided); it does not predict the value of the *actual* outcome.

To summarize, despite the understandable tendency of decision makers to "satisfice," analytic decision making is benefited by systematic consideration of alternatives using quantitative tools such as decision tree analysis. In the final analysis, the key is to at least consider multiple alternatives once a problem has been defined. This is true despite the fact that all weighting schemes involving human judgment are subjective to some degree.

The idea is not to eliminate subjectivity. Rather, the aim of systematic, analytic consideration of alternatives is to reduce adverse effects associated with excessive subjectivity.

Steps Three and Four: Implementation and Evaluation

Implementation. The bridge between making a decision and evaluating the results is the **implementation phase** of the decision-making process. In evaluating the success or failure of any kind of decision, the evaluator should question whether outcomes can be attributed to the quality of the decision or to the quality of execution. Good decisions are sometimes poorly implemented.

Implementation phase: The bridge between making a decision and evaluating results. The actual carrying out of a course of action based on a previous decision or decisions.

Beyond this comment, we will simply note that while implementation is understandably part of the decision-making process, the topic of how to best carry out a decision is not really the purpose of this chapter. (See Chapters Two, Three, Four, and Nine, Communication, Motivation, Conflict and Its Management, and Leadership respectively.)

Evaluation. The importance of assessing the success or failure of a decision cannot be understated. The importance of using good information to formulate problem definition was discussed previously. **Evaluation** of past decisions, as well as other sources of information, should drive future decision making as part of an ongoing decision-making loop.

Evaluation: Assessment of the consequences of past decisions.

Evaluation is sometimes compromised by *rationalization*. When a decision does not work out, decision makers sometimes become even more committed to the poor decision! Rationalization leads decision makers to find illusionary benefit from a past decision. For example, a person might fail at a job selling advertising space for a local newspa-

---

Learning from Past Mistakes

Chrysler once symbolized everything that was wrong with the American automobile industry. The company's costs were out of control, its products were outdated, and red ink had reached $3 billion after three consecutive years of losses. Under the direction of Lee Iacocca, Chrysler turned around. By 1986, Chrysler had repaid $1.2 billion in loans and earned $5.6 billion in profits.

Chrysler learned from poor decisions made in the past. The auto manufacturer saved money by shopping for component parts instead of manufacturing components in-house. The company leased rather than built production facilities. Chrysler was soon able to build cars in U.S. plants for $500 less than G.M. and Ford, contributing to its return to profitability.[11]

Dissonance balancing: The tendency of people to justify or balance the dissonance they feel when things do not go as well as planned.

per, and still justify the decision to go to work for the newspaper based on the perceived quality of sales training that was received. Because the real reason for failure (in this hypothetical situation, let's say poor selling skills were the culprit) was not acknowledged, this unfortunate person might next try his or her hand at selling pots and pans door-to-door!

One reason for rationalization can be found in **dissonance balancing.** People tend to balance dissonance they feel when things do not go as well as planned. In the hypothetical situation described above, finding benefit in failure balanced the dissonance felt by the salesperson (the difference between the salesperson's self-image and actual performance).

Dissonance balancing causes people to remain committed to losing causes, particularly if a decision maker is highly accountable for a previous poor decision.[12] Deciding to stay in a bad marriage, maintaining an unprofitable line, and deciding to continue to commit U.S. ground troops to an unwinnable war in Vietnam are examples of this tendency.

In short, the need to balance dissonance means that decision makers often compound past mistakes by making more serious decision-making errors in the future. The negative effects of dissonance balancing can be moderated by having other informed people, with less at stake in terms of responsibility for the decision, involved in evaluating the outcome of past decisions.

Tips for the Manager.   Managers should learn the steps in the decision-making process outlined in Figure 7–1 and follow these steps, in order, when making analytic decisions. Managers should also realize that not all decisions require the use of an analytic decision-making process. The decision-making process to use depends, in part, on the decision environment (e.g., accountability of the decision maker, resource constraints) and decision characteristics (e.g., ambiguity, complexity).

Managers should define a problem before trying to solve it and should use the best information available. Decision makers should also check assumptions whenever possible and should reframe a problem from several different perspectives. When making analytic decisions, managers should systematically consider multiple alternatives.

Decision makers should determine whether a decision was successful (or not) because of the quality of the decision or because of the manner in which it was implemented. Good ideas are sometimes poorly implemented. It is also beneficial to have people with less at stake involved in evaluating the results of past decisions. Even though it is difficult to accept failure, managers should learn from and accept the lessons of past mistakes.

GROUP CONSIDERATIONS IN DECISION MAKING

Systematic decision making as outlined in Figure 7–1 can also be profitably applied to analytic decision making by groups, though the increased complexity inherent in bringing several people together to make a decision should be recognized. Moderating this complexity requires that group members understand and practice good communication and conflict management skills. (See Chapters Two and Four.) Also, groups are benefited by the understanding and practice of **decision rules,** which guide the group decision-making process. Decision rules are procedural guidelines that direct a group decision-making process.

Decision rules: Procedural guidelines that direct a group decision-making process.

This section on group decision making will cover decision rules. First, however, we will discuss the advantages and disadvantages of using groups, when to use groups for decision making, and how to plan a group meeting.

Group Decision Making: Advantages, Disadvantages, and Planning the Meeting

There are distinct advantages and disadvantages associated with group decision making.[13] Groups accumulate more knowledge and facts, and often consider more alternatives. Participation in group decision making usually leads to higher member satisfaction relative to exclusion. (See Chapter Five, Stress, for further discussion of benefits of participation.) Also, a group process is an effective communications and political device in its own right.

On the other hand, groups make decisions more slowly than individuals. Groups may compromise and, consequently, not make optimal decisions. Also, a "squeaky wheel" in the group may dominate discussions and overly influence results. Overdependence on group decision making can compromise management's flexibility.

Generally, groups make decisions less efficiently than individuals. On the other hand, a group can call on the resources represented by each of its members. Participation in group decision making also has a positive effect on member satisfaction.[14]

Leader Decision Theory. A popular leadership theory developed by Vroom and Yetton provides insight into when a manager should make a decision alone or use a group.[15] (Leader decision theory is covered in detail in Chapter Nine, Leadership.) These researchers identified two sets of concerns regarding the question of whether a manager should rely on a group when making a decision: (1) Is there enough information to make a good decision? and (2) Is acceptance of the decision by subordinates important for effective implementation of the decision? These concerns can be expressed as the *quality rule* and the *acceptance rule*, respectively. Vroom and Yetton have developed a rigorous set of standards pertaining to these two rules. The manager's responses to these questions will determine whether the manager has the group make the decision, consults with the group, or makes the decision alone.

More participative strategies should be used when the manager needs information from group members to improve decision quality and/or when acceptance of the decision by subordinates is important to the success of implementation. (Participation improves member acceptance because, as mentioned previously, it leads to greater satisfaction than exclusion.) Participative strategies also require that the goals of subordinates be congruent with the goals of the organization.

Planning the Meeting. Most analytic decision making by a group is conducted around a table. Beyond the need for a table (and chairs), what else is required for an effective meeting?

An important part of planning a meeting is preparation of an *agenda*. The agenda covers the purpose of a meeting and the items to be considered. The manager should make sure the purpose of the meeting is clear to all participants. He or she should also make sure that participants understand the decision rule to be employed (see below). Meeting characteristics should be specified (physical setting, time, group size) and selection of participants should be determined based on quality and acceptance rules discussed previously.[16]

The points outlined in the previous paragraph may seem obvious.

However, in practice, analytic decision making is often attempted without an agenda; where participant selection is questionable in terms of quality of contribution, representativeness, and/or number of participants. Meetings can drag on too long. This problem is exacerbated when the agenda and/or decision rules are not clear.

Decision Rules

Untrained decision-making groups tend to be ineffective as well as inefficient.[17] As noted previously, group decision making is benefited if managers understand and apply procedural guidelines while conducting a meeting. Decision rules facilitate different parts of the decision-making process outlined in Figure 7–1 or, in the case of consensus decision making, can be used for all steps in the decision-making process.

Brainstorming: An Aid to Creativity. A. F. Osborn, an advertising agency executive, was concerned about encouraging creativity. Osborn subsequently developed **brainstorming** as a solution for encouraging a decision-making group to consider multiple alternatives. (See Chapter Four, Conflict and Its Management, for further discussion of brainstorming.) Brainstorming reduces the tendency of groups to satisfice in considering alternatives. (Recall Simon's observations about the tendency of decision makers to limit consideration of alternatives to the first minimally acceptable course of action.) Four rules guide the brainstorming process.[18]

Brainstorming: Focuses on generating ideas by permitting nonevaluative presentation of alternatives by group members.

1. Freewheeling is OK. Group members are free to offer any suggestions to the facilitator who lists alternatives as people speak.
2. Group members will not criticize alternatives as they are being generated.
3. Quantity of alternatives is encouraged. Get all the ideas on the board!
4. Combination and improvement on previously indicated alternatives is sought (without criticism).

Brainstorming focuses on generating ideas rather than on choosing an alternative. It is a useful technique to use after a problem has been defined and alternatives need to be generated. Brainstorming can also be used to identify a problem.

Consensus Decision Making. Consensus is defined as a collective opinion. Consensus is reached when all group members are able to accept a group decision on the basis of logic and feasibility. The rules for **consensus decision making** include:[19]

Consensus decision making: An interactive group decision-making process where the decision made is a "collective opinion" rather than the result of majority rule (as in voting) or minority rule (as when the leader makes the decision).

1. View differences of opinion as being natural and expected.
2. Do not assume that there must be "winners" and "losers" when discussion bogs down (instead, group members should continue to search for acceptable alternatives).
3. Avoid conflict-reducing techniques such as voting or averaging.
4. Avoid argument for its own sake.
5. Do not change one's mind simply to avoid conflict and to reach agreement. Accept decisions that are acceptable to you (at least in part).

Consensus decision making can be applied to most parts of the decision-making process. Groups can reach consensus on defining the problem, selecting an alternative to implement, and analyzing the outcome of a decision.

Consensus decision making is usually more effective than unstructured decision making.[20] However, consensus is often not easy to reach. It is time consuming and cannot be effectively used to make immediate decisions. Also, as an interactive process, consensus decision making does not entirely eliminate problems associated with interacting groups (e.g., domination of the group by one person). Moreover, effective consensus decision making requires trained or otherwise knowledgeable group members. Group members need to possess communication and conflict management skills, as well as have an understanding of the rules of consensus decision making.[21]

As with other decision rules, it is important that group leaders teach participants "the rules" and practice the rules themselves. Other training, perhaps in communications or conflict management skills, may be necessary to improve the quality of consensus decision making.

Nominal group technique: A structured group decision-making process involving systematic recording of ideas and voting or ranking to reach agreement.

The Nominal Group Technique. A nominal group is a group in name only. The **nominal group technique** (NGT) does not provide group members with the opportunity to interact directly with one another.[22] As with brainstorming, members are asked to generate ideas without direct comment. The idea generation phase of NGT is more confined than it is with brainstorming. Group members present ideas in a round robin rather than through freewheeling. After idea generation, group members vote on or rank the ideas that have been generated. The final decision is thus mathematically derived. Following is a summary of steps in the NGT process:[23]

1. Group members silently record ideas on a notepad.
2. Round-robin recording of ideas on a flipchart or blackboard is done by the facilitator.

3. Each recorded idea is discussed in turn. This step clarifies ideas and provides group members with the opportunity to agree or disagree with an idea. The primary purpose of this step is clarification of ideas, not argumentation.

4. A preliminary vote is then conducted. Delbecq, Van de Ven, and Gustafson recommend that NGT groups conduct a preliminary vote to be followed by a final vote. A typical NGT group will identify 12 to 18 ideas. Use of a preliminary vote allows the group to reduce this number of ideas to about 5 for the final vote. The facilitator asks each member in the group to rank order 5 ideas in order of importance. The leader then records the vote. The top group of ideas is mathematically determined. Serial discussion of the remaining ideas for the purpose of clarification then ensues.

5. The final vote is conducted. This last step determines the decision of the group, provides a sense of closure and accomplishment, and documents the group judgment.

NGT is useful for defining problems and considering and selecting alternatives. This technique controls for problems of interacting groups. It is also very efficient. NGT groups can make decisions more quickly than groups using consensus decision making. Problems with NGT are associated with the rigidity of the process and the restriction of interaction. NGT sometimes does not work well with complex problems within actual organizations.[24]

NGT should be regarded as a decision-making process to be used as special circumstances dictate (e.g., at a planning workshop, with an ad hoc committee working on a well-defined task). Day-to-day group decision making is usually handled more naturally, using consensus or other approaches such as minority rule, as when the leader makes all decisions or voting.

The Delphi Technique. The primary difference between NGT and the **Delphi technique** is that with the Delphi technique participants do not meet face-to-face. Originally used by "think tanks" like the Rand Corporation, the Delphi technique has been used primarily to forecast future events. As with NGT, it can also be used to define problems and to consider and select alternatives. Also, like NGT, the Delphi technique is best used under special circumstances. The process is as follows:

1. A panel of experts is identified.

2. A structured questionnaire is sent to the experts, or the experts are otherwise asked to independently and anonymously provide solutions to the problem at hand.

Delphi technique: A structured group decision-making process where a panel of experts independently analyzes a problem with the assistance of a central facilitator until consensus is reached.

3. Responses are sent to a central location where they are summarized and reproduced. Each expert is sent these summaries.

4. Experts critique responses of other panel members, provide new information, or otherwise work toward solving the problem. These critiques are returned to the central location where responses are again summarized and returned to panel members.

5. Steps 3 and 4 are repeated. Several "Delphi rounds" may take place. The group eventually reaches consensus, or the process otherwise reaches a predetermined stop point.

A significant advantage of the Delphi technique is that it completely avoids group interaction effects. Even NGT is not completely immune to social facilitation pressure that results from having an "important person" in the same room. With Delphi, participants can be thousands of miles apart.

The Oracle at Delphi

The Delphi technique was named after the oracle (or prophet) at Delphi, an ancient Greek city.

The ancient Greeks believed that the site of Delphi was sacred to the god Apollo. At a temple in Delphi, a female oracle named Pythia uttered strange sounds thought to be the words of Apollo (as interpreted by temple priests). City officials and individual citizens sought advice from the oracle. As a result, the oracle at Delphi had significant influence on Greek religion, politics, and economics.

To conclude, coverage of decision rules in this chapter is by no means exhaustive. Groups can come up with their own rules and procedures or modify the methods discussed here. Regardless of the decision rules employed, it is important that groups use decision rules as guideposts to direct deliberations.

Group Dynamics: Problems and Considerations

Group dynamics: Deals with how interaction among individuals within a group affects group processes.

Decision-making groups must also contend with **group dynamics,** which directly affect the quality of the decision-making process. Hence, group dynamics has a direct impact on the quality of group decisions.

Group dynamics is concerned with how interaction among individuals comprising a group affects group processes. For example, have you ever felt reticent to offer an opinion because you thought it would be unpopular with other group members? Have you ever gone along with a group decision because you didn't want to "rock the boat"?

It is impossible to participate in a group decision-making process that is devoid of dynamics. The idea is not to eliminate group dynamics. Rather, effective managers should understand potential problems in order to reduce their adverse effects on decision quality. Following is

Group dynamics can significantly impact decisions of individual group members. In this case, the Sarge might have asked for the meaning of the word *concur* if he had been under less social pressure.

a discussion of problems and considerations associated with group dynamics.

Groupthink: The compromise of critical thinking that occurs within highly cohesive decision-making groups in which members strive for conformity.

Groupthink. Sometimes groups can be too compatible. **Groupthink** describes the compromise of critical thinking that occurs within highly cohesive decision-making groups in which members strive for conformity. (See Chapters Four and Five, Conflict Management and Stress respectively, for further discussion of group cohesiveness.)

The groupthink hypothesis, as described by Irving Janis, asserts that cohesive decision-making groups experiencing groupthink are guilty of (1) an illusion of invulnerability, (2) a belief in the morality of the group, (3) collective rationalization, (4) stereotyping, (5) self-censorship, (6) an illusion of unanimity, (7) applying direct pressure to dissenters, and (8) the emergence of self-appointed mindguards who protect the group from outside information.[25] A lesson to be learned from studying the groupthink phenomenon is that conformity per se is not constructive to group decision making.

Janis developed his ideas after reviewing historical fiascoes and successes, such as the attack on Pearl Harbor which brought the U.S. into World War II, and the Cuban missile crisis during the Kennedy administration which pulled the superpowers from the brink of nuclear war.

Groupthink can be avoided if groups follow decision rules such as consensus, brainstorming, or NGT, which provide for relatively open expression of contrary opinions. Also, groups should keep information channels open. (Recall the previous discussion of the importance of information to analytic decision making. Avoid the garbage in—garbage out syndrome!)

Finally, the appointment or the recognition of a *devil's advocate* effectively counters groupthink. (Devil's advocates were originally appointed by Catholic Church officials to argue against sainthood for candidates being considered for canonization.) If a highly cohesive group lacks a devil's advocate, then the manager or group leader should play that role.

"Squeaky Wheels" and "Social Loafers." As noted in Chapter Two, Communication, an overly dominant group member (a *squeaky wheel*) can compromise the quality of a group's decision. People have an unfortunate tendency to equate the quantity of participation by a group member with the quality of the presentation.[26] Valuable resources within a group may go overlooked because people do not (or cannot) speak up.

Sometimes people do not fully participate within a group because of *social loafing*. People have a tendency to put in less effort when they believe their individual contributions cannot be assessed.[27] You may have experienced this phenomenon while participating in a group activity where individual effort could not be monitored or demonstrated.

Mitigating the negative effects of squeaky wheels and social loafers requires that the group leader seek balanced participation from group members. Slow down the squeaky wheels and invite reticent group members to participate in deliberations! Structure tasks within the group so that individuals are accountable for individual effort (e.g., asking each member of the group to bring two new product ideas to the next meeting). Following decision rules can also help. One of the advantages of the rigidity inherent in NGT is that participation is carefully balanced.

The Group Polarization Effect. Group discussion tends to cause group members to shift toward whatever end of an issue (whether risky or conservative) they already favor.[28] Group discussion seems to have the effect of *accentuating* movement toward individual group member's original postures. This tendency, termed the **group polarization effect,** in turn, leads to a more extreme posture for the group as a whole, particularly when several group members share the same initial view of a problem.

Risky (or conservative) decisions are not always bad. However, groups should take chances because the situation merits taking a chance, not because of a group dynamic. In this regard, a devil's advocate can prove useful by questioning individual and group direction toward a risky or conservative decision.

Also, the leader's initial instructions to a group has a significant effect.[29] This situation is analogous to the instructions a judge gives to a jury. In providing instructions, the judge should try to avoid biasing the jury's verdict. The verdict of a jury, as with the decision of any group involved in analytic decision making, should stand on its own merit.

Group polarization effect: Tendency of groups to shift toward a more extreme decision posture (risky or conservative) relative to the posture that would be taken by individual members.

Tips for the Manager. Having good cause to convene a group, selecting participants on the basis of quality and acceptance rules, planning deliberations, and using decision rules all play an important role in improving the quality of group decisions.

Managers should learn the rules and advantages and disadvantages associated with brainstorming, consensus decision making, NGT, and the Delphi technique. Group members should be taught and encouraged to practice the rules. The appropriate decision rule to use depends on the situation. Consensus decision making and brainstorming used together are appropriate most of the time. However, NGT and/ or Delphi techniques are effective if time is short (NGT); if participants are widely separated (Delphi); and/or if a group is working on a special decision-making task.

Managers should be mindful of group dynamics. To reduce the adverse effects of groupthink, squeaky wheels, social loafing, and the group polarization effect, group leaders should encourage the participation of a devil's advocate within the group, taking on this role if necessary.

Managers should encourage balanced participation from group members by giving assignments to social loafers and by actively soliciting input from relatively silent group members. The tendency of groups to make extreme decisions (the group polarization effect) can be reduced somewhat by giving balanced instructions and guidance to the group and by calling on the devil's advocate.

ORGANIZATIONAL CONSIDERATIONS IN DECISION MAKING

There are significant differences between making decisions at the individual and group levels and doing the same across an organization with thousands of employees, hundreds of departments, dozens of products, and literally hundreds of problems and associated goals. Organizational decision making requires the use of a planning framework which then serves as a guide for decision making at the individual and group level.

Organizational planning framework: Includes determination of mission, the situation analysis, goal setting, strategic and tactical decision making, and a management information system.

Figure 7–4 outlines an **organizational planning framework** that integrates goal setting and decision making across an organization. Note that organizational decision making involves making *process decisions* and *outcome decisions*. Outcome decisions involve setting goals (where do we want to go?) and evaluating results (did we get there?). Process decisions answer questions pertaining to how and what to do to "get there." Process and outcome decisions require individual and/or group decision making using the process outlined in Figure 7–1.

The Situation Analysis

As emphasized throughout this chapter, analytic decision making should be guided by valid information. Decisions concerning future direction (goal setting) should rest on the decision makers' analysis of the situation based on the best information available. Unfortunately, planners sometimes set goals, *then* analyze the situation to determine how goals will be attained. This approach, while intuitively attractive, sometimes leads to the proverbial problem of trying to fit "square pegs into round holes." Determine first if the holes are round (e.g., vis-à-vis a *situation analysis*) *before* designing the pegs (e.g., goal setting).

The situation analysis should include a review of the organization's past history, strengths and weaknesses, and internal and external

Figure 7–4 An Organizational Planning Framework

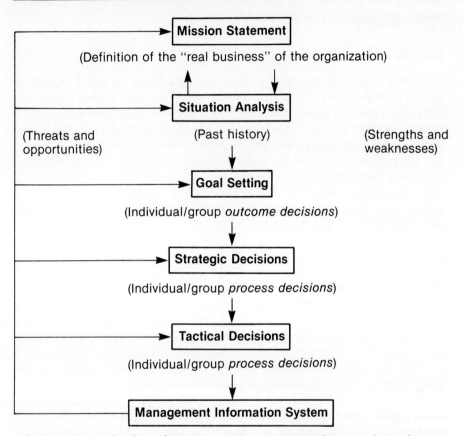

(Systematic evaluation of *process* and *outcome* decisions using relevant, timely data)

This planning framework was inspired by the work of Philip Kotler. See Kotler, P. *Marketing Management, Analysis, Planning and Control.* Englewood Cliffs, NJ: Prentice-Hall, 1980.

threats and opportunities. Out of this analysis should come a clear *mission statement* which articulates the "real business" of the organization. A 1960 article by Theodore Leavitt, concerning the importance of defining the "real business" of the organization, is still highly relevant today.

Leavitt noted the example of the railroad industry which declined because its leaders defined that industry "so narrowly as to guarantee its premature senescence."[30] Had those leaders defined their business to be that of satisfying customers through meeting their transportation needs, rather than just that of building and operating railroads, the railroad industry might have prospered. Who knows? Maybe the railroads would have bought out the fledgling Ford Motor Company and might now control the automobile industry!

Goal Setting

After the situation has been analyzed, goals must be set. Volumes of material have been written on goal setting. (The topic is also covered in Chapters Three and Six, Motivation and Performance Appraisal respectively.) We add to this discussion the observation that goals should be based on the previously defined mission of the organization.

Organizational goal setting should also be viewed as the development of a hierarchy of objectives which cascades down throughout all organizational levels. The basic challenge is to integrate a broad mission statement with organizational goals so that goal-directed behavior of individual employees can be defined.

Strategic and Tactical Decision Making

About 80 years ago the naval historian and theorist, Admiral Alfred Thayer Mahan, defined strategy and tactics: "Strategy is everything up to the point of contact . . . at contact in battle, tactics begin."[31] *Strategic decision making* pertains to *how* the company (or division, or department, or unit . . .) plans to attain goals (e.g., discounting the price of a product to achieve a volume goal). *Tactical decision making*, on the other hand, pertains to *what* will be done in the process of carrying out a strategy. Tactical decision making results in the development of an *action plan* that lays out time frames, costs, personnel, and other resources.

For example, in military terms, if the goal is to "take the hill," a strategic decision would be to conduct a flank assault rather than a frontal assault; tactical decisions and considerations include when the attack will take place, who will be involved, what equipment will be used, and how much the attack will cost. This example can be readily transferred to a business setting: Goals can be tied to sales and profits; strategy can be tied to, say, discounting a product and selling a high volume of units; and tactics can be tied to schedules for conducting retail markdowns, advertising, and deploying personnel. Be sure to make strategic decisions before deciding on tactics. Preparing an effective action plan is difficult if the plan to "take the hill" is unclear.

Decision Support Systems

As can be seen in Figure 7–4, the organizational decision-making process, like individual and group decision making, should be information driven. Information should be collected in a systematic, need-based way for use at all levels of the organization. Consequently, organizations should have in place a **management information system** (MIS).

A MIS is defined as any organized approach for obtaining relevant and timely information on which to base management decisions.[32] Management information systems, together with PC-driven tools, such as spreadsheets, data bases and scheduling and forecasting programs, all serve as *decision support systems.*

Decision support systems enable managers to analyze relevant data before making decisions. A new development has involved the extension of decision support systems to group decision making (group decision support systems or GDSS). A GDSS enables a group to proceed effectively and efficiently through a structured decision task by using software and MIS technology. MIS data are pulled into computers arrayed in a network. Group members massage data, input decision criteria, communicate with other group members, and eventually solve problems through the computer network. Several research efforts have demonstrated the potential inherent in GDSS.[33]

Management information system: Any organized approach for obtaining relevant and timely information on which to base management decisions.

Centralization versus Decentralization

We will conclude by considering the question of **centralization** of organizational decision making. Decentralization of decision making disperses authority (the power to take action) more widely than does centralization of decision making. The advantages of both approaches are outlined in Figure 7–5.

There is no clear-cut way to determine the extent to which decision making should be centralized. Generally, managers should take into account the size and complexity of the organization; dispersion of em-

Centralization: Concerns the dispersement of decision-making authority across an organization.

Decentralized Decision Making at P&G

Procter and Gamble has long been known for slow, centralized decision making. For example, a former brand manager for Prell complained that it took a year and $50,000 in market research before getting approval for a flip-top cap on the shampoo.

The company recently decentralized corporate decision making. On July 1, 1988, P&G took decision-making authority away from its highest-ranking decision-making group—the administrative committee. This group, made up of 40 top executives, used to meet every Tuesday at 10 A.M. to ratify all significant promotions and spending plans. In the future, a 20-member executive panel will meet weekly to deal with only the most important issues.[35]

Figure 7–5 Advantages of Centralization and Decentralization

Centralization:
1. Produces uniformity of policy and action.
2. Results in few risks of errors by subordinates who lack either information or skill.
3. Utilizes the skills of central and specialized experts.
4. Enables closer control of operations.

Decentralization:
1. Tends to make for speedier decisions and actions on the spot without consulting higher levels.
2. Results in decisions more likely to be adapted to local conditions.
3. Results in greater interest and enthusiasm on the part of the subordinate to whom the authority has been entrusted.
4. Allows top management to utilize time for more study and consideration of the basic goals, plans, and policies of the enterprise.

From: Mondy, R. W.; Sharplin, A.; & Flippo, E. B. *Management: Concepts and Practices* (4th ed.). Boston: Allyn and Bacon, p. 254. Copyright © by Allyn and Bacon, Inc. Reprinted with permission.

ployees; competence of personnel available; and the adequacy of the communication system.[34]

The larger and more complex, and more widely dispersed the organization, the greater the need for decentralized decision making. Decentralized decision making does require competent personnel. The extent to which decision making must be decentralized also depends on the quality of an organization's communication system. Good communications reduce the need for decentralized decision making.

Tips for the Manager. Managers should participate in individual and group "outcome" and "process" decision making within the context of a planning framework.

This framework should incorporate a mission statement, a situation analysis, goal setting, strategic and tactical decision making, and a management information system (MIS). Managers should analyze the situation before deciding on goals and make strategic decisions before deciding on tactics. Attainment of process and outcome goals should be assessed through systematic evaluation. Doing this effectively requires the systematic collection and use of relevant and timely information.

Managers should also keep in mind that the larger, more complex, and more widely dispersed the organization, the greater the need for decentralized decision making. This point assumes that there are competent personnel available and that the organization's communication system cannot accommodate a higher degree of centralized decision-making.

SUMMARY: FOCUS ON SKILLS

At the individual and group level, decision making is defined as solving a problem or otherwise attaining a goal by choosing among alternative courses of action. Once an alternative has been selected for implementation, a decision has been made. The decision-making process adds to this definition by including "implementation of an alternative" and "evaluation." At the organizational level, individual and group decision making is tied to an overall planning framework that includes a situation analysis, goal setting, strategic and tactical decision making, and a management information system (MIS).

Following are 23 suggestions for improving the quality of individual, group, and organizational decision making.

Managers should:

1. Learn the steps in the decision-making process (define the problem, consider alternatives, select and implement an alternative, and evaluate) and follow these steps, in order, when making analytic decisions.

2. Realize that not all decisions require the use of an analytic decision-making process. The decision strategy to use depends, in part, on the decision environment (e.g., accountability of the decision maker, resource constraints) and decision characteristics (e.g., ambiguity, complexity).

3. Define a problem before trying to solve it.

4. Avoid the garbage in–garbage out syndrome by using the best information available.

5. Check out assumptions whenever possible.

6. Frame a problem from several different perspectives. Be aware that the way in which a problem is framed influences the decision(s) that are ultimately made.

7. Systematically consider multiple alternatives.

8. Understand and apply the concepts of expected value and the maximization rule.

9. Build a decision tree when considering multiple alternatives. In the process, remember the idea is not to eliminate subjectivity. Rather, it is to control potentially adverse effects of what is an inherently subjective process.

10. Determine whether a decision was successful (or not) because of the quality of the decision, or because of the manner in which it was implemented. Good ideas are sometimes poorly implemented.

11. Try to have other people (with less at stake) involved in evaluating the results of past decisions. Learn from and accept the lessons of past mistakes, even though it is difficult to accept failure.

12. Convene a group if group members have information that would improve the quality of the decision and/or if member acceptance of a decision is necessary.

13. Plan the deliberations! Prepare an agenda, determine decision rules, and set a time, location, and length for the meeting. Select participants based on the need for representativeness (acceptance) and/or information (quality).

14. Learn and apply the rules for brainstorming, consensus decision making, NGT, and Delphi techniques. Also, understand the advantages and disadvantages associated with the use of these approaches.

15. Know that the most appropriate decision rule to use depends on the situation. Keep in mind that consensus decision making and brainstorming used together are appropriate most of the time.

16. If there is a need to convene a group to work on a special task, use NGT and/or Delphi techniques (if time is short—NGT, if participants are widely separated—Delphi).

17. Encourage the participation of a devil's advocate within the group. Take on this role yourself if necessary.

18. Encourage balanced participation from group members. Call on or give assignments to social loafers or to others who are reticent about participating in deliberations. Slow down squeaky wheels by soliciting input from other group members and by enforcing appropriate decision rules.

19. Reduce the tendency of groups to make extreme decisions by giving balanced instructions and guidance to the group. The use of a devil's advocate also reduces the group polarization effect.

20. Participate in individual and group "outcome" and "process"

decision making within the context of a planning framework. This framework should incorporate a mission statement, a situation analysis, goal setting, strategic and tactical decision making, and a management information system (MIS).

21. Analyze the situation before deciding on goals and make strategic decisions before deciding on tactics.

22. Conduct evaluation to assess goal attainment and to otherwise determine the efficacy of strategic and tactical decisions. Doing this effectively requires the use of a management information system. A MIS systematically collects and disseminates relevant and timely information.

23. Keep in mind that the larger, more complex, and more widely dispersed the organization, the greater the need for decentralized decision making. This point assumes that there are competent personnel available and that the organization's communication system cannot accommodate a higher degree of centralized decision making.

■ CASE: "BY THE LIGHT OF THE MOON"

Mark Rhoades, shoe salesman at Shiny Shoe Shop, sat on some cartons in the stockroom with his eyes closed. "Mark, can you come up front? We have some customers," Jack Starr, Mark's boss, called out to him. "You've spent a lot of time in the stockroom lately," Jack continued. "Those shelves must be in perfect order by now." "Yes, they are, Jack; I should have no trouble finding anything in that stockroom now," Mark answered.

Actually, there was nothing out of order in the stockroom. Mark had been dozing in the back. He had been working part-time evenings and weekends at the jewelry counter of Sullivan's department store to try to make ends meet, and he was tired. He couldn't confide in his boss because there was a store policy against moonlighting, and Mark couldn't afford to lose this job. Not yet, anyway.

The jewelry counter was a new department at Sullivan's, and Mark had been promised that if he learned quickly and performed well, he would be promoted to manager of the department within a relatively short period of time. The managerial position paid well and Mark would then be able to give up his job at Shiny. In the meantime, Mark struggled to remain awake.

One Saturday, Jack was looking for a birthday gift for his wife. He noticed that the jewelry counter at Sullivan's was new, and he wandered over to see if there were any bargains. When he came face to face with Mark, it was difficult to tell who was more surprised. While both men searched for something to say, Mark helped Jack pick out a special gift for his wife's birthday.

Finally, Jack spoke. "Mark," he began, "thanks for your help, I think my wife will be pleased, but I think we have something to discuss on Monday." Mark's heart sank. "Yes," he said. "I'll see you Monday."

Early on Monday morning, before the store had opened, Mark met with Jack. Jack spoke first. "Mark, you look exhausted. Why are you trying to wear yourself out? You know the policy against moonlighting. Aren't you happy here? I thought you liked your job."

"I do like my job," Mark responded quickly, "but I need this other job to meet my bills. The raise you gave me is a help, but it's not enough. You see, my kid has been in the hospital for two weeks now and the bills are staggering. Originally, I took the other job just to supplement my salary. Now they tell me that my work is good enough to earn a promotion soon. If I become the manager of the jewelry department, I'll make enough money to quit this job and still pay my bills. I just need some time to prove myself. Jack, are you going to report me?"

Jack wondered what he should do. If he gave Mark a little more time, Mark would probably get the promotion and then leave Shiny, which would mean that Jack would lose a conscientious employee. If he put his foot down but didn't report the moonlighting, Mark would stay at Shiny, but Jack would have an unhappy employee. On the other hand, if management discovered that Mark was moonlighting and that Jack knew about it but had not reported it, both of them could lose their jobs.

By Grace Lander. Reprinted with permission of publisher. From *Supervisory Management,* September © 1984, American Management Association, New York. All rights reserved.

Case Questions

1. What type of decision strategy should Jack use in dealing with this situation?
2. How might "framing" have influenced Jack's decision-making process?
3. To what extent should Jack include Mark in the decision-making process?
4. How might Jack effectively identify alternatives to this problem?

■ EXERCISE: "CONSENSUS BUILDING"

This exercise will provide an opportunity for you to engage in individual and group decision making. You will be able to compare the results of the two approaches. You will then be asked to discuss differences you perceive between individual and group decision-making approaches. So, keep track of what goes on in your group.

As you proceed, keep the following conditions for facilitating a consensus decision in mind (cited in *California Management Review*, Summer 1970, p. 60):

1. There is little expression of personal, self-oriented needs.
2. The self needs that are expressed tend to be satisfied in the course of the meeting.
3. There is a generally pleasant atmosphere and the participants recognize the need for unified action.
4. The group's problem-solving activity is understandable, orderly, and focused on one issue at a time.
5. Facts are available and are used.
6. The chairman, through much probing, helps the group to analyze its problems.
7. The participants feel personally friendly toward each other.

Forms

Your instructor will provide you with all necessary forms and exercise instructions.

ENDNOTES

1. Mintzberg, T. R. "The manager's job: Folklore and fact." *Harvard Business Review* (July–August 1975): 49–61.

2. Agor, W. H. "The logic of intuition: How top executives make important decisions." *Organizational Dynamics* (Winter 1986): 5–18.

3. Cotton, J. L.; Vollrath, D. A.; Froggatt, K. L.; Legnick-Hall, M. L.; & Jennings, K. R. "Employee participation: Diverse forms and different outcomes." *Academy of Management Review, 13* (1988): 8–22.

4. Beach, L. R., & Mitchell, T. R. "Individual and group decision making." In J. E. Garcia, C. T. Lewis, & F. E. Fiedler (Eds.), *People, Management, and Productivity*. Boston: Allyn and Bacon, 1986, p. 57.

5. Beach, L. R., & Mitchell, T. R. "A contingency model for the selection of decision strategies." *Academy of Management Review, 3* (1978): 439–449.

6. Mintzberg, "The manager's job."

7. Miller, A., & Tsiantar, D. "A test for market research." *Newsweek*, December 28, 1987, pp. 32–33.

8. Kahneman, D., & Tversky, A. "Prospect theory: An analysis of decision under risk." *Econometrica, 47* (1979): 263–291.

9. Neale, M. A., & Bazerman, M. H. "The effects of framing and negotiator overconfidence on bargaining behavior and outcomes." *Academy of Management Journal, 28* (1985): 34–49.

10. Simon, H. A. *Models of Man.* New York: Wiley, 1957.

11. Hampton, W. "Chrysler's next act." *Business Week,* November 3, 1986, pp. 66–69.

12. Staw, B. M. "The escalation of commitment to a course of action." *Academy of Management Review, 6* (1981): 577–578. See also: Staw, B. M. "Knee deep in the big muddy: A study of escalating commitment to a chosen course of action." *Organizational Behavior and Human Performance, 16* (1976): 27–44.

13. Maier, N. R. F. "Assets and liabilities in group problem solving: The need for an integrative function." *Psychological Review, 47* (1976): 239–249.

14. Locke, E. A., & Schweiger, D. M. "Participation in decision making: One more look." In B. M. Staw (Ed.), *Research in Organizational Behavior* (vol. 1). Greenwich, CT: JAI Press, 1979. See also: Cotton et al., "Employee participation."

15. Vroom, V., & Yetton, P. W. *Leadership and Decision Making.* Pittsburgh, PA: University of Pittsburgh Press, 1973. See also: Vroom, V., & Jago, A. G. "On the validity of a Vroom-Yetton model." *Journal of Applied Psychology, 63* (1978): 151–162.

16. Stumpf, S. A.; Zand, D. E.; & Freeman, R. D. "Designing groups for judgmental decisions." *Academy of Management Review, 4* (1979): 589–600.

17. Hall, J. "Decisions, decisions, decisions." *Psychology Today* (November 1971): 51–88.

18. Osborn, A. F. *Applied Imagination.* New York: Scribner, 1957.

19. Hall, "Decisions."

20. Ibid.

21. Drake, B. H., & Hansen, D. "Enhancing group decision making: Re-examining process losses." Paper presented at the Western Academy of Management meeting, Big Sky, MT, 1988.

22. Van de Ven, A., & Delbecq, A. L. "The effectiveness of nominal, delphi, and interacting group decision making processes." *Academy of Management Journal, 17* (1974): 605–621. See also: Van de Ven, A., & Delbecq, A. L. "Nominal versus interacting group processes for committee decision-making." *Academy of Management Journal, 14* (1971): 203–214.

23. Delbecq, A.; Van de Ven, A.; & Gustafson, D. "Guidelines for conducting NGT meetings." *Group Techniques for Program Planning.* Glenview, IL: Scott Foresman and Company, 1975.

24. Murningham, J. K. "Group decision making: What strategies should you use?" *Management Review, 70* (1981): 55–62.

25. Janis, I. *Groupthink: Psychological Studies of Policy Decisions and Fiascoes.* Boston: Houghton Mifflin, 1982.

26. Haynes, E., & Meltzer, L. "Interpersonal judgments based on talkativeness: Fact or artifact?" *Sociometry, 35* (1972): 538–561. See also: Baird, J. E., & Weinberg, S. B. *Communication: The Essence of Group Synergy.* Dubuque, IA: Wm. C. Brown, 1977; and Sorrentino, R. M., & Boutillier, R. G. "The effect of quality

and quantity of verbal interaction on ratings of leadership ability." *Journal of Experimental Social Psychology, 11* (1975): 403–411.

27. Latane, B.; Williams, K.; & Harkins, S. "Many hands make light the work: The causes and consequences of social loafing." *Journal of Personality and Social Psychology, 37* (1979): 822–832.

28. McGrath, J., & Kravitz, D. A. "Group research." *Annual Review of Psychology, 33* (1982): 195–230.

29. Miner, J. B. *Organizational Behavior: Performance and Productivity.* New York: Random House, 1988.

30. Leavitt, T. "Marketing myopia." *Harvard Business Review, 38* (1960): 45–56.

31. Cited in Schleh, E. C. "Strategic planning . . . no sure cure for corporate surprises." *Management Review, 68* (1979): 54.

32. Mondy, R. W.; Sharplin, A.; & Flippo, E. B. *Management: Concepts and Practices* (4th ed.). Boston: Allyn and Bacon, 1988.

33. Keleman, K. S.; Garcia, J. E.; & Lewis, L. F. "Group decision support system (GDSS) demonstration project: University human resource planning." Paper presented at the Western Academy of Management meeting, San Francisco, CA, March 1989.

34. Ibid.

35. Schiller, Z. "The marketing revolution at Procter & Gamble." *Business Week,* July 25, 1988, pp. 72–76.

CHAPTER EIGHT

Power

- **Self-Assessment: "Situational Characteristics and the Individual"**

- **Learning about Power**

- **Case: "A Terminal Case"**

- **Exercise: "Bases of Power"**

The fit between organizational and individual characteristics influences the amount of power a manager wields.

Think back to a situation where you were responsible for managing others (e.g., at work, in a school club, organizing a social event). Answer each of the following questions with this particular situation in mind. (Responses to this questionnaire will differ depending on the situation you select.)

1. To what extent were you able to predict events that had an impact on your work group?

Not at All	Somewhat	Very Much
1	2	3

2. How well informed were you, relative to others, about conditions outside of your work group?

Not at All	Somewhat	Very Much
1	2	3

3. Would someone else have been able to assume your duties effectively if you had been suddenly removed from the group?

Not at All	Somewhat	Very Much
1	2	3

4. To what extent were your skills unique to the group?

Not at All	Somewhat	Very Much
1	2	3

5. How much information related to the tasks of your work group channeled through you?

Not at All	Somewhat	Very Much
1	2	3

6. To what extent did group members rely on you for information?

Not at All	Somewhat	Very Much
1	2	3

7. How important was your work to the mission of the group?

Not at All	Somewhat	Very Much
1	2	3

8. To what extent would your group's efforts have been compromised if you left the group?

Not at All	Somewhat	Very Much
1	2	3

Sum the scores obtained from each of the eight items.

■ LEARNING ABOUT POWER

Power—its use and misuse, its balance and imbalance—exacts an unmistakable influence over organizational life. Power determines who gets what, which jobs get done, and which jobs remain incomplete. If you have power, you are more likely to get what you want. But you also have the responsibility to use your power ethically and effectively.

Power is a two-way street in that it both affects and is manipulated by the individuals, groups, and organizations it touches. People frequently struggle for organizational power because its possessor has control over future outcomes. Anyone doubting the dynamism of power need only look at current business news for proof of it in the proliferation of mergers and acquisitions by major corporations.

Management thought has traditionally centered on the concept of formal, legitimate managerial authority in the workplace. But, as you will see, formal authority is only one element of organizational power. We will also discuss influence and politics in organizations, both of which have an impact on the dynamics of power.

WHAT IS POWER?

Power is defined as the *ability* to change the behavior of an individual, group, or organization. Inherent in all power relationships is the element of dependency—a less powerful target is dependent on a powerholder. Power relationships entail a dependency by subordinate parties on more powerful individuals for some necessary resource.[1]

Power: The ability of an individual, group, or organization to change the behavior of others.

Bases of Power

French and Raven identified five **bases of power:** reward, coercive, legitimate, referent, and expert power.[2] (See Chapter Nine, Leadership, for further discussion of bases of power.) Managers have *reward power* when they have control over the disbursement of valued resources such as the assignment of overtime work, bonus pay, or vacation time. In comparison, a police officer's ability to issue a traffic citation is an example of *coercive power. Legitimate power* is derived from the formal assignment of power by an organization, as in the assignment of formal titles and positions such as "production manager" or "director of human resources." Individuals who are admired and respected have *referent power.* Finally, *expert power* is derived from having expert knowledge or skills. Consider how well most people listen to an auto mechanic when their car is in need of repair, or look at the high fees professional consultants often command.

Bases of power: Reward, coercive, legitimate, referent, and expert power account for individual power in small groups.

These bases of power often overlap, thereby collectively contributing to a manager's power. Managers should recognize that power comes from multiple sources, which they should utilize in getting things done.

Pepper . . . and Salt

THE WALL STREET JOURNAL

—Baloo

"This firm is just one big happy family,
Pemberton, and if you don't get your sales
total up, I'm going to spank the living daylights
out of you!"

Coercion is only one base of power. What other bases of power could
(or should) this manager have called upon?

From *The Wall Street Journal*—Permission, Cartoon Features Syndicate.

J. Edgar Hoover: Too Much Power?

J. Edgar Hoover, director of the Federal Bureau of Investigation
for many years, was recognized as a man who sought and ac-
cumulated power. The following story dramatically demonstrates
the power Hoover wielded within his own agency:

A stickler for details, Hoover enforced a rule that limited
interoffice correspondence to one page in length. One enterprising
subordinate was said to have squeezed more than a page's worth of
text onto a sheet of paper by changing the margins on his type-
writer. After reading the memorandum, Hoover complimented the
officer on his work—but added, "Watch the borders."

Word of the mandate spread. The FBI sent a passel of agents
to scour the borders—the U.S.-Mexico and the U.S.-Canada
borders![3]

Power and Ethics

"Power corrupts, absolute power corrupts absolutely." This famous comment by nineteenth-century British historian Lord Acton still rings true today. The mere fact that a powerholder has the capacity to change another's behavior suggests the potential for abuse of power. Indeed, research evidence shows that high inequalities of power lead to the use of more abusive tactics by powerholders over subordinates than do situations with low inequalities.[4] The abuse of power can destroy the integrity of employer-employee relationships within an organization and ultimately between an organization and society. For this reason, **ethical principles** have been developed as guides to moral behavior and the "correct" use of power.

Ethical principles: Guides to moral behavior and the "correct" use of power. Three models of ethical behavior are utilitarianism, justice, and rights.

Gerald Cavanagh describes three ethical models as standards for moral behavior: *utilitarianism, justice,* and *rights.*[5] According to Cavanagh, a managerial action is ethically justified if it satisfies the principles associated with these three models.

The utilitarian model suggests that an action is morally correct if it leads to the greatest good for the greatest number of people. Using power to maximize personal gain at the expense of the organization is inappropriate according to utilitarian values. Instead, power should be used to benefit the organization's constituents as efficiently and effectively as possible.

Commentary: "Power"

Thomas J. Costagliola

I have power and influence because I run a business and have control over my organization. My business has power and influence because it shapes environments for individuals and communities. To use power and influence most effectively, I listen to those affected by my business activities during the planning of projects. I listen to my employees, to the people in the communities in which I work, and, whenever possible, to my customers. By giving people a say in the process, I give people a sense that they have power, and I keep my business moving forward.

I realize, as a builder and real estate developer, that I am influencing the lives of people for generations to come. I believe this because most of us live in edifices that were built by builders and because, except for state and federal highways, real estate developers put most streets in place by giving away some of their land. The guidelines that developers follow often have been set by others—town fathers or town planners. To the extent that developers meet or exceed guidelines, many future lives are influenced. Beyond the guidelines and standards imposed by governmental regulation and social norms, builders and developers wield enormous power.

To me, having power and influence warrants careful thought and as much consensus building as possible. While I potentially have the power to create something wonderful that generations of people will enjoy, I also have the power to wreak havoc on communities and probably, ultimately, on myself. By consensus building and taking into consideration the many effects of my wielding of power, I try to avoid unintended, harmful results.

For example, in a subdivision of land upon which I am currently working, we interviewed as many architects and landscape architects as we found necessary to find one of each that was talented, thoughtful, and, perhaps most importantly, responsive to us. With the idea of sharing power, we asked the landscape architect to come up with several different proposals to address this piece of land. Our objective was simple—to make the development the absolute best from as many people's standpoint as possible, and to earn the most profit.

We worked closely with the architect, neighborhood residents affected by the plan, and public officials. When we formally asked permission of public officials for our project, one individual who had not met with us objected to the project, but was ignored. We received permission to build exactly as we had proposed. We were commended for our approach of talking to neighbors before any of the public hearings.

In this instance, we shared power in a small way at the right time. We received approvals in half the time of our major competitor in the town. In a community that is perceived to be antidevelopment and is less developed than many adjacent communities, we received approvals accompanied by a lot of good will.

Thomas J. Costagliola

Thomas J. Costagliola was born and brought up in Brooklyn, New York. He attended St. Francis Preparatory High and Phillips Academy, Andover, Massachusetts. He finished high school with 11 varsity letters and captained his high-school rugby team. After prep school, Thomas graduated *cum laude* from Harvard University with a degree in fine arts.

The fall of 1974 found Thomas selling artwork and hand-crafted furniture, and building many hundreds of feet of fences. In 1978, a developer for whom Thomas had built a fence gave him a contract to build six townhouses. Thomas promptly hired friends who had built houses before. From those modest beginnings, Infinity Construction (Thomas's company) has constructed over 200 homes. Infinity's most exciting project at present is a seven-lot development in Weston, Massachusetts, where one spec house is on the market for $2.3 million.

Thomas is currently trying to purchase a square mile of land in Massachusetts to build a town. He is married to Wendy Stone, has two children, Eden and Gina, and presently resides in Cambridge, Massachusetts.

The justice model, by comparison, suggests power should be used according to principles of fairness and equity, with rules applied impartially and consistently. Compensation and blame applied under the justice model relates to the amount of control an individual has over his or her actions.

According to the rights model, powerholders should respect the inherent value of others as individuals. This model holds that the use of power is inappropriate if it violates individual rights such as the right to privacy or free consent, and that people should never be used as instruments in attaining a goal.

Applying these ethical models to managerial situations is not a straightforward proposition. "Real-world" circumstances often lead to conflicting recommendations from these models. Imagine having the power to order subordinates to remove hazardous radioactive materials from a nuclear spill—knowing that workers' health and safety will be severely compromised. The utilitarian model would recommend scheduling the workers to the hazardous cleanup only if their work would render a greater benefit to the most people (society, other workers, shareholders) with the least amount of damage. On the other hand, the rights model would recommend against the assignment, because exposing subordinates to hazardous materials that endanger their health would amount to a violation of their rights.

How does one deal with this sort of ethical dilemma? There are no easy answers. Information gathering and soul searching are only a start for the manager faced with complex ethical questions. One structured approach suggests the consideration of "overwhelming factors" that may indicate the superiority of one ethical model over the others in guiding the use of power.[6] Two such overwhelming factors are *incapacitation* and the *double-effect test.*

Incapacitation occurs when the ability to act freely is restricted, as when a manager lacks information or is being pressured by upper management. An incapacitated manager may be justified in choosing one model as a guide for action over the others. For example, you may honestly underestimate the ability of an employee's contracting a terminal illness connected with exposure to radioactive waste, and therefore you would be ethically correct in relying on the utilitarian model instead of the rights model.

The double-effect test is used to determine whether the positive effects of the action outweigh the negative effects, and whether the negative effects are unintentional by-products or instrumental to achieving the benefits of the action. An action passes the double-effect test and is ethical, then, if its benefits outweigh its drawbacks and its negative effects are *unintentional* by-products of the action. So, if you know workers will be sacrificed to complete the cleanup of radioactive materials—meaning the risk of their health is instrumental to the task—the assignment would fail the double-effect test. Ordering workers to participate in such a cleanup would be unethical and an inappropriate use of power.

POWER AND THE INDIVIDUAL

Have you ever wondered why some people are more powerful than others? Although luck and circumstance play a role in the acquisition of power, certain personal characteristics account for the differences in why and how people seek and use power. Without question, personal characteristics such as physical size and communication techniques influence the possession and use of power. There are also several other interesting and significant social and psychological attributes that account for individual differences in the possession and use of power. Among these characteristics are the need for power, Machiavellianism, and skill in the use of influence tactics.

Need for Power

Need for power: An individual predisposition to think and act in ways that lead to a gain in power and influence.

Part of what makes people seek or avoid taking control of situations is personal makeup—more specifically, motivation and personality. David McClelland has found that we develop relatively stable motives that predispose us to act in predictable ways. An important motive identified by McClelland is the **need for power.**[7]

Individuals who have a high need for power spend more time than others thinking of ways to outwit people and to gain formal authority and influence. Their behavior is directed toward the acquisition of power. In fact, power needs have been found to predict occupational choice. People high in power motivation tend to prefer careers such as law, politics, police work, business management, and the military.[8]

The need for power has two dimensions: a *personal power* dimension and a *socialized power* dimension. The personal power dimension refers to a need to use power for personal gain and self-aggrandizement. People with a high need for personal power are likely to exploit others and to work at cross-purposes with an organization. As suggested above, the ethical use of power would argue against this style of power usage. In contrast, socialized power is a need for power congruent with the welfare of the organization. A manager with a strong need for socialized power is likely to care about the organization and to invest in and benefit from the organization's success.[9]

Machiavellianism

The Italian advisor to kings and queens, Niccolo Machiavelli, in his sixteenth-century book, *The Prince*, upheld the use of deceit and manipulation as the ultimate form of power and influence.[10] Today, individuals who use others for their own means have come to be known as Machiavellian.

Researchers Richard Christie and Florence Geis have gone on to identify the characteristics of the **Machiavellian (Mach)** personality.[11] Typically, high Machs tend to be aloof and distant, to take control of unstructured face-to-face interactions, and to use subtle forms of influence to further their own ends. The strategies used by high Machs are similar to those used by someone with high needs for personal power, except high Machs are likely to limit their efforts to situations involving direct interpersonal interaction. High Machs, for example, are especially successful in unstructured negotiations and in bargaining.

Machiavellianism (Mach): A personality trait typified by tendencies to be aloof and distant, to take control of unstructured face-to-face interactions, and to use subtle forms of manipulation to gain influence.

Influence Tactics

Influence is defined as the exercise of power through the use of behavioral techniques. It is through influence that compliance and commitment is obtained from others. Three proven influence tactics are ingratiation, the door-in-the-face technique, and the foot-in-the-door technique. (See Figure 8–1.)

Influence: The use of behaviorally based techniques to engender compliance and commitment from others.

Figure 8–1 Common Influence Tactics

Tactic	Behavior of Influencer	Behavior and Attitude of Person Being Influenced
Ingratiation	Flattery ———⟶	Increased liking of influencer and increased receptivity to a request
"Door-in-the-Face" Technique	Large request ———⟶	Refusal of large request
	Smaller request ———⟶	Increased receptivity to smaller request
"Foot-in-the-Door" Technique	Small request ———⟶	Compliance and shift in self-perception
	Larger request ———⟶	Increased receptivity to a large request

This figure was inspired by communication with Professor Sonia Goltz, College of Business Administration, University of Notre Dame.

Ingratiation: The use of flattery and friendship to influence others.

Flattery will get you somewhere—sometimes. The use of **ingratiation** is a well-known influence technique.[12] Of course, the fame of ingratiation explains both its popularity and its downfall. Flattery will increase your boss's willingness to comply with your wishes, unless he or she is forewarned or suspicious of your motives. "Buttering up" the manager before making a request could backfire; the flatterer may get only resistance to the request and loss of the boss's trust. On the other hand, the general practice of maintaining good interpersonal relationships with others enhances one's sphere of influence or referent power.[13]

Door-in-the-face technique: An influence tactic in which the user begins by making a large request that is likely to be rejected and follows it up with a smaller request.

The second influence tactic, the **door-in-the-face technique,** relies on the importance of reciprocity as a social norm. The person using this technique makes a major request that is likely to be rejected, and then follows it up with a more modest request—which is the intended request. Here is where reciprocity comes into play. In turning down the first request, the target person (who could be the boss) incurs an initial obligation to be responsive to a future request. The influence agent's smaller request then adds to that obligation because it demonstrates a willingness to make concessions. Furthermore, the second request appears that much smaller and easier to comply with because of the contrast with the first request! Although this technique is very effective in eliciting compliance, the manager can defend against it by examining the motives of the influencer.[14]

Foot-in-the-door technique: An influence tactic in which the user begins by making a smaller request that is likely to be granted and following it up with a larger request.

The third influence tactic, the **foot-in-the-door technique,** has been made popular by many door-to-door salespersons. This tactic is the flip side of the door-in-the-face technique: The influence agent makes a minor request that is easy to comply with, and follows it with a greater request. A door-to-door salesperson, for example, would first try to get inside your home and then ask if he or she can perform an elaborate demonstration of the product (encyclopedia set, rug shampoo, stain remover) in order to make the sale. This tactic owes its considerable success to the changes in disposition that occur once the target person has complied with the lesser request: The mere act of compliance leads to a more favorable attitude toward complying with future requests. As with the other influence tactics, forewarned is forearmed. The foot-in-the-door technique can be better resisted by the manager who is aware of its use as a manipulation tactic and who evaluates each request on its individual merits (often easier said than done).[15]

Influence Tactics: Patterns of Use

The three tactics described in the preceding section are only a sampling of techniques used to persuade others. Managers use a variety of tactics that go well beyond ingratiation, door-in-the-face technique, and foot-in-the-door technique.[16] For example, managers may also use reason, facts, negotiation, assertiveness, and coercion.

Influence Tactics

In an effort to clarify the relationship between different influence tactics, Toni Falbo classified them along two dimensions: rationality (e.g., relying upon objective information) and directness:

	Rational	Nonrational
Direct	Bringing up a formal plan	Using threat
Indirect	Hinting at the use of information	Lying

    Falbo found that rationality was the more important dimension. The use of rational tactics were more strongly associated with effective influence than was directness. Also, people who used reason and facts were viewed more positively than were those who used coercion or deceit.[17]

David Kipnis and his associates have discovered that managers tend to rely on favorite patterns of influence tactics.[18] The Kipnis researchers enumerated three basic managerial-influence profiles: the shotgun manager, the tactician and the bystander.

    A **shotgun manager** uses the widest variety of tactics. Ambitious and relatively inexperienced, he or she appears to be searching for tactics that work. Unfortunately, the shotgun approach does not always lead to effective influence efforts. In contrast, a **tactician** relies mostly on reason to influence others. He or she tends to have valued skills and occupy positions of power in the organization. And not surprisingly, a tactician often succeeds in accomplishing his or her objectives. A manager who fits the third profile, **bystander,** makes the fewest attempts to influence others. A bystander tends to have little organizational power and is the most dissatisfied of the three types of manager.[19]

Tips for the Manager.   Managers who have high-power needs tend to seek power and prefer occupations that offer opportunities to accumulate and use power. The need for personal power focuses on individual gain, whereas the need for socialized power is directed toward the

Shotgun manager: An influence profile common to relatively inexperienced managers who use a variety of influence tactics, apparently in search of the one that works best.

Tactician: An influence profile common to more experienced managers who use reason, facts, and logic to influence others.

Bystander: Managers who make infrequent attempts to influence others. Bystanders tend to enjoy little organizational power or satisfaction.

benefit of the organization. To promote the effective use of power, managers should stimulate and reward socialized power and discourage the use of personal power.

High-Mach individuals approach ambiguous interpersonal situations in a cool and detached manner, which enables them to manipulate others who are more emotionally involved. Managers should be advised to structure interpersonal situations with explicit rules to minimize unfair differences that exist between high and low Machs who interact.

People in organizations use influence to get others to comply with their requests. Influence tactics are practiced skills. The frequently used influence tactics of integration, the door-in-the-face technique, and the foot-in-the-door technique have proven effective in increasing a target person's receptiveness to requests. Managers who are aware of these techniques are better able to resist their effects.

Most managers fall into one of three managerial-influence profiles: a shotgun manager, a tactician, or a bystander. To improve one's influence, managers should try to be a tactician, relying on reason and facts to influence others.

GROUP CONSIDERATIONS AND POWER

Anyone who has ever arrived at a party wearing casual attire and found everyone else dressed in tuxedos and evening gowns understands the power of group norms. (See Chapter Three, Motivation, for further discussion of norms.) Pressures to conform with group expectations are very real. This phenomenon is even more pronounced within organizations in which teamwork and the company or department image are formally endorsed.

Group Pressure and Conformity

Conformity: The tendency of individuals to change their behavior as a result of group pressure.

Conformity is a change in individual behavior—either compliance or acceptance—due to group pressure. The effects of conformity are well documented. For example, in decision-making groups the pressure to conform diminishes controversy and the discussion of alternatives (see Chapter Seven, Decision Making, for a discussion of groupthink); in perceptual tasks it leads to inaccurate judgments.[20] People respond to conformity pressures for a variety of reasons. Four such reasons are *normative influence, information influence, self-presentation motives,* and *inattention.*[21]

Normative influence refers to the impact of group norms on individual behavior. As a member of a group, we ascribe to at least some standards of behavior accepted by group members. Our loyalty to and identification with the group predisposes us to accept many practices and beliefs of the group. Normative influence is increased by unanimity and cohesiveness. That is, it is difficult to resist the pressure to conform when everyone agrees or when group members have similar characteristics.

Conformity pressure is also fueled by the need for valuable information supplied by the group (information influence). The information we derive from groups is especially powerful when it bears on a unique situation with which we have little experience. A few informed opinion leaders within a group can induce conformity in others who lack reliable information or relevant experience.

Generally speaking, most people in organizational settings would rather be well regarded by others than not; hence, we see the "self-presentation motive" for group conformity. We try to put our best foot forward and appear competent, attractive, and amiable. Unfortunately, doing the right thing sometimes means deviating from the group, and compromising a preferred image as a team player and good citizen. In the interest of self-presentation, people sometimes succumb to conformity pressures and go along with the group to maintain a positive image in the eyes of our peers. (See the boxed insert below.)

Finally, people frequently conform through inattention. We often do not question why we are engaging in a particular behavior. This mindlessness often reflects a response to the routine nature of everyday organizational life. Only by systematically checking actions can we minimize instances of "falling asleep at the switch."[22]

Keep in mind that high conformity within a group is not necessarily counterproductive or wrong. To the extent that conformity is a problem, managers should promote healthy dissent within the group; focus on clear, specific goals and performance standards; be more accepting of group members; and challenge group members to become more aware of the significance of day-to-day events.

Whistleblowing: Is It Worth It?

Pressures to conform with inappropriate organizational decisions are often quite strong. A recent report on "whistleblowers"—individuals who have publicly revealed information concerning mismanagement and dishonesty in their organizations—indicates that life after whistleblowing is difficult and unpleasant.

Whistleblowers have reported feeling isolated from other people in the organization. They cite frequent attempts by their superiors and others to undermine their credibility, to disrupt their personal lives through active harassment and threats, and to damage their careers through demotion. Perhaps most disturbing about these negative effects is the possible loss of good organizational citizens. Whistleblowers typically have long records of successful employment, hold moderate political beliefs, and have faith in the integrity of their superiors in the organization.[23]

Obedience to Authority

Authority: Tied to legitimate power or power that is expected in a social setting. Usually associated with a formal position in an organization.

Authority relationships exist in every organization. **Authority** gives to an individual legitimate power or power that has been justified and is expected in a social setting.[24] Authority is power associated with a formal position in an organization (discussed previously).[25] Experiences in groups teach people to respect and to obey authority. We learn and relearn obedience in virtually every aspect of social life, including within the context of the family, school, teams, workplace, military, and government.

The extent to which people will subscribe to the dictates of a formal authority figure is a question of significant importance. A number of historical events suggest dramatically that under certain conditions people will obey authority to the extent of committing unthinkable acts. Adolph Eichman, for example, said that when he directed the genocide of Jews in Nazi concentration camps during World War II he did so under orders from his superiors. The massacre of innocent victims by U.S. troops at My Lai was similarly explained as an act of blind obedience. And the mass suicide by more than 900 members of the People's Temple, most responding to Reverend Jim Jones's orders to drink poisoned Kool-Aid, is still another chilling reminder of how responsive people can be in the face of formal authority.

To understand how obedience to authority works, researcher Stanley Milgram conducted a series of studies that required an individual to deliver electric shocks of increasing magnitude to a person situated in another room. Unknown to the subject under study, the "victim" was an actor and was never really shocked.[26] The subject was told the experiment was about learning and punishment, and that whenever the second person—the learner—made a mistake, the subject would be required to deliver a shock to the learner by flipping a switch on a specialized shock generator.

Subjects were paid a nominal fee for their participation; in addition, whenever a subject hesitated or expressed a desire to leave the experiment, the experimenter would prod him or her with one of the following directives:

"Please continue."
"The experiment requires that you continue."

"It is absolutely essential that you continue."
"You have no other choice; you must go on."[27]

Contrary to more optimistic predictions made by a group of experts, all subjects in the experiment delivered shocks to the 300-volt level, and 65 percent of the subjects continued to the 450-volt limit.[28] These studies corroborate the incidents of extreme obedience to authority that have occurred throughout history.

Milgram identified several important factors that affect the likelihood of obedience. His research helps explain the phenomenon of obedience in perhaps more encouraging terms. For example, Milgram found that the amount of feedback subjects received about a learner's condition directly influenced their willingness to obey.

In the original study the subject never saw the learner, but in other studies the subject was required physically to place the learner's hand on the shock pad. Not surprisingly, subjects in this situation were less likely to follow orders. In another rendition, experimenter *prestige* was lowered when the study was conducted in a shoddy downtown office instead of in a university laboratory. Subjects were less likely to obey when experimenter prestige was low. In yet another variation, the subject was paired with a second person—actually an accomplice of the experimenter—who would flip the switch while the subject under study was to keep records. As it turned out, if the accomplice disobeyed, then the subject was also likely to disobey.

Taken together, these results show that strict obedience is not inevitable. Being placed in greater contact with client groups, having greater access to management, and promoting discussions that examine the basis of actions all mitigate adverse effects of strict obedience. Generally, conditions that require people to evaluate their own actions will lead them to act as individuals rather than as blind agents of authority.[29] Fostering these conditions while maintaining an efficient organization is an important challenge for us all.

Coalitions

In many organizational situations, individuals who have little or no formal association form alliances in order to influence the course of events in the organization. These ad hoc groups, known as **coalitions,** are most often linked with organizational politics. **Politics** is the use of power to further individual goals that are incompatible with the goals of others and may or may not be at odds with the goals of the organization.[30] The potential for conflict is inherent in politics. Coalitions provide one mechanism for dealing with conflict situations and achieving political power in an organization.

Formed around issues that cut across departmental and functional divisions within and outside the organization, coalitions often make for

Coalitions: Ad hoc alliances formed with the purpose of influencing the course of organizational events.

Politics: The use of power to further individual ends that are incompatible with the goals of others and may or may not be at odds with the goals of the organization.

strange bedfellows. And since they are inherently temporary groupings, they disband as members seek more profitable alliances or when resources and interests shift.[31]

Don't Discount the Power of a Coalition!

A coalition of environmentalists led by the Sierra Club recently stopped the U.S. Navy in its tracks.

The Navy had planned to build a base for a carrier group in Everett, Washington. All necessary permits had been acquired and the Navy had full support of local business and government officials. Navy officials repeatedly confirmed their optimism regarding the speedy completion of the base. However, environmental groups charged that construction and dredging in Port Gardner Bay would damage local crab, shrimp, and fish populations. Construction was halted several times by court orders resulting from challenges by these groups.

By fall, 1988, work at the site had been indefinitely delayed as the two sides began negotiations. The Navy and environmental groups hope to find an integrative solution to this conflict that will protect the environment and provide a base for the carrier U.S.S. *Nimitz*.[32]

Typically, coalitions are "lean and mean." They are made up only of parties with enough collective resources to maximize the likelihood of reaching their goals. As coalitions increase in size they become too complicated to manage and to maintain, so they seldom grow very large. The transitory nature of coalitions also works against serious growth: They rarely offer parties the opportunity to get to know one another and to build effective long-term relationships.[33] (See Figure 8–2.)

Coalitions are usually composed of individuals with unequal power in the organization. Strong parties prefer weaker partners because they pose little threat to the status of the strong. At the same time, weaker parties know that they must ally themselves with more powerful partners to increase their chances of obtaining valued resources.

The one exception to this rule is that the organization's most powerful party tends to be excluded from coalitions. This is because the other parties are aware that the strongest party can take advantage of the weaker allies. Moreover, the contributions of a very strong party to a political effort could be so great as to entitle that party to the lion's

Figure 8–2 The Anatomy of a Coalition

COALITIONS ACT AS A GROUP AND ARE:

* Issues Oriented

* Interacting Groups

* Deliberately Constructed

* Independent of Formal Organizational Structure

* Lacking Formal Internal Structure

Adapted from Stevenson, W. B., Pearce, J. L., & Porter, L. W. "The concept of coalition in organizational theory and research." *Academy of Management Review, 10* (1985): 256–268.

share of the benefits—leaving little to the weaker allies and creating an even greater imbalance of power. Finally, very strong parties seldom feel a compulsion to form coalitions because they already enjoy strength relative to other groups.[34]

Tips for the Manager. Managers should understand that power relationships within a group influence the extent to which members conform. Group conformity is influenced by pressure to conform to group norms, by individual needs for information, by individual needs to survive, and by inattention. To reduce potentially unproductive group conformity, managers should promote healthy dissent within the group; focus on clear, specific goals and performance standards; be more accepting of group members; and challenge group members to become more aware of the significance of day-to-day events.

Within the context of legitimate (formal) authority, people often follow orders even if the orders are ethically questionable. To maintain appropriate checks and balances on the potential excesses of legitimate authority, managers should consider placing subordinates in greater contact with client groups, increasing subordinate access to management, and promoting discussions that examine the basis for managerial actions. Conditions that require people to evaluate their own actions lead them to act as individuals rather than as blind agents of authority.

Coalitions are made up of individuals who band together to achieve partisan goals. They tend to be temporary in nature, limited in size, and composed of parties with unequal power who together stand a good chance at shifting the direction of the organization. Managers should be aware of the power that can be wielded by coalitions. Coalitions are useful tools for addressing important issues that cut across departmental and organizational boundaries.

ORGANIZATIONAL CONSIDERATIONS AND POWER

Have you ever noticed how power in most organizations tends to concentrate in one or two departments? A number of researchers have suggested that organizational power accrues to departments that have access to resources that are important to the survival of the organization.[35] These departments, thanks to a number of **strategic contingencies,** are positioned to respond to critical events. For example, corporate accounting departments gained power as a result of the tax simplification act enacted in 1986. Similarly, human resource departments gain power during expansion and layoff, when staffing issues become critical to the organization.

Strategic contingencies: Unique qualities that enable a unit to handle critical organizational needs. Important strategic contingencies are the ability to cope with uncertainty, nonsubstitutability, centrality, relevance, and consensus.

By strategic contingencies, then, we mean unique qualities that enable a unit to handle critical organizational needs. Specifically, departments will gain power to the extent they *cope with uncertainty*, are *not substitutable*, are *central to the flow of work, perform relevant tasks* for the organization, and have a high degree of unit *consensus*.[36]

All organizations confront some amount of uncertainty in their environment. As the environment becomes more dynamic, coping with uncertainty becomes more important to the organization. Few airline executives in 1975 would have predicted that controlling terrorist attacks would reach its current level of importance. Yet today, security units have tremendous power and influence over the flow of traffic through airports. Much of their rise to power is due to their ability to cope with the uncertainty of terrorist activity.

Power also accrues to units that perform tasks no other groups can perform. A unit will remain in power as long as no substitute is found for the qualities the group offers. Historically, data-processing departments in many organizations developed significant power bases because other departments, such as payroll and accounting, did not know how to program and operate computers to serve their needs. But since the development and refinement of personal computers and user-friendly software, users can now duplicate the functions of data-processing departments. As a result, many data-processing departments have lost much of their power and, in some organizations, have been replaced with computer support staff who work for the user departments.

The more central a unit's position, the greater its power. A unit may be central by virtue of organizational design or by virtue of functional realities such as communication procedures. *Bureaucratic organizations*, because of their structure, are typically very centralized—so a few centrally placed units have considerable power over organizational activity. For example, an office responsible for issuing checks to all state employees can, because of its central role, effect a statewide change in payroll procedures by implementing new reporting requirements. Such a change would be virtually impossible to effect from a branch location. Another example: College and university scheduling offices have power over professors and students because they are at the hub of information on classroom space throughout the institution.

The capacity to perform relevant tasks refers to how critical a unit's work is to the organization. Could the organization survive if the unit were disbanded or cut back to a "skeleton crew"? If it could, then the unit is not relevant and stands to lose power. In stable manufacturing firms, staff functions such as accounting, human resources, building and grounds, research and development, and legal services have little relevance compared to line functions such as production and sales. On the other hand, research and development will have a great deal of power in a software development firm. Units that match the strategic mission of an organization tend to be powerful.

Finally, the extent to which units have a shared vision—consensus—tempers unit power. Dissension within a department causes energy to be lost to infighting and confusion, weakening the unit's power base. Departments that enjoy consensus, on the other hand, will be able to exploit their special qualities in response to critical events and win or maintain power. (See Figure 8–3.)

Figure 8–3 Strategic Contingencies that Lead to Unit Power

	Ability to Deal with Uncertainty
	Nonsubstitutability
	Centrality
+	Relevance
	Unit Consensus
=	Unit Power

Several factors contribute to the amount of power wielded by an organizational unit.

Organizational Structure and Power Tactics

Although individuals are known to prefer some power tactics over others, managers' selection of approaches is often affected by certain organizational conditions—such as their position in the organization and the direction of their attempts to influence. CEOs, staff managers, and supervisors favor different tactics, as indicated in a survey revealing their divergent perceptions of an effective organizational politician.[37]

In the survey, CEOs generally viewed the successful politician as being articulate, bright, ambitious, and sensitive to the needs of others and to the organization. Meanwhile, staff managers placed special emphasis on the ability to be articulate, logical and socially competent, as well as the ability to fit in. Supervisors saw successful organizational politicians very differently.

Unlike CEOs and staff managers, supervisors emphasized traits such as aggressiveness, popularity, competence, and deviousness. One explanation for these differences is that supervisors, who have less power and fewer personal resources than do CEOs and staff managers, resort out of frustration and lack of formal authority to less rational strategies of influence to achieve political success.

The survey results described above are consistent with the findings on upward and downward influence tactics used by managers in a study by David Kipnis and his associates.[38] These researchers found that managers frequently depended on assertive tactics for downward influence, but for upward influence they relied more heavily on coalition building, a less direct influence tactic. In both situations, however, the use of logic and reason remained the most popular influence tactic.

Political Activity

The amount of energy devoted to political activity varies from one organization to the next. Organizations that engage in high levels of political behavior have been referred to as "snake pits" by at least one researcher.[39] An understanding of what accounts for political activity is just one step toward creating more livable and effective organizations. Prominent among the factors that fuel organizational politics are uncertainty in the organizational environment, organizational complexity, competition for scarce resources, poorly defined decision-making and performance-appraisal processes, and lack of clear goals.[40]

Given the lack of control most organizations have over their environment, and the increasing complexity of modern organizations, we can expect "snake pits" to continue thriving. Managers can help keep politics under control by defining organizational decision-making and performance-appraisal processes and by clarifying and using organizational goals to aid resource allocations. In concert with the development of a less political organizational culture, these efforts will turn attention away from nonessential political activity and toward the organization's mission and goals. (See Chapter Seven, Decision Making, for further discussion of mission and goals.)

Tips for the Manager.   Managers can strengthen their departments by increasing the department's ability to cope with uncertainty, providing expertise for which there is no substitute, keeping central to the flow of communications, performing tasks that are relevant to the organization's mission, and maintaining unity within the department.

Although most upper-level managers prefer the use of reason and logic, managers at the lower levels are prone to use nonrational influence tactics. Influence attempts directed upward are more likely to include indirect tactics such as the building of coalitions, whereas downward influence tactics are more direct. Managers should be aware of these differences and encourage a greater use of reason and logic throughout the organization.

Uncertainty and ambiguity in organizational structure and design will foster dysfunctional political activity. Managers can begin to control the negative elements of political behavior by clarifying departmental goals, performance standards, and decision-making processes, and by trying to alleviate environmental uncertainty and simplify organizational complexity.

SUMMARY: FOCUS ON SKILLS

Power is the ability of individuals, groups, and organizations to change the behavior of others. Power determines who obtains valuable resources and how those resources are used. Following are 18 suggestions for improving the use of power.

Managers should:

1. Recognize that the dependence of one party on another for valued resources creates a power relationship.

2. Recognize that power comes from multiple sources (reward, coersive, legitimate, referent, and expert power), which are used to get things done.

3. Use influence, or the use of behavioral techniques, to effect compliance in others and assert power.

4. Use the ethical principles of utilitarianism, justice, and rights as guides to behavior in the use of power.

5. Promote conditions that reward socialized power needs.

6. Minimize the untoward effects of Machiavellian behavior by clearly defining and structuring interpersonal situations.

7. Resist influence by detecting the techniques and motives of persuasive persons.

8. Increase their own capacity to influence others by building positive interpersonal relationships.

9. Understand that concessions by an influence agent that invoke the norm of reciprocity can trigger compliance in the influenced party.

10. Adopt personal influence tactics that rely on the use of reason and logic to obtain compliance and cooperation from others.

11. Prevent the overwhelming effects of conformity by promoting healthy dissent within the group; focusing on clear, specific goals and performance standards; being more accepting of group members; and challenging group members to become more aware of the significance of day-to-day events.

12. Encourage a climate that supports the responsible use of authority by emphasizing close contacts with client groups, open channels of upward communications, and reviews of management actions.

13. Form healthy coalitions to address issues that have larger organizational impact on the group, and be mindful of the power of a coalition.

14. Be sensitive to the fact that organizational politics often lead to the gain of a few at the expense of the organization.

15. Be aware of unit characteristics such as the ability to cope with uncertainty, nonsubstitutability, centrality, relevance, and unit consensus; and be aware of the impact of such characteristics on the relative power of departments.

16. Note that position in the organization affects the tactics used by managers to influence others.

17. Know that influence techniques directed upward tend to be less rational and less direct than influence techniques directed downward.

18. Control the unwanted effects of political behavior by clearly specifying goals, performance standards, and decision-making processes.

■ CASE: "A TERMINAL CASE"

Jack Jones, supervisor of the back office of the loan department of the Short County Savings Bank, had his hands full.

The receptionist, Diane, who had been doing double duty by working the data terminal since the regular operator left, had flatly refused to continue doing two jobs. She had been working at both positions for about three months, but she disliked the terminal work that she had learned with surprisingly little training and she hoped that a new operator would be soon hired. She was upset because not only was she receiving receptionist's wages even though operator's wages were much higher, but was receiving criticism about the quality and speed of her work on the terminal.

So a new terminal operator had been hired. After two weeks, she suddenly left to join her husband who had just been transferred to another state. Again, the company expected Diane to fill in as terminal operator. But when Diane's supervisor deposited the day's work on her desk, Diane refused to do it. "It's not my job," she said. After a hurried conference, a replacement was borrowed from another division, and Jack called Diane into his office.

"We expect the employees in this office to be cooperative and occasionally do some work outside their job scope," Jack said. "You are relatively new here, and this lack of cooperation would look very bad on your performance appraisal."

Diane exploded. "I spent eight weeks on that terminal doing that job as well as my own. I hated it, but I did it and I didn't get one word of thanks."

Jack replied, "That's true, but sometimes we forget to thank people. We all know you didn't like the work."

Diane fired back, "People may have forgotten to say thanks but they sure knew how to jump all over me when I made a mistake doing the work. I didn't see any extra money in my pay for doing the terminal work, much less two jobs. You don't seem to care very much how hard you push your employees as long as the work gets done. But I don't think I can keep doing two jobs any more. I'm so exhausted I can't eat when I get home."

After a moment, Jack quietly asked, "Will you work on the terminal next week?" Diane said that she would let him know. Jack realized that if he pushed Diane any harder, he would be looking for a new receptionist as well as a terminal operator. But he also knew that the operator he had borrowed would have to return to her own division in a few days.

Case Questions

1. What influence tactic did Jones use to keep Diane working as an operator after the second regular operator left?
2. From what sources does Diane draw her power?
3. Who has the most power in this situation?

■ EXERCISE: "BASES OF POWER"

Listed below are ten occupations. Evaluate each in terms of one of French and Raven's Five Bases of Power (coercive, reward, legitimate, referent, and expert power). Also, provide a brief example of application of the power base for the occupation. For example, you may feel that an army general's predominate base of power is legitimate. Indicate this opinion and then provide a brief example (such as "military people usually adhere closely to the chain of command").

Occupation	Power Base	Example
Accountant	_____	_____
		_____
Actor	_____	_____
		_____
Engineer	_____	_____
		_____
Judge	_____	_____
		_____
Physician	_____	_____
		_____
Police Officer	_____	_____
		_____
Politician	_____	_____
		_____
Professor	_____	_____
		_____
Taxi Driver	_____	_____
		_____
Waiter/Waitress	_____	_____
		_____

ENDNOTES

1. Emerson, R. "Power-dependence relations." *American Sociological Review, 27* (1962): 31–41.

2. French, J. R., Jr., & Raven, B. "The bases of social power." In D. Cartwright (Ed.), *Studies in Social Power.* Ann Arbor, MI: Institute for Social Research, 1959.

3. Feinberg, M. R. "When to engender fear . . . or at least a high degree of anxiety." *The Wall Street Journal,* Oct. 24, 1988, p. A-16.

4. Kipnis, D. "Does power corrupt?" *Journal of Personality and Social Psychology, 24* (1972): 33–41.

5. Cavanagh, G. F. *American Business Values* (2nd ed.). Englewood Cliffs, NJ: Prentice-Hall, 1984.

6. Velasquez, M.; Cavanagh, G. F.; & Moberg, D. J. "Organizational statesmanship and dirty politics: Ethical guidelines for the organizational politician." *Organizational Dynamics, 12* (3) (1983): 68–71.

7. McClelland, D. C. *Power: The Inner Experience.* New York: Irvington, 1975.

8. McClelland, D. C. *Human Motivation.* Glenview, IL: Scott Foresman, 1985.

9. Boyatzis, R. E. *The Competent Manager.* New York: John Wiley, 1982. See also: Chursmir, L. H. "Personalized versus socialized power needs among working women and men." *Human Relations, 39* (1986): 149–160.

10. Machiavelli, N. *The Prince.* (T. G. Bergin, ed.). New York: Appleton-Century-Crofts, 1947.

11. Christie, R., & Geis, F. L. *Studies in Machiavellianism.* New York: Academic Press, 1970.

12. Jones, E. E., & Wortman, C. *Ingratiation: An Attributional Approach.* Morristown, NJ: General Learning Press, 1973.

13. French and Raven, "The bases of social power."

14. Cialdini, R. B. *Influence: Science and Practice.* Glenview, IL: Scott, Foresman, 1988.

15. Ibid.

16. Kipnis, D.; Schmidt, S. M.; & Wilkinson, I. "Intraorganizational influence tactics: Explorations in getting one's way." *Journal of Applied Psychology, 3* (1980): 440–452.

17. Falbo, T. "The multidimensional scaling of power strategies." *Journal of Personality and Social Psychology, 35* (1977): 537–548.

18. Kipnis, D.; Schmidt, S. M.; Swaffin-Smith, C.; & Wilkinson, I. "Patterns of managerial influence: Shotgun managers, tacticians, and bystanders." *Organizational Dynamics* (Winter 1984): 58–67.

19. Ibid.

20. Janis, I., & Mann, L. *Decision Making: A Psychological Analysis of Conflict and Choice.* New York: Free Press, 1977. See also: Asch, S. E. "Opinions and social pressures." *Scientific American, 193* (5) (1955): 31–35.

21. Forsyth, D. R. *An Introduction to Group Dynamics.* Monterey, CA: Brooks/Cole, 1983.

22. Langer, E. J. "Minding matters. The consequences of mindlessness/mindfulness." In L. Berkowitz (Ed.), *Advances in Experimental Social Psychology.* New York: Academic Press, 1989.

23. Glazer, M. P., & Glazer, P. M. "Whistleblowing." *Psychology Today* (August 1986): 36–39, 42–43.

24. Pfeffer, J. *Power in Organizations.* Marshfield, MA: Pitman Publishing, 1981. See also: Bass, B. M. *Stogdill's Handbook of Leadership.* New York: Free Press, 1981.

25. French and Raven, "The bases of social power."

26. Milgram, S. *Obedience to Authority.* New York: Harper & Row, 1974.

27. Ibid.

28. Milgram, S. "Behavioral study of obedience." *Journal of Abnormal and Social Psychology, 67* (1963): 371–378.

29. Milgram, *Obedience to Authority.*

30. Miner, J. B. *Organizational Behavior: Performance and Productivity.* New York: Random House, 1988.

31. Forsyth, *An Introduction to Group Dynamics.*

32. "Warning offered on secret talks." *The Herald* (Everett, WA). October 22, 1988.

33. Forsyth, *An Introduction to Group Dynamics.*

34. Ibid.

35. House, R. J. "Power and personality in complex organizations." (B. M. Staw, & L. L. Cummings, Eds.). *Research in Organizational Behavior 10* (1988): 305–357.

36. Lawrence, P. R., & Lorsch, J. W. *Organization and Environment.* Boston: Harvard Business School, 1967. See also: Hickson, D. J.; Hinnings, C. R.; Lee, C. A.; Schenck, R. H.; & Pennings, J. M. "A strategic contingencies' theory of intraorganizational power." *Administrative Science Quarterly, 16* (1971): 216–229. See also: Pfeffer, *Power in Organizations.*

37. Allen, R. W.; Madison, D. L.; Porter, L. W.; Renwick, P. A.; & Mayes, B. T. "Organizational politics: Tactics and characteristics of its actors. *California Management Review, 22* (1979): 1, 77–83.

38. Kipnis et al., "Patterns of managerial influence."

39. Schwartz, H. S. "The clockwork or the snakepit: An essay on the meaning of teaching organizational behavior." *Organizational Behavior Teaching Review, 11* (1986–1987): 19–26.

40. Beeman, D. R., & Sharkey, T. W. "The use and abuse of corporate politics." *Business Horizons* (March-April 1987): 26–30. See also: Pfeffer, *Power in Organizations.*

CHAPTER NINE
Leadership

- ▆ *Self-Assessment: "The LPC Scale"*

- ▆ *Learning about Leadership*

- ▆ *Case: "The Brains"*

- ▆ *Exercise: "Results-Oriented Leadership"*

■ SELF-ASSESSMENT: "THE LPC SCALE"

Instructions. Throughout your life you have worked in many groups with a wide variety of different people—on your job, in social clubs, in church organizations, in volunteer groups, on athletic teams, and in many others. You probably found working with most of your co-workers quite easy, but working with others may have been very difficult or all but impossible.

Now, think of *all the people* with whom you have ever worked. Next, think of the *one person in your life* with whom you could work least well. This individual may or may not be the person you also disliked most. It must be the one person with whom you had the most difficulty getting a job done, the one single individual with whom you would least want to work—a boss, a subordinate, or a peer. This person is called your "Least Preferred Co-worker" (LPC).

On the scale below, describe this person by placing an "X" in the appropriate space. The scale consists of pairs of words that are opposite in meaning, such as *Very Neat* and *Very Untidy*. Between each pair of words are eight spaces that form the following scale:

Very Neat　　　　　　　　　　　　　　　　　Very Untidy

　　　　　　8　7　6　5　4　3　2　1

Think of those eight spaces as steps ranging from one extreme to the other. Thus, if you ordinarily think that this least preferred co-worker is quite neat, you would write an "X" in the space marked 7, like this:

Very Neat	X							Very Untidy
8	7	6	5	4	3	2	1	
Very Neat	Quite Neat	Some-what Neat	Slightly Neat	Slightly Untidy	Some-what Untidy	Quite Untidy	Very Untidy	

However, if you ordinarily think of this person as being only slightly neat, you would put your "X" in space 5. If you think of this person as being very untidy (not neat), you would put your "X" in space 1.

Sometimes, the scale will run in the other direction, as shown below:

Frustration　　　　　　　　　　　　　　　　Helpful

　　　　　　1　2　3　4　5　6　7　8

Before you mark your "X," look at the words at both ends of the line. There are no right or wrong answers. Work rapidly; your first answer is likely to be the best. Do not omit any items, and mark each item only once. Think of a real person in your experience, not an imaginary character. Remember, it is not necessarily the person whom you liked least, but the person with whom it is (or was) most difficult to work.

Now think of the person with whom you can work least well. He may be someone you work with now, or he may be someone you knew in the past. He does not have to be the person you like least well, but should be the person with whom you had the most difficulty in getting a job done. Describe this person as he appears to you.

Pleasant	8 7 6 5 4 3 2 1	Unpleasant
Friendly	8 7 6 5 4 3 2 1	Unfriendly
Rejecting	1 2 3 4 5 6 7 8	Accepting
Helpful	8 7 6 5 4 3 2 1	Frustrating
Unenthusiastic	1 2 3 4 5 6 7 8	Enthusiastic
Tense	1 2 3 4 5 6 7 8	Relaxed
Distant	1 2 3 4 5 6 7 8	Close
Cold	1 2 3 4 5 6 7 8	Warm
Cooperative	8 7 6 5 4 3 2 1	Uncooperative
Supportive	8 7 6 5 4 3 2 1	Hostile
Boring	1 2 3 4 5 6 7 8	Interesting
Quarrelsome	1 2 3 4 5 6 7 8	Harmonious
Self-assured	8 7 6 5 4 3 2 1	Hesitant
Efficient	8 7 6 5 4 3 2 1	Inefficient
Gloomy	1 2 3 4 5 6 7 8	Cheerful
Open	8 7 6 5 4 3 2 1	Guarded

Reprinted with permission from Fiedler, F. E., & Chemers, M., *Improving Leadership Effectiveness*, 2nd ed. New York: Wiley, 1984, pp. 17–20.

■ LEARNING ABOUT LEADERSHIP

Have you ever:

> Lead a tour group?
> Organized a picnic or pot luck supper?
> Been elected captain of an athletic team or served as an officer in a
>   club?

You have been a leader if you answered "yes" to one or more of these questions.

Leadership is often associated only with famous figures like Mahatma Ghandi or Sir Winston Churchill. Yet, most of us have been or will function as a leader at some point in our lives. Leadership is a much more pervasive concept than most people realize; it is an integral part of everyday life. Without leadership, groups and organizations lack focus. Through leadership, group action is coordinated and directed toward attaining goals.

WHAT IS LEADERSHIP?

Leadership is defined as a relationship between an individual (the leader) and a group (or groups) of followers in which goal attainment of the group is influenced by the leader. *Effective leadership* is further defined in terms of the productivity of the group being led. A leader is effective to the extent that his or her influence on a group results in a desired level of group productivity.

Leadership: A relationship between an individual (the leader) and a group (or groups) of followers in which group productivity is influenced by the leader.

The Difference Between Leadership and Management

What is the difference between leadership and management?

Management is concerned with planning, organizing, directing, and controlling. Effective managers do a good job of setting a course (planning), putting resources together (organizing), leading employees (directing), and following up (controlling). Effective managers are effective leaders because leadership is part of the directing function.

Effective leaders are not always effective managers. Although skilled at influencing followers to attain goals, leaders may influence others to attain the wrong goals. For example, Lee Iacocca of Chrysler Corporation, and Sam Armacost, past CEO of Bank-America, are both effective leaders. Both have proven successful at influencing followers. However, Iacocca has also been an effective manager because his plans for bringing Chrysler back to profitability worked. Armacost, on the other hand, led BankAmerica over a cliff of financial and market share losses and was replaced as CEO during October 1986.

The Leadership Challenge

There are many challenges associated with effectively leading a group or organization. Leaders must contend with the multidimensional nature of leadership (understood as the interplay among characteristics of the leader, the followers, and the situation). Effective leaders also possess considerable skill. Finally, the basis of leader influence is only partially dictated by legitimate authority depicted in an organizational chart. Much of a leader's influence is derived from elements of the informal organization, which can be relatively difficult to control.

The Multidimensional Nature of Leadership. Leadership is a dynamic, multidimensional process influenced not only by *personality traits* of the leader, but also by changing characteristics of a *situation* and of the *followers* being led over time.

For well over 100 years, researchers felt that effective leadership could be defined solely in terms of the personality characteristics or traits of the leader. (This intuitively appealing view was first articulated by Thomas Carlyle in 1841.[1]) In other words, it was believed that effective leaders possess a universal set of common characteristics such as intelligence and compassion. This approach, called by various names including the **trait approach** and "Great Man" theory, simply did not work out.[2]

Trait approach: The belief that effective leaders possess a universal set of common characteristics such as intelligence and compassion.

Too often researchers found that leader traits effective in one situation did not apply or were ineffective in another situation. Leader traits effective in leading a logging crew, for example, may be ineffective in leading office staff involved in the administration of a logging operation.

The nature of those being led has also been found to affect leader effectiveness. Even if the leader possesses the "right" personality traits, changes in the composition of followers could well influence leader effectiveness. For example, one leadership theory recommends that the leader change his or her behavior to match the maturity of those in the group being led.[3]

Changes in the situation also influence leader effectiveness. Even if the leader and the group being led are compatible and effective in terms of past productivity, a changing situation (e.g., new competition, new technology) could compromise the effectiveness of the leader and, consequently, group productivity.

The dynamic and often subtle relationships among characteristics of the leader, the followers, and the situation present a constant challenge. Effective leadership seldom involves the application of simple solutions.

The Importance of Leader Skills. The second leadership challenge we have identified concerns skill requirements of the leader. Effective leaders possess a wide variety of skills.

Consider the chapter content in this book. *Managerial Skills in Organizations* covers skills practiced by leaders pertaining to motivation, performance appraisal, communication, decision making, and conflict management that affect group productivity. Chapters covering organization development and power are concerned with the exercise of influence by leaders in organizations. It could be argued that the content of this entire book is concerned with effective leadership!

Occasionally, leaders come along who seem to be intuitively skilled. However, whether through experience or formal education, most of us require ongoing study and reflection in order to gain and to maintain effective leadership skills.

Commentary: "Leadership"
Governor Booth Gardner

Leadership is a tremendously complex phenomenon and one of the greatest challenges for human endeavor.

The enormous complexity of today's issues and problems—in business, government, education, community affairs, and family life—demands great resourcefulness, flexibility, and imagination from our leaders in order to reach effective solutions.

Successful leadership means results. The achievement of significant goals is the real test of leadership at any level of an organization.

My leadership experience extends from serving as governor of the state of Washington and as president of a large company, to organizing a youth association and coaching women's soccer.

The authors' suggestions concerning ways to improve the quality of leadership are sound. Several of the suggestions in particular reinforce what I have found to be true in leadership situations.

Understanding that Leadership Is a Dynamic, Multidimensional Process.   It is obvious that there is no single, magical leadership skill or component that is guaranteed to be successful in every situation. Experience has taught me that leaders must have as much flexibility as possible in adapting to changing circumstances and differing needs and in determining the most appropriate path to the organization's goals.

For instance, many attributes and tactics can be successful for a coach as well as in high-level positions in government and business. Team-building, inspiration, making evaluations, and choosing other leaders are skills adaptable to many situations.

Convening a Decision-Making Group or Otherwise Soliciting Information.   Leadership that seeks consensus is appropriate to many situations. Listening to followers, incorporating suggestions, and showing a sincere interest in the problems of each part or level of an organization can build deeply rooted organizational support and loyalty.

Communication.   There is perhaps no greater need and no greater strength for a leader to possess than effective communication skills. A successful leader cannot expect the strength of good ideas to carry the day. A successful coach develops a good game plan and then gets that message through to the team; a successful governor creates a vision, builds support for ways to implement that vision through outreach and, in dealing with a Legislature, often has to bring the influence of the public to bear to accomplish important goals.

All of us are called upon to provide leadership in some phase or aspect of life. Every individual has a special talent in which leadership opportunities are available, and seeking out and being successful in such an opportunity can be extremely rewarding.

Governor Booth Gardner

Booth Gardner is in his second term as governor of the state of Washington. He earned a bachelor's degree in business from the University of Washington and a master's degree in business administration from Harvard University and subsequently served as assistant to the dean at the Harvard Business School.

From 1967 to 1972, Gardner served as director of the School of Business and Economics at the University of Puget Sound in Tacoma, and served in the Washington State Senate from 1970 to 1972, chairing the Education Committee. From 1972 to 1980, Gardner was president of the Laird Norton Company, a building supply firm, and he also served as a member of the Weyerhaeuser Company's board of directors.

In 1980, Gardner was elected as the first Pierce County executive, serving until his election as governor in 1984. In addition to his elected and private-sector positions, Gardner co-founded the Central Area Youth Association of Seattle, which provides athletic, social, and educational activities for minority and disadvantaged youths. The governor is also involved in youth sports activities and in 1984, 1985, and 1986, coached a women's soccer team—the Cozars—to the national championship game for its age group.

Legitimate Authority: Only One Base of Leader Power. Finally, leader influence is only partly derived from "legitimate power" that comes from a leader's position (e.g., director, foreman, chairperson, superintendent, team leader, president, officer). Effective leadership requires more than just simple reliance on the power dictated by a position.

Followers are also influenced by a leader's capability to provide rewards and mete out punishment, and by the "referent power" (influence gained from the attractiveness of the leader to followers) and expertise of the leader.[4] (See Chapter Eight, Power, for further discussion of power and influence.) In fact, referent power and expertise may be the most potent bases of influence a leader can exercise. Studies of the effects of expert and referent power of leaders indicate higher levels of follower performance and member satisfaction, and lower absenteeism and turnover.[5]

Bases of Power

Legitimate: Derived from the leader's position in the organization.

Expert: Derived from having special knowledge instrumental to achieving group goals.

Reward: Derived from having valued resources that can be allocated to group members.

Coercive: Derived from the ability to threaten subordinates with punishment.

Referent: Derived from the attractiveness of the leader to followers; put another way—the degree to which followers like and respect the leader.[6]

Expert and referent power are not granted to the leader by the organization. Added to the challenges posed by the multidimensionality of leadership and skills required for effective leadership, is the challenge of contending with bases of power that must be *earned* by the leader. A knowledgeable, well-liked subordinate, for example, may have more influence with group members than the legitimately appointed leader.

LEADERSHIP AND THE INDIVIDUAL

Margaret Thatcher has many unique characteristics that have contributed to her success as prime minister of Great Britain. This statement is equally true of Red Auerbach, general manager of the legendary Boston Celtics basketball team. What makes these very different individuals effective leaders?

We will respond to this question in terms of leader characteristics (who leaders *are*) and leader behaviors (what leaders *do*). The material in this section emphasizes the individual leader rather than characteristics of the group or the situation.

Leader Intelligence

Cognitive resource theory: Proposes that leader intelligence influences group performance when the task requires intellectual ability and the leader acts in a directive fashion, experiences little stress, and has the support of the group.

Leader intelligence is valued as a leadership characteristic. Leaders tend to be selected who are brighter than group members.[7] Yet, leader intelligence has been found to be only weakly associated with group performance.[8] This finding is somewhat suprising. One would expect that groups led by brighter leaders would be more productive. One explanation for this finding is given by the **cognitive resource theory** of leadership.[9] (See Figure 9–1.)

This theory proposes that leader intelligence (1) influences group performance when a task requires intellectual ability and the leader acts in a directive fashion, (2) experiences little stress (especially from a supervisor), and (3) has the support of the group. The cognitive resource theory suggests that under stressful conditions, leader experience, not intelligence, contributes to group performance. This view is consistent

Figure 9–1 The Cognitive Resource Model

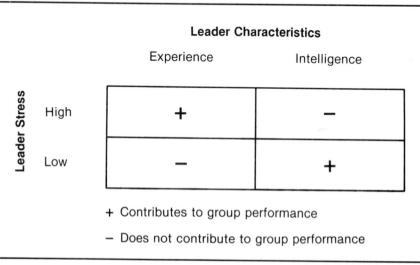

+ Contributes to group performance

− Does not contribute to group performance

Stress plays an important role in determining whether leader experience *or* intelligence contributes to group performance.

with research that demonstrates that stress interferes with thinking, and that performance under stress is significantly affected by the leader's ability to draw from experience.[10]

The cognitive resource theory leads to several implications for managerial practice. First, leaders need to manage stress effectively if their intelligence is to be well deployed in leading a group. Second, leader intelligence only makes a difference if a group is actively directed by the leader. Finally, leader intelligence improves group performance only if the leader can maintain support of the group.

Leader Charisma

Throughout history, **leader charisma** (where followers are influenced by attraction to the leader) has provided leaders with extraordinary power over followers.[11] Charismatic leaders create a special leader–follower relationship through their inspirational efforts and confidence in followers.[12] Examples of charismatic leaders range from Joan of Arc and John F. Kennedy to Martin Luther King. These leaders generated faith, respect, and encouragement by their very presence.[13]

Leader charisma: Leader qualities that are attractive to followers.

Charismatic leadership has been incorporated into the larger framework of **transformational leadership**.[14] Transformational leaders are charismatic and provide followers with intellectual stimulation and consideration. A recent study of transformational leadership showed that transformational leadership had positive effects in increasing satisfaction with performance appraisal and employee performance.[15]

Transformational leadership: Leadership that provides followers with intellectual stimulation and consideration.

A major problem with charisma as a leader characteristic, and transformational leadership as a leadership style, is that they are difficult to assess. Also, as with intelligence, it is virtually impossible to train leaders to become more charismatic. However, leaders could practice basic tenets of transformational leadership by providing intellectual stimulation and consideration to followers. These actions, in turn, could lead to extraordinary effort on the part of followers. An example of transformational leadership can be seen in the remarkable tenure of Golda Meir as a leader of the Israeli people.

Golda Meir was well known for her intellectual prowess. While serving as Prime Minister of Israel during the late 1960s and early 1970s, she encouraged and then benefited from the collective input of her cabinet members. Her debates with U.S. leaders, in support of maintaining the security of Israel, became legendary. Yet, this same woman was also renown for her human touch. She has been described as a person who became one of the political giants of our time without "ever losing the warmth and informality for which she (was) justly celebrated."[16] It is little wonder that the Israel of Golda Meir overcame overwhelming odds to establish a prominent place in the world.

Leader Motivation

The motivation to be a leader also contributes to leader effectiveness. According to John Miner, individuals whose personal motivations match organizational priorities are more likely to be elevated to leadership positions and be evaluated as being more effective.[17] Six motivations were also identified by Miner as being essential to effective leadership within bureaucratic organizational settings. These were the motives to have favorable relations with authority figures, to compete, to exercise power and influence, to take charge, to acquire a specialized position in the organization, and to accomplish required work responsibly.

Miner's findings suggest that effective leaders have personal goals that match organizational goals and have a strong desire to take on responsibility. Effective leaders also have a need to exercise power in carrying out responsibilities and have a strong desire to "get ahead."

Leader motive pattern: According to McClelland, individuals with high needs for power, low affiliation needs, and high self-control are likely to become effective leaders.

Another body of research has led to the notion that a specific set of motives, called the **leader motive pattern,** predisposes individuals to be leaders.[18] According to David McClelland, individuals with high needs for power, low affiliation needs, and high self-control are likely to become effective leaders. In short, effective leaders tend to be interested in gaining influence, maintaining the social distance necessary to make difficult interpersonal decisions, and being willing to work for the good of the organization or group.

Several studies have been conducted that support the leader motive pattern. One study found that sales managers with high motive-pattern scores led subordinates with greater sales and morale compared with equivalent salespeople being led by low leader motive-pattern managers.[19] The success of nontechnical managers at AT&T was predicted by the leader motive pattern in a recent 16-year longitudinal study.[20]

Presidential Leadership and Leader Motivation

Does leader motivation really make a difference? That is the question Professor David Winter asked himself when he decided to take a look at the effectiveness of past U.S. presidents.

Winter found that the presidential need for power, as expressed in inaugural addresses, was positively correlated to historian ratings of decision effectiveness. In other words, presidents who were judged to have a high need for power were regarded to have been effective decision makers. Interestingly, perceptions of presidential popularity were found to be unrelated to motive for

power. Instead, "popularity" was found to be based on the fit between the president's personality and the prevailing values of the
time.[21]

There are circumstances when the motives of the leader are super-
ceded by the need to have a leader with technical knowledge. In effect,
the leader's technical expertise can substitute for leader motivation.[22]
Consider the importance of having a qualified pilot in the cockpit of a
large commercial airplane. Knowing the intricacies of taking off, flying,
landing, and dealing with FAA regulations are of paramount importance. A pilot who knows his or her stuff will have followers who comply
independent of the pilot's personal motives. This is particularly true
during times when the leader's technical expertise is needed, such as
when landing a plane or handling an emergency.

Leader Behavior

Intelligence, charisma, and motivation are inherent leader characteristics that influence leader effectiveness. Again, these characteristics
pertain to who leaders *are*. We now move to consideration of what individual leaders *do*.

What Leaders Do. In the mid-1950s, researchers at Ohio State University discovered that leader behavior could be described in terms of
either *initiation of structure* or *consideration for others*.[23] During the
same period, researchers at the University of Michigan identified *job-
centered* and *employee-centered* leadership styles.[24] Researchers at Ohio
State and Michigan determined that leaders tend to focus on either task
(initiation of structure; job-centered) or people (consideration for
others; employee-centered).

These studies were inconclusive regarding the most effective
leader behavior. The Ohio State University researchers, for example,
placed emphasis on using factor analysis (a relatively sophisticated statistical technique) to find the most prominent categories of leader behavior. It was left to other researchers to develop and test theories
pertaining to the appropriateness of leader behavior.

Tips for the Manager. Managers should understand that legitimate
power is only one of several bases of influence that motivate followers.
Referent power and expertise also have a significant effect on group
productivity, even though people possessing these characteristics may
not appear as leaders in an organizational chart. Leader intelligence,

charisma, motivation, and behavior also contribute to the effectiveness of the individual leader.

The cognitive resource theory proposes that leader intelligence contributes to group performance under limited conditions—when the leader is directive, experiences little or no stress, and has the support of the group. Leader *experience* is a more valid predicator of leader effectiveness under stressful conditions than is leader *intelligence.* The notion of transformational leadership further suggests that leader charisma, when combined with the provision of intellectual stimulation and consideration to followers, accentuates subordinate performance.

Motivation to manage predicts leadership success if the leader's goals fit those of the organization. A need for power, coupled with a low need for affiliation and high self-control, is also associated with effective leadership. However, when technical requirements of the situation are preeminent, leader motivation plays a less important role. Followers are quite willing in this instance to be led by a leader with technical expertise.

LEADERSHIP AND THE GROUP

We now shift from the characteristics and behavior of the leader to theories that are particularly concerned with relationships between the leader and the group, as moderated by the situation.

A High Task–High People Theory

One school of thought that evolved from the Ohio State and Michigan research contends that the most appropriate leader behavior is to be high on both task *and* structure. Robert Blake and Jane Mouton believe that effective leadership *always* involves leader behavior that is high in concern for people and concern for production.[25] Blake and Mouton have arrayed concern for people and task along a nine-point scale. The ideal leader, according to these theorists, is the 9,9 leader who believes that work is accomplished through **team management.** The 9,9 leader has maximum concern for both people and production, and leads a group of committed, motivated followers who share in decision making and are focused on task. A 1,1 leader, on the other hand, leads an uncommitted group that accomplishes very little work.

Team management: According to Blake and Mouton, the most effective leaders always have maximum concern for both people and production (e.g., task).

There is evidence that experienced managers believe that a 9,9 leadership approach works.[26] However, research that tests Blake and Mouton's theory using an organizational index of productivity as a dependent variable is lacking. Sometimes intuitive perceptions of what seems right are inaccurate. Moreover, there are groups and situations where it is very difficult for an effective leader to be high on both people *and* task. For example, a leader placed in a situation characterized by low trust between leaders and followers, and difficult working conditions, may be more effective with a behavioral focus that emphasizes task. It may not be realistically possible to focus on people. Under these circumstances, an emphasis on both people and task might even be contradictory.

Despite these criticisms, Blake and Mouton's theory represents an important application of earlier research. These theorists brought research out of the laboratory and into the workplace. Their framework is also important from the standpoint that it recognizes that effective leadership involves a focus on both people and task, even if the degree of focus on either people or task effective in a given situation is debatable.

The Contingency Model

The contingency model, developed by Fred Fiedler and his associates, proposes that leadership effectiveness is a result of the fit between the leader's personality and the amount of situational control or predictability in the leadership situation.[27] This approach acknowledges that there is no "one best road" to effective leadership. We begin with a discussion of how leader personality influences when a leader will be effective.

The contingency model: According to Fiedler, effective leadership is contingent on the match between the personality of the leader and dictates of the situation.

Leader Personality. Leader personality is defined in terms of either the task or relationship motivation of the leader. Task-motivated leaders are more directive than relationship-motivated leaders. The task-motivated leader is most satisfied with a job well done. Relationship-motivated leaders tend to be more considerate toward their followers. The relationship-motivated leader is most satisfied when the group gets along with each other and with the leader.

After the leader's primary motivation is satisfied, then satisfaction can be derived by the second motivation (e.g., in the case of the task-motivated leader—good interpersonal relationships; for relationship-motivated leaders—task accomplishment).

Situational Control. Situational control is made up of three elements of the situation. In order of importance, these elements are:

1. *Leader-member relations:* The degree to which the leader and group members get along with each other
2. *Task structure:* The degree to which the task can be organized into an orderly sequence or pattern
3. *Position power:* The degree to which the leader has formal recognition and legitimate authority from the organization

According to Fiedler, situational control improves for the leader as leader-member relations improve; task structure becomes better defined and position power increases.

Leader-Match.   The contingency model predicts that task-motivated leaders will have effective groups under conditions of high and low situational control. Groups led by relationship-motivated leaders will be more productive under conditions of moderate situational control. (See Figure 9–2.) This prediction has been supported in a variety of studies.[28]

The contingency model indicates that ineffective leadership is caused by a poor match between the leader and the situation. This model suggests that improvement in group productivity requires that leaders change the situation to match their style rather than try to change their personality.[29] For example, a task-motivated leader in a moderate control situation could improve the situation by setting goals with followers. A relationship-motivated leader in a low-control situation might improve the situation by conducting weekly meetings with

Figure 9–2 The Contingency Model

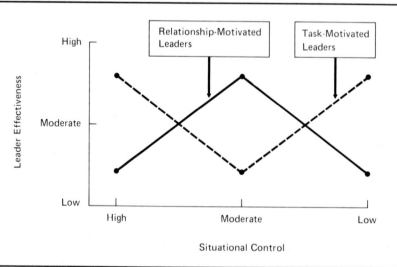

According to Fiedler, leader effectiveness results from an appropriate match between leadership style and situational control. Task-motivated leaders are effective in low- or high-control situations; relationship-motivated leaders perform best in moderate-control situations.

Based on Fiedler, F. E. "The contingency model and the dynamics of the leadership process." In L. Berkowitz (Ed.), *Advances in Experimental Social Psychology* (vol. II). New York: Academic Press, 1978.

followers in a social setting, such as the leader's home or in a local restaurant. The process of monitoring and modifying the situation must be an ongoing one as characteristics of the situation are dynamic and constantly changing.

A primary limitation of the contingency model is that it does not effectively rationalize the effectiveness of leaders who have balanced relationship/task motivations. These leaders may perform well across a wide range of situations.[30] Another limitation of the contingency model is its basic proposition that leader personality cannot be changed. (Another way to look at this limitation is as an understandable constraint caused by the inherent intractability of human personality.)

The contingency model has made significant contributions to the understanding of effective leadership. It was the first theory that confirmed the contribution of factors beyond leader personality or behavior in improving group performance. The contingency model emphasizes the importance of "knowing thyself." Leaders should have an understanding of their primary motivation (whether relationship or task) and should monitor and adjust "fit" between their style and a given situation whenever possible.

Path-Goal Theory

Another leadership theory that emphasizes characteristics of the group being led within a situational context is **path-goal theory.** Path-goal theory is concerned with the relationship between follower characteristics and leader behaviors. It is a follower-driven theory of leadership because it stresses how leader behaviors enable followers to achieve satisfaction by accomplishing their goals.

Path-goal theory: According to House and Mitchell, depending on characteristics of followers, leader behavior should be supportive, directive, participative, or achievement-oriented.

Path-goal theory states that effective leaders show consideration toward subordinates, initiate structure by clarifying paths to goals important to subordinates, and make rewards contingent on goal achievement.[31]

This version of path-goal theory was subsequently modified by Robert House and Terence Mitchell, who provided more detail regarding the fit between specific leader behaviors and specific follower needs.[32] Generally, the validity of House and Mitchell's path-goal theory predictions has been supported.[33] Path-goal theory extends our understanding of the role of leader behaviors far beyond the Ohio State and Michigan studies. This theory provides a higher degree of specificity regarding *how* leaders should behave in a given situation.

Path-goal theory, as formulated by House and Mitchell, predicts that *supportive* leader behaviors are most effective when followers are involved in boring, repetitive, or stressful tasks. *Directive* leadership is effective when the task seems ambiguous to followers who are relatively unskilled. *Participative* leader behavior is effective with followers who

This mail carrier's job is boring, repetitive, and stressful. Path-goal theory indicates that this carrier's boss should be *supportive.*

have a high need for achievement and for control of the task. Finally, an *achievement*-oriented leader sets goals and expects subordinates to perform at a high level. Achievement-oriented leader behavior is indicated when followers can reasonably be expected to work with little supervision doing relatively unstructured work.

One of the strengths of path-goal theory is that it expressly emphasizes the needs of followers in the group being led. This theory focuses on how leaders can provide structure and consideration based on characteristics of followers and the situation, and provide rewards to followers for attaining goals. (Path-goal theory is closely related to the expectancy theory of motivation; see Chapter Three, Motivation, for a discussion of this theory.)

Leader Decision Theory

Leader decision theory: According to Vroom and Yetton, subordinates should participate in decision making to the extent their contribution improves the quality of the decision, and to the extent follower acceptance of the decision is necessary.

Leader decision theory, developed by Victor Vroom and Philip Yetton, is concerned with the role and extent of follower participation in leader decision making.[34] This theory is concerned with decision making as well as leadership; consequently, it is also covered in Chapter Seven, Decision Making, of this book.

According to Vroom and Yetton, follower involvement in decision making should be dependent on two primary criteria: *quality* and *acceptance.* Subordinates should participate in decision making to the extent their contribution improves the quality of the decision, and to the extent follower acceptance of the decision is necessary. (Participation in decision making leads to follower satisfaction; see Chapter Five, Stress, for further discussion of this point.)

Determining the extent to which subordinates should be involved in decision making depends on two considerations: the source of information for the decision and the responsibility for the final decision. From these considerations, Vroom and Yetton developed a set of decision methods that range from extremely autocratic, where the leader has the information and makes the decision alone, to extremely participative, where information and ultimate decision making resides with the group. (See Figure 9–3.)

Vroom and Yetton's leader decision theory was recently revised to incorporate five situational factors: level of subordinate information, time constraints, geographical dispersion of subordinates, leader motivation to conserve time, and leader motivation to develop subordinates.[35]

The validity of the original formulation of leader decision theory has been supported in the literature.[36] This theory has made a significant contribution to understanding of leadership and decision making. The primary implication of leader decision theory is that decision quality, follower acceptance, and situational factors should be considered when deciding who to include in decision making.

Relationships among Leaders and Followers

This section on group considerations will be concluded with a discussion of some of the relationships that evolve among leaders and followers within a group.

Figure 9–3 Leader Decision Theory

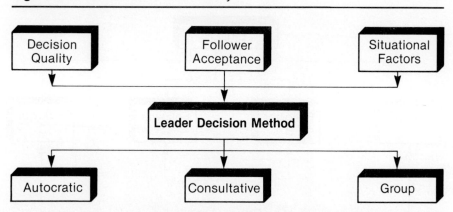

Decision making should become more participatory as the leader requires more information and/or follower satisfaction (an outcome of participation) is necessary.

Leader-member exchange model: Asserts that leaders develop different types of relationships with different followers, resulting in the development of in-groups and out-groups.

Leader-Member Exchange.   Traditional theories of leadership tend to focus on the relationship between the leader and the group as a whole. George Graen and his associates have developed the **leader-member exchange model** to explain the relationships that exist between leaders and individual followers.[37]

This theory places an emphasis on the notion that leaders develop different types of relationships with followers, resulting in the development of in-groups and out-groups. (See Figure 9–4.) Over time, in-group members are given greater attention, information, and responsibility by the leader. Out-group members, in contrast, are less trusted and given less support and less information.

As the relationship develops, in-group members are given more autonomy and access to decision making compared to out-group members. In return for this privileged status, in-group members show greater loyalty and commitment to group success. Compared to out-group members, in-group members are more involved in representing the group to other groups and individuals, and are more likely to serve as volunteers.

Research evaluating the performance of in-group and out-group members indicates in-group member performance is judged to be more effective only when measured by the leader.[38] In spite of this weakness, the leader-member exchange model provides important insights into the leader/individual follower relationship. We know that preferential treatment not only occurs, but is actually institutionalized in organizations.

Figure 9–4 The Leader-Member Exchange Model

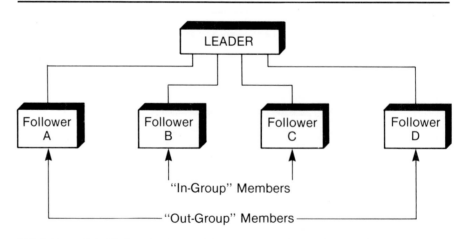

In-group members receive greater attention and support from the leader, whereas out-group members are treated more formally.

Leader Emergence. Often, leaders are not appointed but emerge in a group. **Leader emergence** occurs whenever group members convey authority to a group member by virtue of his or her contribution to the group.

Research indicates that individuals who are more verbally active in a group are more likely to be selected as a leader.[39] In fact, up to a point, quantity of participation is more important than quality of participation in terms of leader selection by members.[40] One explanation for this finding is that participation is interpreted as an index of interest in the group's mission. Active group members are viewed as being more willing to take on the added responsibilities associated with leadership.[41]

Effective leaders, however, are competent as well as actively involved. Members whose participation is irrelevant to achieving group goals are not likely to achieve leadership positions. A longitudinal study of managerial careers, for example, found that competence plays an important role in the prediction of career progression into leadership positions.[42]

Leader emergence: Occurs whenever group members convey authority to a group member by virtue of their contribution to the group.

Tips for the Manager. The implications of different leadership theories are diverse. For the contingency model, the leadership situation (which includes leader-member relationships) should be managed and adjusted to match the leader's style. Path-goal theory suggests that follower characteristics should determine the most effective leader behavior. Leader decision theory suggests that leaders should take into account quality, follower acceptance, and the nature of the situation when deciding who to include in decision making.

An implication of leader-exchange theory is for leaders to avoid playing favorites. Followers who feel left out will demonstrate relatively less loyalty and commitment to the group. Implications of research on leader emergence suggests that managers should carefully assess the quality as well as quantity of subordinate input into a group process. Leaders should not be selected just on the basis of activity.

LEADERSHIP AND THE ORGANIZATION

Naval commanders once had the right to keel-haul and lash errant sailors, and could promote or demote sailors on the spot. Naval commanders are no longer given these leadership rights. The modern naval organization has changed. Promotions and demotions must be approved by a central authority and disciplinary action is subject to military codes and courts. Changing technology, societal values, economics, and government regulation has a significant impact on the way a leader functions within an organization.

The influence of organizational characteristics on leadership was first described in impersonal, formal, and relatively rigid terms by Max Weber.[43] Since Weber, researchers have come to recognize that many different organizational characteristics exist that influence leadership.

Organizational Characteristics

Organizational characteristics: Pertains to the leader's position in the organizational hierarchy, the nature of the leader's jobs, and the nature of the organizational environment.

Organizational characteristics pertaining to the leader's position in the hierarchy, the nature of the leader's job, and the nature of the organization all influence leadership. Organizational characteristics can even serve as a substitute or a supplement, or can enhance the formal leadership role envisioned by Weber.

Hierarchical Considerations.   The leader's position in the organization significantly affects leader activities. Managers at higher levels of the organization tend to be more concerned with broad policy issues and future-oriented issues than lower-level managers who focus on interpreting policy and monitoring work flow.[44] One study of assignments for lower-, middle-, and upper-level managers found that managers were more involved in planning, evaluating, and general managerial activities, and less involved in direct supervision, as level in the organizational hierarchy increased.[45] (See Figure 9–5).

Other studies show that lower-level managers tend to be less participative than upper-level managers.[46] This may be due to the restricted latitude first-line supervisors have to implement work procedures, a high degree of time pressure to accomplish tasks, and the lack of authority to respond to employee concerns. The relatively prescriptive behavior pattern of first-line supervisors is likely to change with the times. (See the boxed insert below.)

First-Line Supervisors in the 21st Century

Work is changing. Computers and automated production processes have proliferated into every nook and cranny of the modern organization. The workforce is more highly educated. Competition in the marketplace is fierce. The importance of human resources to business's bottom-line is being increasingly recognized. How will these trends affect the first-line supervisor?

Some researchers predict that first-line supervisors will become more involved in counseling, nurturing, and group facilita-

Figure 9–5 Managerial Tasks and Organizational Level

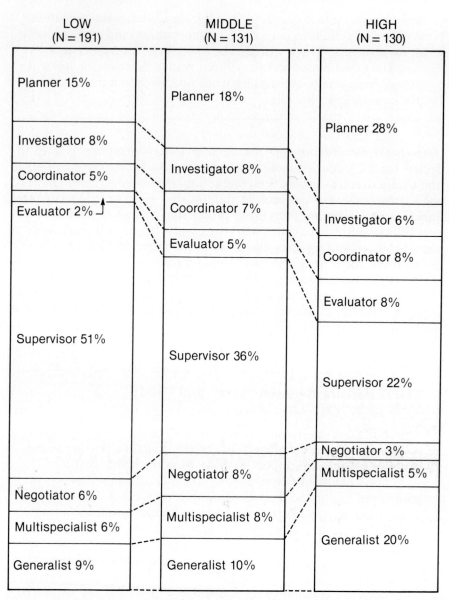

Totals do not add up to 100 percent because of rounding.

Tasks differ as a result of the leader's position in an organizational hierarchy. Notice that higher-level managers tend to be more involved with planning than lower-level managers, who spend more time supervising.

Reprinted with permission from Mahoney, T. A.; Jerdee, T. H.; & Carroll, S. I. "The job(s) of management." *Industrial Relations, 4* (1965): 97–110.

tion in a workplace characterized by more worker participation, work-group self-direction, access to information, and staff specialist involvement. There will also be fewer first-line supervisors.[47]

The first-line supervisor will not vanish. Instead, the job will change from one of controlling work processes to a more consultive human relations role.

Functional Considerations. Leadership in organizations is also affected by the leader's function or what the leader *does* (e.g., whether the leader oversees production, marketing, customer service activities, etc.). One review of research evaluating the effects of departmental function on leadership found that production managers tend to be engaged in directing behavior, supervising work, handling disturbances in the work flow, and working closely with subordinates. Sales managers, in contrast, spend much of their time outside the organization developing sales contacts and spend relatively little time with subordinates.

Leaders in staff departments tend to use participation more than either production or sales managers. They tend to work alone and spend more time working on paperwork. (Much of the staff manager's role is to provide technical advice to other parts of the organization.)[48]

The Difference Between "Line" and "Staff"

Line positions are imbued with decision-making authority that relates directly to the purpose of the organization. Staff positions provide specialized support to those working in line positions.

The CEO, the highest-ranking *line* manager in a business organization, cannot do it all. For example, the CEO of a baseball bat manufacturer may ask *staff* members in human resources to locate candidates for a marketing manager position. The newly hired marketing manager, employed in a *line* position, in turn, may find it necessary to hire *staff* specialists to help conduct marketing research.

Locating candidates for a managerial position and conducting market research do not relate directly to building and actually selling baseball bats. However, specialized staff support helps line managers, such as the CEO and marketing manager, to avoid "striking out."

Finally, a recent study comparing line and staff managers in the same organization found that line managers were more likely to believe that organizing and directing others was desirable and that managerial control over rewards was important to motivation.[49]

Environmental Considerations. The environment of an organization also affects the leader's role. By *environment*, we mean all of the political, legal, demographic, social, technological, economic, and physical influences that affect the organization.

Unstable environments require flexible management, whereas stable conditions require well-structured management.[50] If an organization operates in a stable environment, characterized by stable production processes and markets, then less leadership is necessary.[51] In a turbulent environment, varied leadership behavior is most effective. Also, lower-level managers are more likely to be involved in decision making in turbulent environments, relative to managers working in organizations with stable environments.

One factor that can lead to the instability of a work unit's environment is *task interdependence*. Task interdependence exists to the extent that the unit's activities need to be adjusted to fit the needs of other units. When work activities are interdependent, leaders spend greater amounts of time communicating with other managers, negotiating, and engaging in political activities, especially when resources are scarce. Under these conditions, leaders are expected by subordinates to represent the interests of the group.[52] (See Chapter Four, Conflict and Its Management, for further discussion of interdependent groups.)

Substitutes for Leadership

Characteristics of an organization sometimes serve as **substitutes for leadership.**[53] (This concept was discussed previously when it was noted that the technical expertise of a pilot could substitute for a pilot's personal motives; see page 263.) Clear organizational reward systems, for example, can substitute for leader goal-setting activities. In this case, the leader does not need to formalize goals because the reward structure already provides clear direction for subordinates. Formal procedures and written rules can substitute for leader initiation of structure. In this instance, the leader does not need to initiate structure because formal procedures and written rules already provide structure. (See Figure 9–6.)

Recently the notion of leader substitutes has been expanded to include leader "supplements" and "enhancers."[54] Leader supplements do not replace leader behaviors, as do substitutes. Instead, leader supplements add to the leader's efforts. For example, feedback from customer contact might be considered a leader supplement in that it provides information to sales personnel beyond the feedback a sales manager can provide. Leader enhancers increase the leader's influence on a

Substitutes for leadership: Organizational and follower characteristics, such as reward systems and experience and training of followers, that substitute for actions of the leader.

Figure 9–6 Substitutes for Leadership

Characteristics Listed Below Will Substitute for Leadership which Is . . .	People-Centered	Task-Centered
Characteristics of Subordinates:		
1. Ability, experience, knowledge		x
2. Indifference towards organizational rewards	x	x
Characteristics of the Task:		
1. Routine, unambiguous		x
2. Direct feedback provided		x
3. Intrinsically satisfying	x	
Characteristics of the Organization		
1. Formalized (e.g., explicit plans)		x
2. Inflexibility		x
3. Cohesive work group	x	x
4. Rewards outside of leader's control	x	x
5. Superiors and subordinates physically separated	x	x

Characteristics of subordinates, tasks, and organizations can substitute for leadership. For example, task-centered leadership is unnecessary to the extent able followers are experienced and knowledgeable.

Adapted from Kerr, S., & Jermier, J. M. "Substitutes for leadership their meaning and measurement." *Organizational Behavior and Human Performance, 22* (1978): 375–403.

group. Organizations that give the leader control over reward systems, for example, provide the leader with an enhancer.

Leader substitutes, supplements, and enhancers play an important role in influencing the leader's impact on a group. It is important for managers to recognize that leadership activities are moderated and otherwise influenced by organizational characteristics pertaining to organizational structure, policies, and procedures.

Tips for the Manager. Organizational considerations affect leadership in a number of ways.

Position in the organizational hierarchy influences a leader's activities. Higher-level managerial jobs require more attention to planning, compared to supervisory management positions. Line-supervisors should be more concerned with the directing function of management.

Environmental conditions also influence leader activities. Managers should take into account the degree of turbulence in the organizational environment. As organizational turbulence increases, leaders lower in the organization should become more involved in decision making. Also, as task interdependence increases, more communication should take place between departments or units of the organization.

Finally, various characteristics of the organization substitute, supplement, or enhance the effects of leader behavior. Identifying what characteristics operate in an organization can help a leader direct his or her behavior more effectively and efficiently.

SUMMARY: FOCUS ON SKILLS

Leadership is defined as the relationship between an individual (the leader) and a group (or groups) of followers in which goal attainment of the group is influenced by the leader. Effective leadership is defined in terms of the productivity of the group being led. A leader is effective to the extent that his or her influence on a group results in the desired level of group productivity.

Following are 18 suggestions for improving the quality of leadership.

Managers should:

1. See themselves as leaders, regardless of formal position in the organization. Expertise and referent power also significantly affect the propensity of people to follow a leader.
2. Understand that leadership is a dynamic, multidimensional process. Effective leaders attend to leader, follower, and situational characteristics.
3. Learn skills associated with effective leadership (e.g., skills pertaining to communication, conflict management, performance appraisal, decision making, and motivation). Study the other chapters of this book!
4. Remember that leader intelligence enhances group productivity to the extent that the leader is assertive, experiences little stress, and has group support.
5. If leading other leaders, provide a supportive atmosphere so these leaders can effectively use their intelligence. In highly stressful situations, select experienced leaders.
6. According to dictates of transformational leadership, provide

followers with a vision of possible futures, stimulate their thinking, and be supportive.

7. Have goals that are congruent with the organization's goals. Motivation to manage predicts leader success only if the leader's goals fit the goals of the organization.

8. Don't forget the importance of the situation! Change situational elements such as leader-member relations, task structure, and position power to match leadership style (e.g., task-motivated or relationship-motivated).

9. Match leader behavior with follower needs. Provide support for followers doing boring tasks, direction for unskilled followers doing ambiguous tasks, participation for achievement-oriented followers, and a goal-directed achievement orientation when followers require little or no direction.

10. Convene a decision-making group or otherwise solicit information from individual subordinates, if followers have information that enhances the quality of the decision, and/or if subordinate acceptance of the decision is necessary.

11. Adopt and adapt group leadership approaches that best fit a particular leadership situation. Appreciate that no one model or theory applies in all situations.

12. Avoid playing favorites. Followers who feel left out demonstrate relatively less loyalty and commitment.

13. Carefully assess the quality as well as quantity of participation of prospective leaders. Avoid selecting leaders just on the basis of high activity.

14. Keep in mind that hierarchical rank in an organization affects leader behavior. For example, higher-level managers should be more involved in planning activities relative to line supervisors.

15. Know that functional specialty influences leader beliefs and behavior. Relative to staff managers, line managers tend to be more directive and believe in structuring the work of subordinates.

16. Provide for active subordinate participation to the extent the organizational situation is turbulent. Autocratic leadership is relatively ineffective under turbulent circumstances.

17. Actively communicate with other organizational leaders when tasks are interdependent between organizational units.

18. Assess characteristics of the situation to determine substitutes, supplements, and enhancements for leadership in order to best direct your efforts.

■ CASE: "THE BRAINS"

"Listen, Mitch, I'll do all the thinking; you just do as you're told," Don shouted. Mitch shrugged and rejoined his co-workers on the loading platform. Ever since he had become familiar with the routine in the package express and baggage department at the bus terminal, Mitch had been discovering procedures that seemed inefficient. He had thought his supervisor would at least listen to his suggestions for improvements.

The workers laughed as Tim Brooks mimicked Don, "I got all the brains around here." Mitch laughed and sat down. "Well, that's the last time I ever make a helpful suggestion. From now on, I'll do exactly what Don says—even when I know he's wrong."

"Hey, Mitch," Tim said, stopping his laughter for a moment, "why is Don so uptight? What did you say to him anyway?"

"Oh, I just told him we wouldn't have to be busy as we are sometimes and twiddling our thumbs other times if we just changed a couple of procedures. But he didn't even want to listen to my ideas; he didn't give me a chance.

"Just once I'd like to hear him say, 'Hey, that sounds like a good idea. Let's try it and see if it works. If it does, well do it that way from now on.' "

Don looked up from his work and saw the crew sitting idle. He knew the work was light right now, but there were still a few things to be done. He resented workers who goofed off one minute and started telling him how to run things the next. And he felt that Mitch was presumptuous to make suggestions when he had been on the job for only two months. Angry and impatient, Don glanced quickly at his work schedule and strode out to the dock.

"O.K., let's get going. Mitch, that's the 10:06 from D.C. You're in charge of unloading. Let's get that baggage in here pronto." Don went back to his office, congratulating himself on the way he had controlled his temper. He hoped that putting Mitch in charge would show him that Don didn't hold anything against him. Don recognized Mitch's leadership abilities, and he didn't want to alienate a good worker.

While Don busied himself with paperwork, Mitch glanced at the other workers. "He said to unload it, right?"

"That's what he said."

"O.K., everybody, we're going to unload it—even though it's not the 10:06 from D.C. We'll let Don do the thinking, and we'll do the unloading. Since that's the way he wants it, that's the way he's going to get it."

"Hey, Mitch, do you think we should do this? Don will have a coronary when he finds out this stuff should have been transferred. . . ."

"I'll do the thinking around here, Brooks," Mitch mocked.

The crew laughed sardonically as they busied themselves unloading the luggage. They hoped Don would be jolted off his high horse when he started getting angry phone calls from people whose baggage was lost or delayed.

Case Questions

1. What has Don done to "earn" his leadership status in the group? How might he improve his position in the group?
2. How does Don's behavior influence follower motivation?
3. Given his task-oriented leadership style, what could Don do to make the situation work for him?

■ EXERCISE: "RESULTS-ORIENTED LEADERSHIP"

In this exercise your instructor will assign you to a production unit in a paper airplane manufacturing company. One person in your unit will be designated as the Unit Manager, who has responsibility for planning, organizing, directing, and controlling for your unit. All unit members report to the Unit Manager. The primary objective of your unit is to produce as many paper airplanes as you can in the time allotted. Other units will also be working at the same time.

Your unit manager will inform you of your production task at the appropriate time.

ENDNOTES

1. Carlyle, T. *Heroes and Hero Worship.* Boston: Adams, 1907.

2. Bass, B. M. *Stogdill's Handbook of Leadership: A Survey of Theory and Research.* New York: Free Press, 1981.

3. Hersey, P., & Blanchard, K. "Life cycle theory of leadership." *Training and Development Journal,* 23 (1969): 26–34.

4. French, J. P., & Raven, B. "The bases of social power." In D. Cartwright (Ed.), *Studies in Social Power.* Ann Arbor: University of Michigan Institute for Social Research, 1959.

5. Yukl, G. A. *Leadership in Organizations.* Englewood Cliffs, NJ: Prentice-Hall, 1981.

6. French and Raven, "The bases of social power."

7. Bass, *Stogdill's Handbook.*

8. Fiedler, F. E., & Garcia, J. E. *New Approaches to Leadership: Cognitive Resources and Organizational Performance.* New York: John Wiley & Sons, 1987.

9. Ibid.

10. Sarason, I. G. "Stress, anxiety, and cognitive interference: Reaction to tests." *Journal of Personality and Social Psychology, 46* (1984): 929–938. See also: Zajonc, R. B. "Social facilitation." *Science, 149* (1965): 269–274.

11. Weber, M. *The Theory of Social and Economic Organization.* New York: Oxford University Press, 1947.

12. Bass, B. M. *Leadership and Performance Beyond Expectations.* New York: Free Press, 1985.

13. Ibid.

14. Ibid.

15. Waldman, D. A.; Bass, B. M.; & Einstein, W. O. "Leadership and outcomes of performance appraisal processes." *Journal of Occupational Psychology, 60* (1987): 177–186.

16. Meir, G. *My Life.* New York: G. P. Putnam's Sons, 1975. See also: Slater, R. *Golda: The Uncrowned Queen of Israel.* New York: Jonathan David Publishers, Inc., 1981.

17. Miner, J. B. "Twenty years of research on role motivation theory of managerial effectiveness." *Personnel Psychology, 31* (1978): 79–760.

18. McClelland, D. M. *Power: The Inner Experience.* New York: Irvington-Halstead-Wiley, 1975.

19. McClelland, D. C., & Burham, D. "Power is the great motivator." *Harvard Business Review, 25* (1976): 159–166.

20. McClelland, D. C., & Boyatzis, R. E. "Leadership motive pattern and long term success in management." *Journal of Applied Psychology, 67* (1982): 737–743.

21. Winter, D. M. "Leader appeal, leader performance, and the motive profiles of leaders and followers: A study of American presidents and elections." *Journal of Personality and Social Psychology, 52* (1987): 196–202.

22. Kerr, S., & Jermier, J. M. "Substitutes for leadership: Their meaning and measurement." *Organizational Behavior and Human Performance, 22* (1978): 375–403.

23. Fleishman, E. A.; Harris, E. F.; & Burtt, H. E. *Leadership and Supervision in Industry.* Columbus: Ohio State University, 1955. See also: Stogdill, R. M., & Coons, A. E. "Leader behavior: Its description and measurement." *Research Monograph No. 88.* Columbus: Ohio State University, 1957; and Korman, A. " 'Consideration,' 'initiating structure,' and organizational criteria—a review." *Personnel Psychology, 19* (1969): 349–362.

24. Szilagyi, A. D., & Wallace, M. *Organizational Behavior and Performance.* Santa Monica, CA: Goodyear Publishing Co., 1980.

25. Blake, R. R., & Mouton, J. S. *The Managerial Grid III: The Key to Leadership Excellence*. Houston, TX: Gulf, 1985.

26. Blake, R. R., & Mouton, J. S. "Theory and research for developing a science of leadership." *Journal of Applied Behavioral Science, 18* (1982): 275–291.

27. Fiedler, F. E. *A Theory of Leadership Effectiveness*. New York: McGraw-Hill, 1967.

28. Strube, M. J., & Garcia, J. E. "A meta-analytic investigation of Fiedler's contingency model of leadership effectiveness." *Psychological Bulletin, 90* (1981): 307–321. See also: Peters, L. H.; Hartke, D. D.; & Pohlman, J. T. "Fiedler's contingency theory of leadership: An application of the meta-analysis procedure of Schmidt and Hunter." *Psychological Bulletin, 97* (1985): 274–285.

29. Fiedler, F. E., & Chemers, M. M. *Improving Leadership Effectiveness: The Leader Match Concept* (2nd ed.). New York: John Wiley & Sons, 1984.

30. Kennedy, J. K. "Middle LPC leaders and the contingency model of leadership effectiveness." *Organizational Behavior and Human Performance, 39* (1982): 1–14.

31. Evans, M. G. "The effects of supervisory behavior on the path-goal relationship." *Organizational Behavior and Human Performance, 55* (1970): 277–298.

32. House, R. J., & Mitchell, T. R. "Path-goal theory of leadership." *Journal of Contempory Business, 3* (1974): 81–97. See also: House, R. J. "A path-goal theory of leader effectiveness." *Administrative Science Quarterly, 16* (1971): 321–338.

33. Indvik, J. "Path-goal theory of leadership: A meta-analysis." In J. A. Pearce & R. B. Robinson, Jr. (Eds.), *Academy of Management Best Papers Proceedings*. Chicago: Academy of Management, 1986, pp. 189–192.

34. Vroom, V. H., & Yetton, P. W. *Leadership and Decision Making*. Pittsburgh, PA: University of Pittsburgh Press, 1973. See also: Vroom, V. H., & Jago, A. G. *The New Leadership: Managing Participation in Organizations*. Englewood Cliffs, NJ: Prentice-Hall, 1988.

35. Jago, A. G.; Ettling, J. T.; & Vroom, V. "Validating a revision to the Vroom/Yetton model." *Academy of Management Proceedings, 45* (1985): 220.

36. Field, R. H. "A test of the Vroom-Yetton normative model of leadership." *Journal of Applied Psychology, 67* (1982): 523–532.

37. Graen, G., & Cashman, J. F. "A role-making model of leadership in formal organizations: A developmental approach." In J. G. Hunt & L. L. Larson (Eds.), *Leadership Frontiers*. Kent, OH: Kent State University Press, 1975.

38. Dienesch, R. M., & Liden, R. C. "Leader-member exchange model of leadership: A critique and further development." *Academy of Management Review, 11* (1986): 618–634.

39. Bass, *Stogdill's Handbook*.

40. Sorrentino, R. M., & Boutillier, R. G. "The effect of quality and quantity of verbal interaction on ratings of leadership ability." *Journal of Experimental Social Psychology, 11* (1975): 403–411.

41. Hollander, E. P. *Leadership Dynamics: A Practical Guide to Effective Relationships*. New York: Free Press, 1978.

42. Bray, D. W.; Campbell, R. J.; & Grant, D. L. *Formative Years in Business: A Long Term AT&T Study of Managerial Lives*. New York: Wiley-Interscience, 1978.

43. Weber, *Theory of Social and Economic Organization*.

44. See Bass, *Stogdill's Handbook*, and Yukl, *Leadership in Organizations*.

45. Mahoney, T. A.; Jerdee, T. H.; & Carroll, S. I. "The job(s) of management." *Industrial Relations, 4* (1965): 97–110.

46. Yukl, *Leadership in Organizations*.

47. Kerr, S.; Hill, K. D.; & Broedling, L. "The first-line supervisor: Phasing out or here to stay?" *Academy of Management Review, 11* (1986): 103–117.

48. Yukl, *Leadership in Organizations*.

49. Nystrom, P. C. "Comparing beliefs of line and technostructural managers." *Academy of Management Review, 29* (1986): 812–819.

50. Burns, T., & Stalker, G. M. *The Management of Innovation*. Chicago: Quadrangle Books, 1961.

51. Bass, *Stogdill's Handbook*.

52. Yukl, *Leadership in Organizations*.

53. Kerr & Jermier, "Substitutes for leadership."

54. Howell, J. P.; Dorfman, P. W.; & Kerr, S. "Moderator variables in leadership research." *Academy of Management Review, 11* (1986): 88–102.

CHAPTER TEN

Organization Development

- ■ *Self-Assessment: "Growth Needs"*
- ■ *Learning about Organization Development*
- ■ *Case: "The Incredible Rumor"*
- ■ *Exercise: "Force Field Analysis"*

■ SELF-ASSESSMENT: "GROWTH NEEDS"

For each question, two different kinds of jobs are briefly described. You are to indicate which of the jobs you personally would prefer—if you had to make a choice between them.

In answering each question, assume that everything else about the jobs is the same. Pay attention only to the characteristics actually listed.

Two examples are given below.

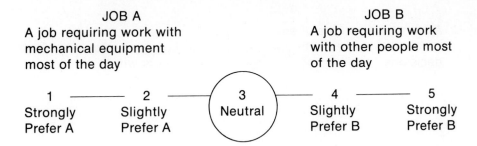

JOB A			JOB B	
A job requiring work with mechanical equipment most of the day			A job requiring work with other people most of the day	
1	2	3	4	5
Strongly Prefer A	Slightly Prefer A	Neutral	Slightly Prefer B	Strongly Prefer B

If you like working with people and working with equipment equally well, you would circle the number 3, as has been done in the example.

Here is another example. This one asks for a harder choice—between two jobs which both have some undesirable features.

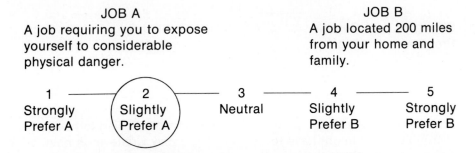

JOB A			JOB B	
A job requiring you to expose yourself to considerable physical danger.			A job located 200 miles from your home and family.	
1	2	3	4	5
Strongly Prefer A	Slightly Prefer A	Neutral	Slightly Prefer B	Strongly Prefer B

If you would slightly prefer risking physical danger to working far from your home, you would circle number 2, as has been done in the example.

Please ask for assistance if you do not understand exactly how to do these questions.

JOB A

JOB B

1. A job where the pay is very
   good.

A job where there is
considerable oppor-
tunity to be creative
and innovative.

1	2	3	4	5
Strongly Prefer A	Slightly Prefer A	Neutral	Slightly Prefer B	Strongly Prefer B

2. A job where you are often
   required to make important
   decisions.

A job with many
pleasant people to
work with.

1	2	3	4	5
Strongly Prefer A	Slightly Prefer A	Neutral	Slightly Prefer B	Strongly Prefer B

3. A job in which greater
   responsibility is given to
   those who do the best work.

A job in which greater
responsibility is given
to loyal employees
who have the most
seniority.

1	2	3	4	5
Strongly Prefer A	Slightly Prefer A	Neutral	Slightly Prefer B	Strongly Prefer B

4. A job in an organization
   which is in financial
   trouble—and might have to
   close down within the year.

A job in which you are
not allowed to have any
say whatever in how
your work is scheduled,
or in the procedures to
be used in carrying
it out.

1	2	3	4	5
Strongly Prefer A	Slightly Prefer A	Neutral	Slightly Prefer B	Strongly Prefer B

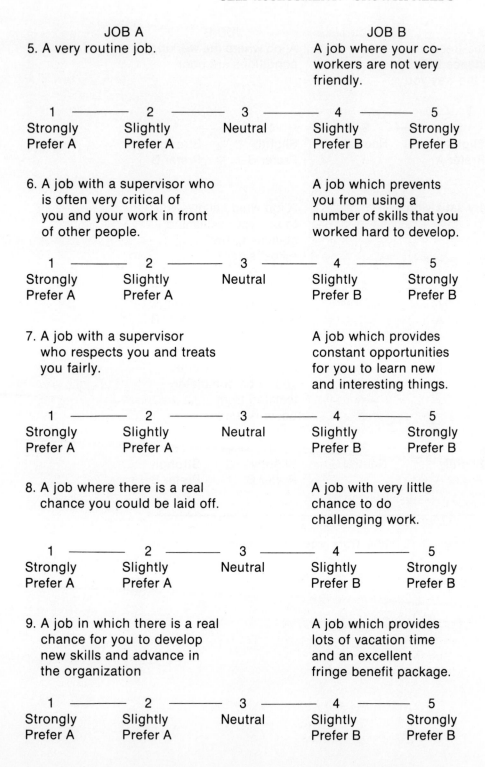

JOB A
5. A very routine job.

JOB B
A job where your co-workers are not very friendly.

1 ———— 2 ———— 3 ———— 4 ———— 5
Strongly   Slightly   Neutral   Slightly   Strongly
Prefer A   Prefer A   Prefer B   Prefer B

6. A job with a supervisor who is often very critical of you and your work in front of other people.

A job which prevents you from using a number of skills that you worked hard to develop.

1 ———— 2 ———— 3 ———— 4 ———— 5
Strongly   Slightly   Neutral   Slightly   Strongly
Prefer A   Prefer A   Prefer B   Prefer B

7. A job with a supervisor who respects you and treats you fairly.

A job which provides constant opportunities for you to learn new and interesting things.

1 ———— 2 ———— 3 ———— 4 ———— 5
Strongly   Slightly   Neutral   Slightly   Strongly
Prefer A   Prefer A   Prefer B   Prefer B

8. A job where there is a real chance you could be laid off.

A job with very little chance to do challenging work.

1 ———— 2 ———— 3 ———— 4 ———— 5
Strongly   Slightly   Neutral   Slightly   Strongly
Prefer A   Prefer A   Prefer B   Prefer B

9. A job in which there is a real chance for you to develop new skills and advance in the organization

A job which provides lots of vacation time and an excellent fringe benefit package.

1 ———— 2 ———— 3 ———— 4 ———— 5
Strongly   Slightly   Neutral   Slightly   Strongly
Prefer A   Prefer A   Prefer B   Prefer B

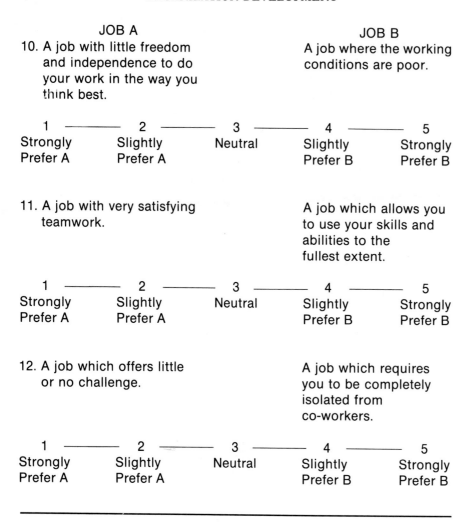

JOB A
JOB B

10. A job with little freedom and independence to do your work in the way you think best.

A job where the working conditions are poor.

1 ——— 2 ——— 3 ——— 4 ——— 5

Strongly Prefer A   Slightly Prefer A   Neutral   Slightly Prefer B   Strongly Prefer B

11. A job with very satisfying teamwork.

A job which allows you to use your skills and abilities to the fullest extent.

1 ——— 2 ——— 3 ——— 4 ——— 5

Strongly Prefer A   Slightly Prefer A   Neutral   Slightly Prefer B   Strongly Prefer B

12. A job which offers little or no challenge.

A job which requires you to be completely isolated from co-workers.

1 ——— 2 ——— 3 ——— 4 ——— 5

Strongly Prefer A   Slightly Prefer A   Neutral   Slightly Prefer B   Strongly Prefer B

Hackman, J. R., & Oldham, G. R. (1980). *Work redesign.* Reading, MA: Addison-Wesley Publishing Co.

■ LEARNING ABOUT ORGANIZATION DEVELOPMENT

Andcom's rise to prominence was meteoric. Starting in her garage, Sheila Weeks built the communications company from scratch. Now, the company is international, has over 3,000 employees on the payroll, and grosses more than $167 million per year.

For the first seven years, all went smoothly at Andcom. However, the rapid growth, expansion into new countries, and change in technology soon took their toll. Andcom's executive team acknowledged at a recent staff meeting that morale was poor, quality was suffering at the newest facilities, and profits were slipping even though market studies had confirmed a high demand for Andcom's products. The management team concluded that they needed to plan to cope with the pressures of a turbulent environment and rapidly growing company.

The management team decided to create an organization development department to study the company's problems—its technology and systems, hierarchy, work groups, reporting lines, turnover, productivity, and profits. The organization development staff would be responsible for making recommendations and preparing appropriate programs to get Andcom back on track.

Although fictitious, the story about Andcom is typical of real dilemmas that organizations face. Organizations change. They change not only for their own internal needs but also in order to better serve customers in an environment characterized by technological advances, economic demands, and competition. Adapting to these demands requires that successful organizations constantly plan and carry out necessary change at the individual, group, and organizational levels.[1] In short, successful organizations are concerned with **organization development (OD).**

WHAT IS ORGANIZATION DEVELOPMENT?

Organization development (OD) is the implementation of planned interventions designed to manage change effectively. Warren Bennis calls OD "a response to change, a complex educational strategy intended to change the beliefs, attitudes, values, and structure of organizations so that they can better adapt to new technologies, markets, and challenges, and the dizzying rate of change itself."[2] The focus of OD is on the organization itself. When well-implemented, **OD programs** improve an organization's ability to solve problems and to adapt. Well-constructed OD programs also improve quality of life for employees.

Organization development: The implementation of planned interventions designed to manage change effectively.

OD programs: Consists of three components: diagnosis, intervention, and evaluation.

Commentary: "Organization Development"

Tom Green

Fred Meyer recently changed chief executive officers. The new CEO, F. M. Stevens, determined that change was needed if the company, and the people within it, were to realize their potential. From a series of two-day workshops, Fred Meyer's top 32 executives developed a strategic plan. The goals and objectives included in the plan required extensive organizational change.

Through a series of workshops, managers at every level and from all divisions learned the importance of sharing the new corporate mission, vision, goals, and strategies with company employees. Managers were charged with the responsibility of enabling employees to achieve personal goals compatible with newly formed corporate direction. The overall effectiveness of this process is that corporate goals and objectives addressed in the newly created strategic plan will be achieved in thousands of small bits, each time by the employee responsible. Consequently, it became crucial that managers create an environment where "ownership" occurs with every employee in the company.

Having spent a good deal of time with the employees of Fred Meyer, I am confident that the specific objectives of the plan will be met. Managing the chaos inherent in any major organizational change is never easy. There will be dropouts, casualties, and setbacks. There will be "winners" and "losers." There will be fairness and, at times, "unfairness." However, there will also be important challenges successfully met. Eventually a stronger organization will emerge.

This chapter relates that "where impor-

tant changes in the life of an organization are being considered, there are seldom simple solutions." Organizations are complicated. Despite the inevitable difficulties, top management, as is stated in the chapter, must remain committed to maintaining the health of their organization. Doing this effectively requires that top management regularly take time to listen to feedback from the lower ranks.

In this regard, the process of evaluation is extremely important during the course of organizational change. The burden is heavy at every level of an organization during times of change and upheaval. Perhaps more attention should be given to evaluation than was initially given to planning and implementation. Coaching and feedback skills require review and must be drawn out of supervisors throughout the entire organization.

All major organizational changes concern people and their personal orientation to their workplace. Personal goals and directions are directly challenged and vitalized. Organizational change remains a growth experience. Management skills facilitating the process can be the measure of success or failure. Organizational change deals with "growth." Though growth, at times, seems painful, it still remains necessary to the ongoing health of the organization.

To close, it is my sincere hope that the employees of Fred Meyer can achieve and maintain their vision of being "the most creative, customer-respected, financially responsible retailer in America."

Tom Green

Tom Green worked for Fred Meyer for 13 years. He began, after college, as a management trainee in General Merchandise, moved up through store operations to become General Merchandise Manager and Divisional Productivity Manager. After spending a year as Divisional Productivity Manager, Tom assumed the duties of Hardlines District Manager where he was responsible for expanded store operations involving General Merchandise and Home Improvement Centers. In this capacity, Tom supervised 15 store managers. In the summer of 1989, Tom left Fred Meyer to accept a position with Senn-Delaney Management Consultants in Long Beach, California.

Tom earned a BA in liberal arts from the Evergreen State College (Olympia, WA) in 1973. He is committed to promoting personal growth through positive, supportive leadership.

OD programs involve three different components: diagnosis, intervention, and evaluation. *Diagnosis* determines where change is needed and what kind of change will best serve organizational needs. *Interventions* stimulate and focus change; *evaluation* determines the success of change and the need for future interventions. (See Figure 10–1.)

OD programs help individuals and groups to be aware of organizational objectives, to evaluate needs, to diagnose impediments that are frustrating goal achievement, to reevaluate needs, to learn necessary skills through training, and to implement change.

Change Agents

OD programs are usually facilitated by a **change agent**—a consultant or facilitator who moves participants from all organizational levels through each phase of the change process. Since the 1970s, an increasing number of organizations have relied on the use of internal change agents (rather than external consultants).[3] Today, most of the Fortune 500 companies have one or more OD specialists.[4] OD has become a necessity rather than a luxury in competitive, healthy organizations. Often, human resource and training managers take on the role of change agent and practice some form of OD as part of their normal duties.[5]

Change agent: A consultant or facilitator who facilitates change in an organization.

Managers as Change Agents. Midmanagers are important change agents. As the vital link between top and supervisory management,

Figure 10–1 The Process of Organization Development

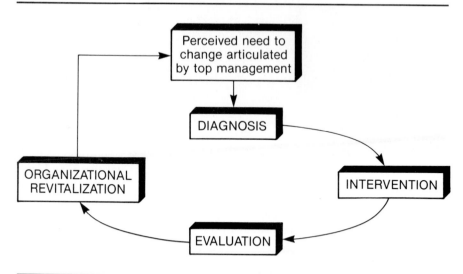

All organization development programs should be managed from the top and provide a means of diagnosing needs, planning and carrying out interventions, and conducting evaluation at all levels of the organization. The process of OD leads to organizational revitalization and should be regarded as cyclical.

Unfreezing, Moving, and Refreezing: Lewin's Change Process

In 1946, Kurt Lewin and several colleagues pioneered unstructured, small-group laboratory training to help individuals change. Lewin and his colleagues found that small-group discussion sessions provided participants more insight into individual and group behavior than did lectures and seminars.

These small-group, unstructured training sessions facilitated change. Participants seemed to accept new ideas and organizational change more readily.

Lewin described change in organizations as a three-step process, requiring: (1) "unfreezing" old systems through training, (2) "moving" toward more effective participative systems through the intervention of change agents, and (3) "refreezing" these new systems through reinforcement provided by the organization.[6]

midmanagers provide for supervisor needs and serve as role models. Midmanagers spend a great deal of time making sure that supervisors are properly trained, have correct up-to-date information, perform as expected, and are satisfied with their jobs.

Top-management commitment is essential to the success of an OD program. As with our fictitious company, Andcom, many OD programs start with a realization by top management that change is necessary. Although the top echelon is not the only place where change can be initiated, it is the place where *major* changes should begin. OD programs should be *managed from the top*.[7]

Major organization changes require reallocation of resources and top-management commitment to succeed. If top management does not support change, support dwindles and lower-tier managers and workers end up ignoring change or attending to alternate priorities. Successful OD programs are also deliberate, well thought out, and supported at all levels of the organization. They can be proactive as well as reactive. That is, OD programs help a company to ready itself for growth and change or to overcome the potentially negative effects of rapid growth and change.

A Caveat. As you probably have noticed, this book treats each topic *from the bottom up;* that is, from the individual, to the group, and then to the organizational level. However, as noted, OD programs are planned and carried out organizationwide, *from the top down.* As you read this chapter, keep in mind that, regardless of the order of topics presented, interventions at individual and group levels are intended to facilitate *organizationwide* change and to improve *organizational* effectiveness.

The individual, group, and organizational sections of the chapter will begin by discussing diagnosis, and then will cover a variety of interventions. The chapter will conclude with a discussion of evaluation.

INDIVIDUAL CONSIDERATIONS IN MANAGING CHANGE

Before an OD intervention can be effectively implemented, one has to know what the problems are and the intent of the intervention. Although OD programs affect change across the whole organization, their focus ultimately begins (and ends) with the individual. A diagnosis of the situation is an important part of beginning OD interventions with individuals.

Organizational Diagnosis: The Individual Perspective

Action research: A method for diagnosing individual problems, such as low morale and poor production.

Action research is a method managers use to understand problems such as low morale, poor production, and other difficulties that arise among individuals. Action research means simply looking at all possible areas of a problem to try to determine its source (i.e., does the individual lack enough information? skills? self-confidence?) and possible solutions. The manager then identifies and tests interventions that will solve the problem, and implements the change.[8]

One distinguishing feature of action research is its emphasis on *collaboration* between change agents and individuals. Collaboration facilitates the change process. People tend to support what they help to create. When individuals are allowed to collaborate extensively in action research, they are more likely to participate fully in identifying the cause of a problem, in finding ways to end it, and in following through with change.[9] Therefore, collaboration is a key ingredient that makes action research successful.

Baby-Busters—The New Generation Poses New Challenges[10]

A new breed of workers are entering the marketplace. For the most part, they are under age 25. They're hard-driving, ambitious, and acutely aware of their place in the scheme of things. They want visibility. Yet paradoxically, they're also less wedded to their jobs, less motivated by money, and more willing to gamble their careers than their parents were. Meet the newcomers known as "baby-busters."

These new generation workers are definitely new wave. Said an AT&T district manager in New York, "They're not asking so much what the pension plan is like as 'Do you have a fitness center?' They're not asking how they can go up the corporate ladder; they want to know about the environment they'll be working in. These younger employees don't want to know the pecking order as much as they want to know if they'll have access to the top."

Intense competition for the best and brightest employees make it easy for new generation workers to leave employers they dislike. If a company isn't a good place to work, people move on.

What do the baby-busters value? More than money, they want an opportunity for promotion. They're anxious to learn and they want to work with top management early in their careers. Participation in decision making is their cup of tea.

> Another major priority is lifestyle. Baby-busters have more to do with their time than just to work! Leisure-time activities and health, fitness, flextime, and child care at the worksite are important to the new generation.

OD Interventions for Individuals

OD interventions for individuals *place* and *maintain* job candidates and incumbents in appropriate positions, facilitate *life* and *career planning*, improve employee *skills* and *knowledge*, and generally improve employee *motivation* through workplace flexibility.

Many problems are avoided when a company selects and/or promotes the right people for a job and helps employees to meet career goals. Skill development includes teaching interpersonal skills—skills that help employees work more effectively with others, and technical skills that help employees perform more effectively. As employees have more control over their work schedules, they become more motivated to be on the job and to avoid being absent.

Keeping People in Jobs.   Job seekers know how difficult it is to find one that is just right; it is also hard for organizations to maintain the right people in some jobs—especially jobs that are routine or require unskilled labor. Organizations often experience high turnover with these kind of jobs.

John Wanous found that when new recruits were told exactly what a job entailed, including positive and *negative* aspects of a position through a **realistic job preview** (RJP), turnover was reduced significantly.[11] When applicants understand and agree to take a position with no surprises, commitment increases. The RJP reduces substantial costs of hiring and training by reducing turnover, and by helping the organization to hire the right people in the first place.

Life and Career Planning.   Helping individuals to achieve life goals is an important part of maintaining the quality of work life, a major focus of OD programs. **Life and career planning**—discovering one's strengths, aspirations, and achieving life goals—is an active rather than a passive process.[12]

Life and career planning helps individuals to assess skills, to clarify work values, and to implement career decisions. With career planning, individuals grow and develop within the organization according to goals and timetables that they set. As individuals succeed, they move up the career ladder. Career planning improves retention (as employees are promoted from within) and enhances interest in and commitment to the organization. Life and career planning is especially

Realistic job preview: The practice of telling new recruits exactly what a job entails, including both positive and negative aspects in order to clarify expectations, build commitment to the organization, and reduce turnover.

Life and career planning: Interventions to help individuals assess skills, clarify work values, and implement career decisions.

helpful for individuals who find themselves in a rut, who are contemplating a career change, or who have seldom thought about their life-style and career plans.[13]

There are many career development strategies. *Job rotation* provides individuals an opportunity to explore interests and potential by working in a number of different jobs within the organization. Employees rotate through selected jobs at a predetermined schedule and may apply to take advantage of such an opportunity. *Job posting* announces job openings to employees within the organization before they are announced to the public. This practice gives employees an opportunity to apply and compete for higher-level jobs within the organization. Job posting can also pinpoint problems! When a posted position fails to attract applicants, managers should try to determine why.

Management development is training to help employees learn managerial skills before they assume new managerial duties. *Upward mobility training programs* assist employees with little education and few skills to increase both, and *career counseling* gives employees the opportunity to use test and interview results to examine career choices. *Preretirement counseling* prepares individuals to enter the retirement phase of life and to enjoy the change.

Improving Employee Skills and Knowledge.   Job skills training is a major part of many OD programs. Surveys indicate that over 90 percent of private corporations have such training programs.

*On-the-job training:
Training that helps
employees learn
about a job while on
the job.*

On-the-job training (OJT) is a common training method used by organizations. Quite simply, OJT is learning how to do a job while on the job. Properly implemented, OJT is formal, has training objectives, employs standardized lessons, and includes evaluation of trainee performance. Unfortunately, OJT is often informal, not standardized, unplanned, and trainees learn by watching an experienced worker who may not do a job according to specifications.

When effectively applied, OJT is as successful as other formal training approaches. Research has shown that OJT significantly improves employee retention as well as employee productivity.[14]

OJT has many advantages over other types of training. It is usually conducted in the same setting where new skills will be applied, so trainees have an opportunity to practice new behaviors in realistic settings which improves the transfer of learning to the job. Because OJT is job specific, evaluation measures can be accurate reflections of learning in a "real-world" setting.

*Programmed in-
struction: Training,
carried out by
automated teaching
machines, which
presents material
in short, complete
modules.*

Since the 1950s, self-instructional materials, automated teaching machines (including computers), and programmed learning texts have become increasingly popular. These various materials, known as **programmed instruction,** provide the learner with information organized in short, complete modules. Programmed learning uses principles of reinforcement to help students remember the material presented.

Programmed learning has many advantages for organizations. It allows students to learn at their own pace—a major advantage when training many people of varying abilities. Training materials are standardized, which reduces the variability of instructional methods. Evaluation is straightforward since the training materials are developed around specific learning goals.[15]

Modifying Work Schedules to Improve Motivation. Motivation and productivity are sometimes improved when individuals are allowed alternatives to the eight-hour workday. Employees react favorably to the *compressed workweek* and *flextime*. The **compressed workweek** allows employees to work a standard number of hours per month in fewer days. Rather than working eight hours, five days per week, employees might work ten hours, four days per week, or up to twelve hours per day, alternating three to four days per week. The compressed workweek has been successful in companies where workers requested or had a say in implementing the change.[16]

Flextime means that an employee has some discretion over the starting time of a full eight-hour day, when lunchtime will begin, and when he or she will go home. Some flextime schedules require all employees to be at work during certain hours, such as 10:00 A.M. until noon, and 2:00 P.M. until 4:00 P.M. Others have fixed schedules, each beginning at different hours (i.e., a 7:00 A.M. starting time versus an 8:00 A.M. or 9:00 A.M. starting time), and employees can choose the schedule best fitting their needs and habits.

Companies who need an expanded work force for only a few hours per day (e.g., during peak hours) particularly benefit from the use of flextime. These companies often provide higher pay to make a limited workday worthwhile for part-time employees. The result is increased customer service during peak hours, reduced salary costs for the company, and flexible work schedules that meet special needs of employees.[17]

In general, flextime has been shown to be more effective than the compressed workweek in reducing absenteeism and accidents, and in increasing quality and quantity of work.[18] Flextime is also particularly useful when many people need to use limited resources (i.e., employees who share equipment). Employees are less likely to accept overtime when a compressed workweek schedule is used. However, the compressed workweek can be beneficial to jobs that require or are facilitated by long periods of concentrated effort (e.g., the computer industry, nursing).

Compressed workweek: A work schedule that allows employees to work a standard number of hours per month in fewer than the standard number of working days.

Flextime: A scheduling method that allows employees to start and end their workday at variable times.

Tips for the Manager.   Managers should use action research to identify problems among individuals. Its emphasis on collaboration between change agent and individuals facilitates the change process.

Conducting a realistic job preview (RJP) provides job applicants with a good understanding of both the positive and negative aspects of a position. Because satisfied employees are inclined to stay with an organization, managers should use career development strategies such as job rotation, job posting, management development, upward mobility training programs, and career and preretirement counseling to improve the fit between employee life and career goals and opportunities afforded by the organization.

On-the-job training and programmed instruction improve employee knowledge and skills. OJT provides good transfer of learning to an actual work setting and is particularly amenable to evaluation. Programmed instruction makes it possible to concurrently train many employees with varying skill levels.

Employees react favorably to compressed workweek and flextime if they have been involved in developing the system. These schedule modifications improve attendance and employee productivity, allow better use of limited resources, and better serve customer demand during peak hours.

GROUP CONSIDERATIONS IN ORGANIZATION DEVELOPMENT

You probably belong to many groups—each having different purposes—and have noticed that groups are as distinctive as you are. Very little would be accomplished without groups, yet group efforts (especially the efforts of committees) are often the basis of jokes (Do you know what a camel is? A horse designed by a committee).

OD Programs for Groups

One cannot convene talented people and always produce a talented group. A group assumes a character all its own, quite independent of the characteristics of individual members. To really be effective, group *members* must accept responsibility for the way the group acts and works; in other words, group members must function as a *team*. The goal of OD interventions within groups is to build **teamwork** so, together, groups achieve desired goals.

Teamwork is an understanding and commitment to group goals on

Teamwork: An understanding and commitment to group goals by all members and a maximum utilization of each member's resources.

the part of all members of the team. Effective teamwork requires maximum utilization of each individual member's resources. It is achieved when flexibility, sensitivity to others' needs, and creativity are encouraged; and it is most effective when the leadership role is shared. Effective teamwork is characterized by a group's ability to examine its processes in order to improve performance.[19]

Effective teams are not built overnight. Building a productive team requires mutual acceptance on the part of individual members, open communication, clear expectations and goals, support of members for each other, and a willingness to take risks.[20] Members need to focus on attaining group goals and on making each member maximally effective.

Group productivity is often greater than the sum of individual contributions. Managers should remember that many outstanding teams are little more than a group of ordinary individuals who believe that *together* they can get a job done.

The manager can facilitate team building by getting all members to commit to team goals, by providing necessary resources, or by getting together the necessary resources to help members help themselves to reach goals. By giving praise to all group members for team accomplishments, and by getting members to solve their problems together rather than by imposing managerial solutions, a sense of teamwork and group cohesiveness is fostered.

Anatomy of a Team

Years ago, Douglas McGregor described characteristics of well-functioning, effective groups as follows:

- The atmosphere is relaxed, comfortable, and informal.
- The group's task is well understood and accepted by members.
- Members listen well to each other; there is much task-relevant discussion in which most members participate.
- Members express both feelings and ideas.
- Conflict and disagreements are present but are centered around ideas and methods, not personalities and people.
- The group is self-conscious about its own operation.
- Decisions are usually based on consensus, not majority vote.
- When actions are decided upon, clear assignments are made and accepted by the members.[21]

Organizational Diagnosis: The Group Perspective

A number of diagnostic methods are effective for helping groups to identify impediments to effective performance.

Group diagnostic meeting: A diagnostic strategy carried out by the manager and group members to analyze performance problems.

The **group diagnostic meeting** is a diagnostic strategy carried out by the manager and group members to analyze problems. The purpose of the meeting is to evaluate how well the group is meeting organizational objectives, whether it is functioning to potential, what problems need attention, whether opportunities are being missed, and specifically what the group is doing well and not so well.[22]

The diagnostic meeting can be conducted three different ways. The whole group can analyze problems together, two or more subgroups can analyze problems and report to the larger group, or the larger group can be broken down into dyads (two-person groups) who interview each other, discuss issues, and then report back to the larger group.[23]

There is an important side benefit to the group diagnostic meeting that is not as prevalent in other diagnostic approaches. It builds a sense of unity among members: "When a team engages in problem-solving activities directed toward task accomplishment, the team members *build something together.* It appears that the act of building something together also builds a sense of camaraderie, cohesion, and esprit de corps."[24]

OD Interventions for Groups

After diagnosis, interventions help groups achieve needed change. In this section, three different interventions are presented and each is appropriate for different organizational situations.

Role analysis technique: An intervention designed to clarify role expectations and obligations of team members to improve team effectiveness.

Role analysis technique (RAT) clarifies role expectations and obligations of team members to improve team effectiveness. This technique is particularly effective with *special teams* (new teams with no or limited history), but also helps *established teams* (groups who have worked closely together over time) when role ambiguity or confusion exists.

While using RAT, a group member defines the role requirements of his or her job as it fits with roles of other group members and with the organization. The individual and team members negotiate and agree upon appropriate expectations that should be fulfilled on both sides (i.e., expectations the individual should fulfill for team effectiveness, and expectations that the team should meet to enhance individual performance toward team goals).

This intervention can be extremely effective. The collaborative nature of the analysis, together with the ability to negotiate expectations and responsibilities, clarifies roles within a group that must be filled in order to maximize group productivity.

Role negotiation technique serves different organizational needs than role analysis technique. Whereas RAT works in situations where group members want to change, role negotiation technique provides for intervention in power struggles where group members do *not* want to change because change would lead to a loss of power or influence.[25]

Role negotiation technique: An intervention that facilitates negotiation in power struggles where group members do not wish to give up power and influence.

This technique is based on the assumption that most people prefer a fair negotiated settlement, and would rather invest time and make concessions to achieve a solution than to live with uncertainty.

The technique allows team members to negotiate how they will work together in a highly structured meeting. Each makes concessions until an agreement (that everyone can live with) is reached. As the facilitator, the manager or change agent plays a pivotal role in helping opposing sides to negotiate concessions, and is a critical part of the evaluation procedure. Within one or two months, the negotiated outcomes are evaluated to make sure that all bargains have been kept, that initial problems have been resolved, and that further refinement of the agreements is not necessary.

Just as you use a mirror to see how you look, the **organization mirror technique** uses the opinions of other groups to "see" how a target group is perceived and regarded. This intervention is designed to improve working relationships among three or more groups.[26]

Organization mirror technique: An intervention that allows a host group to use the opinions of other groups to analyze and solve performance deficiencies.

The intervention is usually planned and is requested by a group that is experiencing difficulties. The group asks others for an honest evaluation of their performance.

A manager or change agent conducts interviews with "other" group members prior to a diagnostic meeting to determine the source and magnitude of problems facing the target group. The change agent then prepares "other" group members to give constructive feedback to the target group. At the diagnostic meeting, the target group listens and learns. After all major problems are presented, the target group restates what they have heard and seeks clarification regarding problems identified during the meeting.

Next, solutions to problems are proposed by subgroups comprised of a member from the "other" group and target group members. Each subgroup identifies workable solutions, determines a plan of action, and makes a report to the total group. The total group then assigns tasks and agrees on target completion dates.[27]

This intervention is simple and effective for well-functioning groups experiencing temporary difficulties. New groups or fast-growing companies facing constant employee turnover or change benefit from this technique.

Tips for the Manager. The goal of OD programs for groups is to develop teamwork. Team building is facilitated by getting members to commit to goals, by providing necessary resources to achieve those goals, by praising the group rather than by praising individuals, and by allowing members to solve their own problems rather than by imposing managerial solutions.

Use the group diagnostic meeting to diagnose group problems while building camaraderie and espirit de corps. The role analysis technique (RAT) should be used to clarify role ambiguity and build consensus on what member roles should be. Use role negotiation technique to overcome power struggles among group members and evaluate concessions members have made to each other to assure that bargains have been kept. The organization mirror technique should be used with well-functioning groups that are experiencing temporary difficulties. This technique allows other groups to assess how a target group is performing.

ORGANIZATIONAL CONSIDERATIONS IN OD PROGRAMS

To reiterate, the focus of organization development concerns the health of the total organization. The impact of OD programs should cascade down throughout the entire organization. Some OD interventions should affect literally every person in the organization, regardless of the organization's size.

Organizational Diagnosis: An Organizational Perspective

Organizationwide OD programs should be created after considerable diagnosis of organizational needs, conducted through *interviews, tests, questionnaires,* and *surveys* of organizational members. The purpose of this phase of an OD program is to determine relevant attitudes, perceptions, and beliefs, skills, abilities, and performance of key individuals and groups. Evaluation of *organizational data,* including employee turnover, productivity, profit, market trends, and organizational structure, *before* an intervention provides change agents with valuable information on where the organization is, and where it should be after an OD program has been completed. (See Figure 10–2.)

Confrontation meeting: A meeting in which the entire management team discusses and evaluates the organization's health.

The next step in organizational diagnosis can include a **confrontation meeting** where the entire management group meets to evaluate the organization's health. It is similar to the group diagnostic meeting described on page 302, but is attended only by the management team. It focuses on change; problems are discussed in depth, solutions are

Figure 10–2 Diagnostic Tools for Organization Development

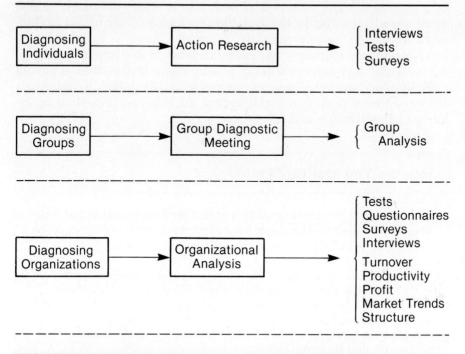

Effective diagnosis is carried out at the individual, group, and organizational levels using a variety of techniques and measures.

identified, and adoption of change becomes a major priority of all members. Diagnostic procedures at the organizational level require considerable expertise and are often conducted by trained OD specialists.

Organizational Interventions

One way to find out what does and does not motivate employees across an organization is to ask them. As simple as that statement sounds, it had not been done in the work setting prior to the mid-1950s. Frederick Herzberg, in an attempt to clarify conflicting studies on job satisfaction, asked 203 Pittsburgh engineers and accountants what they liked and disliked about their jobs. (See Chapter Three, Motivation, for further discussion of Herzberg's work.)

One of the startling findings Herzberg reported was that money was not a main motivator to work. People said they would rather have interesting work at which they could receive recognition than to engage in dull, boring work at a similar salary.[28] Herzberg's work led to the OD intervention called **job enrichment** (also discussed in Chapter Three).

Job enrichment: An intervention that provides employees with more control over their jobs.

Job enrichment is an intervention designed to motivate employees by giving them more control over their job. It is also called *vertical job enlargement*, referring to the fact that enriching a job means adding more responsibility and authority (typically given to higher-echelon jobs) as opposed to simply adding more tasks. According to Herzberg, job enrichment is more cost effective and longer lasting than is paying more in salary and benefits in an attempt to satisfy unhappy employees. Job enrichment results in psychological growth—an important determinant of motivation and job satisfaction.[29]

How Do You Motivate Employees?

How does one motivate employees? In a well-known *Harvard Business Review* article, Herzberg listed seven principles of vertical job loading or job enrichment that motivate employees.

1. Remove some of controls but retain accountability.
2. Increase the accountability of individuals for their own work.
3. Give a person a complete natural unit of work.
4. Grant additional authority or freedom to employees.
5. Make periodic reports directly available to workers rather than routing them through supervisors.
6. Introduce new and more difficult tasks.
7. Assign individuals to specialized tasks enabling them to become experts.[30]

Job Enrichment: A Caveat.   Some theorists, like Herzberg, tend to believe that everyone wants to develop in their job and is motivated to take on more responsibility. However, research shows that only employees who seek intrinsic rewards (interest in the work itself, the challenge), rather than extrinsic rewards (pay, vacation benefits), are likely to respond to job-enrichment strategies.[31]

Job-enrichment strategies must be supported and desired by employees who have high *growth needs*. (See Chapter Three, Motivation, for further discussion of growth needs.) Some individuals select a job that demands little of them so that they can pursue outside interests. Job enrichment is not likely to work well for such individuals because growth needs are met by outside interests—not by the job.[32] Individual worker reactions can also limit the effect of job enrichment. Anxiety, fear of failure and inadequacy, increased reliance on supervision, and dislike of change hamper acceptance of job-enrichment strategies.[33]

Herzberg recommended that job enrichment be used for those jobs in which technical changes can be made at a minimum of expense, where satisfaction is currently low, where pay and additional incentives are expensive, and where improved motivation will affect performance.

Restructuring Work: Alternatives to Job Enrichment. There are other ways to *restructure work* (i.e., to change aspects of the job) that can be useful to improve productivity and motivation, but do not require individual growth needs that are associated with job enrichment.

Job rotation, discussed earlier in this chapter, is also an effective organizational intervention. Job rotation is motivating in that it provides variety for workers who are in relatively dull or repetitive jobs such as assembly lines. Job rotation has a side benefit in that it prepares employees to take over another position in case of emergency or turnover.

Another way to reorganize work and increase job satisfaction is to create **autonomous work groups.**[2] These are generally small work groups that have responsibility for a specific task and that tend to manage themselves. (Although it sounds like a group-intervention strategy, creating autonomous work groups requires considerable support from the organization and is done organizationwide.) Autonomous work groups determine pace of work and member task assignments; they may be responsible for selecting new members and they determine when breaks and lunch hours will begin. In other words, autonomous groups are "in charge" of themselves.

Autonomous work groups: Small work groups that have responsibility for a specific task and manage themselves within limits defined by the organization.

These work groups have been successfully used in organizations where tasks are well defined, where the company supports group rather than individual incentives, and where groups have the expertise and capability to carry out assignments. In such cases, forming autonomous work groups has increased motivation, job satisfaction, and productivity; has reduced use of sick leave; and has improved mental health. Sometimes, an entire level of supervision can be eliminated. When autonomous work groups function well, they supervise themselves.[34]

Autonomous work groups have been popular in Sweden for several decades. (Volvo automobile manufacturing company is a notable example.) In the United States, Procter & Gamble established its first autonomous work groups in plants during the 1960s. P & G now has 18 plants employing such groups. P & G's autonomous work group plants are 30 to 40 percent more productive than their traditional counterparts and are significantly more able to adapt quickly to the changing needs of business.[35]

Making Change Work in Organizations

One of the more difficult challenges of an organizationwide OD program is to overcome resistance to change. Resistance to change stems

Poorly managed change is disconcerting to employees.

from a contradiction between existing beliefs and new ideas. People seldom accept change at its face value or see its possibilities. Rather, people often attempt to determine whether a hidden agenda is driving change. The mere belief that a hidden agenda exists is enough to convince some that change will result in a personal work-related loss. Communicating with key members at all levels of an organization when implementing an OD intervention helps to curb this resistance to change.

Overcoming Resistance to Change: Changing Push to Participation

The following 12 steps help to overcome resistance to change in organizations that encourage participation, value employees, and are committed to growth. Without such corporate values, these steps for reducing resistance to change will be more difficult to implement.

1. Encourage participation.
2. Start change with top officials.
3. Demonstrate that change will reduce rather than increase burdens.
4. Connect proposed with traditional corporate values.
5. Highlight novel and exciting aspects of the change.
6. Assure that autonomy will not be threatened.
7. Include participants in diagnostic efforts.

8. Try to get consensual decisions.
9. Empathize with resistors to reduce their fears.
10. Build in feedback mechanisms to detect problems before they become serious.
11. Build mutual trust among participants.
12. Build a mechanism for reappraisal and revision.[36]

Evaluation: A Tool for Organizational Change

Performance appraisal is the formal assessment of employee performance. (See Chapter Six, Performance Appraisal, for further discussion of this topic.) From an OD perspective, performance appraisal helps managers assess the effectiveness of interventions.

Effective performance appraisal reinforces appropriate employee behavior and helps to change or stop ineffective behavior. Performance appraisal builds rapport and communication between a manager and employees. Performance appraisal also helps managers to identify employee potential for future promotions.

Survey feedback technique, useful for organizational diagnosis, also allows a manager to collect data about an intervention and to share it with the appropriate groups for analysis and corrective action. Data are collected through a survey instrument and results are discussed at workshops and meetings. When used consistently, survey feedback is a powerful tool for evaluating change and modifying relationships.

Survey feedback technique: An evaluation strategy in which a manager collects data about the organization and feeds it back to appropriate work groups for analysis and corrective action.

Although not a formal OD evaluative strategy, regular *staff meetings* or cross-group meetings (i.e., getting all support staff across departments together) help managers to evaluate the effectiveness of OD interventions and to resume OD interventions should the need arise.

A Final Comment on OD—No Simple Solutions

To conclude, just as effective people continually strive to improve skills, abilities, and less-than-perfect habits, so too should effective organizations adopt the same behavior. When organizations begin an OD program, they embark on an odyssey. This odyssey does not stop after the last OD intervention is finished. In fact, the odyssey is just beginning. The evaluation process ending the last "OD program cycle" provides data for the next cycle of planned change.

OD programs fail when they lack support, when goals are not well defined, when planning is faulty, when an OD program is prematurely introduced, when the organization fails to follow through, when people resist change, and when evaluation is done infrequently or ineffectively. In short, there are no shortcuts, no simple "off-the-shelf" solutions, and no end to the care and feeding that an effective OD program requires.[37] (See Figure 10–3.)

Figure 10–3 Reasons Why OD Programs Fail

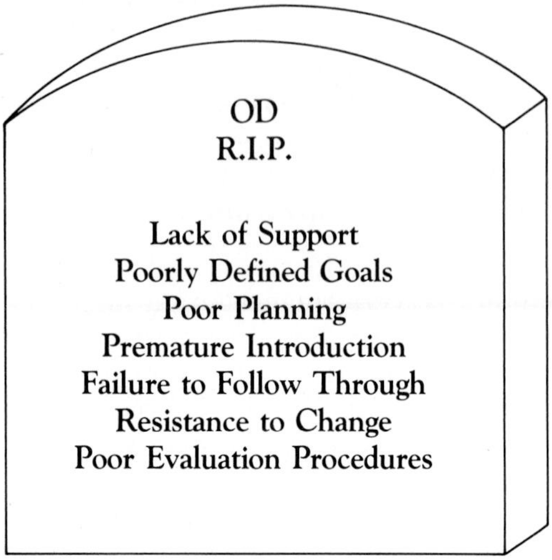

```
OD
R.I.P.

Lack of Support
Poorly Defined Goals
Poor Planning
Premature Introduction
Failure to Follow Through
Resistance to Change
Poor Evaluation Procedures
```

When changes are not well-supported, planned, or evaluated, OD programs cannot produce desired results.

Tips for the Manager.   A confrontation meeting should be used to identify organizational problems through management discussion. Remember that organizational diagnosis should be carried out by a specialist or person who is trained in OD.

Job enrichment will provide employees with more control over their jobs. Job enrichment works best in settings where employees are willing and able to accept increased responsibility, technical changes can be made at a minimum of cost, satisfaction is low, salary and benefits are expensive, and intrinsic motivation will improve performance.

Job rotation is moving employees through different jobs. It also adds variety and prepares employees to move to another position if necessary.

Autonomous work groups allow organizations to restructure tasks and assign them to small groups that manage their performance, productivity, and scheduling of assignments. The success of autonomous work groups depends on a supportive corporate environment and rewards for group rather than for individual performance.

To overcome resistance to change, allow key employees at all levels of the organization to participate in diagnosing needed change. Assure employees that their autonomy will not be compromised and that change is consistent with closely held values that permeate the organization. Obtaining the support of the informal leadership within the organization helps organizational members to accept change.

Use performance appraisal to evaluate the effectiveness of an intervention and how well an employee has met objectives associated with a particular job. Survey feedback should be used by managers to stay in touch with group attitudes and enable employees to analyze survey feedback data and implement corrective action. Conduct regular staff meetings in order to keep abreast of needs and problems of group members and to determine the effectiveness of OD interventions over time.

SUMMARY: FOCUS ON SKILLS

Organization Development (OD) is defined as the implementation of planned interventions designed to manage change effectively in an organization.

The purpose of OD is to change beliefs, attitudes, values, and structures of an organization and its members so that the organization can better adapt to new technologies, markets, economic pressures, and other challenges. Following are 19 suggestions managers should keep in mind when planning or implementing an OD program.

Managers should:

1. Remember that organizational change is best managed from the top down. Top management support is essential to the success of an OD program.

2. Know that OD programs at the individual, group, and organizational levels have three components: diagnosis, intervention, and evaluation.

3. Use the realistic job preview (RJP) to improve individual job commitment. Describe the negative as well as the positive aspects of a job during the interview process.

4. Strive to improve the fit between an employee's life and career goals and opportunities provided within the organization.

5. Plan formal, standardized on-the-job training (OJT) which can be evaluated in order to help individual employees to easily transfer learning to the job.

6. Use programmed learning to teach skills to large numbers of individuals who need to learn at their own pace.

7. Modify work schedules to increase individual motivation. Use flextime and compressed workweek strategies for full-time employees. Make part-time schedules to cover limited peak hours more attractive to employees by paying higher hourly wages.

8. Facilitate team building by getting group members to commit to group goals. Praise the team rather than individual members, and encourage members to collaborate in solving problems.

9. Use role analysis technique (RAT) to build working relationships within groups. RAT involves having members clarify role requirements and expectations with each other.

10. Use role negotiation technique to reduce power struggles when group members are not cooperating. This technique has members negotiate concessions in order to create acceptable role requirements for all.

11. Use organizational mirror technique with groups experiencing temporary difficulties. This technique allows other groups to identify performance problems in a target group and to identify solutions.

12. Diagnose needed organizational change by using tests, surveys, interviews, and questionnaires in order to determine employees' attitudes, perceptions, beliefs, skills, and abilities.

13. Use measures such as employee turnover, productivity, profit, market trends, and structure to determine organizational productivity.

14. Use job enrichment to make organizationwide changes for employees with high growth needs.

15. Rotate jobs to increase task variety and to improve employee productivity.

16. Change work flow in organizations by forming autonomous work groups. Do this when tasks can be logically divided into subunits, and work groups have the skill and ability to perform assigned tasks with minimum supervision.

17. Overcome resistance to change by communicating with key members at all levels of the organization.

18. Evaluate the results of organizationwide change with performance appraisal and survey feedback. Conduct performance appraisal to evaluate the effectiveness of interventions across the organization. Use survey feedback data to evaluate group attitudes and to help employees implement change. Also use frequent, focused staff meetings to monitor group change.

19. Remember, where important changes in the life of an organization and its members are being considered, there are seldom simple solutions.

■ CASE: "THE INCREDIBLE RUMOR"

The Shorey Hotel has been a Center City landmark for the last 50 years. In all that time it has changed little; it has the same management and the same art deco interior it had back in the thirties. Lately, however, management has begun to realize that, to remain competitive with more recently designed or refurbished hotels, the Shorey will have to go through an extensive period of renovation.

Somehow or other, the rumor mill transformed management's decision to renovate into a decision to close the hotel. The rumor is completely untrue, but everyone from the desk clerk to the busboys believes they'll soon be out of a job. It's got everybody preoccupied and is creating a degree of antagonism toward management.

The Shorey's largest and most loyal department, housekeeping, also has the most senior employees. It has always functioned well, but since Wally Ging took over as executive housekeeper the staff has done an even better job. Not only has management noticed the difference, but letters from recent guests also acknowledge the fine job Wally is doing. The department should have an appropriately high level of motivation, but the rumors of the Shorey's closing have Wally's people worried, too.

When Wally found out what was causing the anxiety among the staff, he assured everyone that no one's job was in danger. "Believe me," he told his employees, "management is thinking of knocking down some walls and putting on some fresh paint. And that's it." Before the week was out, however, a memorandum was distributed outlining the need for layoffs in some departments—including housekeeping—while the renovation was under way.

The reaction was immediate within the housekeeping department. Wally felt not only embarrassed but guilty for having misled his staff members. Their hostility and their indifference to their jobs escalated following the memorandum. They were not only angry at Wally but worried about who would be laid off. If the quality of their work deteriorates, and it seems to have already started, Wally knows he'll soon be worrying about his job, too.

But Wally doesn't know what to do. His staff's declining performance is difficult to discipline since the problem is not one of insubordination but of generally low morale. And that problem, Wally knows, can only be resolved by removing the insecurity his employees feel. But how can he persuade them that they will be dealt with fairly when his credibility is already shot?

Case Questions

1. How could Shorey's management have done a better job of overcoming resistance to the changes that management was planning?

2. How do you think management's actions affected Wally's feelings toward Shorey? What could he have done to avoid this situation?

3. What must Wally do after the remodel to rebuild department morale?

■ EXERCISE: "FORCE FIELD ANALYSIS"

Managing change in organizations requires an understanding of driving (i.e., change creating) and restraining (i.e., change limiting) forces which affect the status quo. Kurt Lewin's force field analysis methodology provides a way to identify driving and restraining forces. Once identified, removing a restraining force may be the best way to manage change because it is often less stressful to remove an obstacle to change than it is to impose a solution for change.

In this exercise you will have an opportunity to analyze a current problem at your college or university using force field analysis.

Forms

1. Describe the problem briefly.

2. List each of the forces *driving* change below.
   a.
   b.
   c.
   d.
   e.
   f.

3. List each of the forces *restraining* change.
   a.
   b.
   c.
   d.
   e.
   f.

4. List the driving and restraining forces of the problem on the chart below in order of their degree of impact on change.

Force Field Analysis

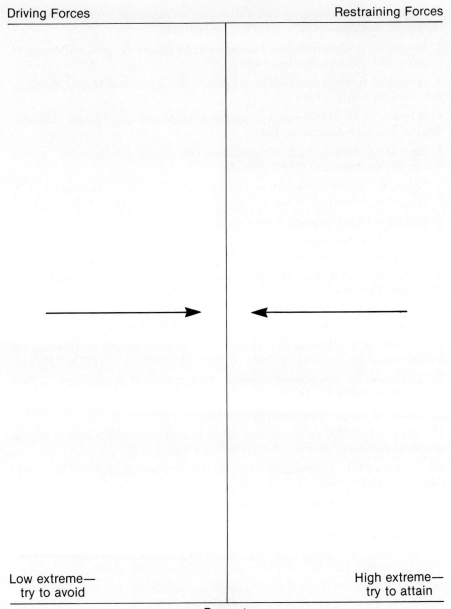

Driving Forces   Restraining Forces

Low extreme—
try to avoid

High extreme—
try to attain

Present
balance point

ENDNOTES

1. Lippitt, G. *Organizational Renewal: A Holistic Approach to Organization Development.* Englewood Cliffs, NJ: Prentice-Hall, 1982.

2. Bennis, W. G. *Organizational Development: Its Nature, Origins, and Prospects.* Reading, MA: Addison-Wesley, 1969.

3. Beckhard, R. *Organizational Development: Strategies and Models.* Reading, MA: Addison-Wesley, 1969.

4. Warrick, D. D. *Managing Organization Change and Development.* Chicago: Science Research Associates, 1984.

5. Beer, M., & Walton, A. E. "Organization change and development." *Annual Review of Psychology, 38* (1987): 339–367.

6. Lewin, K. "Group dynamics and social change." In G. E. Swanson & E. L. Hartley (Eds.), *Readings in Social Psychology.* New York: Holt, 1952.

7. Beckhard, *Organizational Development.*

8. Weisbord, M. R. *Organizational Diagnosis: A Workbook of Theory and Practice.* Reading, MA: Addison-Wesley, 1978, pp. 69–70.

9. French, W. L., & Bell, C. H., Jr. *Organization Development.* Englewood Cliffs, NJ: Prentice-Hall, 1978.

10. "The baby-busters," *The Wall Street Journal* (the Western Edition), October 26, 1988, p. 1. This discussion is an adaptation of the news article.

11. Wanous, J. P. "Effects of a realistic job preview on job acceptance, job attitudes, and job survival." *Journal of Applied Psychology, 58* (1973): 327–332.

12. Lippitt, G. L. "Integrating personal and professional development." *ASTD Journal* (May 1980): 12–18.

13. French & Bell, *Organization Development.*

14. Lefkowitz, J. "Effect of training on the productivity and tenure of sewing machine operators." *Journal of Applied Psychology, 54* (1970): 81–86.

15. Goldstein, I. L. *Training: Program Development and Evaluation.* Monterey, CA: Brooks/Cole, 1974.

16. Latack, J. C., & Foster, L. W. "Implementation of compressed work schedules: Participation and job redesign as critical factors for employee acceptance." *Personnel Psychology, 38* (1985): 75–92.

17. Gray, J. L., & Starke, F. A. *Organizational Behavior Concepts and Applications.* Columbus, OH: Merrill Publishing Company, 1988, p. 642.

18. Greene, C. N. "Effects of alternative work schedules: A field experiment." *Academy of Management Proceedings, 44* (1984): 269–273.

19. Lippitt, *Organizational Renewal.*

20. Francis, D., & Young, D. *Improving Work Groups: A Practical Manual for Team Building.* San Diego, CA: University Associates, Inc., 1979.

21. McGregor, D. *The Human Side of Enterprise.* New York: McGraw-Hill, 1960.

22. French & Bell, *Organization Development.*

23. Ibid.

24. Ibid.

25. Harrison, R. "When power conflicts trigger team spirit." *European Business* (Spring 1972): 27–65.

26. Fordyce, J. K., & Weil, R. *Managing with People.* Reading, MA: Addison-Wesley, 1971, pp. 101–105.

27. Ibid.

28. Herzberg, F.; Mausner, B.; & Snyderman, B. B. *The Motivation to Work.* New York: John Wiley, 1959.

29. Buchanan, D. A. *The Development of Job Design Theories and Techniques.* Westmead, England: Saxon House, 1979.

30. Herzberg, F. "One more time: How do you motivate employees?" *Harvard Business Review* (January-February 1968): 53–62.

31. See: Centers, R., & Bugenthal, D. E. "Intrinsic and extrinsic job motivations among different segments of the working population." *Journal of Applied Psychology, 50* (1966): 193–197; and Blood, M. R., & Hulin, C. L. "Alienation, environmental characteristics, and worker responses." *Journal of Applied Psychology, 51* (1967): 284–290.

32. Hackman, J. R., & Oldham, G. R. *Work Redesign.* Reading, MA: Addison-Wesley, 1980.

33. Reif, W. E., & Luthans, F. "Does job enrichment really pay off?" *California Management Review, 15* (1972): 30–37.

34. Toby, D. W.; Kemp, N. J.; Jackson, P. R.; & Clegg, C. W. "Outcomes of autonomous work groups: A long-term field experiment." *Academy of Management Journal, 29* (1986): 280–304.

35. "Management discovers the human side of automation." *Business Week,* September 29, 1986, pp. 70–75.

36. Lippitt, *Organizational Renewal.*

37. Pfeiffer, W. J., & Jones, J. E. "A current assessment of OD: What it is and why it often fails." *The 1976 Handbook for Group Facilitators.* University Associates, Inc., 1976.

Io Enterprises:
A Microcomputer Simulation

Version prepared for *Managerial Skills in Organizations*

Software created by:

Philip C. Lewis
Gemini Software, Training & Development

I/O: *Often used as the acronym to describe "industrial organizational psychology." I/O is concerned with the "people side" of organizations. This includes theory and practice in areas such as motivation, conflict management, leadership, communication, and decision making.*

Io: *The fifth moon of Jupiter. Located deep within the magnetic field of Jupiter, Io is the most volcanically active moon or planet in the solar system. This volcanic activity makes Io one of the most lethal places in the solar system for man. The Ionian sky is dominated by the bloated, red and yellow striped presence of Jupiter, the largest of the planets.*

One day on Io lasts 42 Earth hours. Gravity on Io is roughly equivalent to that of Earth's moon. Average temperatures on Io range from −318 to −295° F.

Welcome to *Io Enterprises: A Microcomputer Simulation!*

Soon, you will travel to Io where you will serve as part of the management team of a titanium mine. Your objective is to earn the highest profits of all mines on Io. Profits are maximized to the extent the productivity (and revenues) of your mine are increased relative to expenses.

Improvements in mine productivity depend on whether you and your teammates make correct "people decisions." Decisions are made each fiscal quarter during the Earth year 2086. Consequently, you will make decisions for four periods. Each simulated fiscal quarter:

1. You and your teammates will receive a set of ten scenarios. The scenarios are based on the content of your text, *Managerial Skills in Organizations,* or other material your instructor has covered. Your instructor determines the content of the scenarios you will face during each decision period.

    You must understand the material covered by your instructor in order to respond correctly to scenarios. For example, if your instructor announces that scenarios will contain motivation and leadership content, then you should carefully study Chapters Three and Nine in *Managerial Skills in Organizations,* and/or other relevant course material, prior to making simulation decisions.

    You will also receive a management report each period which includes a simple income statement, a production report, an absenteeism report, and a status report (which reports present, past, or future conditions affecting the productivity of all mines on Io). You need not be an accountant in order to understand the financial information included in the management report. All terms and reports are defined in these instructions.

2. After analyzing your management report and scenarios, you and your teammates will respond by deciding on the correct course of action for each scenario. You also make financial decisions pertaining to wages, bonuses, and training, which also affect productivity. Each period, your decisions are entered on team decision forms (TDFs) located in Appendix B.

3. The information on TDFs will be entered into a microcomputer by your instructor (or by a member of your team at your instructor's option). The computer program determines the effectiveness of your decisions and produces management reports and scenarios to be used by each management team for the next round of decisions. (See Figure 1.)

The remainder of these instructions includes sections pertaining to the environment, the management report and scenarios, and the decisions you must make each period.

Figure 1 The Process

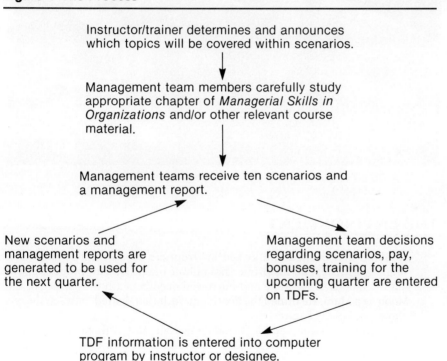

Instructor/trainer determines and announces which topics will be covered within scenarios.

Management team members carefully study appropriate chapter of *Managerial Skills in Organizations* and/or other relevant course material.

Management teams receive ten scenarios and a management report.

New scenarios and management reports are generated to be used for the next quarter.

Management team decisions regarding scenarios, pay, bonuses, training for the upcoming quarter are entered on TDFs.

TDF information is entered into computer program by instructor or designee.

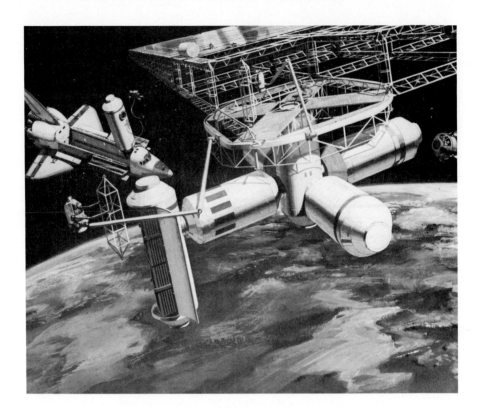

THE ENVIRONMENT

> Mankind had pushed and kicked his frontiers beyond the confines of a single world, beyond his primordial bubble of air. He sent probes searching the moons of Neptune and burrowed deep beneath the surface of the Moon and Mars. He mined the floating wealth that drifted between the red planet and giant Jupiter.
>
> All were harsh and bleak and dangerous. But of them all, none was worse than Io . . . Io was a place to work, and to do your best to survive."[1]

In the year 2084, 12 billion people lived on Earth.

Mankind avoided nuclear holocaust during the particularly dangerous time toward the end of the last century. The information revolution helped to bring together the countries of the world, as people found it necessary to cooperate for the common good. The world economy also stabilized. The purchasing power of the dollar remained relatively constant from the closing decades of the twentieth century to the present day.

Still, as the twenty-first century began, there were problems to overcome. Besides a burgeoning population to feed and house, the mineral resources of the planet were rapidly being depleted. Technology could solve many problems, but it could not replace planetary reserves of important minerals such as lead, nickel, and iron. Market forces, driven by the insatiable hunger of Earth industry, dictated a movement outward toward the stars.

The Overlake Mining Company actively participated in the outward metamorphosis of the Earth economy. Started as a coal-mining operation in the middle part of the last century, The Overlake Mining Company grew into the multinational conglomerate known today as The Overlake. The Overlake's strategic mission continued to be mining, but the scope of corporate operations eventually grew to include all areas of planetary natural resources management as well.

The Overlake took the lead in the private exploration of outer space. The first successful retrieval of an asteroid was accomplished in 2012 by a team of 12 Overlake astronauts. This asteroid, known then as 4242 RD, but later nicknamed "Prometheus," was captured and redirected toward on Earth orbit. After a 30 million-mile journey, Prometheus was docked in a high Earth orbit in the year 2015.

Prometheus was the first of many asteroids to be captured, transported to Earth, and mined by The Overlake. Metals and glass, processed in space by using continuous solar energy, were taken from the asteroids and used to build solar power collectors. These collectors produced electric power, which soon replaced the coal, nuclear, and oil plants that had supplied Earth's energy needs. Agricultural stations in space were also built from asteroidal materials and relieved the hunger of billions of people.[3]

By the year 2060, however, it became apparent that asteroid mining technology was insufficient. New and pressing needs for mineral resources had developed. Of particular concern was an acute shortage of titanium. Titanium ore reserves had long been depleted on Earth, and asteroidal titanium deposits were insufficient. Titanium, as strong as tempered steel but 40 percent lighter, was in high demand, particularly in the spacecraft construction industry. In 2065, an Overlake exploration party found huge high-grade deposits of titanium ore on Io, the fifth moon of Jupiter.

The decision was made by top management of The Overlake to establish a permanent mining colony on Io. This colony would be comprised of 2 to 12 separate titanium mines, administered by separate managements. This autonomy was necessary because magnetic interference from Jupiter made communication through space impossible, and the geological instability of the moon surface precluded the laying of communications cables. Each mine would be on its own.

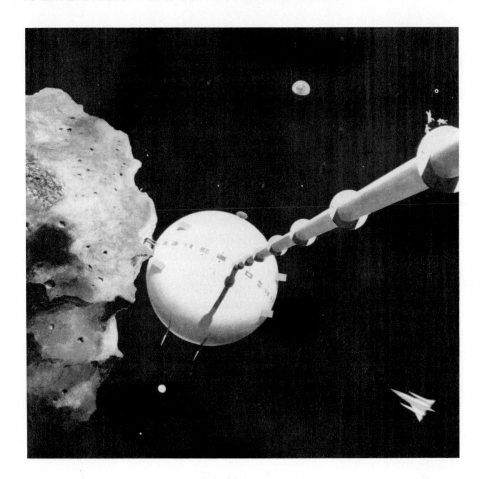

Could It Happen?

Engineering studies conducted by NASA engineers during 1976–77 at NASA's Ames Research Center concluded that lunar mining and space processing could begin during the early 1990s at a cost of $60 billion spread over 15 years. The mining of Earth-approaching asteroids is another option which has been actively explored.

   Astrophysicist Eric Jones, of the Los Alamos National Laboratory, believes that within the next 500 years, one trillion human beings will inhabit the solar system's planets, moons, asteroids, and comets. Jones believes that a moon base outfitted with mines, smelters, and a power station would enable pioneers to build space cities and launch them cheaply into the solar system. He predicts that within eight million years our decendants will have colonized the entire galaxy.[3]

The Mines

The Io mining colony was finally completed in 2080 and was established as a wholly owned subsidiary of The Overlake. This subsidiary was named Io Enterprises.

Each mine on Io had the same facilities. These facilities included locker and equipment rooms, a library, a gymnasium, screening and social gathering rooms, housing, and a cafeteria. Living and administrative facilities were located underground, protected from Ioquakes by massive hydraulic supports. The mill and other "tipple" operations for the mine were placed on the moon surface.

Top management decided to organize and staff all mines the same way. Figure 2 shows an organizational chart.

A total of 250 miners were assigned to work in each mine. Titanium ore was mined above ground in open pits as well as underground. Mining was accomplished through blasting, using low-yield fusion nuclear explosives and lasers. The ore was scooped up on the surface by using specially adapted power shovels, or gathered and transported from underground by using highly reliable robotic muckers and electronic conveyors.

Ore was transferred to a surface mill where it was milled and readied for shipment to Earth. Life-support systems on Io were powered by orbiting solar collectors. Each mine was assigned its own solar collector.

Employees remained on Io for one Earth year before being replaced. Each shift of new employees, consequently, represented a "rotation." An Earth calendar was used to track time. An hour on Io was 60 minutes long, a day 24 hours long, and so forth.

The Io project presented two different work environments. Interior work was primarily administrative and relatively safe. Exterior work was physically and technically demanding and dangerous. Most employees on Io were technical specialists.

In 2076, a space station was placed in orbit around Io. This station served as a central supply for all mines on Io. Supplies, equipment, and electronic mail from Earth were routinely shuttled down from this station to the moon surface. This space station represented the only contact individual mines had with the outside. Interference from the Jovian magnetic field required that messages and mail be physically transported by shuttle to each mine.

Figure 2

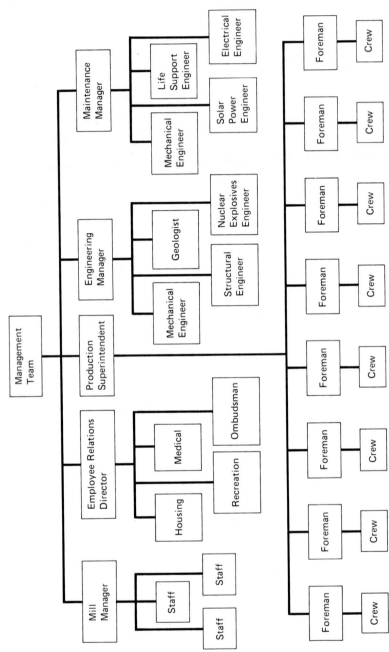

Figure 2 (Continued)

Job Descriptions, Io Enterprises Mines (Line Positions)

a. *Management Team*—Responsible for setting policy and directing all mining operations.

b. *Production Superintendent*—Oversees day-to-day mining operations. This responsibility includes mine safety and injury control.

c. *Engineering Manager*—Responsible for assaying ore deposits, blasting, and all technology related to ore extraction and transfer to the Mill.

d. *Maintenance Manager*—Responsible for maintaining structural and life support integrity of all mine structures and equipment, and living quarters.

e. *Employee Relations Director*—In charge of off-work environment for all staff. This responsibility includes supervising the ombudsman, as well as all recreation, medical cafeteria, and housing staff. The Employee Relations Director also arbitrates employee grievances.

f. *Mill-Manager*—Supervises all titanium ore crushing and milling operations, and off-moon loading of ore to Earth transport ships.

g. *Crew Foremen*—Line supervisors; each foreman has a span of control of ten miners. This is one of the most difficult and important jobs on Io.

The Current Situation

By 2082, all mines had attained comparable levels of titanium ore production. Top management was pleased with the application of technology. Moreover, *all* ore mined on Io was sold immediately into a titanium-starved market. However, productivity of the miners failed to meet expectations.

Top management eventually, and reluctantly, concluded that low productivity was caused primarily by on-site management of miners living and working on Io. Managers at all levels in the organizational hierarchy in all mines on Io were lacking in "people skills."

Accordingly, top management decreed that all future rotations on Io would be supervised by a management team trained in "people skills." You, your teammates, and the other management teams in your rotation, are the first teams to have received such training.

You just left Earth. After a two-year journey, you will arrive on Io, ready to begin managing a mine during the first quarter of 2086. During your trip, you will be oriented to the decisions to be made by the orientation materials that follow. Your success and the safety of miners depend on your understanding of this information.

Have a good trip!

IO ENTERPRISES ORIENTATION MATERIALS

Top management decided to let each management team name their mine. It was felt that this action would help build rapport among management team members and esprit de corps among mine personnel. This name is in effect during each management team's one-year rotation.

One of your first decisions, then, is to name your mine. This is a one-time decision. Name your mine the first time you complete a team decision form (TDF). Names cannot exceed 20 characters, including spaces. A discussion of decisions you must make each period follows.

Your Decisions

The equipment, technology, and resources of all mines on Io are identical. Any improvements in productivity and profits depend entirely on your management of human resources. Refer to the organizational chart on page 328 if you have questions regarding formal relationships between personnel while responding to scenarios.

Each period, you enter decisions pertaining to scenarios, compensation, and training on team decision forms (TDFs) found in Appendix B. Your management team will submit one completed TDF each period.

The Scenarios

Each quarter, your management team will be confronted with "people situations" to resolve. Scenarios come to you on a printout separate from your management report. These situations pertain to any combination of "people skills" your instructor wishes to provide. All management teams face the same scenarios. Unless indicated otherwise, all mines are affected by scenarios equally.

Scenarios include personnel shown in the organizational chart on page 328. Support and administrative staff are included in scenarios because the productivity of miners is affected by the contributions of these employees.

Unless changed by your instructor, content of scenarios will pertain to either situations requiring immediate *action* or to the *diagnosis* of a past, present, or future situation. Both types of scenarios involve the use of effective managerial skills. Scenarios involving diagnosis require understanding which is important to taking correct action in the future. Action scenarios involve actual decisions affecting productivity in the present.

Following is a representative "action" scenario pertaining to leadership:

> The top-producing crew's foreman was lost in a crevice, during an Io-quake. This crew gets along well and has well-defined tasks. A relationship-motivated crew member has applied for the foreman's job. According to the contingency model of leadership, would this replacement be successful?
> A. Yes.
> B. No.
> C. No theory covers this contingency.

According to Fiedler's contingency model (circa 1965), the best answer to the question posed in this scenario is item B.[4]

Following is a "diagnostic" scenario pertaining to motivation:

> Your lowest-producing and most poorly trained crew puzzles you. Crew members like and can rely on rewards for high performance. The definition of high performance is well understood. Crews on Io can count on being rewarded for performance. The primary problem here is with:
> A. Valence.
> B. Instrumentality.
> C. Expectancy.

The correct or best answer to this scenario is item C (based on Vroom's expectancy theory, circa 1964).[5]

During each decision period, you and your teammates will respond to 10 such scenarios. (*Note:* You will usually not have access to textbooks or other materials during a decision period.) The productivity of your mine will increase to the extent your management team makes correct responses to scenarios.

Pay ($50.00–$75.00)

Compensation practices on Io are intended to motivate miners in order to increase productivity. A mine's contribution to company profits is improved if increases in productivity outstrip increases in compensation and other expenses. The previous rotation of miners was paid $54 per hour during the last period.

The management team for each mine has the freedom to set hourly wages for miners within the range provided by corporate top management. This range is set for the present rotation at \$50.00–\$75.00 per hour. (*Note:* The cost-benefit associated with paying miners outside a \$55–\$65 range is usually not good.) Once a raise is given, it *cannot be retracted.* Each miner works a 30-hour week. There is no overtime.

What Is Productivity?

Productivity is concerned with the *efficiency* of production. Productivity gains represent improvements in efficiency. An improvement in productivity means that more has been produced relative to the amount of resources used (e.g., time, labor, capital).

Productivity on Io is defined as average tons of titanium ore produced per quarter per miner. This figure is computed by dividing total tons of output for a quarter per mine by 250 (number of miners assigned each mine who are paid wages each period).

Pay as a Motivator on Io

There was considerable controversy regarding the effect of pay as motivator during the heyday of human resources research (1960–1990).[6]

Some theorists believed that pay could be used only to stave off dissatisfaction or that pay primarily contributed to meeting primary needs. That is, pay could motivate only if a person lacked basic essentials such as food, shelter, and protection. Higher-order needs, such as the need for recognition, were seen to be stronger motivators than pay.

Other twentieth-century theorists argued that pay could be a motivator if tied to such factors as highly valued goals of employees. Edward Lawler contended that pay could motivate performance of adequately trained employees if they held these values:

1. Valued pay highly
2. Believed that good performance could result in high pay
3. Believed that by exerting effort they could improve performance
4. Believed that the advantage of working hard, performing well, and obtaining high pay exceeded disadvantages and psychic opportunity costs
5. Saw good performance as the most attractive of all possible behaviors in a given situation.[7]

On Io, all employees value pay highly. In many respects, a one-year rotation on Io can only be justified on the basis of pay.

The Ionian environment is dreary and the work is hard. There are few attractions on the moon beyond the momentary excitement new arrivals feel when they first witness the red, yellow, black, and white Ionian moonscape (vivid colors due to chemical reactions caused by the sulphur content in the atmosphere and on the surface) and the red and yellow mass of Jupiter hanging directly over their heads.

Some mine personnel do enjoy playing "moonball," a modification of field hockey adapted to the low gravity of Io. (Moonball rules adapted to Earth gravity are found in Appendix A.) Nevertheless, this enjoyment does not fully compensate for the very difficult living and working conditions on Io. In short, compensation, in the form of wages and bonuses, is an important motivational tool on Io. As noted previously, the wages paid to miners at competing Io Enterprises mines also has an influence on pay as a motivator.

Pay Equity. In time, all the miners on Io learn of the wages paid at other mines. This information is usually conveyed by space station employees to staffers working for maintenance or mine supervisors. From there, the information travels informally through the grapevine to foremen who then pass it on to miners. Miners determine the equity of pay practices from this information, and this determination can significantly affect productivity and absenteeism.

Miners are motivated to the extent they are paid adequately and equitably. Remember, once a pay raise is given, it cannot be taken back.

Bonuses (Optional; $5.00–$10.00 *if paid*)

You can also provide bonuses to miners. Bonus payments are optional and are tacked on to hourly wages. The previous rotation of miners did not receive bonus payments.

Like hourly wages, the allowable range of bonus payments is determined by top management. That range is presently defined as $5.00–$10.00 per hour. Bonuses for less than $5.00 hourly are not allowed.

Bonuses are temporary "incentive money." The effect of a bonus on productivity is enhanced to the extent *you respond correctly to scenarios*. The effect of bonus payments on productivity declines with each incorrect response to a scenario during each period. If you provide incorrect responses to more than two scenarios, the effect of bonus payments on productivity will be *significantly* reduced.

Productivity cannot be increased simply by "throwing money" at miners. Bonus payments must work in concert with correct responses to scenarios. Otherwise, miners receive mixed messages, which can obviate the positive impact of a bonus.

Bonus payments can be withdrawn or reduced from one period to the next. This action will not cause a decrease in productivity. Also, bonuses will not be paid to miners absent from work.

Training ($0–$99,999)

Top management has also provided each management team with a training budget not to exceed $99,999 per quarter. (Trainers and high-tech training materials are available on-call from the space station orbiting Io.) Expenditure of any amount up to the ceiling is acceptable. Investment in training is optional. The previous rotation of miners did not receive training during the last period.

It may seem like $50,000, $60,000, or even $99,999 is a large amount to spend per quarter for training, however, each new rotation of miners is entirely new to the Ionian environment. Consequently, training is individualized and intensive, which adds to its cost.

Training has two positive effects on productivity. First, training assists miners to make better use of equipment and other resources, thereby increasing productivity. Second, there is evidence that training reduces injuries.[8]

Injured workers cannot work, yet Io Enterprises has contracted to provide injured (as well as otherwise absent) workers *full pay* (but not

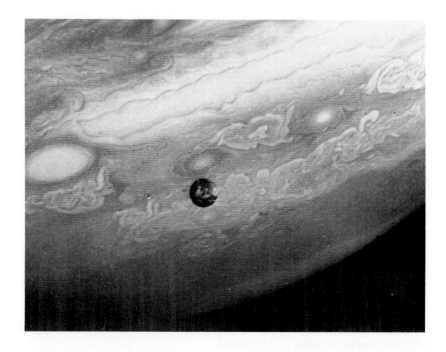

bonuses!) for work days missed. This provision was necessary in order to attract miners to Io. Consequently, injured workers are included in productivity calculations. In this sense, training expenditures increase mine productivity if miners, who might otherwise have been injured and unable to work, are able to work.

Avoiding injuries to miners is important. Of all miners injured during a period, 20 percent will never return to work during their one-year rotation. The number of injured miners unable to work can accumulate rapidly and can significantly reduce productivity.

The effect of training dollars builds *after* an initial investment. (It takes time for people to benefit from training.) This means that an initial training investment does not appear to have much of an effect (the effect will come later). It also means that training dollars spent during the final period are of little benefit. Training investment is also "layered," with the effects from previous periods being added to current investment.

Earning Profits

You're probably wondering how a management team could lose money. Based on your orientation to this point, it might seem easy to earn profits. Simply handle "people situations" correctly, and invest the maximum amount possible in pay, bonuses, and training.

The problem with this perspective is that you could have the most productive miners on Io, but still earn relatively less profit because your miners have essentially been overpaid and/or overtrained relative to their productivity. Always keep in mind that you are charged with earning satisfactory *profits*. Your goal is to outearn all mines on Io.

It is for this reason that you should not simply maximize pay, bonus, and training expenditures.

Take a look at the income statement in the last rotation's management report (page 337). Increasing compensation (pay and bonuses) of miners will increase "total expenses." The income statement formula is revenue minus expenses equals profit (or loss). Put another way, tons of ore mined times $200 (revenue) minus cost of production and total operating expenses (expenses) equals your mine's contribution to company profits.

Increasing your expenses (e.g., providing a wage increase or training) can only be justified to the extent a proportionately greater increase occurs in revenues. In other words, there is a law of diminishing marginal returns that affects profits. At some point, a dollar spent on compensation and training will bring less than a dollar back in the form of productivity increases. One of your tasks will be to determine where that point lies for your mine.

Since you have never managed a titanium mine on Io, and the previous management team paid an insufficient wage and did not invest in training and bonuses, you will have to determine the best mix of compensation (wages and bonuses) and training for your employees.

Some advice: Look at the company averages column found in the management report to see what your competition is doing. This is particularly important for maintaining wage equity. Training expenditures also have the most impact early in your rotation. Try to keep hourly wages between $55 and $65 and pay a modest to moderate bonus. Finally, respond correctly to scenarios! Correct application of "people skills" is vitally important to your success.

Now on to the management report!

THE MANAGEMENT REPORT

Following is a management report from the last quarter for the mine you inherit. You will use this report, together with scenarios provided by your instructor, to make decisions for the first period.

Coincidentally, all mines on Io performed exactly the same last quarter! As you can see, the last rotation of management teams didn't fare too well. They lost $300,000 during the quarter. Top management's concern about the Io mining colony is well founded!

Feedback

As you can see, the last management team responded incorrectly to three scenarios pertaining to motivation during the last period.

The feedback section of the management report refers you to a page number in a twentieth-century text titled *Managerial Skills in Organizations* published by Allyn and Bacon. The company was never able to duplicate the quality of this text. Consequently, it is used to this day by The Overlake in all of its mining divisions and subsidiaries, including Io Enterprises. (If no page number appears in the management report, it means your instructor developed a scenario using his or her own material.)

Refer to the page number indicated if you responded incorrectly to a scenario. Discuss incorrect responses with team members and your instructor. You may disagree with the rationale provided in the text or other written materials used by your instructor. Some disagreement is to be expected when "people skills" involving human behavior and interaction are at issue. However, don't dwell on any disagreements you may have. Instead, try to understand the rationale for the preferred answer to the scenario.

IO ENTERPRISES MANAGEMENT REPORT
FOURTH QUARTER, OCTOBER-DECEMBER, 2085

Class: Not Assigned   **Instructor: Not Assigned**
ALL MINES

—FEEDBACK—

Scenario #	Responses Actual	Preferred	Pages	Scenario #	Responses Actual	Preferred	Pages
1	C	C	57	6	B	B	65
2*	C	B	73	7	B	B	61
3	B	B	71	8	B	B	70
4	B	B	65	9	C	C	70
5*	A	B	60	10*	C	B	59

*INDICATES INCORRECT RESPONSE   Total Correct: 7

—INCOME STATEMENT—

Revenue (37,550 tons at $200/ton)		$7,510,000
Production costs	6,760,000	
plus bonus pay	0	
Gross Margin		$ 750,000
Expenses		
Selling	$200,000	
Administrative	500,000	
Insurance	200,000	
Training	0	
Miscellaneous	150,000	
Total Expenses		$1,050,000
Contribution to Profit		$ −300,000
Contribution to Profit (YTD)		$100,000

—PRODUCTION REPORT—

	Ore Produced	Company Av.
Ore Produced	37,550	37,550
Productivity	150.20	150.20
Hourly Pay	$54.00	$54.00
Bonus	$0.00	$ 0.00
Training	$0.00	$0.00

—ABSENTEEISM REPORT—

	Last Quarter	Company Av.
Noninjury-Related		
Causes: Missed scenarios	2	
Wage inequity	0	
Other	2	
Total Noninjury-Related	4	4.0
Injury-Related		
Causes: Missed scenarios	2	
Inadequate training	2	
From previous quarters	5	
Other	1	
Total Injury Related	10	10.0
Injuries (To-Date) 28		7.0
Total Absenteeism	14	14.0

—Status Report—
WELCOME TO IO ENTERPRISES: A MICROCOMPUTER SIMULATION!

The Income Statement

The income statement reports revenues, expenses, and profits. Following are definitions of each part of the income statement:

Revenue: Defined as the number of tons of titanium ore mined times the price per ton ($200.00). This is the contract price negotiated by The Overlake. This price is maintained for the entire year. Revenue for the past quarter was $7,510,000.

Cost of Production: Includes fixed cost of $1,900,000 plus wages for miners during the period. *Wages* are defined as 250 (number of miners) times quarterly hours per miner of 360, times an hourly wage ranging from $50.00–$75.00. Remember: Wages must be paid to miners even if they are absent!

Bonus Pay: Bonuses are optional. If paid, bonus pay is defined as the number of *working* miners for a period times quarterly hours of 360 times an hourly bonus ranging from $5.00–$10.00. Bonus payments below $5.00 are not allowed. Bonuses are also *not* paid to miners who are absent. No bonuses were paid to the previous rotation of miners during the last period.

Gross Margin: The difference between revenue and cost of production and bonus payments, sometimes called "gross profit." Gross margin last quarter was $750,000.

Selling Expenses: Fixed amount of $200,000 each period.

Administrative: Fixed amount of $500,000 each period.

Insurance Premium: A fixed amount of $100,000 per quarter, *unless* injuries of miners (year-to-date) exceed 13. If this total is exceeded, your insurance premium is doubled for the duration of your rotation. Consequently, increases in insurance premiums reduce profits. Premiums were doubled during the last quarter of last year.

Training: Expenditure of up to $99,999 is allowed each period. Last period, no investment in training was made.

Miscellaneous: Fixed amount of $150,000.

Total Expenses: The sum of all selling, administrative, insurance, training, and miscellaneous expenses. Total expenses last quarter were $1,050,000.

Contribution to Profit: This is the amount your mine contributed to Io Enterprises profits for the quarter. Last quarter, the management team of each mine on Io lost $300,000.

Contribution YTD: This is your mine's cumulative contribution year-to-date (from the beginning of the year, January 1, 2086, to the present). You begin your rotation with a Contribution YTD of zero.

The Production Report

The production report includes information for your mine, plus company averages.

Ore Produced: Total tons of titanium ore extracted from your mine during the quarter. Last period, the previous rotation extracted 37,550 tons of ore.

Productivity: As defined on page 332, productivity on Io is computed by dividing the total tons of ore produced for a quarter per mine by 250 number of miners compensated for the period. Productivity last period for the previous rotation was 150.2.

Hourly Pay: As defined on page 331, hourly pay is $50.00–$75.00. Hourly pay last period was $54.

Bonus: As defined on page 333, bonus pay is $5.00–$10.00 per hour (if paid). Note: Only mines paying bonuses are included in the "company average" figure. Last period, none of the mines on Io paid a bonus.

Training: As defined on page 334, any amount up to $99,999 per quarter may be invested in training. Training expenses are also included on the income statement. Last period, none of the mines on Io invested in training.

The Absenteeism Report

Total absenteeism is *equivalent* to the number of full-time miners lost during the quarter due to absenteeism. Absenteeism on Io occurs for one of two reasons. Either the miner has reported sick or the miner has been injured. Sometimes miners reporting sick are actually sick, but sick leave is also used by dissatisfied miners as a means of avoiding work.

You must still pay wages to miners even if they are absent, so absenteeism maintains expenses without contributing to revenue. This reduces total productivity because fewer miners are available to extract titanium ore.

Absenteeism: Noninjury Related.   Absenteeism is a multidimensional phenomenon. Dissatisfied workers tend to be absent more than satisfied workers. However, people are not always absent from work because they are dissatisfied.

Sometimes a positive attraction to an alternative activity is the cause of absenteeism rather than avoidance of a working environment. There are also other nonwork-related reasons for absenteeism. For instance, an absence is required for a doctor's appointment. (As you know, advances in dentistry made this occupation obsolete around the year 2005.)

On Io, there are simply no attractive options that would cause a miner to take a day off (like going fishing). Other reasons for absenteeism, such as medical appointments, are scheduled by management so that the productivity of the mines is not compromised.

To keep noninjury-related absenteeism down, and to maintain or increase productivity, you must *make correct decisions on scenarios* and *keep your wages for miners adequate and equitable.* There will, however, be some absenteeism that is uncontrollable (noted under "other" in the absenteeism report).

Absenteeism: Injury Related.   Miners are also absent when they have been injured. If "injuries to date" exceed 13, your mine's insurance premiums will double for the remainder of the year. This will reduce future profits proportionately.

Injuries on Io are very serious. You will lose 20 percent of miners injured during a period for the remainder of the year (indicated under "from previous quarters" in the absenteeism report). Injured miners who are unable to work because of injuries from previous quarters will accumulate.

Titanium mining in the vacuum of deep space is extremely dangerous. Underground miners can be injured by "cave-ups" and malfunctioning equipment. Surface miners are prone to injury because of the instability of the moon surface and the difficulty of moving tons of ore in a low-gravity environment. Injuries can also be caused by carelessness in an environment where nuclear detonations are commonplace.

There are two ways to reduce injuries and thereby maintain or improve productivity. The first approach is, again, to *respond correctly to scenarios.*

There is evidence that high absenteeism and high injury rates are associated.[9] Consequently, you will find that incorrect responses to scenarios will lead to increases in absenteeism which, in turn, are associated with increases in injury rates. The more errors on scenarios the management team makes, the more miners will be injured.

Another way to reduce injuries is to *invest in training.* Training helps miners to avoid errors that cause injuries. Of course, training expenditures also increase expenses that can reduce profits if productivity increases are not proportionately greater.

As with noninjury-related absenteeism, there will usually be some injuries that are uncontrollable (noted under "other" in the "injury-related" section of the absenteeism report).

The Status Report

The last section of the management report is a status report. Here, you will learn of past, present, or future conditions that could affect the productivity and profitability of your mine. Unless indicated otherwise, all mines on Io are affected equally by status report information. You will face any of a number of conditions that have the potential of affecting the safety, working conditions, or general satisfaction of miners.

Now that you are approaching Jupiter's orbital system, you would do well to review the management report format once again. You will need to interpret this report with confidence as you make decisions in the year ahead.

CONCLUSION

Tighten your seat belts! You're about to land and begin your one-year rotation on Io.

If your responses to scenarios are correct, if the full impact of bonus payments can be felt, if wages are adequate and equitable, if training expenditures are sufficient, and if miners are not absent or injured, productivity and profits will be maximized.

Refer to Table 1 on page 342. This table summarizes decisions and considerations you will face.

To conclude, we hope that the experience gained from *Io Enterprises: A Microcomputer Simulation* serves you well in the years ahead.

You may never experience space travel, but your children might, and your grandchildren most certainly will. The management of human resources will continue to be a concern, regardless of where future generations travel, work, and live.

Good Luck!

Table 1 Summary of Decisions

Decision	Considerations
Responses to scenarios.	Correct responses lead to productivity increases.
	To the extent responses are correct, injuries and absenteeism are reduced which also increases productivity.
Pay	$50.00–$75.00
	Pay is highly valued on Io. A pay raise can lead to a productivity increase by itself.
	Equity of pay practices is also an important consideration. Keeping wages competitive will increase productivity by reducing miner dissatisfaction.
	Equitable pay practices also reduce absenteeism which, in turn, improves productivity.
	Once given, a pay raise cannot be taken back.
Bonus payments	$5.00–$10.00 per hour (if paid).
	Bonus payments are not required.
	Bonuses are one-time "incentive money" intended to increase productivity.
	The impact of bonus payments is influenced by correct responses to scenarios. Incorrect responses reduce the impact of bonuses. If more than two scenarios for a period are answered incorrectly, the effect of the bonus upon productivity of miners during that period will be *significantly* reduced.
	Reducing bonus payments from one period to the next will not adversely affect miner's perceptions of equity.

Training   0–$99,999 per period.

Training expenditures are not required.

Training increases productivity and profits by reducing injuries. If cumulative injuries exceed 13, insurance premiums will be doubled for the remainder of the year.

20 percent of miners injured during any period will be lost for the remainder of the year.

Training also contributes to an increase in productivity by itself.

The effect of training expenditures builds *after* the initial investment, there is a residual training effect from one period to the next.

ENDNOTES

1. Foster, A. D. *Outland*. New York: Warner Books, 1981.

2. The travels of the asteroid "Prometheus" and the future use of solar power collectors was inspired by: O'Leary, B. "Asteroid mining." *Astronomy*, 6 (1978): 6–17.

3. O'Leary, "Asteroid mining." See also: "Space colonies are ahead, but no ET, scientist says." *Everett Herald* (Washington), May 30, 1984.

4. Fiedler, F. E. "Engineer the job to fit the manager." *Harvard Business Review*, 43 (1965): 115–122.

5. Vroom, V. *Work and Motivation*. New York: Wiley, 1964.

6. The decline in human resources research began during the 1990s as government funding sources and the priorities of research institutions moved completely away from the study of organizational behavior to the study of technology. Productivity problems on Io are but one result of the shortsightedness of this emphasis.

7. Lawler, E. E. *Pay and Organizational Effectiveness: A Psychological View*. New York: McGraw-Hill, 1971.

8. Fiedler, F. E.; Bell, C. H.; Chemers, M. M.; & Patrick, D. "Increasing mine productivity and safety through management training and organizational development: A comparative study." *Basic and Applied Psychology*, 5 (1984): 1–18.

9. Goodman, P. S., & Atkins, R. S. *Absenteeism*. San Francisco: Jossey-Bass, 1984.

APPENDIX A
Moonball

MOONBALL RULES (ADAPTED TO EARTH GRAVITY)

Moonball is an important part of life in the mining colonies on Io. A formal moonball league exists. Teams, representing different Io Enterprises mines, compete every Saturday from March until December. Intramural moonball tournaments are also conducted and, like league games, provide respite from the dreariness and hardship of the Ionian environment.

Miners who return to Earth after a one-year rotation on Io often miss the sport. A few years ago, a group of moonball aficionados adapted the sport so that it could be played in Earth gravity. The Earth version is not as exciting as the Ionian version. You see, on Io, moonball is played as much above as on the ground.

The following version has still proven satisfying to the many now Earth-bound men and women who were accomplished moonball players during their time on Io.

The Rules

Moonball is very simple. It is similar to field hockey in that the objective of the game is to place the ball in the enemy's goal. (Except in moonball, the objective is to hit the opposing team's "point stand." On Io, point stands are electronic touch-sensitive standards about the size of a chair. On Earth, an actual chair is used.)

There are eight rules:

1. Official Earth-bound moonball equipment *must* be used. That equipment is as follows:
   a. A large fully inflated beach ball.
   b. One nerf bat per player.

   Any number from 4 to 20 per side can play. The moonball playing field (whether outdoors or indoors in a gymnasium) should be 20 to 80 yards long, or whatever happens to be available. Out-of-bounds should be defined. Point standards (chairs) should be placed in the middle of both goal-lines. Moonball games are comprised of two 20-minute halves with a 5–10-minute rest period (and pause for refreshments) in between halves.

2. A coin toss determines which team puts the ball into play.

3. The losing team must bat the ball from mid-field to the receiving team (in moonball, hitting the ball is referred to as "batting"). The receiving team must be at least 5 feet from where the ball is batted. Note: If the ball strikes the ground on the bat-off, without being touched by the receiving team, the bat-off must be repeated.

4. The receiving team then attempts to bat the ball, without the ball touching the ground, towards the opposing team's point standard.

5. One player cannot bat the ball more than three times in succession. He or she must pass the ball to a teammate, or try to hit the point standard, on at least the third bat.

6. If a player bats the ball more than three times, if the ball touches the ground or goes out of bounds, or if the ball is batted with something (hand, foot, head) other than the bat, the opposing team takes over on offense.

   One player from the offensive team (selected by his/her team) is then allowed to bat the ball into play from the point where the infraction occurred. On out-of-bounds calls, the ball is batted into play from the sideline. Defensive players must be at least 5 feet from this player when the ball is finally batted into play.

   The opposing team also takes possession if successful in intercepting the ball. Play should not be interrupted after an interception.

   Time-outs may be called at any time, but only by the offensive team (except in the case of injury to a player). The offensive team must bat the ball back into play out-of-bounds and parallel to the point on the field where the time-out was called (following the out-of-bounds procedure outlined above).

7. Play continues until a point standard (chair) is actually struck with the ball. One point is scored for the offensive team. Play resumes when the team which scored bats the ball from mid-field to the opposing team.

   Note: No more than two members of the defending team can be within 10 feet of the point standard at any time. This is a very important rule of moonball. A team guilty of "standard stacking" forfeits the game the second time the infraction occurs. There is no penalty for the first violation, play simply continues.

8. Lastly, referees are not used in moonball. Players are expected to resolve differences in a constructive manner using good human relations skills.

   Traditionally, particularly in the intramural leagues on Io, the losing team treats the winning team to refreshments.

Team Decision Forms

Io Enterprises
TEAM DECISION FORM

PERIOD: January–March, 2086

Team Name _____

Team Number _____

SOLUTIONS (place a check mark next to the most correct response)

ONE			SIX		
A. _____	B. _____	C. _____	A. _____	B. _____	C. _____
TWO			SEVEN		
A. _____	B. _____	C. _____	A. _____	B. _____	C. _____
THREE			EIGHT		
A. _____	B. _____	C. _____	A. _____	B. _____	C. _____
FOUR			NINE		
A. _____	B. _____	C. _____	A. _____	B. _____	C. _____
FIVE			TEN		
A. _____	B. _____	C. _____	A. _____	B. _____	C. _____

PAY? ____.____
(Range $50.00–$75.00)

TRAINING? _____
(Range $0–$99,999)

BONUS ____.____
(Range $5.00–$10.00)

A Summary of Decisions

Responses to scenarios.

Correct responses lead to productivity increases.

To the extent responses are correct, injuries and absenteeism are reduced which also increases productivity.

Pay

Pay is highly valued on Io. A pay raise can lead to a productivity increase by itself.

Equity of pay practices is an important consideration. Keeping wages competitive increases productivity by reducing miner dissatisfaction.

Equitable pay practices reduce absenteeism which improves productivity.

Bonus payments

$5.00–$10.00 per hour (if paid).

Bonus payments are not required.

Bonuses are one time "incentive money" to increase productivity.

Incorrect responses to scenarios reduce the impact of bonuses. If more than two scenarios for a period are answered incorrectly, the effect of the bonus upon productivity of miners during that period will be *significantly* reduced.

Reducing bonus payments from one period to the next will not adversely affect miner's perceptions of equity.

Training

0–$99,999 per period.

Training expenditures are not required.

Training increases productivity and profits by reducing injuries. If cumulative injuries exceed 13, insurance premiums double for the rest of the year.

20 percent of miners injured during any period will be lost for the remainder of the year.

Training contributes to an increase in productivity by itself.

The effect of training builds *after* the initial investment; there is a residual training effect from one period to the next.

Io Enterprises
TEAM DECISION FORM

PERIOD: April–June, 2086

Team Name _____

Team Number _____

SOLUTIONS (place a check mark next to the most correct response)

ONE

A. _____   B. _____   C. _____

TWO

A. _____   B. _____   C. _____

THREE

A. _____   B. _____   C. _____

FOUR

A. _____   B. _____   C. _____

FIVE

A. _____   B. _____   C. _____

SIX

A. _____   B. _____   C. _____

SEVEN

A. _____   B. _____   C. _____

EIGHT

A. _____   B. _____   C. _____

NINE

A. _____   B. _____   C. _____

TEN

A. _____   B. _____   C. _____

PAY? _____._____
(Range $50.00–$75.00)

BONUS _____._____
(Range $5.00–$10.00)

TRAINING? _____
(Range $0–$99,999)

A Summary of Decisions

Responses to scenarios.

Correct responses lead to productivity increases.

To the extent responses are correct, injuries and absenteeism are reduced which also increases productivity.

Pay

Pay is highly valued on Io. A pay raise can lead to a productivity increase by itself.

Equity of pay practices is an important consideration. Keeping wages competitive increases productivity by reducing miner dissatisfaction.

Equitable pay practices reduce absenteeism which improves productivity.

Bonus payments

$5.00–$10.00 per hour (if paid).

Bonus payments are not required.

Bonuses are one time "incentive money" to increase productivity.

Incorrect responses to scenarios reduce the impact of bonuses. If more than two scenarios for a period are answered incorrectly, the effect of the bonus upon productivity of miners during that period will be *significantly* reduced.

Reducing bonus payments from one period to the next will not adversely affect miner's perceptions of equity.

Training

0–$99,999 per period.

Training expenditures are not required.

Training increases productivity and profits by reducing injuries. If cumulative injuries exceed 13, insurance premiums double for the rest of the year.

20 percent of miners injured during any period will be lost for the remainder of the year.

Training contributes to an increase in productivity by itself.

The effect of training builds *after* the initial investment; there is a residual training effect from one period to the next.

Io Enterprises
TEAM DECISION FORM

PERIOD: July–September, 2086   Team Name _____

                                                Team Number ____

SOLUTIONS (place a check mark next to the most correct response)

ONE			SIX		
A. ____	B. ____	C. ____	A. ____	B. ____	C. ____
TWO			SEVEN		
A. ____	B. ____	C. ____	A. ____	B. ____	C. ____
THREE			EIGHT		
A. ____	B. ____	C. ____	A. ____	B. ____	C. ____
FOUR			NINE		
A. ____	B. ____	C. ____	A. ____	B. ____	C. ____
FIVE			TEN		
A. ____	B. ____	C. ____	A. ____	B. ____	C. ____

PAY? ____.____   TRAINING? _____
(Range $50.00–$75.00)   (Range $0–$99,999)

BONUS ____.____
(Range $5.00–$10.00)

A Summary of Decisions

Responses to scenarios.

Correct responses lead to productivity increases.

To the extent responses are correct, injuries and absenteeism are reduced which also increases productivity.

Pay

Pay is highly valued on Io. A pay raise can lead to a productivity increase by itself.

Equity of pay practices is an important consideration. Keeping wages competitive increases productivity by reducing miner dissatisfaction.

Equitable pay practices reduce absenteeism which improves productivity.

Bonus payments

$5.00–$10.00 per hour (if paid).

Bonus payments are not required.

Bonuses are one time "incentive money" to increase productivity.

Incorrect responses to scenarios reduce the impact of bonuses. If more than two scenarios for a period are answered incorrectly, the effect of the bonus upon productivity of miners during that period will be *significantly* reduced.

Reducing bonus payments from one period to the next will not adversely affect miner's perceptions of equity.

Training

0–$99,999 per period.

Training expenditures are not required.

Training increases productivity and profits by reducing injuries. If cumulative injuries exceed 13, insurance premiums double for the rest of the year.

20 percent of miners injured during any period will be lost for the remainder of the year.

Training contributes to an increase in productivity by itself.

The effect of training builds *after* the initial investment; there is a residual training effect from one period to the next.

Io Enterprises
TEAM DECISION FORM

PERIOD: October–December, 2086   Team Name _____

Team Number ____

SOLUTIONS (place a check mark next to the most correct response)

ONE			SIX		
A. ____	B. ____	C. ____	A. ____	B. ____	C. ____
TWO			SEVEN		
A. ____	B. ____	C. ____	A. ____	B. ____	C. ____
THREE			EIGHT		
A. ____	B. ____	C. ____	A. ____	B. ____	C. ____
FOUR			NINE		
A. ____	B. ____	C. ____	A. ____	B. ____	C. ____
FIVE			TEN		
A. ____	B. ____	C. ____	A. ____	B. ____	C. ____

PAY? ____ . ____   TRAINING? _____
(Range $50.00–$75.00)   (Range $0–$99,999)

BONUS ____ . ____
(Range $5.00–$10.00)

A Summary of Decisions

Responses to scenarios.

Correct responses lead to productivity increases.

To the extent responses are correct, injuries and absenteeism are reduced which also increases productivity.

Pay

Pay is highly valued on Io. A pay raise can lead to a productivity increase by itself.

Equity of pay practices is an important consideration. Keeping wages competitive increases productivity by reducing miner dissatisfaction.

Equitable pay practices reduce absenteeism which improves productivity.

Bonus payments

$5.00–$10.00 per hour (if paid).

Bonus payments are not required.

Bonuses are one time "incentive money" to increase productivity.

Incorrect responses to scenarios reduce the impact of bonuses. If more than two scenarios for a period are answered incorrectly, the effect of the bonus upon productivity of miners during that period will be *significantly* reduced.

Reducing bonus payments from one period to the next will not adversely affect miner's perceptions of equity.

Training

0–$99,999 per period.

Training expenditures are not required.

Training increases productivity and profits by reducing injuries. If cumulative injuries exceed 13, insurance premiums double for the rest of the year.

20 percent of miners injured during any period will be lost for the remainder of the year.

Training contributes to an increase in productivity by itself.

The effect of training builds *after* the initial investment; there is a residual training effect from one period to the next.

Glossary

Action research: A method for diagnosing individual problems, such as low morale and poor production (p. 296).

Active listening: Involves the timely and appropriate provision of feedback that facilitates achievement of meaning between communicators (p. 19).

Alternative pay practices: Complement or otherwise modify traditional pay plans (such as cafeteria-style benefit programs, lump-sum salary increases, and skills-based evaluation) (p. 74).

Attitudinal restructuring: Intended to build bonds between negotiating parties by building trust and favorably influencing the attitudes of participants toward each other (p. 99).

Authority: Tied to legitimate power or power that is expected in a social setting. Usually associated with a formal position in an organization (p. 238).

Autonomous work groups: Small work groups that have responsibility for a specific task and manage themselves within limits defined by the organization (p. 307).

Bases of power: Reward, coercive, legitimate, referent, and expert power account for individual power in small groups (p. 227).

BATNA: "Best alternative to a negotiated agreement" (p. 103).

Behavior observation scales (BOS): Requires that raters respond to all behaviors associated with a job dimension. In doing so, raters indicate the frequency with which behaviors occur (p. 155).

Behaviorally anchored rating scales (BARS): Requires that raters judge behavior associated with a dimension of a job (p. 155).

Bounded rationality model: People tend to focus on only a few alternatives and eventually select the first alternative minimally sufficient to solve a problem (p. 197).

Brainstorming: Focuses on generating ideas by permitting nonevaluative presentation of alternatives by group members (p. 203).

Bystander: Managers who make infrequent attempts to influence others. Bystanders tend to enjoy little organizational power or satisfaction (p. 235).

Centralization: Concerns the dispersement of decision-making authority across an organization (p. 213).

Change agent: A consultant or facilitator who facilitates change in an organization (p. 293).

Coalitions: Ad hoc alliances formed with the purpose of influencing the course of organizational events (p. 239).

Cognitive resource theory: Proposes that leader intelligence influences group performance when the task requires intellectual ability and the leader acts in a directive fashion, experiences little stress, and has the support of the group (p. 260).

Commission pay: A compensation system where pay is based on a percentage of output (e.g., sales) (p. 73).

Communication: A process whereby symbols generated by people are received and responded to by other people (p. 16).

Communication networks: Depict the flow of communication between and among members of a group. In centralized networks, communications flow through a focal person; in decentralized networks, group members have direct access to each other (p. 33).

Communication rules: Define the communication process to be used by group members (p. 35).

Compressed workweek: A work schedule that allows employees to work a standard number of hours per month in fewer than the standard number of working days (p. 299).

Conflict: Occurs when there is an incongruity of fit between the aspirations of interdependent parties (p. 91).

Conflict management strategies: Include avoidance, competitiveness, compromise, collaboration, and accommodation. These strategies involve different degrees of assertiveness and cooperativeness (p. 95).

Conformity: The tendency of individuals to change their behavior as a result of group pressure (p. 236).

Confrontation meeting: A meeting in which the entire management team discusses and evaluates the organization's health (p. 304).

Consensus decision making: An interactive group decision-making process where the decision made is a "collective opinion" rather than the result of majority rule (as in voting) or minority rule (as when the leader makes the decision) (p. 203).

Contingency approach: Indicates that the performance appraisal method used should be based on the capability to define work outcomes and behaviors associated with a given job or job family (p. 172).

Contingency model: According to Fiedler, effective leadership is contingent on the match between the personality of the leader and the dictates of the situation (p. 265).

Contrient organizational climate: An organizational climate where interdependent parties perceive that one party's gain will be another party's loss (p. 110).

Coping: The dynamic efforts one makes in response to stressors (p. 130).

DAP-MAP-RAP: A performance review method that bases timing, content, and action following a review on past employee performance. Reviews are developmental, maintenance, or remedial in nature, depending on performance (p. 164).

Decision making: Involves solving a problem or otherwise attaining a goal by choosing among alternative courses of action (p. 190).

Decision-making process: Steps are: definition of the problem, consideration and selection of an alternative, implementation, and evaluation (p. 190).

Decision rules: Procedural guidelines that direct a group decision-making process (p. 201).

Decision strategies: The decision strategy selected (aided analytic, unaided analytic, or nonanalytic) should be based on the decision environment and characteristics of the decision (p. 191).

Degree of interdependence: The degree of interdependence between groups in an organization. Groups have pooled (low), sequential (moderate), or reciprocal (high) interdependence with other groups (p. 104).

Delphi technique: A structured group decision-making process where a panel of experts independently analyzes a problem with the assistance of a central facilitator until consensus is reached (p. 205).

Dissonance balancing: The tendency of people to justify or balance the dissonance they feel when things do not go as well as planned (p. 200).

Distributive bargaining: A traditional approach to bargaining that results in the distribution of limited resources and "win-lose" outcomes (p. 99).

Door-in-the-face technique: An influence tactic in which the user begins by making a large request that is likely to be rejected and follows it up with a smaller request (p. 234).

Equity theory: States that people are motivated by fairness. Perceptions of fairness are based on comparisons made by employees with "comparison others" in terms of the ratio between job inputs and outputs (p. 64).

ERG theory: Proposes three levels of human needs: existence, relatedness, and growth. Asserts that individuals move down the needs hierarchy if needs at a higher level have been frustrated (p. 59).

Ethical principles: Guides to moral behavior and the "correct" use of power. Three models of ethical behavior are utilitarianism, justice, and rights (p. 229).

Evaluation: Assessment of the consequences of past decisions (p. 199).

Evaluation criteria: Evaluative standards against which to assess an employee's attributes, motives, abilities, skills, knowledge, or behavior (p. 153).

Expected value: The expected value of an alternative is a function of the probability that a given action will lead to an outcome, and the value of the outcome to the decision maker(s) (p. 197).

Expectancy theory: Asserts that the force of motivation is a function of expectancy (belief that effort will lead to performance); instrumentality (that performance will lead to an outcome); and valence (value placed upon the outcome) (p. 60).

Feedback: Occurs during two-way communication when a receiver responds to the original sender of a communication (p. 19).

Flextime: A scheduling method that allows employees to start and end their work day at variable times (p. 299).

Foot-in-the-door technique: An influence tactic in which the user begins by making a smaller request that is likely to be granted and following it up with a larger request (p. 234).

Formal group: A group comprised of members brought together for the sole purpose of making decisions and solving problems (p. 30).

Gain-sharing plans: Group or organizational pay plan that allows employees to share in the gains (profits) of a business enterprise (e.g., Scanlon Plan, ESOPs) (p. 74).

Garbage in—Garbage out syndrome: All steps in the decision-making process benefit from using relevant, valid information. If you put "garbage in" you'll usually get "garbage out" (p. 193).

General Adaptation Syndrome (G.A.S.):   A generalized physical response to a stressor. The three stages are alarm (fight or flight), resistance, and exhaustion (p. 127).

Goal setting: The process of setting goals. Goals are statements of direction that describe desired states or end results (p. 152).

Goal-setting theory: According to this theory, setting specific, hard-but-achievable goals, accepted by subordinates, leads to higher performance than do vague goals or having no goals at all (p. 61).

Grapevine: The communications channel that connects the informal organization (p. 39).

Graphic rating scale: Displays a continuum or discrete categories of potential performance for each job dimension. Scales can be anchored using adjectives, numbers, or descriptions of behavior (p. 153).

Group cohesiveness: The atmosphere of closeness that results in a group from common beliefs, attitudes, and goal directedness (p. 107).

Group communication: Three or more persons who are interacting with one another in such a manner that each person influences and is influenced by each other person (p. 30).

Group diagnostic meeting: A diagnostic strategy carried out by the manager and group members to analyze performance problems (p. 302).

Group dynamics: Deals with how interaction among individuals within a group affects group processes (p. 206).

Group objectives: Objectives set for the entire group. Particularly relevant for interdependent work groups (p. 170).

Group polarization effect: Tendency of groups to shift toward a more extreme decision posture (risky or conservative) relative to the posture that would be taken by individual members (p. 209).

Groupthink: The compromise of critical thinking that occurs within highly cohesive decision-making groups in which members strive for conformity (p. 208).

Hardiness: A personality trait associated with feelings of control, commitment, and challenge (p. 128).

Hierarchy of needs: Purposes that human needs are arrayed in a hierarchy ranging from primary needs (physiological and safety needs) to higher-order needs (social, esteem, and self-actualization needs) (p. 58).

Horizontal communication: Communication across individuals and work groups at the same level within an organization. Facilitates coordination of efforts among organizational members (p. 38).

Implementation phase: The bridge between making a decision and evaluating results. The actual carrying out of a course of action based on a previous decision or decisions (p. 199).

Influence: The use of behaviorally based techniques to engender compliance and commitment from others (p. 233).

Informal organization: Is determined by the status, power, and politics of organization members (p. 39).

Ingratiation: The use of flattery and friendship to influence others (p. 234).

Integrative bargaining: A cooperative and assertive negotiation strategy used to maximize joint gains of negotiating parties. Synonymous with *constructive collaboration* (p. 98).

Interdependent relationships: Relationships where both (or all) parties must rely on one another to attain respective goals (p. 92).

Interpersonal communication: Communication between two people (p. 17).

Interrole conflict: Exists when a person is expected to play two or more incompatible roles (p. 135).

Intraorganizational bargaining: Involves intragroup negotiation so that group members will accept outcomes negotiated with other groups by the group leader or negotiator (p. 108).

Intrarole conflict: Exists when different people expect incompatible behaviors from the same role (p. 135).

Job analysis: Involves the measurement and recording of work activities associated with a job. This analysis includes determination of tools used and assessment of working conditions (p. 152).

Job characteristics model: An approach to redesigning jobs. Jobs with a high degree of skill variety, task identity, task significance, and autonomy are considered to have high motivating potential for employees with high growth needs (p. 67).

Job description: A written description of all work activities associated with a job (e.g., responsibilities, duties, reporting lines) (p. 152).

Job enrichment: An intervention that provides employees with more control over their jobs (p. 305).

Job specifications: Indicate minimum qualifications, such as work experience and education, necessary for an employee to perform a job adequately (p. 153).

Kinesics: Nonverbal communication (p. 26).

KISS principle: Keep It Short and Simple (p. 21).

Leader charisma: Leader qualities that are attractive to followers (p. 261).

Leader decision theory: According to Vroom and Yetton, subordinates should participate in decision making to the extent their contribution improves the quality of the decision, and to the extent follower acceptance of the decision is necessary (p. 268).

Leader emergence: Occurs whenever group members convey authority to a group member by virtue of their contribution to the group (p. 271).

Leader-member exchange model: Asserts that leaders develop different types of relationships with different followers, resulting in the development of in-groups and out-groups (p. 270).

Leader motive pattern: According to McClelland, individuals with high needs for power, low affiliation needs, and high self-control are likely to become effective leaders (p. 262).

Leadership: A relationship between an individual (the leader) and a group (or groups) of followers in which group productivity is influenced by the leader (p. 255).

Life and career planning: Interventions to help individuals assess skills, clarify work values, and implement career decisions (p. 297).

Life change events: Incidents that cause individuals to make major adjustments in their lives (p. 129).

Listening: A skill involving accurate receipt and interpretation of a communication (p. 31).

Machiavellianism (Mach):   A personality trait typified by tendencies to be aloof and distant, to take control of unstructured face-to-face interactions, and to use subtle forms of manipulation to gain influence (p. 233).

Management by objectives (MBO):   Performance appraisal that uses output as an evaluation criterion. Managers and subordinates participate in setting objectives, review progress periodically, and adjust activities and/or objectives as necessary (p. 158).

Management information system: Any organized approach for obtaining relevant and timely information on which to base management decisions (p. 213).

Mechanistic organization: Characterized by relatively stable technology and markets (p. 172).

Motivation: Psychological state that predisposes people to pursue or avoid certain activities and goals. Energy and direction are essential components of motivation (p. 53).

MUM effect: Tendency of subordinates to be hesitant to pass on bad news to superiors (p. 39).

Need for achievement: The need to exceed a performance standard. High achievers tend to assume responsibility for tasks, seek task-relevant feedback, and prefer moderate-risk situations (p. 57).

Need for power: An individual predisposition to think and act in ways that lead to a gain in power and influence (p. 232).

Negotiation jujitsu: When negotiating with a difficult opponent, involves asking questions, seeking clarification, and reframing personal attacks as an attack on the problem (p. 103).

Nominal group technique: A structured group decision-making process involving systematic recording of ideas and voting or ranking to reach agreement (p. 204).

Norms: Standards of behavior expected for an individual within a group (p. 106).

OD programs: Consists of three components: diagnosis, intervention, and evaluation (p. 291).

Office design: Layout of office furniture into a relatively open or closed format (p. 29).

On-the-job training: Training that helps employees learn about a job while on the job (p. 298).

Organic organization: Characterized by unstable, rapidly changing technology and markets (p. 172).

Organization development: The implementation of planned interventions designed to manage change effectively (p. 291).

Organization mirror technique: An intervention that allows a host group to use the opinions of other groups to analyze and solve performance deficiencies (p. 303).

Organizational behavior modification (OB Mod):   An approach to worker motivation based on principles of operant conditioning. OB Mod holds that organizational productivity can be improved by reinforcing desired employee behavior across the organization (p. 70).

Organizational characteristics: Pertains to the leader's position in the organizational hierarchy, the nature of the leader's job, and the nature of the organizational environment (p. 272).

Organizational communication: Is concerned with formal and informal, horizontal and vertical communication within an organization (p. 37).

Organizational planning framework: Includes determination of mission, the situation analysis, goal setting, strategic and tactical decision making, and a management information system (p. 210).

Organizational structure: The formal allocation of work, responsibility, and authority in an organization (p. 139).

Organizing principles: Conflict-reducing principles that focus on organizational structure. Include unity of command, the scalar principle, maintaining balance between authority and responsibility, and maintaining a manageable span of control (p. 111).

Paraphrasing: Repeating back in your own words what you thought you heard the sender of a communication say (p. 20).

Participation: Direct involvement in the processes of goal setting, problem identification, decision making, and implementation in work processes (p. 138).

Path-goal theory: According to House and Mitchell, depending on characteristics of followers, leader behavior should be supportive, directive, participative, or achievement-oriented (p. 267).

Pay: Monetary compensation (p. 73).

Peer evaluation: Performance appraisal conducted by co-workers (p. 169).

Perception checking: Involves checking out what you thought another person meant by a communication (p. 20).

Performance: Actual output. Effective performance requires both motivation and ability, as moderated by situational factors (p. 53).

Performance appraisal: The assessment of employee performance (p. 151).

Performance review: Occurs whenever a manger and a subordinate discuss performance appraisal results (p. 161).

Piece-rate pay: A compensation system where pay is based on the number of units produced (p. 73).

Politics: The use of power to further individual ends that are incompatible with the goals of others and may or may not be at odds with the goals of the organization (p. 239).

Power: The ability of an individual, group, or organization to change the behavior of others (p. 227).

Principled negotiation: When negotiating, involves separating the people from the problem; focusing on interests, not positions; inventing options for mutual gain; and using objective criteria (p. 100).

Programmed instruction: Training, carried out by automated teaching machines, that presents material in short, complete modules (p. 298).

Promotive organizational climate: An organizational climate where interdependent parties perceive that gains or losses by one will result in gains or losses by another (p. 110).

Proxemics: Study of the way people and animals use space (p. 28).

Rating error: A systematic recording of invalid impressions by raters. Examples of rating errors include contrast effects, leniency, central tendency, severity, halo effects, and attributional biases (p. 165).

Realistic job preview (RJP): The practice of telling new recruits exactly what a job entails, including both positive and negative aspects, in order to clarify expectations, build commitment to the organization, and reduce turnover (p. 297).

Role ambiguity: A state of confusion about the nature of a role (p. 135).

Role analysis technique: An intervention designed to clarify role expectations and obligations of team members to improve team effectiveness (p. 302).

Role negotiation technique: An intervention that facilitates negotiation in power struggles where group members do not wish to give up power and influence (p. 303).

Role overload: A condition in which role demands exceed the individual's ability to respond (p. 134).

Role underload: A condition in which the individual's abilities are under-utilized due to a lack of expectations (p. 134).

Roles: Standards of behavior expected for individuals working in a given position (p. 107).

Schedule of reinforcement: A plan used to distribute reinforcement. Includes continuous, intermittent, ratio, and interval schedules (p. 71).

Scientific management: A methodology used for optimizing work processes and reducing inefficiency through techniques such as work simplification (p. 137).

Sender-receiver model: Depicts parts of the interpersonal communication process: thought or feeling, encoding, transmission of a message, decoding, and thought or feeling (p. 17).

Sensitivity audit: Periodic assessment of what your nonverbal communication might be communicating to others (p. 28).

Shift work: A work schedule in which employees work different hours or shifts, rotating from one set of work hours to another at regular time intervals (p. 137).

Shotgun manager: An influence profile common to relatively inexperienced managers who use a variety of influence tactics, apparently in search of the one that works best (p. 235).

Social facilitation effect: Is demonstrated when the presence of others increases arousal and facilitates performance on simple or well-learned tasks, but interferes on complex or unfamiliar tasks (p. 65).

Social learning theory: Contends that behavior is influenced by observing the behavior of others (p. 72).

Social loafing: Occurs when the presence of others in a group leads to reduced individual effort and performance (p. 66).

Social support: The helpfulness derived from others in a group (p. 136).

"Squeaky wheel": A talkative group member (p. 31).

Strategic contingencies: Unique qualities that enable a unit to handle critical organizational needs. Important strategic contingencies are the ability to cope with uncertainty, nonsubstitutability, centrality, relevance, and consensus (p. 242).

Stress: A condition in which demands threaten an individual's ability to obtain valued outcomes (p. 126).

Stressors: Events that place demands on the individual (p. 126).

Substitutes for leadership: Organizational and follower characteristics, such as reward systems and experience and training of followers, that substitute for actions of the leader (p. 275).

Superordinate goals: Higher-order goals that transcend differences between groups and lead groups to work together to solve a common problem (p. 108).

Supportive communication: Is descriptive, problem oriented, honest, empathetic, equal, and tentative. Supportive communication is also timely and "soft on people and hard on the problem" (p. 24).

Survey feedback technique: An evaluation strategy in which a manager collects data about the organization and feeds it back to appropriate work groups for analysis and corrective action (p. 309).

Systems perspective: Views the different parts of an organization in terms of how they function together (p. 171).

Tactician: An influence profile common to more experienced managers who use reason, facts, and logic to influence others (p. 235).

Team management: According to Blake and Mouton, the most effective leaders always have maximum concern for both people and production (e.g., task) (p. 264).

Teamwork: An understanding and commitment to group goals by all members and a maximum utilization of each member's resources (p. 300).

Training programs: Systematic, structured attempts to improve the validity of performance appraisal ratings by training raters (p. 166).

Trait approach: The belief that effective leaders possess a universal set of common characteristics such as intelligence and compassion (p. 256).

Transformational leadership: Leadership that provides followers with intellectual stimulation and consideration (p. 261).

Two-factor theory: Contends that hygiene factors (e.g., pay, working conditions), at best, reduce job dissatisfaction. The presence of motivators (e.g., recognition), on the other hand, improves job satisfaction and motivation (p. 60).

Type-A behavior pattern: A set of personality traits typified by competitiveness, achievement focus, fatigue suppression, persistence, and impatience (p. 128).

Vertical communication: Communication that flows through the organization in an upward or downward direction. Usually consists of management directives, information regarding changes in the environment (downward), or feedback (upward) (p. 38).